Regulating Labour in the Wake of Globalisation

In recent decades, the prevailing response to the problem of unacceptable labour market outcomes in both Europe and North America—national regulation of labour standards and labour relations, coupled with collective bargaining—has come under increasing pressure from the economic and technological forces associated with globalisation. As those forces have shifted power away from national governments and labour unions and toward capital, the appropriate institutional locus of labour regulation has become hotly contested. There have been efforts to move the locus of regulation downward to smaller units of governance, including firms themselves, upward to larger units such as regional federations and international organisations, and outward to non-governmental organisations and civil society. In this volume, labour relations scholars from North America and Europe examine the efficacy of these emerging forms of labour regulation, their democratic legitimacy, the goals and values underlying them, and the appropriate direction of reform.

Columbia-London Law Series

General Editors:

George A Bermann
Walter Gellhorn Professor of Law and Jean Monnet
Professor of European Union Law, Columbia Law School
and
Terence Daintith
Emeritus Professor of Law, University of London,
formerly Director, Institute of Advanced Legal Studies

Volume 1: Party Funding and Campaign Financing in International Perspective
Edited by Keith Ewing and Samuel Issacharoff.

Volume 2: Regulating Labour in the Wake of Globalisation: New Challenges, New Institutions
Edited by Brian Bercusson and Cynthia Estlund

Regulating Labour in the Wake of Globalisation

New Challenges, New Institutions

Edited by

BRIAN BERCUSSON AND CYNTHIA ESTLUND

·HART·
PUBLISHING

OXFORD AND PORTLAND, OREGON
2008

Published in North America (US and Canada) by
Hart Publishing
c/o International Specialized Book Services
920 NE 58th Avenue, Suite 300
Portland, OR 97213-3786
USA
Tel: +1-503-287-3093 or toll-free: (1)-800-944-6190
Fax: +1 503 280 8832
E-mail: orders@isbs.com
Website: www.isbs.com

Hart Publishing, 16C Worcester Place, Oxford, OX1 2JW
Telephone: +44 (0)1865 517530 Fax: +44(0)1865 510710
E-mail: mail@hartpub.co.uk
Website: http://www.hartpub.co.uk

British Library Cataloguing in Publication Data
Data Available

ISBN: 978-1-84113-766-7

Typeset by Hope Services, Abingdon, Oxon
Printed and bound in Great Britain by
TJ International Ltd, Padstow, Cornwall

GENERAL EDITORS' PREFACE

With volume 2 in our Columbia–London Law Series—a path-breaking comparative study of contemporary workplace law—we continue the remarkable collaboration between our colleagues, respectively, in the Columbia University School of Law and the law schools of the different colleges of the University of London. The model of direct collaboration between the faculties through the media of workshops and publication has again proved its worth, though all recognition for bringing this chapter in the collaboration to fruition belongs to Cynthia Estlund, of Columbia, and Brian Bercusson of Kings College, respectively.

We are grateful to our own home institutions—including the Institute of Advanced Legal Studies of the University of London—for supplying the essential administrative support without which the intellectual input of the participants in this workshop and publication enterprise would not have yielded the excellent results it has.

The genius of the model is demonstrated by the fact that several other collaborative research projects between Columbia and London law faculty are underway within this series, as future volumes in this book series will record.

As before, recognition is owed to Richard Hart and Hart Publishing of Oxford for having undertaken the publication of this series of volumes and for manifesting the confidence that this commitment implies.

The quality of the present volume further reveals 'the spirit of joint study, reflection and problem-solving' to which we referred in our Introduction to the inaugural volume. We look forward to the further fruits of this collaboration.

George A Bermann
Walter Gellhorn Professor of Law and Jean Monnet Professor of European Union Law, Columbia University School of Law

Avrom Sherr
Woolf Professor of Legal Education, Director, Institute of Advanced Legal Studies University of London

CONTENTS

1

Regulating Labour in the Wake of Globalisation: New Challenges, New Institutions

BRIAN BERCUSSON* AND CYNTHIA ESTLUND**

By the mid-twentieth century most North American and European societies had converged upon a model of national regulation of firms' labour standards and labour relations, coupled with collective bargaining, as the response to unacceptable labour market outcomes. Regulation and collective bargaining occupied largely separate spheres, within which firms were seen as the objects of 'command-and-control' regulation and as the sites of industrial self-governance respectively. Subnational and supranational levels of government played only a very marginal role in labour relations or in labour regulations.

In recent decades, however, the viability of both national regulation and collective bargaining has come under increasing pressure, and the appropriate institutional locus of workplace and labour regulation has become hotly contested. The forces at work are familiar: cross-border mobility of capital, goods and services, and to a lesser extent labour; the rise of multinational corporate entities; intense product market competition from outside the wealthy West; rapidly changing technology, shorter product cycles, and the resulting clamour for flexibility; and the growing importance of information and intellectual capital relative to physical capital. As the balance of power has shifted away from national governments and labour unions, on the one hand, and toward capital, on the other, employers have ratcheted up the demand for deregulation while gaining the practical ability in many sectors to circumvent or escape regulation by outsourcing production.

In response to these forces, there have been efforts to move the locus of regulation 'downward' to smaller units of governance, including firms themselves, 'upward' to larger units such as regional federations and international organisations, and 'outward' to non-governmental organisations (NGOs) and civil society. Institutional actors at every level of governance—the International Labour Organisation, NAFTA and the European Court of Justice, national regulatory agencies, state and local governments, trade associations, labour unions, corporations, and NGOs—are all

* Professor of Law, King's College London
** CA Rein Professor, New York University School of Law.

jostling for a role in the emerging regulatory regimes. Actors at disparate levels, from the firm to the ILO, are linking up to form novel regulatory approaches that do not depend on the efficacy of traditional national regulatory institutions. The efficacy of these emerging forms of labour regulation, their democratic legitimacy, the goals and values underlying them, and the direction of reform are all in dispute.

With this as our very large theme, we and our colleagues at the School of Law of King's College London, the University of London's Institute of Advanced Legal Studies and the Columbia University School of Law convened an accomplished group of European and North American labour law and labour relations scholars. The group met twice, in 2003 and 2004, to discuss and compare emerging developments on both sides of the Atlantic and beyond. This book is the product of those presentations and discussions.

Globalisation and the Challenge to National Labour Regulation

Globalisation of the economy challenges established national approaches to governing labour standards and labour relations. The primary challenge that globalisation poses to labour regulation lies in the organisation of production itself. Because many goods are manufactured in different countries and marketed globally, often by multinational corporations, employers are not practically bound by the labour standards applicable to production in any one nation. A Report in 1997 of the Director-General of the ILO pointed out that globalisation threatens the autonomy of states to maintain labour standards:[1]

> Implicit in the [ILO] Constitution is the notion that the context in which social justice is to prevail is that of each State, which is to be democratic . . . Globalisation destroys this framework by placing greater emphasis on comparisons between workers in the same trade or industrial group and not only within the same country. Within the deepening inequalities in the developed countries, there is a danger that globalisation might increasingly make this principle seem a threat rather than a promise.

So globalisation tends both to undermine national labour standards as an economic matter and to weaken the control that democratic institutions exercise over market activity.

Globalisation is not, of course, simply a disembodied process; it has its agents, chiefly the multinational corporations (MNCs) and their global production networks. Much of the debate over globalisation is essentially about whether and how citizens, organised geographically or otherwise, can effectively govern the conduct of the MNCs and their supply chains, or 'whether global competition spells the end of national economic strategy and the welfare state'.[2]

[1] *The ILO, Standard Setting and Globalisation*, Report of the Director-General, International Labour Conference, 85th Session, 1997, Geneva, 'Introduction', p 5.

[2] D Held and A McGrew, 'The Great Globalisation Debate: An Introduction', pp 1–50 in D Held and A McGrew (eds), *The Global Transformations Reader* (2nd edn), (Polity Press, Cambridge, 2003), at p 19.

There is no doubt that MNCs play a central role in globalisation and global competition:[3]

> In 2001 there were approximately 65,000 MNCs worldwide with 850,000 foreign subsidiaries selling $18.5 trillion of goods and services across the globe (UNCTAD 2002). Today transnational production considerably exceeds the level of global exports ($7.4 trillion) and has become the primary means for selling goods and services abroad. Multinational corporations now account, according to some estimates, for at least 20 per cent of world production, 11 per cent of world GDP (compared to 7 per cent in 1990), 54 million direct jobs and 70 per cent of world trade . . .

Manuel Castells confirms the place of MNCs in the global economy, but highlights the more recent 'organisational transformation of the production process, including the transformation of multinational corporations themselves'.[4] He points out that:

> Global production of goods and services, increasingly, is not performed by multinational corporations, but by transnational production networks, of which multinational corporations are an essential component, yet a component which could not operate without the rest of the network . . .
>
> Thus, the new international division of labor is increasingly intra-firm, or, more precisely, intra-networks of firms. These transnational production networks, anchored by multinational corporations, unevenly distributed across the planet, shape the pattern of global production, and, ultimately, the pattern of international trade.

Transactions within these 'transnational production networks', both among different units of a MNC and within networks coordinated by MNCs and other large firms (sometimes called 'transnational corporations' or TNCs[5]) account for the bulk of world trade.[6]

Another primary facet of economic globalisation, besides MNCs and integrated production chains, is global financial integration. Together with trade liberalisation and expanded foreign investment, 'the emergence of massive cross-border financial flows' made global markets more competitive, and 'created the enabling conditions for the onset of globalisation'.[7]

The combined result of these developments has been intense international competition and an erosion of the ability of individual states to enforce their own labour standards. Nowhere is this more evident than in the sphere of international

[3] Held and McGrew, *ibid*, p 26.

[4] See M Castells, 'Global Informational Capitalism', *ibid*, pp 311–34, at pp 317–20.

[5] P Dicken thus defines the transnational corporation (TNC) as one that '*has the power to co-ordinate and control operations in more than one country, even if it does not own them*'. 'A New Geo-economy', *ibid*, pp 303–10, at p 306.

[6] Castells, *op cit*.

[7] *A Fair Globalisation: Creating Opportunities for All*, Report of the ILO World Commission on the Social Dimension of Globalisation, 2004, paragraph 132. See also 'Introduction', in D Held and A McGrew (eds), *Governing Globalisation: Power, Authority and Global Governance* (Polity Press, Cambridge, 2002), pp 1–21, at p 3. Also JA Scholte, 'Governing Global Finance' in the same volume, pp 189–208.

capital transfers. The details are almost impenetrably complex, but the basic problem, as Fritz Scharpf explains, is painfully simple:[8]

> While governments and workers are indeed without alternatives, capital owners do have a choice. If they find it unattractive to invest in job-creating productive assets, they may instead opt for speculative or interest-bearing financial assets, they may buy gold or other value-conserving assets, or they might simply consume, rather than invest, their savings . . . At the same time, technological innovations and the increasing importance of multinational firms undercut the effectiveness of national controls over capital transfers . . . As a consequence, financial assets are now mobile around the globe, and the minimal rate of return that investors can expect is again determined by global financial markets rather than by national monetary policy.

Geoffrey Garrett affirms that '[t]he potential for massive capital flight acts as the ultimate discipline on governments' and, ending on a lighter note, he quotes the Clinton political strategist James Carville: 'I used to think that if there was reincarnation, I wanted to come back as the president or the pope. But now I want to be the bond market: you can intimidate everyone'.[9]

While the proponents of free trade and freer markets in labour and products hold out the promise of expanding global prosperity, workers and their allies see the spectre of a 'race to the bottom' in labour standards—a globalised version of the same 'race to the bottom' that prompted states on both sides of the Atlantic in the last century to assert control over largely unregulated labor markets, to put a floor on 'destructive competition', and to foster the development of labour market institutions that could generate more socially acceptable labour and living conditions. The globalised flow of capital, goods, and services is increasingly running circles around the regulatory systems put in place in the last century. The result might be best described as a 'race to the rising bottom': There is evidence of economic gains in the countries to which production is flowing; but the gap in wages and living standards between workers in those countries and those in the developed countries is so dramatic that this 'rising bottom' does little to assuage the latters' fears about the downward spiral. Given the unprecedented wealth that is being generated at the top of the emerging global economic hierarchy, there must be a better way of improving living standards in the developing world without impoverishing the workers of the developed world.

More than economic well being is at stake: Production is flowing toward nations and parts of the world where democracy has at best a tenuous hold. But

[8] 'Globalisation and the Political Economy of Capitalist Democracies', in Held and McGrew, *op cit* 2003, pp 370–8, at pp 370, 372, 374–5.

[9] 'Global Markets and National Politics', pp 384–402, in *ibid*, at p 386. TI Palley refers to 'the emergence of a new regulatory paradigm. The old paradigm (call it the New Deal paradigm) had government regulating finance, with finance being harnessed to work for full employment. The new paradigm works in reverse, with finance now regulating government. This is an important part of the new political economy espoused by the IMF where open international financial markets are seen as a means of disciplining governments'. 'Industrialised country financial markets: the missing dimension in the stabilising global finance debate', in D Foden, J Hoffmann and R Scott (eds), *Globalisation and the Social Contract* (ETUI, Brussels, 2001), pp 55–73, at p 63.

even if democracy spreads to more of those nations, global capital is not governable within national boundaries. And we do not yet see the advent of genuinely democratic mechanisms of governance that operate above the national level. Even within Europe—a highly-evolved aggregation of firmly democratic states—there is concern about the 'democratic deficit' of the European Union. So if national governments lose their grip on labour standards and workplace governance, then so do the people within those nations.

Globalisation and Workers' Organisations: European and North American Perspectives

Alongside national labour standards, the second pillar of workplace governance has been organisation of labour through trade unions capable of representing workers at the workplace level and beyond. Trade unions are by far the dominant, and in some places the only, institutional vehicle for workers *qua workers* to influence not only their own working conditions but also the legal regime governing working conditions. Trade unions function in democratic societies as supplemental vehicles of democratic accountability and control within the economic sphere. So one might ask whether trade unions can take up some of the regulatory functions of national governments and serve as an alternate vehicle of democratic control.

Unfortunately, globalisation and cross-border mobility of trade and capital pose a threat to trade unionism and traditional collective bargaining strategies that is similar to, and stems from a similar asymmetry as, the threat to national regulation. Since labour is relatively immobile, and tends to be organised geographically, it is losing the capacity to bind increasingly footloose and transnationally organised employers.

Trade unions face challenges not only from the relative immobility of labour (relative to capital), but also from labour's increasing mobility and resultant diversity across both Europe and North America. Traditional labour unions were founded on assumptions of demographic and cultural homogeneity and virtual identity of interests among the workers represented. Globalisation has contributed to changes in the nature of the labour force, the widely noted erosion of the 'standard employment relationship', increasing fragmentation of the workforce and demographic changes. The rise of workforce diversity and employment discrimination as major regulatory concerns parallel the simultaneous influx of women into the workforce, bringing to the fore issues of work/life balance and working time. Increasing diversity of those workers and their interests poses a serious challenge to any effort to give collective voice to the workers in any particular workplace or sector.

At least within the US, the predicament of organised labour is aggravated by the willingness and ability of employers to combat and avoid unionisation when they perceive it in their interests to do so; resistance to unionisation has hardened in the US as competitive pressures on firms have intensified and globalised.

If trade unions lose their capacity to aggregate and amplify workers' own voices in the regulation and governance of work, that will further undermine the democratic character of workplace governance. And there is no doubt that trade union membership and power in Europe and North America have eroded to some degree under the pressure of global competition. Unions have traditionally been particularly strong in manufacturing, which is the sector most exposed to global competition. Declining employment in manufacturing alone will lead to declining union density.

There are, however, important differences between the American and European experiences, and indeed among the EU Member States, in this regard. For example, while trade union density—ie, union membership as a proportion of the working population—is down both in the US and across most of the EU, the variation in union density is striking. The author of one study points out that '[t]he range of variation in unionisation levels among advanced industrial societies is larger than in any other social-economic or political indicator'.[10]

The following table sets out union density in 2000:[11]

Country	Union Density (%)
Denmark	87.5
Finland	79.0
Sweden	79.0
Belgium	69.2
Luxembourg**	50.0
Ireland	44.5
Austria	39.8
Italy**	35.4
Greece	32.5
Portugal*	30.0
Germany**	29.7
UK	29.0
Netherlands	27.0
Spain	15.0
USA	13.5
France	9.1
Unweighted EU avg.	43.8
Weighted EU avg.	30.4

* 1999 figure ** 1998 figure

[10] J Visser, *In Search of Inclusive Unionism*, Bulletin of Comparative Labour Relations, no. 18, 1990, Kluwer, Deventer, at p 36.

[11] Source: European Foundation for the Improvement of Living and Working Conditions, Dublin; European Industrial Relations Observatory (EIRO) on-line; comparative overview of 'Industrial relations in the EU, Japan and USA, 2000', Table 2.

Within the EU, four countries maintain a high union density (ranging from 69.2 per cent in Belgium up through the Nordic countries to 87.5 per cent in Denmark), and two big countries have low levels of union density: Spain with 15 per cent and France with only 9.1 per cent union density. Most countries are in between, with the three big economies of Italy (35.4 per cent), Germany (29.7 per cent) and the UK (29 per cent) at around 30 per cent. The unweighted average of the EU-15 (the 15 EU Member States prior to the enlargements of 2004 and 2007 to 27 Member States) countries is 43.5 per cent; but because the biggest countries are clustered below that level, the weighted EU average union density is only 30.4 per cent. In contrast, trade union density in the USA in 2000 was 13.5 per cent, lower than any EU country except France.

The impact of the higher levels of unionisation in the EU is magnified by the degree of centralisation of collective bargaining in most EU-15 Member States. Because of the predominance of centralised bargaining on pay in Europe, collective agreements tend to cover all employers in the sector or the country, even where workers are not members of trade unions, employers are not members of employers' organisations, and no collective agreement is in effect. That is in striking contrast to the USA (as well as the UK and France), where the bargaining takes place almost entirely at the individual company level, with only limited instances of 'pattern bargaining' in some industries. As a result, the disparity between US and European levels of collective bargaining coverage is even more striking than the disparities in union density. The following Table illustrates this:

Collective bargaining coverage, Europe, Japan and USA

Country	Coverage
Austria	98%
France	90%–95%
Belgium	90%+
Sweden	90%+
Finland	90%
Italy	90%
Netherlands	88%
Portugal	87%
Denmark	83%
Spain	81%
Average of 13 EU Member States	*c* 80%
Germany	67%
Luxembourg	58%
Average of 9 (then) candidate countries	*c* 40%
UK	36%
Japan	21%
USA	15%

Sources: figures for EU Member States and candidate countries—referring to various years from 1999–2002, and in some cases estimates—are in most cases as calculated by EIRO for TN0301102S and TN0207104F; figure for Japan (2001) is from JIL; figure for USA (2001) from BLS.

Beyond the higher levels of union density and a collectivised system of pay determination, there is yet another dimension along which working life in Europe, far more than in the US, is determined through collective processes. A European Directive was finally adopted in 2002, after many years of deliberations, established a general framework for improving information and consultation rights of employees at workplace level, supplementing and reinforcing the levels above.[12] In the US, by contrast, there is no legal mechanism for worker participation in the workplace outside the small and shrinking ambit of collective bargaining. (Indeed, neither individual states nor employers within the US could lawfully institute 'works councils' on their own without an amendment—an extraordinarily unlikely one—to the national labor laws).

There is, finally, the institutionalised participation of the major trade union confederations, as leading 'social partners', in the 'social dialogue' that operates within many EU member states and that is part of the evolving European policymaking process. The pervasive presence and role of workers' organisations at both EU and Member State levels, in the form of macro-level national dialogue, collective bargaining at intersectoral and sectoral levels, and collective participation in decision-making at the workplace, is the most salient quality distinguishing the European social model, particularly from the US model. These differences between European and American experience in levels and forms of labour representation and regulation surfaced as a prominent theme in our workshops and a focus of our discussions of labour regulation in an internationalised and globalised economy.

So the two great pillars of 20th century labour regulation—of democratic control over markets and capital—have been national labour standards and nationally-governed collective bargaining through trade unions. While there are important differences between the US and Europe in this regard, on both sides of the Atlantic, both of those institutions are being undercut and weakened by globalisation and outmaneuvered by the chief agents and beneficiaries of globalisation, the transnational and multinational corporations. What is growing up, and what can be cultivated, to take the place of or to strengthen these institutions and restore the power of workers to have a say in their own economic destinies?

The contributions by the North American and European labour law scholars in this book focus on two general substantive themes in relation to the labour dimension of international economic regulation: institutional design and democratic legitimacy.[13]

[12] See the Preamble to the final directive, particularly Recital 17: '. . . the object is to establish a framework for employee information and consultation appropriate for the new European context described above [in Recitals 6–16] . . .'. Council Directive No 2002/14 establishing a framework for informing and consulting employees in the European Community. OJ 2002, L80/29.

[13] Other scholars have similarly identified three 'primary and interrelated concerns . . . in debates about global regulation': 'First comes the question of how institutions emerge and evolve in mediating the dynamic of the global marketplace. Secondly, there is . . . the problem of the appropriate level for public governance of economic activities. . . . Thirdly, there is a problem of democratic deficit. This stems from a perception that internalised economic activities are no longer subject to control or facilitation by national governments acting alone, while international structures are institutionally underdeveloped'. W Bratton, J McCahery, S Picciotto, C Scott (eds), *International Regulatory*

Labour Regulation in a Global Economy: Institutional Design and Levels of Governance

Our first and most explicit mission was to explore matters of institutional design, and specifically the efficacy of different regulatory mechanisms, techniques, and institutions for the attainment of the objective of real rights and protections for workers. How viable and effective are emerging mechanisms of 'soft law' and internalised 'self-regulation' by firms themselves as compared to more traditional forms of state-centered 'hard' regulation? Is 'soft law' and 'self-regulation' a trap and a delusion or can it deliver real rights and protections to workers? Are we seeing hybrid forms of soft and hard law that can improve upon both?

In this volume, for example, Professor Susan Sturm argues that complex and subtle forms of employment discrimination have proven resistant to formal equal employment mandates in the US; but that informal mechanisms—both within firms and among public and private actors in the aftermath of litigation—have extended the law's reach and its efficacy. She argues for a reflexive conception of law that includes 'creating occasions and incentives for non-state actors to deliberate about norms in context, and to construct conditions of permeability between legal and non-legal actors so that formal law can legitimately and effectively take account of informal normative activity and vice versa'.

Professor Harry Arthurs, in his contribution, takes a more pessimistic view of 'reflexive law', with its decentering of the state, its encouragement of self-regulation, and its deemphasis on hard law. He suggests that the reflexive move in legal theory follows the Reagan-Thatcher romance with deregulation and coincides with rising corporate power, and that the purportedly positive claims of reflexive legal theory risk becoming normative, and legitimating the withdrawal of the state from its hard-won role in protecting workers from the ravages of the market.

Professor Cynthia Estlund aims for a compromise that taps into the self-regulatory capabilities of major employers while preserving a major role for both the state (including, in the US, through private litigation) and organisations representing workers. She contends that conventional legal pressures should be designed and deployed as leverage to secure more effective forms of 'self-regulation' in which workers themselves, through organisational intermediaries, help to monitor compliance with legal norms.

Central to the issue of institutional design is the question of the appropriate level or levels of regulation. Apart from the question of whether some regulatory functions can be devolved effectively to firms themselves, there is the question of

Competition and Coordination: Perspectives on Economic Regulation in Europe and the United States (Clarendon Press, Oxford, 1996), p 2. These same authors note, too, that the European Union 'continues to occupy a central position as a catalyst and a precursor of global institutional developments'. (p 4).

which levels of government should exercise external regulatory authority. Should and must regulation aspire to global reach to match the reach of capital and product markets? Or is there still an enduring role for national regulation? What is the appropriate role of subnational—ie, regional and local—regulation, or for supranational—eg, European—regulation?

Clearly no single level of regulation, nor even any single configuration of multiple levels of regulation, will be able to respond to the variety of regulatory challenges posed by workplace and labour issues. On the one hand, the ever-increasing mobility of capital, of products and services, and of production itself seems to militate for higher and broader levels of regulation. Yet much economic activity remains highly local. The need for physical proximity to customers, to suppliers, to concentrations of skilled and knowledgeable workers continues to constrain capital's ability to seek less regulated or less unionised environments. That creates both acute regulatory challenges and surprising opportunities, and helps account for the sheer variety of regulatory experiments and proposals.

Professor Simon Deakin's analysis of the origins of the contract of employment aims to illustrate his conclusion that 'the institutional underpinnings of capitalism are perhaps more diverse, and more contingent, than some current theories allow'. The institutional design appropriate for labour protection in the early period of capitalist development in Britain is characterised by a contract of employment whereby, in return for subordination, workers were offered only much later protection through fiscal legislation, social insurance and collective bargaining. In contrast, on the European continent, there was earlier 'recognition of the role of the contract of employment as a mechanism of economic integration within the enterprise and of social cohesion beyond it'. This dynamic conflict is evident in continuing debates over the 'European social model', itself in competition with other institutional designs for worker protection in a globalised economy.

In his analysis of the changing institutional architecture of the European social model, Professor Brian Bercusson explores the interaction of different techniques of enforcement of labour law at different levels, primarily the national and the EU levels. New techniques of labour regulation at EU level include the 'open method of coordination' (OMC) of Member State labour administrations and the transnational social dialogue between European organisations of trade unions and employers. His analysis of the European social dialogue focuses on the interaction of representative organisations of workers at EU, national and sectoral levels, in order to highlight issues of the democratic legitimacy of transnational mechanisms of labour regulation.

One example of the regulatory opportunities created by globalisation is found within corporate governance structures. In Europe, corporate governance encompasses the institutional voice of workers through works councils. So, for example, the EU Directive on European Works Councils (EWCs) requires firms to provide information and consultation on financial issues: 'in particular . . . the structure, economic and financial situation, the probable development of the business and of production and sales, the situation and probable trend of employment, investments, and substantial changes concerning organisation . . .'.[14] The first three cases decided by the European Court of Justice involving the EWCs directive were concerned with disclosure of information about the financial links between different enterprises.[15]

Professor Marie-Ange Moreau uses the case of the European Works Councils Directive to focus on the central role of multinational corporations (MNCs) as illustrating the transformation whereby norms elaborated by a central state are now created by private actors. She identifies a 'principle of concordance' as a tool to confront the challenge of MNCs' power: concordance of scope, whereby norms must match the transnational scope of MNCs; concordance of time, whereby enforcement of norms must match the swiftness of MNC decision-making; and concordance of action, whereby transnational norm-creating actors representing employees have the freedom and power to act at the level of the MNC.

Such developments show that globalisation does not only erode national-level controls on capital and labour conditions; it also potentially extends the reach of the advanced economies, and potentially of their social norms, beyond national (and European) boundaries. To the extent that multi- and transnational firms make their home or maintain establishments in Europe, for example, European labour legislation, and particularly EWC provisions, have the potential to fill part of the emerging governance gap—and particularly the 'participation gap'—that globalisation has opened up.[16] This is an illustration of how a regional federation can intervene into the internal governance of firms themselves, and then potentially use the firm's own global organisation to extend the reach of regional labour norms. National regulation and trade unions, the traditional actors in labour regulation, may play a supporting role, but the leading actors in transnational labour

[14] Council Directive 94/45/EC of 22 September 1994 on the establishment of a European Works Council or a procedure in Community-scale undertakings and Community-scale groups of undertakings for the purposes of informing and consulting employees. OJ L 254/64 of 30.9.94. Annex, 'Subsidiary requirements', paragraph 2.

[15] *Betriebsrat der bofrost Josef H Boquoi Deutschland West GmbH & Co. KG, Straelen v bofrost Josef H Boquoi Deutschland West GmbH & Co. KG Straelen*, Case C-62/99, [2001] European Court Reports I-2579. *Gesamtbetriebsrat der Kuhne & Nagel AG & Co KC v Kuhne & Nagel AG & Co KC*, Case C-440/00, decided by the ECJ, 13 January 2004, *Betriebsrat der Firma ADS Anker GmbH v ADS Anker GnbH*, Case C-349-01, ECJ, 15 July 2004.

[16] See B Bercusson, 'Labour and multinational capital: the potential of European Works Councils', in P Humblett and L Lenaerts (eds), *Arbeid en Kapitaal: (on) verzoenbaar?*, Tegenspraak-Cahier 19; 1999, Ghent, pp 103–20. EWCs need to be perceived in this context of the precise role of MNCs in the global economy. As indicated, the scope for EWCs may have to extend beyond the boundaries of the MNC itself and link up with the integrated production chains in which the MNC plays a central role. See, for example, 'The TNT European information and consultation committee', *European Works Councils Bulletin*, Issue 4 (July/August 1996), pp 11–14; 'Nissan agreement', *European Works Councils Bulletin*, Issue 18 (November/December 1998), pp 17–20; 'Nortel agreement', *European Works Councils Bulletin*, Issue 19 (January/February 1999), pp 17–20.; 'American Express agreement', *European Works Councils Bulletin*, Issue 20 (March/April 1999), pp 18–20; AM Artiles, 'Working for Big Brother Ford: limits to the effectiveness of the European works councils?', *Transfer*, vol 5, no 3 (Autumn 1999), pp 394–9; T Royle, 'Avoidance strategies and the German system of co-determination' (on MacDonalds in Germany), (1998) *The International Journal of Human Resource Management* (December), pp 1026–46; *cf* M Whittall, 'The BMW European Works Council: A Cause for European Industrial Relations Optimism?' (2000) 6 *European Journal of Industrial Relations* (No 1), pp 61–83.

regulation are regional and corporate entities, and the worker-participants in European works councils.

The role of regional integration in the process of economic globalisation is a well-known theme in the literature. As stated by Bjorn Hettne: 'The basic issue is the relationship between forces of globalisation and forces of regionalisation. Regionalism is one possible approach to "a new multilateralism" . . .'. He adds that 'Europe represents the most advanced regional arrangement the world has seen . . .'.[17]

The emergence of the European Union as the world's largest trading bloc holds particular interest, not least due to the EU's development of transnational labour standards applicable to its Member States. EU law regulates the largest economy in the world. The economic integration of twenty-seven sovereign states requires a legal framework which allows for transnational business activity. The development of this legal framework illustrates the complexities of transnational public institutions regulating international business activity. The EU is the most advanced modern example of *regional* economic integration providing a legal framework for the regulation of international business. At regional level, the EU has developed a growing body of regulations governing employment standards and industrial relations. As the EU develops labour standards applicable to transnational economic activities, the EU's role in the global economy may offer valuable lessons in techniques linking labour standards to transnational economic activities. The case of labour regulation in multinational enterprises is but one example. The continuing continent-wide debate over a new Constitutional Treaty for the European Union has raised popular consciousness and stimulated discussion of the future of labour regulation as well as the place of labour organisations in the overall institutional design of a European Union. Both regulatory techniques (legislation, the 'open method of coordination', social dialogue) and levels of regulation ('subsidiarity', vertical and horizontal, and federalism) have been central issues in that debate.

Still, European social norms and governance institutions are not going to match the reach of global capital. So, inevitably, the problem of globalisation leads to an exploration of international labour standards, and international organisations—the United Nations, the ILO, even the World Trade Organisation (WTO)—as mechanisms of governance.

The paper by Professor Bob Hepple examines how the objectives of raising labour standards in exporting countries, or to secure compliance with international labour standards, or at least to secure adequate enforcement of domestic labour standards have been pursued in both the USA and in Europe through various measures: unilateral measures (the Generalised System of Preferences), bilateral and regional agreements (the North American Agreement on Labor Co-operation of NAFTA and the EU's external trade agreements) and multilateral

[17] 'Global market versus the New Regionalism', in Held and McGrew, *op cit* 2003, pp 359–69, at pp 359, 362.

trade agreements. However, detailed analysis of the WTO and its precursors leads him to conclude that '[t]he real impact of the WTO is its potential for undermining such positive developments as the EU GSP and some of the bilateral trade agreements made by the US'.

Of course, most international organisations have been formed, and continue to function, largely as treaty-based creatures of states. So the weakness of states has implications, as well, for international organisations that traditionally have functioned through states. A report to the ILO recognised this problem: 'the object would be, first, to go beyond the limits inherent in its dependence upon the action of States, in a world in which the realities of globalisation know no borders . . .'.[18] The weakness of individual states led the ILO to identify an alternative: 'The mobilisation of non-governmental actors'—'in particular manufacturing enterprises, wholesalers and retailers, and consumers . . .'.[19]

One striking development has been the rise of consumer pressure, orchestrated through NGOs, in support of improved labour conditions in the developing world. On the one hand, the rise of multinational brands that sit atop elaborate transnational production networks and supply chains epitomises the threat of the 'race to the bottom'. Yet globalised competition has also helped to give these brands the potential means and incentive to become effective regulatory actors. The brands have developed sophisticated methods of monitoring the speed, cost, and quality of production that could be readily extended to encompass labour standards at the bottom of those supply chains. And the brands' acute sensitivity to customer tastes makes them vulnerable to pressure from consumers who care about labour standards (whether out of solidarity with distant workers or out of a desire to mitigate the downward pressure that sweatshop conditions elsewhere put on labour conditions in their own societies).

Those circumstances have opened the door to a variety of efforts to tap the sympathies of consumers in the developed world in support of improved labour conditions in the developing world. The rise of 'labour codes of conduct' and no-sweat labelling schemes, along with increasingly sophisticated monitoring systems, is the most visible of those developments. However, some sympathetic critics of those efforts contend that they do too little to engage and empower local workers, undermining both their efficacy and their democratic legitimacy. A pioneering effort by the Worker Rights Consortium, which works with US universities and colleges to police the production of apparel bearing university logos, aims to cultivate rather than circumvent both local labour activists and local regulatory officials. That system, and its operation in two case studies, is explored here by Professor Mark Barenberg, a participant-observer and a theoretician of emerging models for improving labour standards in the developing world and in the eclipse of command-and-control models.

[18] *Op cit*, 1997, p 8.

[19] *Ibid*, p 27. For an analysis along similar lines, see B Bercusson, 'Economic Policy: State and Private ordering', in TC Daintith (ed), *Law as an Instrument of Economic Policy: Comparative and Critical Approaches*, W de Gruyter, 1988, pp 359–420.

Labour Regulation in a Global Economy: Democratic Legitimacy

A second related theme developed around issues of democratic legitimacy. What role do and should (and can) workers and their organisations have in these emerging regulatory mechanisms, techniques, and institutions? As the boundaries of product markets expand beyond the reach of national trade unions, the traditional tools of collective bargaining, and thus the traditional forms of democratic participation in workplace governance, are under increasing pressure. That has implications both for the changing shape of citizenship and of democracy itself and for the efficacy of the new regulatory techniques and institutions. For it is nearly axiomatic—and was in any event a shared assumption among this group of labour law scholars—that no system of labour regulation that purports to protect workers can be effective unless the affected workers themselves have a voice and real influence within the system.

Indeed, one might generalise this observation to what could be considered an axiom of labour regulation—one that joins the themes of institutional design, and especially the appropriate level of regulation, and legitimacy: that the efficacy and legitimacy of regulation is in inverse relation to the distance between those who formulate the rules and those to whom they are applied; the greater the distance, the less effective and legitimate, and vice versa. But if that is the case, the challenge of designing effective institutions of labour regulation in an increasingly global economy appears daunting indeed.

The participants debated whether and how democratic participation can be re-envisioned, and institutions for employee participation can be reconstituted, in the wake of declining unionisation. Does the solution lie in bolstering traditional unions, or perhaps in reorganising them to match the global reach of their employer counterparts? Or do employees need radically different institutions for participation within the firm and the polity? Keith Ewing explores the potential of 'international framework agreements' by which some unions are seeking to meet the challenges posed by MNCs. But he finds that the lack of a transnational legal regime behind these agreements is a serious hindrance to this otherwise salutary development.

One problem is that unions' experience in representing employees has been mainly in relation to employers and their federations. But employers are no longer the sole or even the most important interlocutors for those who represent workers. For example, the financial institutions that control multinational enterprises make many of the decisions that affect workers in both the developed and the developing world. Yet these financial institutions have different cultures, decision-making criteria and processes from those of the enterprises they control.[20]

[20] See H Gospel and A Pendleton (eds), *Corporate Governance and Labour Management: An International Comparison* (Oxford, Oxford University Press, 2005), who track the influence of financial institutions on corporate structures, and their influence on corporate decision-making on employment and labour relations.

Trade union methods of influencing decision-making need to adapt to reach levels of financial decision-making currently beyond the reach of traditional structures and institutions of industrial relations.[21] They may do so in part by expanding their representational compass to include employees' identities as pension fund members, bank account holders, shareholders, etc, as well as their identities as workers. Other associations and organisational forms (eg ethical trading/socially responsible investment NGOs at sector, local, regional, national and international levels) open possibilities for alliances with workplace based representative organisations.

Again, what are the appropriate levels at which participation is effective? As with employing enterprises, it may be that workers and their institutions must seek participation and influence not at the level of individual financial institutions but at higher levels of aggregation: sectoral, national or even international institutions. The 'representation gap' at the level of individual institutions could perhaps be filled by effective representation at higher levels. Currently, however, the representation gap is compounded by the absence of effective actors or effective representation at those higher levels (eg on the employees' side, international trade unions).[22]

The welfare state grew in response to workers' realisation that power at the work site could not always defend against risks of unemployment, old age, accidents and disease. Workers mobilised their power as voters through political organisations (political parties) that were capable of influencing state institutions to provide protection against these risks. Workers now need to seek equivalent leverage within or against controlling financial institutions. For example, however centralised their internal governance structures, the dispersed ownership of organisations of capital (eg pension funds, insurance companies) may offer scope for mobilisation and organisation of workers to participate in their governance and influence their decision-making. Multinationals unresponsive to trade union pressures have been shown to be vulnerable to pressure from consumer or environmental NGOs. Are financial institutions similarly vulnerable?

The challenge for labour and its allies lies in monumental shifts in decision-making power. The locus of economic decision-making is shifting away from the individual worksite and toward MNCs and financial institutions. The locus of political control, if it is to remain effective at all, must shift from individual states to regional and international bodies. If workers are to have any effective role in these emerging structures of decision-making, the locus of worker participation and the structures of worker representation need to evolve accordingly.

[21] A number of major problems are anticipated. For example, the nature of 'controlling financial institution' itself needs to be analysed. This could look to definitions of 'controlling undertaking', for example, in the European Works Councils directive, Article 3(1), as developed in ECJ case law and other related literature. See, eg B Bercusson, 'The significance of the legal form of the group enterprise in the United Kingdom', in D Sugarman and G Teubner (eds), *Regulating Corporate Groups in Europe* (Nomos Verlag, Baden-Baden, 1990), pp 267–84.

[22] For a discussion of different systems and logics of representation in the context of governance of the EU, see GP Cella, 'European governance, democratic representation and industrial relations', (2003) 9 *Transfer: European Review of Labour and Research* (No 2) (Summer), pp 196–207. N Kluge, 'Workers' involvement in Europe—a still unfinished jigsaw', in H. Jorgenson et al (eds), *European Trade Union Yearbook 2003/2004*, ETUI (Brussels, 2004), pp 115–136.

Both economic and political decision-making processes vary along a number of dimensions. There are *time and process dimensions of decision-making*; when does decision-making start, and finish? Does decision-making follow a fixed procedure or an indeterminate timetable? How long does the process last, and how important is speed? There are also *structure and level dimensions of decision-making*. Who are the persons and structures engaged and at which levels? Do they act through formal or informal structures or both?

It may seem obvious that, to be meaningful, the timing, structures, and levels of workers' participation in decision-making must be aligned with the decision-making process itself. But that simple observation has important implications for how participation can take place—for when participation should start (at the earliest opportunity) and finish (reaching a final decision), and at what levels it should take place. If the decision-making process is flexible, then so must be the participatory process. If speed of decision-making is important, then forms of participation that permit expedition must be developed. When time is money, participation may be costly, and may be compressed in exchange for concessions. If decision-making requires the coordination of plant-level and corporate-level inputs, then workers' participation must take place at both levels as well. And since workers' participation can generally take place only through representatives, the institutions of worker representation must develop along all of these same dimensions. There must be structures of representation at the global, regional, and sectoral levels, as well as firm-level and plant-level. Traditional trade union structures must evolve, but that may not be enough. For workers' voices to be heard within the decision-making processes that matter to them, we may need new institutions to supplement even the more versatile and wide-reaching organisations that some trade unionists envision.

Professor Ulrich Mückenberger examines the world of work in the context of the failure of 'old governance' mechanisms of labour regulation in Europe, the starting point of which is the failure of the nation state as the focal point of socio-economic security. The crisis of 'old governance' is identified as the result of three trends—'decentration': the state and the economy moving to both global and local levels, 'individualisation': the loss of governing structures, and 'dualisation': multiple divisions within society, all of which impact on the regulatory possibilities for labour's voice. Each poses challenges for the democratic legitimacy of 'new governance' mechanisms which require that the world of work and labour be linked to the wider life-worlds of civil society.

Professor Katherine Stone approaches much the same problem from the US perspective. She identifies three dynamics that are coalescing to reshape labour relations in the United States: First, *flexibilisation*, or the decline of internal labour markets in favour of flexible employment relations that permit employers to expand or shrink their workforces, and reassign and redeploy employees with ease; second, *globalisation*, or the increase in cross-border transactions in goods and services that facilitates firm relocation to low labour cost countries; and third, *privatisation*, or the dismantling of the social safety net. All three of these dynamics have been detrimental to US employment standards and union strength. At the same time, however, Professor Stone identifies many areas of social life in which the spread of the global leads to the re-emergence of the local. She argues that the response to the global threat to labour standards lies in a revival of collective action at the local level. She further contends that the combined forces of flexibilisation, globalisation, and privatisation make collective action at the local level not only necessary, but also possible.

Conclusion: Collective Frameworks of Labour Regulation

There is an inescapable comparative dimension to both of our larger themes of institutional design and democratic legitimacy. For example, the question of institutional design is intimately tied up with the strength and shape of labour unions. A society in which unions are strong and are regarded as the legitimate representatives of working people will (or should) design institutions of labour regulation in which unions play a central role. While levels of unionisation have been declining throughout the developed world, unions in Europe have tended to maintain both broader membership and a more institutionalised role within political and governmental institutions than in North America, and especially in the United States. The concepts of 'social dialogue' among 'social partners'—concepts with Northern European origins that have gained considerable resonance within the European Union—simply have no counterpart in the US. The European institution of the 'works council' not only has no counterpart but is barely imaginable in the US. The decline of collective bargaining in the US thus precipitates both a more acute crisis of democratic legitimacy and a greater challenge to the design of regulatory institutions than it does in Europe, where workers *qua* workers have other institutional mechanisms of political and social voice and engagement.

Cutting across both the substantive themes and the comparative dimension of our discussions was a recurring motif of 'pessimism versus optimism'—or perhaps 'pessimism versus hope'—regarding the possibilities for effective protection of workers' interests within global capitalism. For every one of the trends that have undermined the mid-20th century system of national labour regulation and collective bargaining seems to enhance the power of capital relative to labour and relative to any bounded jurisdiction. Are the concepts of 'self-regulation' and 'corporate responsibility' a dangerous delusion in that context? Is any form of governmental regulation with less than global reach an invitation to circumvention? Is global regulation even conceivable in the foreseeable future, absent the conventional accoutrements of state power?

The problem underpinning all of labour law, as stated by Otto Kahn-Freund, is the imbalance of power between the employer, the collective embodiment of capital, and the individual employee.[23] Redressing this imbalance of power in the capitalist economic organisation of society was the function of collective organisations of workers and of democratically-driven regulation. Depending on the different political and economic trajectories of the nation states, collective actors and processes met with different mixtures of legal support, obstruction, or repression; and regulatory institutions encountered varying levels of hostility, commitment, and support.[24] The variety of collective frameworks that exist now within the developed world reflect historical conjunctures and contingencies that will continue to influence the evolution of new institutions even under the pressure of global capitalism. It is not clear which, if any, of the existing models will survive and what will evolve alongside them or in their place. What is clear is that new solutions are needed to the abiding problem of protecting and empowering workers in a capitalist economy.

[23] O Kahn-Freund, *Labour and the Law* (1972), 3rd edn, edited and with an introduction by PL Davies and MR Freedland, Stevens (London, 1983). See also, Lord Wedderburn, R Lewis and J Clark (eds), *Labour Law and Industrial Relations: Building on Kahn-Freund* (Clarendon Press, Oxford, 1983).

[24] C Crouch, *Industrial Relations and European State Traditions*, Oxford, Clarendon Press, 1993; PA Hall and D Soskice, *Varieties of Capitalism: The Institutional Foundations of Comparative Advantage* (Oxford, Oxford University Press, 2001).

2

Corporate Self-Regulation: Political Economy, State Regulation and Reflexive Labour Law

HARRY ARTHURS*

In their introductory essay, Brian Bercusson and Cynthia Estlund note:

> Actors at disparate levels . . . are linking up to form novel regulatory approaches. . . . The efficacy of these emerging forms of labour regulation, their democratic legitimacy, the goals and values underlying them, and the direction of reform are all in dispute.[1]

The ambition of this chapter is to explore one such 'novel regulatory approach'—reflexive labour law—and to assess not only its efficacy, legitimacy and normative aspirations, but also its intellectual origins, assumptions and implications.

The growing corpus of reflexive labour law scholarship comprises foundational essays by Gunther Teubner,[2] an extensive body of work by Drs Rolf Rogowski and Ton Wilthagen as well as several volumes edited by them,[3] and a number of books and articles which engage with their work and Teubner's.[4]

* University Professor Emeritus and President Emeritus, York University. I am grateful to Freya Kodar and David Doorey for their research assistance, to the Social Sciences and Humanities Research Council of Canada for its financial support, and to the Hugo Sinzheimer Institute and the University of Amsterdam, my hosts at a conference on Reflexive Labour Law in 2001, where I presented an earlier version of this essay.

[1] This volume at p 2.

[2] See, eg, G Teubner, 'The Transformation of Law in the Welfare State' and 'After Legal Instrumentalism? Strategic Models of Post-regulatory Law' in G Teubner (ed), *Dilemmas of Law in the Welfare State* (Berlin/NY, DeGruyter, 1985); 'Industrial Democracy Through Law' in T Daintith and G Teubner, *Contract and Organization: Legal Analysis in the Light of Economic and Social Theory* (Berlin/NY, DeGruyter, 1986); *Juridification of Social Spheres: A Comparative Analysis in the Areas of Labor, Corporate, Antitrust and Social Welfare Law* (Berlin/NY, DeGruyter, 1987); *State, Law and Economy as Autopoietic Systems: Regulation and Autonomy in a New Perspective* (Milan, Giuffrè, 1992) (with Alberto Febbrajo); *Law as an Autopoietic System* (London, Blackwell, 1993).

[3] Their English-language publications include: R Rogowski and T Wilthagen, 'Reflexive Labour Law: An Introduction' in R Rogowski and T Wilthagen (eds), *Reflexive Labour Law: Studies in Industrial Relations and Employment Regulation* (Deventer/Boston, Kluwer, 1994); M Aalders and T Wilthagen, 'Moving Beyond Command-and-Control: Reflexivity in the Regulation of Occupational Safety and Health and the Environment' (1997) 19 *Law and Policy* 415; R Rogowski, 'Autopoietic Industrial Relations and Reflexive Labour Law' in T Wilthagen (ed), *Advancing Theory in Labour Law and Industrial Relations in a Global Context* (Amsterdam, North-Holland Press, 1998); R Rogowski, 'Industrial Relations as a Social System' (2000) 7 *German Journal of Industrial Relations* 97; R Rogowski,

While reflexive law belongs to a family of post-modern socio-legal theories which dispute the state's centrality in the administration of law's empire, it is distinguished by several controversial features: its claim that legal and other social systems are closed and autonomous; its demarcation of system boundaries on the basis of functional differentiation rather than stipulated or a priori characteristics; its identification of legal discourse as the trigger for a binary distinction between law and non-law; its insistence on the autopoietic—self-referential, self-regulating and self-reproducing—character of law; and its novel hypothesis that law acts not so much by imposing itself on other social domains directly as by regulating their self-regulatory processes as well as its own.[5]

I will explore some of these ideas in greater detail below. First, however, I will sketch out three case studies of self-regulation in the labour sphere which will hopefully bring into focus these features of reflexive law. Next, I will consider reflexive labour law from the perspective of legal theory and political economy, with particular emphasis on the marginalisation of the state in both domains. And finally, I will explore the possibility that the normative implications of reflexive labour law may turn out to be even more important than its descriptive insights

Three Case Studies

Case study no 1—Voluntary codes of conduct[6]

As has been widely remarked, many global corporations have recently adopted voluntary codes of conduct. Labour standards feature frequently in these codes,

'The Concept of Reflexive Labour Law: Its Theoretical Background and Possible Applications' in J Priban and D Nelken, *Law's New Boundaries: The Consequences of Legal Autopoiesis* (Aldershot, Ashgate/Dartmouth, 2001).

[4] See, eg, C Barnard, S Deakin, R Hobbs, 'Reflexive Law, Corporate Social Responsibility and The Evolution of Labour Standards: The Case of Working Time', in O De Schutter, and S Deakin (eds), *Social Rights and Market Forces: Is Open Coordination the Future for European Employment and Social Policy?* (Brussels, Bruylant, 2005) [available at: http://www.cbr.cam.ac.uk/pdf/wp294.pdf]; J Cohen, *Regulating Intimacy: A New Legal Paradigm* (Princeton, Princeton UP, 2002); H Collins, 'Is there a Third Way in Labour Law?' in A Giddens (ed), *The Global Third Way Debate* (London, Blackwell, 2001) 300; D Doorey, 'Who Made That? Influencing Foreign Labour Practices Through Reflexive Domestic Disclosure Regulation' (2006), 44(1) *Osgoode Hall LJ* [forthcoming]; O Lobel, 'The Renew Deal: The Fall of Regulation and the Rise of Governance in Contemporary Legal Thought' (2004) 89 *Minn L Rev* 262 esp at 328–43; D O'Rourke, 'Outsourcing Regulation: Analyzing Nongovernmental Systems of Labor Standards and Monitoring' (2003) 31 *Policy Studies J* 1; S Smisman, 'Reflexive Law in Support of Directly Deliberative Polyarchy: Reflexive-Deliberative Polyarchy as a Normative Frame for the OMC' in O De Schutter and S Deakin (eds), *Social Rights and Market Forces: Is the Open Coordination of Employment and Social Policies the Future of Social Europe?* (Brussels, Bruylant) [forthcoming].

[5] See generally N Luhmann, *Essays on Self-Reference* (New York, Columbia UP, 1990); G Teubner (ed), *Autopoietic Law: A New Approach to Law and Society* (Berlin/New York, W de Gruyter, 1988); J Priban and D Nelken (eds), *Law's New Boundaries*, above, n 3. For a root-and-branch critique, see A Beck, 'Is Law an Autopoietic System?' (1994) 14 *OJLS* 401.

[6] For a fuller development of these ideas, and more extensive references, see HW Arthurs, 'Private Ordering and Workers' Rights in the Global Economy: Corporate Codes of Conduct as a Regime of Labour Market Regulation' in J Conaghan, K Klare, M Fischl (eds), *Labour Law in an Era of*

which also often encompass environmental practices, commercial honesty, consumer protection and integrity in dealings with government officials. What does this sudden upsurge in the use of voluntary codes signify? Opinions vary: codes represent the principled acceptance by corporations of their social obligations; they are a fig leaf used to conceal corporate exploitation; they fill a regulatory gap caused by the inability of states to regulate the actions of corporations outside their own boundaries; they signal an innovative shift in the modalities of market regulation from a pure state-based command model to new hybrid models involving a mix of public and private initiatives; they are a concession wrung from governments and corporations as a result of pressures generated by political and social actors concerned about exploitation and abuse; and—perhaps—they are evidence of the existence of autopoietic systems and of the ubiquity of reflexive law.

The use of the term 'voluntary' to describe these codes requires some explanation. They are typically adopted without compulsion of law; thus in a juridical sense they are indeed voluntary. But in a practical sense, they are generally less so. They are often adopted only after a corporation has been accused of exploiting or abusing its workers, either at home or abroad. Adverse publicity ensues, and the corporation is confronted by threats of moral, economic or political sanctions such as consumer boycotts, sympathetic industrial action, denial of government loans and procurement contracts, or (infrequently) legislation barring its goods from market. If these threats are deemed credible, the corporation must respond. One response is to adopt a 'code' which declares its commitment to respect fundamental labour rights such as freedom of association, a safe work environment and the absence of coercion and discrimination. In a variant of this scenario, corporations which are not themselves the immediate target of censure or pressure, but are potentially vulnerable to it, may proactively adopt a code developed by a sectoral organisation, an international agency, a national government, or their professional advisors. Or they may adopt a code entirely on their own initiative, in an effort to secure whatever market or moral rewards accrue to exemplars of corporate social responsibility. In a final variant, corporations may be drawn into collaboration with NGOs in drafting, administering and even monitoring a code.[7] To reiterate, in these scenarios,

Globalization: Transformative Practices and Possibilities (Oxford, Oxford University Press, 2001) and 'Corporate Codes of Conduct: Profit, Power and Law in the Global Economy' in W Cragg (ed), *Ethics Codes, Corporations and the Challenges of Globalization* (Edward Elgar Press, 2005).

[7] For an overview of codes and their contents, see K Gordon and M Miyake, *Deciphering Codes of Corporate Conduct: A Review of their Contents* (Paris, OECD Directorate for Financial, Fiscal and Enterprise Affairs, Working Papers on International Investment No 99/2, 1999); *Report of the Working Party of the Trade Committee of the Trade Directorate, Codes of Corporate Conduct—An Inventory* (Paris, OECD TD/TCWP(98)74, 1999). For a discussion of labour codes in particular, see United Nations Commission on Trade and Development (UNCTAD), *World Investment Report 1994—Transnational Corporations, Employment and the Workplace* (New York/Geneva, United Nations, 1994) 349 *ff*; ILO, *Overview of Global Developments (Working Party on the Social Dimensions of the Liberalization of Trade* (Report to the International Labour Office Nov. 1998, GB.273/WP/SDL/1) (available at www.ilo.org.ch/public/english/20gb/docs/gb273/sdl-1.htm); J Diller 'A Social Conscience in the Marketplace? Labour Dimensions of Codes of Conduct, Social Labelling and Investor Initiatives' (1999) 138 *International Labour Rev* 99.

codes are 'voluntary' in the sense that corporations do not adopt them under compulsion of state law. But of course they are also 'non-voluntary', in the sense that they are adopted out of fear of sanctions or hope of reward.

Whether voluntary or not, however, corporate codes are indisputably 'corporate'. That is to say, their drafting, administration and enforcement reflect the fact that they originate in the realm of private, rather than public, regulation.[8] This shapes their architecture in several important ways. First, their substantive provisions are typically vaguely worded, perhaps to allow for their application in diverse economic, socio-cultural and legal contexts; as a result, it is difficult to identify clear violations. Second, responsibility for code administration is seldom fixed on any specific corporate officer, nor are procedures mandated whereby adherence is promoted or compliance monitored; as a result, corporations often fail to publicise codes internally, train their employees to respect them, clarify vague language through information bulletins, or report on overall code compliance to their boards of directors.[9] Third, sanctions for non-compliance are seldom specified, nor is machinery established whereby sanctions can be imposed on non-complying employees, subsidiaries, suppliers or affiliates. Given these characteristics, codes often appear to be—and are—ineffectual, if not actually counter-productive.[10] This is obviously not to suggest that all corporations with codes are guilty of egregious behaviour, only that codes per se do not seem to not seem to be an efficient or contributing cause of higher labour standards.[11]

However, reflexive law makes us sensitive to the possibility that the very appearance of a code may be evidence of a pattern of adaptive behaviour, of a learning

[8] See generally M Priest, 'The Privatization of Regulation: Five Models of Self-Regulation' (1997) 29 *Ottawa L Rev* 233; N Gunningham and J Rees, 'Industrial Self-Regulation: An Institutional Perspective' (1997) 19 *Law and Policy* 364.

[9] A recent survey of major Canadian companies doing business abroad discloses that over 85% professed to have a written document dealing with corporate ethics relating to labour, environmental and business practices, including about 50% which described such statements as 'rules of conduct' or 'guidelines'. However, over 60% did not train their staff to administer such documents; virtually all those which did spent 4 hours per year or less on such training; that only 15–25% of such companies applied any aspect of their ethics codes to suppliers; only 2–12% reported to their Boards of Directors on compliance; and similarly low rates of Board oversight were exercised even with regard to the firms' own practices. Bribery stands apart as receiving somewhat more intensive and extensive scrutiny. KPMG, 'Ethics Survey 2000—Managing for Ethical Practice' (available at http://www.kpmg.ca/english/services/docs/fas/ethicssurvey2000e.pdf).

[10] A King and M Lenox, 'Industry Self-Regulation without Sanctions: The Chemical Industry's Responsible Care Program' (2000) 4 *Academy of Management Journal* 698.

[11] Of course, this is an empirical question in each case, and therefore likely to involve controversial issues of evidence interpretation. For a rather poignant example of such a controversy, contrast the honestly optimistic view of the chair of the Independent Monitoring Council responsible for ensuring implementation of Mattel Inc's 'Global Manufacturing Principles' with the critical comments of the representative of an independent monitoring group (Asia Monitor Resource Centre) concerning non-compliance with those principles in Mattel factories in Thailand. See SP Sethi, 'Corporate Accountability through International Codes of Conduct—Theoretical Implications and Challenges to Cross-Cultural Applications: The Case of Mattel, Inc' (Sao Paolo, Second World Congress, International Society of Business, Economics and Ethics—'The Ethical Challenges of Globalization', July, 2000, unpublished) and S Frost, 'Factory Rules versus Codes of Conduct: Which Option makes Sense for Business?' (2000) 2:4 *Human Rights Dialogue* 3 (Carnegie Council on Ethics and International Affairs).

process which over time will reshape the law of the corporation and its workplaces. Indeed, while I have accurately described the first generation of corporate codes, I believe, a second generation of codes is said to be emerging. This second generation is characterised by several innovations, designed to give greater credibility to codes, if not actually to enhance their effectiveness. First, transnational advocacy organisations—unions and social movements—are claiming a greater role in the formulation and administration of codes. Second, the monitoring or auditing of code compliance has become a discrete and increasingly professionalised function, often contracted out to specialist commercial or non-profit agencies which operate at arm's length from the corporation itself. Third, in a few cases, senior management and boards of directors are becoming more heavily invested in the exercise, responsibilities are fixed on a compliance officer and the code itself becomes a standing item on the directors' agenda. Fourth, proactive steps are being taken to ensure that suppliers and other elements in the production chain do not embarrass the company by violating code standards. Fifth, less frequently, the language of the code is re-written to provide more explicit guarantees of a broader range of employment standards, occasionally even including a 'living wage' or a 'fair wage'. And finally, sanctions are built into some code regimes in the form of compliance marks or labels whose presence or absence will trigger positive or negative consumer reactions.

It is too early to assess what practical consequences—if any—might flow from these second generation corporate codes. However, a third generation may be just over the horizon. One distinguishing feature of third generation voluntary corporate codes would be that they cease to be purely 'corporate'; states and civil society actors would be equal partners or even prime movers in their drafting, promulgation, administration and enforcement.[12] The other is that they would no longer be purely 'voluntary'; they would be mandated and enforced by law. Legislation has been proposed in both the United States and Australia which would require that all corporations doing business abroad adopt a code, ensure its transparent administration, and be subject to sanctions for non-compliance in the form of loss of access to government export loan guarantees, procurement contracts and other forms of government support.[13] And several legal scholars and advocates have suggested that corporate codes might be used by courts as evidentiary or normative standards designed to establish, diminish or eliminate

[12] R O'Brien, 'NGOs, Global Civil Society and Global Economic Regulation' and R Mayne, 'Regulating TNCs: The Role of Voluntary and Governmental Approaches' in Picciotto and R Mayne, *Regulating International Business—Beyond Liberalization* (New York, St. Martin's Press, 1999); K Gordon, 'Rules for the Global Economy: Synergies between Voluntary and Binding Approaches' Unpublished paper, Conference on Corporate Citizenship: Linking CSR business strategies and the emerging international agenda (London, 8–9 November, 1999).

[13] In the United States, see the Corporate Code of Conduct Act, HR 4596 IH (Rep McKinney) introduced June 7, 2000. Complying corporations would receive preferential treatment in the awarding of federal contracts, participation in trade and development programs and access to export-import credits and loan guarantees. In Australia, a similar Corporate Code of Conduct Bill 2000 was introduced by Senator Vicki Bourne as a private member's bill. See http://search.aph.gov.au/search/parlinfo.ASP?action=browse&Path=legislation/. Neither is likely to be enacted in the foreseeable future.

corporate civil or criminal liability for wrongful conduct, even though the codes themselves are not directly enforceable as such.[14] But so far, neither legal approach has made much headway.

If indeed a third generation of codes does emerge, with the imprimatur of state law and the involvement of civil society and state—as well as corporate—actors, this would represent a genuine innovation. It would also constitute a convenient site for empirical investigation of the hypothesis that regulatory efficacy will increase as successive generations of codes move up a rising gradient of state involvement. But we may not be able to investigate this hypothesis for some time yet. State-mandated codes so far remain below the horizon and, for reasons canvassed in a subsequent section of this chapter, they are unlikely to surface soon. Codes, therefore, remain no more than a potentially interesting example of how reflexivity and change may occur in a closed normative system.

Case study no 2—Ratcheting Labour Standards

An important recent academic article has proposed that leading corporations should commit themselves to 'ratcheting labour standards' permanently upward. The essence of this 'RLS' proposal is to create a system for:

> . . . monitoring and public disclosure of working conditions [which would] . . . create official, social and financial incentives for firms to monitor and improve their own factories and those of their suppliers.

This would be accomplished by creating

> . . . an easily accessible pool of information with which the best practices of leading firms could be publicly identified, compared and diffused to others in comparable settings . . . The combination of firm-level monitoring and an infrastructure for pooling results would help to set provisional minimum standards of corporate behaviour, upon which competition—driven by social and regulatory pressures—would generate improvements that then 'ratchet' standards upwards.[15]

The key features of the RLS proposal—transparency, competition, continuous improvement and sanctions ('social and regulatory pressures')—mark it as worthy

[14] See, eg, for international law perspectives: N Horn, *Legal Problems of Codes of Conduct for Multinational Enterprises* (Deventer, Kluwer, 1980). For domestic perspectives, see, eg, HL Pitt and G Groskuafmanis, 'Minimizing Corporate Civil and Criminal Liability: A Second Look at Corporate Codes of Conduct' (1990) 78 *Georgetown LJ* 1559; C J Walsh and A Pyrich, 'Corporate Compliance Programs as a Defense to Criminal Liability: Can a Corporation Save Its Soul' (1995) 47 *Rutgers L Rev* 605; K Webb, 'Voluntary Approaches, the Environment and the Law: A Canadian Perspective' in C Carraro and F Lévéque (eds), *Voluntary Approaches in Environmental Policy* (Deventer, Kluwer, 1999); S Lu, 'Corporate Codes of Conduct and the FTC: Advancing Human Rights Through Deceptive Advertising Law' (2000) 38 *Columbia J of Transnational Law* 603.

[15] A Fung, D O'Rourke and C Sabel, 'Realizing Labor Standards' (2001) available at http://bostonreview. mit.edu/BR26.1/fung.html; see also C Sabel *et al* 'Ratcheting Labor Standards: Regulation for Continuous Improvement in the Global Workplace' (2000) available at http://www.law.columbia.edu/sabel/papers/ratchPO.html.

of attention from students of reflexive labour law. However, it has already received attention—unflattering attention—from labour and academic commentators, who have dubbed it 'wishful thinking'.[16] As one such commentator has noted, there is little empirical evidence that RLS will in fact produce the desired results:

> . . . of 61 factories 'certified' by SA8000 [a standard such as those proposed by the authors of RLS], 34 of them are in China. In the SA8000 code there is very strong language about freedom of association. If any workers in those 34 factories were to try and exercise the rights spelled out in the code, they would find themselves in jail or an insane asylum.[17]

At the very least, then, RLS raises in different form issues similar to those posed by the 'third wave' of voluntary codes, what is the relationship between self-regulation and state regulation? To what extent is it possible to think about RLS in isolation from the political economy and legal system of each state in which this approach is to operate? For example, if states tolerate or even insist upon a low level of workers' rights, how likely are corporations operating there to adhere to a higher standard even when formally committed to RLS? And, conversely, if states insist on decent labour standards, what need is there for RLS?[18]

The RLS proposal itself is less than clear on these questions. Its proponents insist that RLS '. . . aims not to deregulate, but rather to redeploy public power in ways that extend its regulatory reach and wisdom', that it is not 'a concession to unfettered markets' but rather that it will 'strengthen the hands and extend the horizons of those who have long championed workplace improvements'.[19] However, state action is clearly not an intrinsic feature of RLS. On the one hand, RLS rests on the fundamental assumption that conventional regulation by the state has proved incapable of achieving its objectives, and that it must be replaced or supplemented by new regulatory strategies which are more compatible with the political economy of globalisation. For that reason, the design of RLS begins not with state initiatives or in state institutions but with private initiatives and in the corporate context. On the other hand, RLS proponents do make passing reference to 'a more ambitious' model of their project. In this more ambitious model, they suggest, states might enact legislation requiring domestic firms to participate in RLS, might promulgate performance standards and benchmarks generated by RLS procedures as their own official labour standards, might 'transform their own

[16] M Levinson, 'Wishful Thinking' available at http://bostonreview.mit.edu/BR26.1/levinson.html. *Cf* J Murray, 'The Sound of One Hand Clapping?' The 'Ratcheting Labour Standards' Proposal and International Labour Law' (2001), 14 *Aust J Labour L* 306.

[17] Levinson, above n 16.

[18] A less polemical, recent empirical study of codes operating in four Chinese footwear factories which supply footwear to US-based transnational corporations concluded: 'The absence of de facto supporting institutions and norms at the national and local level in China militated against workers' awareness and support for workers' rights, as enshrined in labour legislation and the codes of practice. For the codes to be effective . . . institutional supports in the form of labour law enforcement, some kind of legitimate, independent workers' institution, and procedures for skill enhancement, will be necessary . . .'. S Frenkel, 'Globalization, Athletic Footwear Commodity Chains and Employment Relations in Southern China' (2001) 22 *Organizational Studies* 531 at 558.

[19] Fung *et al*, above n 15, at p 17.

regulatory systems from fixed-rule to ratcheting by requiring domestic firms to score high on RLS measures or face sanctions', and might (one can infer) impose sanctions which are of a 'regulatory' as well as a 'social' character.[20]

In short, even in the eyes of its proponents, for RLS to become 'more ambitious', it must become more state-centred. But here there is a potential contradiction: state law, state institutions, state policies may endanger reflexivity. This may happen in several ways. State policies may force social actors such as corporations to abandon their efforts to ratchet labour standards upwards, as in the Chinese example cited above. State regulatory institutions in countries with politically accountable legislatures may brush aside corporate regimes of self-regulation which are deemed unambitious, insincere or inefficacious. Or state law may encumber reflexive systems with constitutional, procedural and substantive requirements—formal promulgation, clear definitions of conduct, predictable sanctions—which are inconsistent with their implicit, allusive and inchoate character.

Case study no 3—The United Nations Global Compact

Self-regulation has perhaps reached its apotheosis in the Global Compact signed by the Secretary General of the United Nations, more than fifty of the world's most powerful corporations and a number of unions and social movements.[21] Like the RLS proposal, the UN Global Compact displays some characteristics of reflexive law. It is driven by the techno-professional discourse of a dialogic community; it is a closed system capable of receiving and responding to external stimuli; its success depends on the willingness of participants to engage in a transparent exchange of opinions and information; and it is designed to regulate not conduct per se but other normative systems, especially those embedded in corporate relationships.

The Global Compact declares nine substantive principles—two concerned with human rights, four with the environment and four with labour standards.[22] It commits signatories to advocate the principles of the Compact to both internal and external audiences; to 'embrace, support and enact' these principles 'within their sphere of influence'; to submit once each year 'a concrete example of progress made or a lesson learned in implementing the principles'; to promote positive behaviour by their own employees; to participate in an exchange of information with other companies; and to enter into a dialogue with their social partners concerning further measures.[23]

Finally, the Compact initiates various processes—a learning forum, policy dialogues, company and partnership initiatives and outreach—through which it seeks to promote the dissemination of best practices, to encourage their adoption

[20] Fung *et al*, above n 15, at pp 17–18.

[21] See http://www.unglobalcompact.org.

[22] Freedom of association and effective recognition of the right to collective bargaining (principle 3); elimination of forced and compulsory labour (principle 4); effective abolition of child labour (principle 5); and elimination of discrimination in respect of employment and occupation (principle 6).

[23] Global Compact, above, n 21.

by subscribing corporations, and to foster cooperation amongst corporations, governments, unions and civil society.[24]

On its face, the UN Global Compact seems at worst innocuous, and at best a modest step towards promoting global corporate accountability. Indeed, it is likely the most ambitious initiative that the Secretary General could hope to undertake, given the adamant refusal of many states to accept any measures which might compromise their sovereignty or their competitive edge.[25] However, some civil society actors have been critical of the Compact from its inception, claiming that corporations have become 'tangled up in blue'—accorded recognition and prestige through their association with the Secretary General and the UN itself. These critics argue, for example, that membership of the Global Compact should not have been extended to corporations which have been guilty of egregious abuses of workers, human rights or the environment; that the relationship of such corporations to the UN and civil society actors should not be described as a 'partnership'; that the image of the UN has been sullied by its deferential attitude towards these corporations; and that the Compact establishes no monitoring or enforcement procedures.[26]

As the Compact was signed only in mid-2000, and is not yet fully operational, it is impossible to evaluate its positive or negative impact.[27] However, it does constitute a highly visible experiment whose results will contribute to a better understanding of the potential and the limits of self-regulation and reflexive labour law.

The Significance of Self-Regulation, Several Observations in Search of an Hypothesis

These brief sketches of experiments in corporate self-regulation suggest that reflexive labour law may be becoming more commonplace, that it may indeed

[24] *Ibid.*

[25] The inability of the UN—for over 35 years—to agree upon even a non-binding code of conduct for multinational corporations is some evidence of the difficulties which confronts such measures. See D Kinley, 'Human Rights as Legally Binding or Merely Relevant?' in S Bottomley and D Kinley (eds), *Commercial Law and Human Rights* (Aldershot, Ashgate/Dartmouth, 2001). For an account of other difficulties precluding more conventional strategies, see J Ruggie, 'Global_governance.net: The Global Compact as a Learning Network' (2001) 7 *Global Governance* 371. Ruggie was one of the architects of the Global Compact.

[26] See Transnational Resource and Action Center (TRAC), *Tangled up in Blue: Corporate Partnerships at the United Nations*, available at http://corpwatch.org/trac/globalization/un/tangled.html (Sept 6, 2000).

[27] The early literature—'A Symposium on the Global Compact' in (2001) 34 *Cornell International LJ*—is perforce largely descriptive and speculative. For a guardedly optimistic view of the Global Compact from the perspective of critical legal pluralism, see A Blackett, 'Global Goverance, Legal Pluralism and the Decentered State: A Labor Law Critique of Codes of Corporate Conduct' (2001) 8 *Indiana J of Global Legal Studies* 401 at 440 *ff.*

emerge as the characteristic legal form of the future.[28] This makes it especially important to explore why self-regulation and reflexive labour law seem so relevant at this particular moment in history. Note first that many of the post-modern socio-legal theories[29] which have emerged in recent decades display characteristics associated as well with reflexive law. (They also exhibit fundamental differences, reflecting the diversity of intellectual provenances and socio-political milieux in which they first appeared.)[30] These theories in general challenge the conventional 'command model' of law; emphasise the normative fecundity of social fields; insist on the pluralistic character of legal systems; acknowledge the role in law-making, -interpreting and -enforcing of discursive communities and other agents not formally mandated by the state; and regard the close alignment of state and law as an historical contingency of the modern era. In various ways, then, they share an attitude of scepticism about the state's central role in the meta-narrative of law.

And now a second observation. The de-centring of the state is not only an important issue for socio-legal scholars. It is the defining issue of political life in most countries. The notion that the state should intervene actively to promote the public interest and distribute public goods has been the subject of relentless, often irrational and sometimes cogent criticism for almost as long as activist government has been advocated and practised. However, especially since the Thatcher and Reagan administrations of the 1980s, this criticism has become particularly strident in the English-speaking world. It has produced disenchantment with the state, and apathy—even hostility—towards electoral politics not least, ironically, amongst marginalised groups which are the principal clients of state intervention and amongst the political and technocratic elites which have been shaping state policy and directing state administration.

Disenchantment, hostility and apathy have transformed the discourse of labour law. It is no longer a given that the state can or should ensure minimum labour standards, promote countervailing power, redistribute wealth or coordinate corporatist strategies which feature labour as a prominent contributor and principal beneficiary. Instead, the state is now to be assigned the more mundane tasks of providing infrastructure, supporting human resource development, blaming refugees and immigrants for labour market dislocations caused by structural adjustment to technology and globalisation, and imposing economic and legal discipline on assertive workers. Likewise, the key participants in the formation of labour policy have changed. Labour lawyers (now 'employment lawyers'), industrial relations managers (now 'human resources' officers), trade unionists (still 'trade unionists',

[28] W Scheuerman, *Liberal Democracy and the Social Acceleration of Time* (Baltimore/London, Johns Hopkins UP, 2004) 210 *ff.*

[29] This includes work on jural polycentricity or legal pluralism; Bourdieu's emphasis on the constitution of the 'legal field', studies by Burawoy and Stuart Henry on workplace normativity; the governance school which derives from the work of Foucauld; analyses of the emergence of 'soft law', especially in transnational relationships; and elements of critical legal studies. For references to this work see H Arthurs, 'Landscape and Memory: Labour Law, Legal Pluralism and Globalization' in T Wilthagen (ed), *Advancing Theory*, above, n 3.

[30] See generally D Nelken, 'Changing Paradigms in the Sociology of Law' in G Teubner (ed), *Autopoietic Law—A New Approach to Law and Society* (Berlin/NY, de Gruyter, 1988).

but fewer in number) and labour ministries (where they still exist) no longer play key roles, if any; economists, corporate lobbyists, central bankers, Treasury officials and Ministries of Trade and Industry now control the agenda.[31] And that agenda itself has changed, both for policy makers and scholars. Considerable anti-labour legislation has been enacted by neo-liberal, centrist and social democratic governments around the world; progressive reforms are at best a remote possibility in most countries;[32] and in many benign neglect is the most labour can hope for. In much of North America (though perhaps not in Europe)[33] the intense and highly politicised debates over workers' rights which once raged within academic labour law have been largely superseded by yet more intense and highly politicised controversies over gender, race and disability;[34] and within the residual domain of labour law, individual employment law—for practical reasons, the law of privileged categories of workers—attracts more attention than collective labour law.

In short, the de-centring of the state has altered power relations. Most states are now unwilling or unable to confront powerful global corporations, which can disinvest with relative ease, which can relocate production to more business-friendly jurisdictions, and which can destabilise share prices and national currencies. In fact, in most states, the shift of political power away from labour is accepted, however glumly, as a fact of life. Governments confront only sporadic protests against the loss of labour's entitlements, only plaintive pleas for protection against the dislocations which result from the 'creative destruction' of global capitalism. Even the traumatic anti-globalisation protests in Seattle, Prague, Genoa, Quebec and elsewhere have not so far produced organised, sustained, mass support for laws and policies which protect workers. For all of these reasons, workers—even those who populate the thinning ranks of unions—are reluctant to challenge their employers. This, I suggest, is the context within which we must understand the recent proliferation of experiments in corporate self-regulation.

The Political Economy of a Reflexive Labour Law System

Against this background, one may ask—If socio-legal theory and political economy are being transformed in the same moment, in the same direction, does one have something to do with the other, and if not, what does their coincidental convergence imply for an understanding of reflexive labour law?

[31] HW Arthurs, 'What Immortal Hand or Eye?—Who Will Redraw the Boundaries of Labour Law?' in G Davidov and B Langille, *Boundaries and Frontiers of Labour Law: Goals and Means in the Regulation of Work* (Hart, 2006).

[32] See, eg, C Estlund, 'The Ossification of American Labor Law' (2002) 102 *Columbia L Rev* 1527.

[33] See, eg, A Supiot, with ME Casas *et al*, *Beyond Employment: Changes in Work and the Future of Labour Law in Europe* (Oxford, Oxford University Press, 2001).

[34] For a rather dyspeptic view of this tendency, see M Finkin, 'Reflections on Labor Law Scholarship: The Reveries of Monsieur Verog' (1992) 46 *University of Miami L Rev* 1101.

In an important recent piece, Rogowski argues that '. . . a major function of reflexive law is to stimulate and instigate self-reflection and self-regulation in other social systems . . .'.[35] Taking the three episodes of self-regulation described above as examples of reflexive labour law operating in this way, we can next explore what Rogowski describes as his 'research hypotheses', as trends which he detects in the regulation of labour and employment conflicts:

—the emergence of increasingly specialised and autonomous labour tribunals, which become the primary locus of innovation in the labour law system
—enhanced proceduralisation of labour law, in part reflecting a growing disenchantment with instrumentalism, formalisation and materialisation
—self-regulation leading to mutual recognition amongst the multiple systems of social ordering which impinge on the workplace, with a view to facilitating their autonomy and self-reproduction and with a commensurate decline in judicial regulation.[36]

Rogowski does not suggest, of course, that these are the only possible manifestations of reflexivity in labour law whether in its conflictual or non-conflictual aspects. Nor does he have much to say specifically about corporate codes or other forms of corporate self-regulation. Nonetheless, the three case studies summarised above—of corporate codes, of RLS and of the UN Global Compact—generally support Rogowski's 'research hypotheses'. However, in each case one must enter a serious *caveat.*

It is true that voluntary code-based systems are totally or largely 'autonomous', that they are closed systems and that tribunals associated with them—though rare—are indeed highly specialised. But there is little evidence that code-based systems actually produce innovation, except to the extent that by masking or cosmeticising the decline of state labour law they help to facilitate and normalise the shift of power from unions and workers to employers.

As Rogowski predicts, these new regimes of corporate self-regulation—unlike state law—are often neither rational nor instrumental nor formal in their operation and effects. Their mandates tend to be expressed only in vague and modest aspirational terms; their capacity to initiate action or pursue complaints is circumscribed; their remedial powers are negligible or non-existent; their professional character is typically underdeveloped; their activity levels are low; and their capacity or ambition to actually shape the conduct of the corporations which promulgate them appear to be minimal. Consequently, as near as anyone can tell, they have produced little change in the workplace.[37]

[35] Rogowski in Wilthagen (ed), *Advancing Theory*, above, n 3, at 73–4.

[36] *Ibid* at p 74–7.

[37] In fairness, while claims and counter-claims abound concerning the efficacy or inefficacy of self-regulatory regimes, the literature does not provide much empirical evidence one way or the other. The most sophisticated empirical study to date, however, concludes that companies which have subscribed to a code of self-regulation in the US Chemical Industry have a worse environmental record than those which did not. See A King and M Lenox, above, n 10.

To compensate, as Rogowski points out, these regimes are often heavily 'proceduralised', in the sense that they seek to achieve their objectives by emphasizing transparency, the promotion of cooperation and the dissemination of best practices. Their proceduralism is fraught with great symbolic significance. Performances of the rituals of self-regulation—the well-publicised adoption of a code, for example, or the blessing conferred on the exercise by senior government officials, the undertaking of annual compliance audits, the occasional solemn exorcism of an offending contractor, the publication of self-congratulatory reports—tell us a great deal about the values and interests which shape labour market regulation today.[38] They remind us that states and their voters seem content that corporations should create and administer their own standards, that they should be trusted and admired for their conscientious behaviour, and that while workers should benefit from such behaviour, they should play no role in shaping or censuring it. And they remind us, as well, that to the extent that reflexivity is accomplished by such symbolic strategies, we must ask ourselves what are its prospects for improving on the outcomes achieved by more conventional regulatory regimes.

Rogowski hypothesises that workplaces are increasingly regulated by multiple regimes—including 'company procedures and other mechanisms of self-regulation'—which contribute to legal complexity, and ultimately to the 'juridification of social regulations'.[39] Because these multiple regimes interact with but do not control each other, he suggests, state courts tend to concentrate on the necessary task of resolving conflicts amongst them rather than regulating employers and workers directly. A reasonable hypothesis: but what does it imply?

On the one hand, courts may use state laws of general application or broad concepts such as 'jurisdiction' to mediate inter-systemic conflicts by limiting the autonomy of one system or enlarging that of another. In given circumstances, this may protect workers' rights and limit corporate power. Or courts may use concepts such as 'due process' or 'reasonableness' to ensure that all systems—state or private—conform to minimal standards of fairness. Again, in given circumstances, workers may be the beneficiaries. However, even such well-meant curial mediation may undermine or over-burden the fragile procedures, doctrines and discourses of reflexive workplace systems and render them incapable of performing the protective functions for which they were originally designed.[40] On the other hand, when courts decide to simply take a hands-off attitude to reflexive regimes, the result can also be prejudicial to workers.[41] Everything depends on the nature of the systems in question.

[38] Compare A Hyde, 'Labor Law as Political Symbol—A Critical Study of Labor Legislation' in Rogowski and Wilthagen (eds), *Reflexive Labour Law*, above, n 3 at 173.

[39] Rogowski in Priban and Nelken (eds), *Law's New Boundaries*, above, n 3 at 191 *ff.*

[40] H Arthurs, 'Protection Against Judicial Review' (1983) 43 *Rev du Barreau* 277, reprinted in *CIAJ, Judicial Review of Administrative Rulings* (Montreal, Editions Yvon Blais, 1984); H Arthurs, 'The New Economy and the New Legality: Industrial Citizenship and the Future of Labour Arbitration' (1999) 7 *Canadian Employment & Labour L J* 45.

[41] For example, several recent US Supreme Court decisions have held that employees must honour provisions in their employment contracts which require them to arbitrate statutory claims against their

Likewise, courts may decide to attempt to resolve inter-systemic conflicts not by adjusting reflexive workplace regimes to conform to the mediating principles of state law, but rather by mobilizing the power of state law to reinforce the values and assumptions of those reflexive regimes. For example, as noted earlier, courts might decide to hold corporations liable under state criminal, tort, contract or regulatory law for violations of their own codes of conduct.[42] Or they might actually mandate the creation of new reflexive systems of self-regulation, which would operate under court auspices on an ongoing basis,[43] much as legislatures did in encouraging or requiring the practice of grievance arbitration in North America. Again, in terms of the consequences for workers, everything depends on the quality of those systems.

It seems clear, then, that Rogowski is right in his fundamental insight that the existence of normative pluralism raises issues of legal complexity and internormativity which in turn invite mediation by state courts. But it is now important to add that there is no single set of appropriate organizing principles which must inform such mediation, that there is no way of predicting whether mediation will work in favour of particularistic, indigenous or reflexive law rather than in favour of state laws of general application, and that there is no necessary assurance that the resulting social outcomes are likely to be favour workers rather than employers.

From Rogowski's perspective, systemic mediation is driven by a tendency towards the reduction of legal complexity. However, as he acknowledges, the reduction of legal complexity may amount in practice to deregulation of the labour market. This is clearly a matter of concern to Rogowski who distinguishes 'reflexive deregulation' of the workplace from that driven by neo-liberal ideology. Indeed, Rogowski's own preference is for an approach which '. . . pursues not only economic but also wider social goals, . . . [which] tries to strike a balance between employer demands of reduced levels of protection and the employees' interests to find and keep a secure job'.[44] This formulation is important. It suggests that while proponents of the theory of theory of reflexive law begin by stating that their aims are purely descriptive or analytical, they themselves acknowledge that in practice reflexive labour law systems may produce effects with real-life political, social or moral consequences which they regard as undesirable. I will return to this point in my conclusion.

employer rather than seek recourse through government agencies. K Stone, 'Mandatory Arbitration of Individual Employment Rights: The Yellow Dog Contract of the 1990s' (1996) 73 *Denver University L Rev* 1017; K Stone, 'Rustic Justice: Community and Coercion under the Federal Arbitration Act' (1999) 77 *North Carolina Law Review* 77.

[42] See above, n 12.

[43] An American federal district court has been asked to issue a consent decree approving the settlement of litigation by some 50,000 Asian migrant workers against a group of garment manufacturers in the Marianas, an offshore US dependency. The proposed decree would mandate the adoption of a code of conduct to prevent continuation of egregious employment practices by the employers, require that the code contain effective monitoring, complaint and remedial procedures, and place the whole arrangement under the ongoing surveillance of specially-trained court monitors. For a history of the litigation, see Sweatshop Watch, 'Summary of the Saipan Sweatshop Litigation', available at http://igc.org/swatch/marianas/summary10_00.html.

[44] Rogowski in Priban and Nelken (eds), above, n 3 at 192.

Finally, as Rogowski remarks, reflexive systems are not only autonomous in their operation; they have an extensive capacity for self-reproduction.[45] States have so far generally not captured them; they proliferate; they mutate in successive generations; and they maintain remarkable isolation from the adjacent state systems, whose incursions they are designed to forestall. They operate, in other words, in much the same way as lethal viruses and dangerous new drug-resistant strains of bacteria. Of course, reflexive systems of labour law are not inherently lethal or dangerous to the well-being of workers and the health of unions. But it is not irrelevant that the proliferation of regimes of corporate self-regulation—of reflexive labour law regimes, in other words—seems to have no necessary connection with an improvement in labour standards for workers employed by corporations which have adopted codes of conduct, committed themselves to 'ratcheting' standards upwards through the sharing of best practices, or signed on to the UN Global Compact.

Even more cynical interpretations are possible. Perhaps there is a connection between reflexive labour law and enhanced labour standards. Reflexivity, after all, implies learning. In the new labour law dispensation of corporate self-regulation, employees are indeed learning: to accept that the state cannot or will not protect them; to applaud employers whose adoption of voluntary codes certifies that they are responsible corporate citizens; to subject themselves willingly to governance by those codes and, by extension, by the other normative systems promulgated by their employer; and ultimately to abandon the notion that they can shape their own fate by supporting unions or political parties committed to aggressive state regulation of the labour market.

Conclusion: Beyond Reflexivity, Beyond Labour Law

The three sketches of corporate self-regulation which introduce this essay do not so much challenge the hypotheses of reflexivity as expose their potential dark side. However, one should not criticise theories of reflexivity for what they do not claim and therefore do not accomplish. As noted, Rogowski and Wilthagen maintain that the theory of reflexivity is intended to be descriptive rather than prescriptive.[46] That is to say, it is meant to help us better understand socio-legal phenomena, not to enlist support for specific regulatory strategies or programs, much less for ultimate political or social values. To that extent, I have been somewhat unfair in stressing that reflexive labour law may express, legitimate and even reinforce corporate power. On the other hand, for several reasons, it is important for reflexive labour lawyers to come to grips with the issue of power more explicitly than they have done so far.

45 Rogowski in Wilthagen (ed), above, n 3 at 71.
46 Rogowski and Wilthagen (eds), above, n 3 at 7–8.

Rogowski aptly cites Hegel's famous aphorism that '. . . philosophy [a]s the thought of the world . . . appears only at a time when actuality has gone through its formative process and attained its completed state. . . . [T]he owl of Minerva begins its flight only with the onset of the dusk . . .'.[47] The idea of reflexivity, I wish to suggest, arrives at the dusk of post-war optimism about the potential of electoral politics and the activist state, about social democracy, about the emancipatory potential of collective workers action, about law's rationality and practical attainments. It would therefore be helpful if reflexive labour law had more to say about the events which characterise this neo-liberal dusk, and about what Minerva's owl portends for relations of power in the workplace.

This shortcoming is no reason to resist reflexive labour law as a descriptive or explanatory theory. Indeed, the crisis of theorisation in industrial relations, in law generally, and in labour law in particular amply justifies all attempts to develop new scientific critiques and new theoretical perspectives.[48] Reflexive labour law clearly responds to this crisis. However, let us revisit the context. Like other theories associated with post-modernity, reflexive law assumes—but does not insist—that the state and its legal system are historically contingent and increasingly irrelevant. Fair enough: but note that theories of neo-liberalism and globalisation also dismiss the state and its legal system—or at least the social democratic state and transformative legal strategies. Is this mere coincidence? Or is there a connection—consequential, ideological or epistemological—between reflexive law and neo-liberalism?

At the least, it seems that the post/modern view of the state and the reflexive analysis of law may become self-fulfilling prophecies. Theories such as reflexivity are not parthenogenic: they do not create themselves, write themselves, disseminate themselves. They are produced by human intelligence and propagated by human agents—by scholars like us. But scholars like us are also—inescapably—political actors: we write books and articles and shape the thinking of students, lawyers and judges; we advocate public policies and advise governments and civil society organisations; we prepare legal opinions and draft legislation. My concern is that our scientific work will—even against our intentions—come to affect our political work, so that our descriptive hypotheses about how law works will become prescriptive. After all, if we believe in autopoiesis, what can we say about legislation or rights-based litigation or other purely instrumental approaches to law? If we believe in legal reflexivity, how can we be critical, much less cynical, about corporate self-regulation which, after all, is a text-book example of the phenomenon? At some point, then, what we believe as scholars is likely to impinge upon what we do as political actors. When it does, the activist state is going to suffer the defection of some of its most influential and knowledgeable supporters—a loss it can ill afford in this era of neo-liberal ascendancy.

[47] G Hegel, *Elements of the Philosophy of Right* (Cambridge, Cambridge University Press, 1991) at 23 (A Wood, ed, originally published 1820), cited by Rogowski in Wilthagen (ed), above, n 3 at 67.

[48] H Arthurs, 'Landscape and Memory: Labour Law, Legal Pluralism and Globalization' in Wilthagen, above, n 3 at 21 *ff*.

Finally, in this scenario, it is not just the state and its legal system which are being transformed by the simultaneously assault of neo-liberalism and post-modern theorizing. The metaphoric death of the state is likely to have the same disconcerting effects on labour lawyers and scholars as the death of God had on theologians and members of religious orders. In the end, some of us may cling mindlessly to the old church; others may abandon labour law entirely; still others may embrace new economic faiths, new political values, new scientific revelations or new legal rituals. Will reflexive labour law rise to the challenge of this new era to provide us with a narrative of workplace normativity which is not only helpful in a descriptive and explanatory sense, but which provides a basis for evaluation and critique? And will those of us who persevere with scholarship in the field be able to build again—with new insights, in new historical circumstances—a new regime of state labour law which speaks social justice to corporate power? Or does the very formulation of these questions mark me as someone who has failed to grasp the fundamental insights of reflexive labour law?

3

Toward a Democratic Model of Transnational Labour Monitoring?

MARK BARENBERG*

In the field of international labour law, the International Labour Organisation (ILO) is the predominant actor. A specialised agency of the United Nations, the ILO enacts and 'supervises' the enforcement of global labour rights. But in light of manifest weaknesses in the ILO's enforcement function, the last decade has seen the emergence of two new developments in the transnational enforcement of labour rights and standards. The first is the inclusion of labour rights provisions in bilateral and plurilateral trade agreements. The second is the diffusion of privatised systems for enforcing labour rights across borders, through corporate codes of conduct monitored by corporate managers, for-profit consultants, and non-profit consortia.

This Chapter assesses the performance of the privatised systems of labour monitoring. It does not purport to offer an overall survey of the field. Instead, it examines the most rigorous model of monitoring that has yet to emerge. Using an ethnographic method, the Chapter presents two case studies in which that model was implemented and tested. The case studies, in which I was a participant-observer, describe interventions at factories in Mexico and Indonesia by the Worker Rights Consortium (WRC), an organisation supported by more than one hundred universities and colleges in the United States.

The Chapter highlights those aspects of the two case studies that may shed light on two practical questions: What are the key institutional challenges to conducting transnational labour monitoring in a manner that is not only effective in enforcing basic rights but also meets basic norms of democratic governance? Are the decisions of local monitoring teams accountable, either to one another or to a legitimately constituted central organ that announces evolving understandings of the universal norms in light of their local specifications and re-specifications?[1]

* Professor of Law, Columbia Law Shool.

[1] The cases raise other crucial questions of legitimacy and effectiveness. The WRC monitors factories through multiparty teams that include Northern labour-rights experts representing the university communities, and representatives of local workers and their communities. As the WRC has evolved, local representatives have constituted a growing super-majority of team membership. This methodology raise several questions: To what degree do the WRC teams in fact constitute effective, participatory arenas for the specification of norms? Do the teams include and empower representatives of all relevant local interests to deliberate over norm-specification and remediation—to make autonomous

To answer these questions, I focus on the WRC teams' investigation in the area of freedom of association—a basic right that many private monitors fail to address. More specifically still, I examine the WRC's encounter with company-dominated or state-dominated unions. In both cases, the WRC teams achieved substantial improvements in working standards—such as overtime hours and pay, safety and health, and sexual and physical abuse. But it is the WRC's assessments of the legitimacy of labour organisations that most pointedly test the teams' own legitimacy. The implications for institutional design of transnational labour monitoring are significant, in light of the pervasive problem of 'protection unionism' in both the export and non-export sectors in low-wage countries.

The Chapter concludes that the WRC teams have taken some significant steps toward effective, democratic monitoring at the local level, but are likely to fulfil that potential only if they are integrated with democratic national or regional bodies.

'Managerialist' and 'Participatory' Models of Labour Monitoring

There is general recognition among corporate monitors, non-governmental organisations, and academicians that the WRC has developed the most effective, transparent, and 'participatory' model of transnational labour monitoring. But then, it may not take much to surpass the performance of other private monitors, which generally adhere to a 'managerialist' model.[2] In fact, the WRC's participatory model emerged self-consciously in response to the flaws of the managerialist models. A quick description of the WRC's genesis, then, reveals the key distinctions between the two models.

Universities and colleges in the United States organised the WRC in 2000, largely in response to student protests over 'sweatshop' conditions in the factories that produce apparel bearing university names and logos. Those goods are sold to students, faculty, and alumni, and have a high profile among American consumers more generally, especially among supporters of the big-name college football and basketball teams. The universities act as licensors or buyers vis-à-vis manufactur-

choices about the organisation of production, distributional shares, tradeoffs between levels of employment and wages, and ultimately the path of local development? Are the composition and methods of the teams well-suited to draw on local knowledge of worker preferences, production systems, and market constraints? A reader seeking decisive answers to these questions might justifiably demand ethnographic 'thick description' of (1) the actual interaction and deliberations among team members over the weeks and months of fact-finding, norm-specification, and remediation, and (2) the organisational norms of the factory and their transformations. I save these issues for another time.

[2] The description of managerialist monitoring in this subsection is based principally on the author's in-depth interviews with eighty-seven social-compliance managers of factories and multinational brands in the apparel, footwear, and retail sectors in Thailand, Hong Kong, Mexico, Indonesia, China, and the United States over the period 2001 to 2003.

ers. Manufacturers out-source their production of collegiate merchandise to factories owned by vendors, whose headquarters are most frequently found in South Korea, Taiwan, Hong Kong, and Singapore. Conceptually, universities can be viewed either as retailers that serve as the final step in global supply chains, or as collective consumers, analogous to government procurement departments.

In response to student protests in the late 1990s, many US universities announced their intention to affiliate with the Fair Labour Association, a US-based labour-monitoring consortium. The student protestors found the FLA unacceptable. Their objections were similar to those levelled against the FLA by several human rights, religious, and labour organisations.[3] They objected to: (1) the financial and voting power of major manufacturers in FLA governance, creating a conflict of interest with the FLA's mandate to report on those corporations' own factories ('the fox guarding the henhouse', according to FLA critics); (2) a second conflict of interest stemming from the manufacturers' right to choose and pay the particular second-party monitor to audit any given factory (a practice that the FLA ultimately abandoned in spring of 2002); (3) the limits that the FLA placed on full reporting of data gathered by factory auditors; (4) the absence of a 'living wage' requirement in the FLA code of conduct; and (5) the FLA's authorisation of factories to operate in countries with highly repressive labour policies, so long as factory managers do not actively aid those policies. Many universities responded to the student protests by affiliating with both the FLA and the newly established WRC.

The WRC governing board comprised representatives of three constituencies—university administrators; an advisory council made up of faculty and independent specialists in labour-rights; and graduate and undergraduate students. The three groups reached agreement on a set of principles that would animate the WRC—and that would sharply distinguish it from the FLA and other managerialist monitors.

The WRC would remain independent of management and labour-union interests in the apparel industry, in terms both of voting rights within the WRC Board and of WRC funding sources;[4] would engage, to the maximum feasible extent, local workers and communities in the process of factory assessment and in revision of the substantive terms of the WRC Code; would strive to ensure that factories provide a 'living wage' to their workforces; would insist that retailers and vendors maintain or increase their investment while improving labour

[3] Based on these objections, the organisations refused to participate in FLA. Several other important human-rights and labour-rights groups supported the FLA.

[4] The establishment of the WRC as a counter-model to the industry-supported FLA had the tacit support of US labour unions. But once the WRC became a functioning organisation rooted in the university community, it kept its distance from both industry and labour unions as a matter of internal governance, although it necessarily interacted with companies and unions in the course of its monitoring activities. Unlike other private monitors, the WRC does not take funding from corporations or unions. Although one member of its 15-member Board of Directors is a union official, she sits as an expert in labour rights and not as a representative of her organisation. No other union or corporate official sits on the WRC Board.

compliance in factories being assessed, rather than 'cutting and running' at the expense of local job-creation; would afford full public access to information gathered in factory assessments; and would seek to improve those conditions given highest priority by a factory's workforce but would not seek to 'certify' that a factory, product line, or brand was comprehensively compliant with labour rights.

The latter principle entails that, unlike most managerialist monitors, the WRC will not provide 'no-sweat' labelling or its equivalent to university licensees and factories. The WRC maintains, accurately, that any such warrant of full compliance will likely give consumers a misleading picture. Private monitors currently lack the capacity to investigate all potential claims of non-compliance, across all areas of labour and employment law and across all domestic and international codes, covering the months or years since the previous audit. These are tasks that have proven difficult even for multiple sovereign agencies such as, in the United States, the National Labour Relations Board (covering collective bargaining), the Equal Employment Opportunity Commission (covering antidiscrimination rights), the Department of Labour (covering wages, hours, and child labour), the Occupational Safety and Health Administration, and so on. These agencies have many professionally trained investigators and adjudicators who can devote days and weeks to single claims of non-compliance. By contrast, managerialist auditors generally spend one or two person-days on each factory audit. Interviews of workers generally occur on company property and last only 15 to 30 minutes. Workers' interviews are not preceded by periods of trust-building between auditors and workers. Although auditors select workers to be interviewed, workers are pulled from their stations by managers and fear they will be held responsible for any loss of purchase orders or other adverse consequences that may result from auditors' negative findings. Auditors are generally not professionally trained in labour law enforcement or industrial health and hygiene. They lack the power to subpoena documents and cross-examine witnesses under oath, in the face of predictable conflicts in testimony among workers and managers over sensitive subjects.

Rather than claiming to engage in comprehensive audits of factories' compliance with all labour and employment rights over the relevant audit period, the WRC prioritises workers' grievances based on the workforces' own preliminary complaints. The WRC then seeks to investigate and remedy only those problems, or other high-priority problems that emerge during the assessment, within the concededly limited resources of a private monitoring organisation.

At the same time, the WRC seeks to conduct audits that are particularly (1) resource intensive and (2) participatory, compared to managerialist monitors. The WRC assembles teams of five to eight members, who undertake hundreds of hours of interviews during four to eight days of on-site fact-finding and months of subsequent remediation activity for a single factory assessment. Prior to the formal interviewing, WRC staff, consultants, or allied non-governmental organisations may spend weeks or months in trust-building communication with local workers, managers, and civil-society groups. Following the on-site investigation, the WRC maintains regular contact with on-site groups of workers, labour organisations, community members, local academics, and supply-chain managers.[5]

The composition of the WRC teams is designed to maximise participation by representatives of worker and community interests most vitally affected by the operation of the factory—worker advocates, women's organisations, village associations, informal worker organisations, and others. In composing the teams, the primary goal is to embody within the team a 'deliberative arena' in which local actors may participate equally with US-based or other Northern-based team members. Each day of the week-long, on-site assessment, the team members conduct several hours of interviews and several hours of discussion within the team. Within that social space, the relatively abstract norms embodied in international labour rights and university codes of conduct, and the less abstract norms embodied in domestic law will be given specific local content and effect—as team members deliberate over fact-finding, interpretation and application of labour rights, and recommendations for remediation. The substantive goal is to generate compliance norms that are, in some meaningful sense, *autonomously* shaped by local interests, and *pragmatically* suited to local problem-solving within the functional constraints and 'moral codes' of the factory organisation and supply chains—but also accountable to the more general international and domestic legal norms.[6]

In addition to interviewing managers and workers, the WRC teams interview local government officials, including labour ministers, conciliation boards, labour judges, economic development officers, and police. Although the WRC is, of course, a private organisation, it has a paradoxical attitude toward privatisation of labour-rights enforcement. It seeks to develop an intensive model of private monitoring, but it opposes the displacement of legitimate sovereign authorities and workers' organisations by private organisations. It therefore seeks to cooperate with and build the capacity of local labour ministries and tribunals, just as it and other private monitors attempt to build the capacity of local NGOs.

Unlike managerialist monitors, the WRC assesses workplace grievances in contexts where local workforces are 'in motion'—that is, where factory workers are in

[5] The WRC seeks to develop a global network of NGOs, experts, and labour-rights advocates who can collaborate with the WRC in the assessment process as well as in other educational, outreach, and capacity-building activities.

[6] Before, during, and after each factory assessment, the WRC staff presents the university constituents with Reports that include fact-finding, findings of compliance or non-compliance with Codes, and recommendations for remediation. The WRC staff as well as officials of the affiliated universities communicate with manufacturers, vendors, and factories about the unfolding assessment processes and means of remediation. The authority to deploy the leverage of university licensing or buying power vis-à-vis the manufacturers, however, rests only with the universities, not with the WRC Board or staff.

In practice, a sub-group of university administrators plays a proactive role in demanding that licensees take the remedial measures recommended by the WRC; and the university administrators authorise the WRC Executive Director to communicate directly with the brands and factories to achieve remediation. At the same time, student activists and interested faculty members independently point to the WRC Reports in their frequent campaigns urging the university administrators and licensees to act aggressively toward factories that are found non-compliant.

fact attempting to address factory non-compliance through their own associational activities. The WRC attempts to engage in robust enforcement of labour rights and thereby 'open political space' for legitimate public authorities, worker organisations, and other collective actors to engage in long-term, self-sustained monitoring.

The principle of maximum local participation is constrained by three other objectives: First, the WRC teams include experts on international labour rights and domestic labour rights of the host country, and on technical matters such as occupational safety and health and wage-and-hour compliance—in order to conduct the investigation effectively and to ensure credibility in the eyes of the US media and university officials. Second, while the teams include worker representatives from the local area, they do not include workers employed at the factory or union officials seeking to organise the factory—in order to avoid conflicts of interest. Third, each team includes at least one staff member or board member of the WRC—since the WRC is ultimately responsible for the findings of fact and law and recommendations for remediation that it forwards to the university licensors.

From the point of view of the WRC's strategies, the role of the mass media is complex.[7] The WRC does not seek consumer boycotts of university licensees, since the WRC does not aim to take jobs away from non-compliant factories. Nonetheless, media coverage of WRC factory reports undoubtedly increases the pressure on licensees to take remedial action at factories and to follow the WRC recommendations to 'stay and improve' rather than 'cut and run'. In addition, media coverage shines an international spotlight on factories where workers face imminent threats and abuse, thereby protecting workers against such intimidation. Favourable stories about WRC efforts in *The New York Times*, *The Washington Post*, and other influential newspapers also played an important role in establishing the legitimacy and credibility of a monitoring organisation devoted to robust monitoring of rights that, at least in the United States, are politically controversial—particularly workers' right of association. Establishing this kind of credibility was especially important for the WRC, which, as a matter of principle, had no organisational ties to corporations and unions and which had emerged as a result of protests by 'militant' students.

Kukdong

The Kukdong factory is located in Atlixco, a village in the Mexican State of Puebla. It is owned by a South Korean corporation that also has apparel facilities in other

[7] The mass media are generally not viewed as a constitutive actor in the field of social compliance; yet their role is often important and sometimes decisive. This role stems from the fundamental fact that private monitoring gains much of its leverage over factories through the actual or latent purchasing decisions of consumers. The mass media, as the term suggests, are the central channel for transmitting information from monitors to consumers, alongside the increasingly important channel of websites created by monitors and independent NGOs.

low-wage countries. In late 2000 and early 2001, the facility employed approximately 900 workers, mostly very young women recruited from small rural villages within a two-hour drive from the factory. It produced sweatshirts for Nike, under license from universities affiliated with the WRC. Kukdong also produced for Reebok and other retailers.

On January 18, 2001, Kukdong workers filed a complaint with the WRC, alleging that the factory violated Mexican and international law and university codes of conduct in several areas: sick leave, maternity leave, minimum wages, physical assault and abuse, child labour, food provision, and rights of association. A large segment of the Kukdong workforce sought to organise an independent union and oust the incumbent CROC union, an affiliate of a government-controlled federation. The workers charged that the CROC was a corrupt 'protection union' that signed a contract with Kukdong managers, took payments from the factory, but provided no benefits or services to the workers.

The complaint to the WRC was triggered by the factory's discharge of five leaders of the independent union on January 3, 2001. A large majority of the Kukdong workers began a strike in protest of the discharges and other grievances, and in support of the independent union drive. On January 11th, Kukdong managers and CROC officials led a violent police action against the striking workers.[8] On January 13th, as transnational scrutiny of the dispute began, Kukdong managers signed an agreement to reinstate all striking workers without discrimination. Subsequently, the managers required returning workers to sign loyalty oaths to the CROC and refused to reinstate several hundred workers who were active in the strike.

The WRC assessment team spent five days in the State of Puebla, beginning eight days after the January 11th police action against the striking workers (January 19–23).[9] During that time, the team interviewed fifty-eight workers in six of their home villages, including both supporters and opponents of the strike; five Kukdong managers, including the general manager, human resources manager, and labour attorney; the chief officers of the incumbent union and other unions in

[8] As is customary in Mexico, the striking workers did not leave company property, but instead stayed within the factory compound, standing in an area between the factory and the compound fence. Riot police entered the compound and forced the workers off of company property, striking workers with batons.

[9] Because the Kukdong assessment was its first and because the WRC had not yet formulated its Protocols of Assessment, the composition of the assessment team was somewhat improvised. The membership of the team also reflected the still sensitive political relations among the WRC's internal constituencies. Apart from the WRC Executive Director, the team included representatives of all three WRC constituencies—university administrations, the advisory council (including university faculty), and students. Only one team member was a local worker advocate—a former worker and Mexican labour lawyer affiliated with a Jesuit-based organisation that focused on the rights of women workers. The WRC Board viewed this as a significant defect, of course, in light of the organisation's aspirations to create a participatory model of monitoring. Drafted after completion of the Kukdong assessment, the WRC Protocols of Assessment required that at least half of team members represent local parties. The Protocols mandate that the WRC Executive Director appoint team members, drawing from local and foreign labour-rights experts, community advocates, women's organisations, village associations, and other non-governmental organisations, with priority given to local over foreign representatives.

the region; officers of the Puebla Conciliation and Arbitration Board and the Ministry of Economic Development; local academic researchers, worker advocates, and others. The team also conducted an inspection of the factory premises.[10]

After completing the five days of interviews, the team deliberated and concluded that there was substantial evidence that workers' right of association would be irreparably harmed if Kukdong did not take immediate remedial action. The team's Preliminary Report,[11] issued on January 24th, stated:

> [I]f the idled workers are not quickly reinstated, there is a great risk of irreparable damage to their right of association. To the extent that the idled workers are disproportionately supporters of an independent union at Kukdong, failure to reinstate those workers will likely extinguish the associational activities of those Kukdong workers—whether idled or still working—who seek an alternative to the CROC union, which they firmly believe to be corrupt and undemocratically entrenched . . . [A] failure to reinstate idled Kukdong workers will also likely chill the associational activities of workers throughout Puebla who wish to replace unions they perceive to be corrupt and illegitimate with democratic unions of their own choosing.[12]

The Report concluded that it was necessary to undertake a proactive program of 'outreach' to idled workers, and urged 'a cooperative effort among itself, locally affected workers, local workers rights and other human rights organisations, the Fair Labour Association, the International Labour Rights Fund, Nike and Reebok'. The brands did not accept the WRC's invitation to establish a formal remediation program. Instead, the WRC worked with local village and worker organisations to help strikers return to their jobs, while university administrators and students maintained pressure on the brands and factory managers to take positive action.

In a Second Report issued in June, 2001,[13] the WRC team reached findings on issues ranging from minimum wage to new questions of freedom of association, and recommended a democratic process to determine the workers' genuine preference as between the CROC and the independent union.

[10] The WRC team interviewed workers in groups of two to eight in locations outside the factory, mostly in homes, courtyards, and cafes in the workers' villages. The interviews ranged from one to three hours in length. The interviews combined 'structured' and 'unstructured' methodologies. That is, workers were asked a series of common questions, but were also encouraged to give testimony about events that they had experienced, followed by questions designed to clarify, probe, and test those narratives. The team interviewed top managers, supervisors, legal counsel, and incumbent union officers in the factory itself.

[11] The team collected further testimonial and documentary evidence before releasing a Second Report making final findings of fact and recommendations on June 20, 2001. This two-stage model is analogous to the practice of the US and other legal systems, in which judges order preliminary relief where there is a probability that rights are being violated and where damage to those rights will be irreparable if not remedied prior to the court's final ruling in a case. This model was logically adapted to the WRC's intervention in a 'real time' dispute. In subsequent assessments, the WRC continued to follow this two stage procedure, releasing a First Report that makes recommendations for remediation necessary to avoid irreparable harm to workers' rights and a Second Report that makes recommendations for remediation as to all allegations. In practice, the Second Report also assesses the degree to which the factory has implemented the recommendations in the First Report.

[12] Worker Rights Consortium, 'Kukdong Investigation: Preliminary Findings and Recommendations' (January 21, 2001).

[13] Worker Rights Consortium, 'Kukdong Investigation: Second Report' (June 20, 2001).

Intervention by a Private Monitor on Behalf of Freedom of Association.

The WRC intervention into the events at Kukdong was not a typical instance of private monitoring. The managerialist model of monitoring takes the form of routinely scheduled audits that check for compliance with a list of rights and standards. The WRC assessment at Kukdong, to the contrary, was a 'real time' intervention into allegedly ongoing labour-rights violations—namely, Kukdong's failure to reinstate strikers.

The WRC decided to intervene in real time because of the nature of the right of association.[14] It is a commonplace among industrial relations scholars and practitioners that a mass discharge of workers striking in support of unionisation must be remedied immediately or it is unlikely to be remedied at all. The Kukdong case was a classic illustration. It was likely that many Kukdong workers would simply give up their effort to return to a factory where they had faced so much intimidation and fear; the young women workers could return to their village lives or seek employment in other factories or in the informal sector. As a result, the campaign to oust the incumbent union and establish an independent union would dissipate and would not be easily revived for a long time to come.

Indeed, many managerialist monitors take the position that they should distance themselves from questions of freedom of association because questions of the validity of union formation—including requirements that employers not support or dominate incumbent unions—are not only too difficult to remedy but too sensitive to decide. Other managerialist monitors, on the other hand, take the position that freedom of association is easily measurable and reportable through quantitative 'metrics'. Some monitors, for example, measure freedom to organise unions by a proxy indicator of 'good labour-management communication', without inquiring into compliance or non-compliance with specific rules of free unionisation and collective bargaining.

The WRC, to the contrary, chooses to treat 'freedom of association' like any other worker right or standard in the sense that it is a right that can be defined with sufficient precision to allow a determination whether the factual record indicates compliance or non-compliance. On the other hand, the WRC recognises that freedom of association is a qualitative, multidimensional right that requires fact-intensive, context-specific inquiry and is not reducible to a quantitative metric in individual cases (even if compliance may be measured quantitatively in aggregate

[14] The WRC's intervention in a situation in which workers were exercising their right of association would, as mentioned above, set a pattern for the WRC's early work that distinguished it from other private monitoring organisations. Before its decision to launch an assessment, the WRC communicated with workers and their local advocates to ensure that Kukdong workers fully understood the potential risks and benefits of such an intervention and consented to it—a practice later codified in the WRC Protocols of Assessment. This type of intervention poses organisational risks as well. If a WRC assessment is followed by increased managerial repression or job loss, the hard-won credibility and legitimacy of the organisation may erode.

samples). In the Kukdong case, therefore, there was no escaping an inquiry into whether the CROC union had in fact been established and administered in compliance with the Mexican labour code, ILO conventions, university codes, and the WRC code. At the same time, the WRC team was cognisant that the very nature of that right (freedom of association) requires external organisations—whether public labour boards or private monitors—to defer to expressed preferences and practices of local workforces.

The WRC team therefore reached a finding that questioned the *factual* basis of the CROC's bargaining relationship with Kukdong only after taking meticulous testimony and gathering corroborating evidence from multiple credible sources. Equally important, after the factual investigation, the WRC team reached a *legal* conclusion that the CROC's bargaining relationship was invalid only after finding a 'clear and incontrovertible basis' for that conclusion.

In light of the sensitivity of the question and the relative rarity of this type of inquiry by a private monitor, it is worth summarising the WRC's inquiry. The WRC team began with lengthy interviews with members of the Puebla Conciliation and Arbitration Board (CAB), the body that oversees unionisation in the State of Puebla. The CAB is a classic tripartite body, comprised of representatives of government, employers, and unions. The particular members of the Puebla CAB were representatives of the ruling party and of labour unions affiliated with the ruling party—to which, of course, the CROC was affiliated. The WRC team then closely questioned CROC officials about the process through which the Kukdong-CROC bargaining relationship was allegedly established. Finally, the team questioned Kukdong managers and attorneys. The testimony of these three actors—managers, union officials, and CAB members—was mutually contradictory and incredible in the extreme.[15] Their testimony pointed clearly to the conclusion that the CROC had not met the legal formalities of entering into a collective bargaining relationship with Kukdong.

There was also overwhelming evidence that the CROC had carried out no functions of a labour union. No Kukdong worker—whether a supporter of CROC or the new independent union—had heard of the CROC union prior to March 2000, long after the CROC officers signed the collective agreement with Kukdong. Thereafter, according to dozens of workers, agents of the CROC threatened workers with firing and worse, if they did not sign membership statements. The CROC-Kukdong contract afforded workers no rights or benefits beyond those already provided by Mexican statutory law. According to workers' testimony, the CROC had pressed no grievances on behalf of Kukdong workers. Even when workers complained that Kukdong supervisors struck them with hammers as a disciplinary measure (a shocking practice that Kukdong managers admitted to the WRC team), CROC officers failed to pursue the grievance. Further, the CROC officers denied any knowledge of such physical abuse, even though it was among the most

[15] The team's close interrogation of these parties, their contradictory testimony, and the crucial role played by the Mexican member of the team, are chronicled in detail in the Kukdong Preliminary Report, above.

widely discussed issues at Kukdong—discussed not only among workers but among Kukdong managers and supervisors as well.

Perhaps most important, there was overwhelming evidence that the vast majority of Kukdong workers had 'cast their votes' against the CROC by joining the walkout in support of a new union. And the CROC officers had instigated and marched in the lead of the violent police action against their own 'members'. This direct evidence that the CROC was a protection union made it unnecessary for the WRC team to rely on the large body of secondary documentation and evidence that the CROC had acted in this corrupt and violent manner for many years and at many factories in Puebla, under the protection of the ruling party in that state.[16]

The corrupt alliance between the CROC and the state government was also corroborated during the remediation phase of the WRC assessment. To unclamp the CROC's grip on the factory, it was necessary for Nike and Kukdong managers to use their economic clout to obtain the *de facto* approval of state party officials, local notables, and CROC officials.

Nike would not have used its considerable economic and political leverage to crack open the labour-repressive regime in Puebla if not for the second-order leverage exerted by the WRC assessment, as described in the next section.

Remediation—Transparency, Legal Competence, and Economic Leverage.

In March, 2000—several months before the mass walk-out—Pricewaterhouse-Coopers (PWC), a financial accounting firm, conducted a labour audit at Kukdong on behalf of Nike. The PWC Report stated that Kukdong management 'has established relations with employees that are both flexible and transparent' and that 'workers felt they could air their grievances in a fair and effective way'. That Report did not address what the WRC assessment team identified, nine months later, as the most important ongoing question involving the right of association at Kukdong—the question of the collective bargaining relationship between Kukdong and the CROC.

On January 14, 2001, the WRC sent a letter to Nike's Global Director of Labour Practices informing Nike of the complaint submitted to the WRC by Kukdong workers and assuring Nike that the WRC had 'reached no conclusions concerning the accuracy' of the allegations of labour-rights violations at Kukdong.[17] The WRC also initiated communication with Reebok's regional compliance officer.

[16] Under the pressure of WRC scrutiny, Nike chose the respected Mexican labour lawyer and democratic activist Alturo Alcalde to make a preliminary investigation of the Kukdong dispute. Alcalde rendered an even broader judgment against the CROC and its relationship with local authorities. See 'Opinion Presented by Arturo Alcalde Justiniani Regarding the Case of Kuk Dong International', January 30, 2001.

[17] Letter from Scott Nova, WRC Executive Director to Nike, Global Director of Labour Practices (January 14, 2001).

In its initial responses, Nike harshly attacked the WRC, questioned the WRC's objectivity and fact-finding methodology, and demanded that it not 'politicis[e]' the dispute.[18] The industry-governed FLA—in which Nike played a substantial role—chose not to formally intervene in the dispute, on the grounds that its function was to conduct routine auditing and not dispute-resolution. At the same time that Nike expressed concerns about the fact-finding methodology of the WRC, however, Nike publicised a press release by the Executive Director of the FLA who—prior to any fact-finding by any organisation—called for the extraordinary remedial measure of a new process for Kukdong workers to elect their union representative.[19]

Nike managers announced that, rather than cooperating with the WRC, they would 'work with' a Mexican attorney in order to 'gather information' and 'assist in the resolution of this [Kukdong] situation'. The attorney briefly visited the factory and received reports from an associate who observed workers' attempt to enter the factory on another occasion. His January 30th Opinion, was consistent with the WRC team's Preliminary Report issued on January 24th.[20] Nike, however, did not undertake effective remediation based on its own investigators' fact-finding until the WRC and affiliated universities applied sustained pressure and the US media gave attention.

The WRC urged Nike and Reebok to help the WRC assessment team gain access to the Kukdong factory and help to make Kukdong managers available for interviews. Nike initially refused, but, after the urgings of university licensors, allowed the WRC team to interview Kukdong managers and CROC union officials. This represented the first vital concession by Nike and Kukdong to the universities' transnational scrutiny.

As recounted above, Nike declined the WRC's recommendation that a proactive remedial program of outreach to workers' home villages be implemented through a cooperative effort with the WRC and other groups. Instead, with the approval of Reebok and the Kukdong management itself, Nike selected and paid a US-based, FLA-certified auditor to undertake the two distinct tasks of (1) 'observing' the reinstatement process at Kukdong and (2) conducting a general 'audit' of Kukdong's practices regarding 'child labour, working conditions, disciplinary practices, grievance procedures, harassment and abuse, wages and compensation'.[21] The Kukdong managers gave the auditors access to the factory to observe the reinstatement process but denied such access to WRC observers.

Nike warned its auditors that they were contractually bound to maintain the confidentiality of all information gathered inside the factory. Upon learning of the confidentiality requirement, the WRC advised the auditors that failure to publicise conditions in the factory on a continuing, real-time basis would defeat the avowed purpose of the 'observation'. The purpose was precisely to provide immediate,

[18] See Nike Statement, 'Update on Labour Dispute at Kukdong Apparel Factory' (January 16, 2001).
[19] See Statement of Sam Brown (FLA), 'Attachment to Nike Statement Update' (January 16, 2001).
[20] See note 16, above.
[21] See Nike Press Release (February 8, 2001).

credible, public assurance to workers outside the factory that returning workers were not subject to intimidation or discrimination inside the factory. This assurance would be meaningless if it were never published or were contained in public reports issued days or weeks after workers—owing to prior intimidation—abandoned their efforts to exercise their legal right to return to the factory and to continue their associational activities. After the WRC Executive Director and university administrators communicated their concerns about its confidentiality policy, Nike authorised its auditors to issue daily 'Activity Reports' during the observation period.

This change in policy—affording (limited) transparency—was the second constructive action taken by Nike, again under the pressure of independent monitoring by the WRC. However, Nike prohibited the auditors from answering questions or otherwise communicating or cooperating with representatives of the WRC and other organisations on the ground. Informal communication nonetheless continued among the WRC Executive Director and representatives of Nike, Reebok, and the auditors. At that level, the WRC and Nike's auditors developed good working relationships while conducting their 'parallel' activities at Kukdong.

Nonetheless, the WRC team's specialists on Mexican labour law and the Nike auditors (who lacked professional training in labour law) took differing positions about the fundamental legal issues at stake. First, in their daily Activity Report of February 6th, Nike's auditors stated that their first goal was to '[o]bserve and note how workers who had left the factory during the work stoppage were being received when re-applying for a job at the factory'.[22] The WRC assessment team took the position that the legal remedy for Kukdong's illegal discharge of five workers on January 3rd was *reinstatement* to their existing jobs, not '*re-appl[ication]* for a job at the factory' and that Kukdong's legally binding agreement of January 13th similarly required Kukdong to reinstate, not to accept re-applications from, the hundreds of participants in the work stoppage. The WRC team believed that the distinction between reinstatement and re-application constituted the heart of the substantive dispute over labour rights at Kukdong. The Kukdong managers demanded that returning workers re-apply for a job at the factory and await notice from Kukdong whether their applications had been accepted. On the occasion of their reapplication, Kukdong denied jobs to many strike-supporters. The WRC team concluded that Kukdong's imposition of *any* process of re-application itself constituted a continuing violation of workers' right of association and right to be free of discrimination, and could not constitute a *remedial process*, contrary to Nike's auditors' statement that its primary objective was to observe a process of reapplication on behalf of Nike.

Second, Nike's auditors stated that all of a large contingent of Kukdong workers had 'resigned'. The WRC concluded, to the contrary, that as a matter of Mexican labour law those workers had been 'constructively discharged' and therefore had no obligation to reapply. The auditors' intervention on behalf of Nike and

[22] See Verite, 'Activity Report' (February 6, 2001).

Kukdong seemed to mark a step backward, as a result of their manifest lack of legal competence. Indeed, the auditors' first Activity Report conceded that they had not yet consulted any specialists in Mexican labour law although they 'hoped' they would have the chance to do so at some later time.

Alongside these interactions among the WRC, Nike, and Nike's auditors, there were also communications between the AFL-affiliated Solidarity Center and Nike, including disagreements about the proper application of Mexican law regarding closed shops. In a statement dated February 1, 2001, a Nike public relations officer stated that Kukdong was permitted to require returning strikers to sign loyalty oaths to the incumbent union, since Mexican law permitted the CROC to implement a closed shop.[23] In an email dated February 3, 2001, a representative of the AFL's Solidarity Center stated: 'In this case, the Kukdong workers who are seeking to return to work were long ago forced to become members of the CROC, and were forced to pay dues to the CROC up to their last pay check. The only way they could be considered to be required to re-join the CROC is if they were fired for participating in the walkout, and are now being rehired as new workers, a clear violation of Nike and Kukdong's commitment to return workers to their original jobs without discrimination or reprisals'.[24]

On February 6th, Kukdong refused to reinstate 70 workers who attempted to return to their jobs. This was publicly reported, and on February 9th, Nike finally took decisive action—the third major instance when Nike used its economic leverage as a result of the WRC's scrutiny in the remediation phase. On that date, Nike sent an email to Kukdong managers asking that they take three remedial steps that the WRC had urged in its January 24th Preliminary Report: (1) reinstate all striking workers without discrimination or preconditions, (2) extend a specific invitation to return to work to the five worker-leaders discharged on January 3rd, and (3) make a public announcement that Kukdong was dropping criminal charges against Kukdong workers.[25]

Substantial numbers of workers returned to Kukdong during the next several weeks. Under the supervision of Nike, Reebok, and Professor Huberto Juarez (who undertook continued observation of the factory at the request of Reebok and with the support of the WRC), two of the five discharged leaders reached a negotiated reinstatement agreement with Kukdong managers. Another of the leaders had tried but not succeeded to gain reinstatement; and approximately two hundred of the rank and file strikers had not returned to the factory.

Throughout these events, the WRC Executive Director was in regular contact with the university and student representatives sitting on the WRC Board of Directors. The administrators of several university affiliates took an active interest and repeatedly communicated their own concerns about the workers' grievances to the licensees and the factory managers. A student organisation with chapters on individual campuses, United Students Against Sweatshops, launched activist

[23] See Nike, 'Update Regarding Kukdong Mexico Factory' (February 1, 2001).
[24] See Email, Jeff Hermanson to Nike (February 3, 2001).
[25] See Email, Nike to Kukdong Managers (February 9, 2001).

campaigns to press university administrators to act more aggressively. These interventions by students and university administrators, and the latent threat of more bad press, induced Nike to take the decisive remedial action on February 9th, and to take the political action ultimately required to remove the CROC from the factory. Without the WRC's intensive investigation, transparent reporting of 'real time' events, and economic pressure, Nike and its chosen monitors would almost certainly have failed to exert the necessary leverage against the factory and vendor managers and the authoritarian ruling party in Puebla.

Long-term Accountability—Local Monitoring Capacity and Transnational Media Politics

An independent monitor such as the WRC does not have automatic, continuing access to a factory in the way that a brand's internal supply-chain monitors or industry-governed consortia generally do. In each case, the WRC must therefore construct a system for follow-up monitoring of remediation efforts at a factory, after the period of intensive on-site interviewing by the WRC assessment team. In the case of Kukdong, the WRC's long-term remediation efforts were channelled through a two-member team located in the region—a United States researcher and a Mexican Professor of Economics specialising in the manufacturing clusters in the State of Puebla. They conducted more than 150 worker interviews in the months after the WRC assessment team's on-site fact-finding. The WRC staff and Board kept apprised of developments at the Kukdong facility through their reports and through less formal communication with advocates, managers, trade unionists, and workers located in the region.

In September, 2001, Kukdong managers revoked their collective agreement with the CROC (after Nike brokered a deal between Kukdong managers, officials of CROC, and the Puebla political elite). Kukdong workers formally elected an independent union that had the support of eighty percent of the workforce. The newly established union of Kukdong workers succeeded in securing a collective agreement with Kukdong, now re-incorporated under the name Mexmode. The rights and benefits in the collective agreement substantially exceeded those in the previous contract. At the same time, Nike insisted that Mexmode managers recommit themselves to adherence to the Nike code and to intensified monitoring through Nike's compliance system.

The WRC intervention and continued scrutiny appeared to achieve a combination of long-term 'accountability from below' (through a democratic union), 'accountability from above' (through more rigorous Nike and Reebok compliance systems), and 'lateral accountability' (through the local advocacy of Professor Huberto Juarez's team)—the three-fold system of long-term accountability and remediation that the WRC team had proposed in its two reports.

As noted above, the mass media play a constitutive role in the success or failure of private monitoring, since the media may (a) legitimate the work of particular monitoring organisations and (b) act as a transmission belt carrying factory information from transparent monitors such as the WRC to consumers, the ultimate 'sanctioning' actors. It was a significant development, then, when elite media in the United States recognised the success of the WRC model. In a long feature story, the *New York Times* concluded: 'The cross-border campaign [by the Worker Rights Consortium and the United Students Against Sweatshops] prompted Nike to press managers at [Kukdong] to reinstate the ousted workers, to create a formal grievance process, to address complaints of harassment by its managers and to improve cafeteria conditions', in addition to replacing the CROC with an independent union.[26] The editorial page of the *Washington Post* cited the WRC's intervention at Kukdong as a model for transnational enforcement of labour rights.[27]

These and other major media reports made university administrators much readier to put pressure on Nike and other brands—and made it more difficult for the brands to dismiss the WRC as a 'radical' outlier on the spectrum of compliance organisations.

PT Dada—Organisational Intervention and Interaction

The PT Dada factory, a South Korean-owned factory, is located in Purwakarta (two-hours outside Jakarta) and employs between 3000 and 5000 workers, predominantly young women. In 2001, the facility produced for major manufacturers such as The Gap, Adidas, and Disney. Two other manufacturers—Top of the World and American Needle—produced baseball caps and stuffed toys under license for more than twenty-five universities affiliated with the WRC.

In July, 2001, the entire PT Dada workforce walked out in protest over an array of grievances about non-compliance with labour rights and standards, including safety and health problems;[28] forced homework, often without pay; denial of full annual leave; corporal punishment against workers who took sick leave; and other forms of physical and verbal abuse. After the July strike, three different unions sought to organise the newly active workforce. Factory managers strongly supported one of the three unions and made public a collective bargaining agreement of which the workforce had no prior knowledge. Managers also launched a campaign of reprisals against workers who supported the protest, especially those who became leaders of the two independent unions.[29]

[26] G Thompson, 'Mexican Labour Protest Gets Results', *The New York Times* (October 8, 2002) at A3.

[27] 'Editorial: How to Battle Sweatshops', *The Washington Post* (February 2, 2001) at A22.

[28] The safety and health complaints included inadequate ventilation and drinking water, unsafe machine guarding, roofing, and cable lifts, failure to provide personal protective equipment, and denial of the right to wear shoes during work.

[29] Managers interrogated many workers about their union allegiance, demanded they renounce their membership in two unions disfavoured by management, and threatened to fire those who refused to join the management-favoured union. Over a two-week period, one young woman was sequestered

Prior to the WRC's on-site assessment of PT Dada, in February, 2002, the WRC undertook a preliminary investigation lasting several months.[30]

Evolving Forms of Participatory Monitoring and Remediation.

The composition of the WRC's PT Dada assessment team reflects the organisation's decision, after the Kukdong Assessment, to ensure that local workers, NGOs, and experts were represented at least equally with their 'Northern' counterparts. The six-member team was composed of: a senior WRC staff person; a professor of comparative and international labour law from the United States (this author); a resident expert in Indonesian occupational health and safety; a Staff Attorney of the Legal Aid Foundation (Labour Division) of Indonesia; a former garment-industry worker and Indonesian labour-rights specialist affiliated with the Sedane Institute for Labour Information (an Indonesian NGO); and a South Korean labour-rights specialist affiliated with the Asian Monitoring Resource Center.

The team spent six days on-site (February 17th through 22nd), conducting interviews, gathering documents, and inspecting the factory. In light of numerous allegations of intimidation of workers by local police, paramilitaries, and *preman* (thugs), the team interviewed workers in confidential locations away from the factory, including small cafes, courtyards, and private offices. The team interviewed production and supervisory workers, including supporters of each of the three unions that sought the allegiance of PT Dada workers after the mass walkout of July 2001.[31] The WRC team ultimately relied on over 150 worker interviews. The team also interviewed five PT Dada managers, including the President of Dada (Korea), the vendor; fifteen union officials; officials of the Purwakarta Ministry of

by security guards in 'solitary confinement' in a factory storage space, and was subsequently discharged. Managers filed a criminal complaint against a worker on the ground that her grievance letter alleging labour rights violations constituted defamation; local police officers thereafter began menacing interrogations and surveillance. Workers and union officers alleged that they were subject to similar intimidation by local thugs-for-hire (known as *perman* in Indonesian). Two workers who took education leave to attend union training were discharged.

[30] An independent researcher conducted interviews with workers at PT Dada and another facility from January through May 2001 and forwarded transcripts of those interviews to the WRC. Students from the United States conducted further interviews under the auspices of the Collegiate Apparel Research Initiative (CARI) and these too were made available to the WRC. After review of those interviews, the WRC retained a consultant, a United States researcher fluent in Bahasa Indonesian and well-versed in Indonesian culture and political economy. She conducted further preliminary interviews with workers, union officials, and advocates in the region.

In December, 2001, the WRC Executive Director sent a letter to PT Dada management seeking its view of grievances raised by PT Dada workers. After PT Dada responded, the Executive Director made the requisite findings to launch a formal WRC Assessment: First, he found that the preliminary investigation yielded evidence of probable cause to believe that PT Dada was non-compliant with workers rights in several areas, including occupational safety and health, wage and hours, physical abuse, and freedom of association. Second, he found that the PT Dada workforce overwhelmingly desired that the WRC undertake the Assessment.

[31] Workers were interviewed in groups of 2 to 6, for periods of time ranging from one to four hours. As in the Kukdong Assessment, interviews combined structured and unstructured methodologies.

Manpower, Police Department, and People's Parliament; four members of Adidas' Department of Social and Environmental Affairs, including the two ground-level auditors responsible for the factory inspections of PT Dada; and several local and international human-rights groups.

The team drafted and published a Preliminary Report in March, 2002. The Report found that there was a risk of particularly severe irreparable harm in five areas, including impairment of freedom of association by intimidation of union supporters by means of interrogations, threats of violence, abusive filing of criminal charges, solitary confinement, and various acts of favouritism and support toward the union dominated by supervisory personnel.[32]

As recounted above, during the Kukdong investigation the WRC proposed the formation of a cooperative remediation program among the WRC, the FLA, ILRF, Nike, Reebok, and local groups. That proposal was taken up by the local groups but not by the others. In the PT Dada case, the WRC instead proposed the formation of a local 'accountability team' comprised of representatives of Indonesian non-governmental organisations with expertise in labour rights, and urged the factory to grant the accountability team reasonable access to the factory, especially for the purpose of ensuring that factory managers and the company-favoured union did not have unfair and intimidating access to the workforce throughout the workday.

The WRC proposed and implemented the more narrowly drawn accountability team for several reasons. First, of course, the Kukdong case showed the difficulties of achieving cooperation among managerialist monitoring teams and organisations, with their own interests, methodologies, personnel, and philosophical commitments. Second and conversely, the Kukdong case had shown that much constructive improvement could be achieved through informal, rather than formal, interaction among the WRC and the compliance personnel of the brands and other monitoring groups.

Third, the experience of the Kukdong assessment had shown that local actors—with knowledge of local production systems, labour relations, legal practices, and political constellations—are more effective than external auditors affiliated with supply chains or transnational NGOs.

Fourth, the concept of the accountability team was adapted to the particular remedial requirements at PT Dada. In particular, the three unions at PT Dada were in the initial phase of efforts to establish a coordinated strategy, and perhaps a unified structure, to bargain a new collective agreement with PT Dada. Since the collective bargaining process was both the appropriate and legally mandated

[32] The other four areas requiring immediate remediation were: (1) abusive physical punishment and humiliation of workers who exercised their sick-leave entitlements; (2) danger of severe heat stress due to inadequate ventilation; (3) structural hazards, including dangers of roofing cave-ins and sub-standard cable lifts; and (4) factory requirements that workers take work home at night, often for sub-standard or no pay. In addition to these highest-priority items, the Preliminary Report identified many other areas of non-compliance in the areas of health and safety, wages and hours, discrimination, and freedom of association.

forum to address many of the WRC's remedial recommendations, the WRC did not wish to establish a 'parallel' process beyond the accountability team's authority to ensure that the factory met minimum statutory standards and treated each of the three unions fairly in unionisation and collective bargaining.

Fifth, the WRC's experience suggested that a structure like the accountability team could ensure flexible and effective remediation when implemented alongside other channels of continuing communication between the WRC team and local actors. At the end of the five days of on-site assessment, the WRC team set up two such channels. A 'rapid response' channel was designed to transmit information about events in the factory as quickly as possible to members of the team, once they returned to their respective offices in Indonesia, South Korea, and the United States. That is, it seemed vital for the team to have continuous and rapid updates on fast-changing developments that might require immediate recommendations for new or revised remedial steps—in the event, for example, that new disputes or crises broke out between management and union supporters. A second channel was designed to allow the team members to communicate rapidly with 'elder strategists'—politically independent Indonesian advocates who had played prominent roles in the pre- and post-Suharto democracy movements and who could provide broader strategic evaluation of the complex events unfolding in Purwakarta.

Private Monitoring of Fluid Public Rights of Association.

The PT Dada case presented the WRC team with a particularly difficult problem of freedom of association. In the Kukdong case, the WRC had already faced a contest between a company-favoured union and an independent union movement. The PT Dada case was more complex, however, for at least three reasons. First, there were three unions vying for collective bargaining rights at PT Dada; and it appeared that no single union could claim an overwhelming majority. One was the SPSI, affiliated with a union that had had close relations with the former Suharto regime. The second was affiliated with SBSI and its sectoral union in the textile sector known as Garteks. The third union, SPBDI, was affiliated with a small independent organisation.

Second, the union favoured and supported by the company—the SPSI—was not as deeply integrated with managerial authority as was the company-dominated union at Kukdong.[33] There remained the possibility that that union might evolve into a bargaining representative with greater genuine autonomy, especially in light of competition for worker allegiance from the two other independent unions.

[33] It is true that, after the July 2001 strike, PT Dada managers played the lead role in 'reviving' the SPSI and bringing forward a collective agreement about which the workforce remained unaware. The national SPSI, however, had a significant reform wing; the leaders of the factory-level SPSI were among the leaders of the July strike; and the fluidity of events at PT Dada made it unclear whether the factory-level SPSI would develop in the reformist direction.

Third, the new, post-Suharto Indonesian Trade Union Law no 21 of 2000 provided rights of worker association in sweeping, abstract terms, but did not specify the rights and obligations of managers, unions, and workers in a context of multiple unions. Indonesia had also recently ratified ILO conventions on collective bargaining and freedom of association. PT Dada managers themselves offered three competing interpretations of managers' rights and obligations, during in-depth interviews by the WRC team. One manager asserted that PT Dada was obligated to bargain with the company-supported union with which a majority of workers had affiliated (notwithstanding the substantial evidence that those workers had affiliated under duress) and could not legally bargain with the other two unions. A second manager asserted that PT Dada was obligated to bargain with the company-supported union and could, but was not required by law, to bargain separately with the others. A third manager asserted that PT Dada was obligated either to bargain or consult with all three unions.

The WRC therefore faced the *reality* of labour-union 'pluralism' in the factory and the *formality* of a labour code that authorised but had not yet institutionalised concrete measures for implementing union pluralism. The situation at PT Dada was a closely watched case throughout Indonesia, precisely because it might become a model for institutions of pluralist bargaining under the new Indonesian law.

In his interview with the WRC team, the head of the regional Ministry of Manpower (the one-man equivalent of a combined Labour Ministry and Labour Board) expressed an opinion that Trade Union Law no 21 had priority over any ILO interpretations of conventions ratified by the Indonesian government. He interpreted the associational rights in Law no 21 to be sufficiently broad to allow managers and unions to choose among several options: exclusive negotiations with the majority union; negotiation with the majority union and consultation with minority unions; separate negotiations with each of the majority and minority unions; or unified bargaining with all unions. He made clear, however, that there was no precedent under the new domestic labour code for the situation prevailing at PT Dada and that his own expressed views on the matter were not legally binding.

This left the WRC team with the problem of interpreting a domestic code that had not yet been authoritatively interpreted by sovereign bodies—apart from the question whether the WRC or university codes might yield conflicting mandates on the question or pluralist bargaining. The view of the Indonesian 'elder strategists' was that the PT Dada rank-and-file workforce might well have strongly unified interests, even though the workforce had splintered into three different organisations following the July 2001 walkout. They convincingly based this view on the nature of the walkout itself. All workers had spontaneously walked out behind a single set of grievances; and they had elected a unified team of negotiators (to resolve the immediate strike) that included individuals who only later were recruited by the three separate organisations (to renegotiate the regular collective agreement). The elder strategists believed that the PT Dada workers, if given the opportunity, would likely choose a single, unified bargaining structure that included representatives of all three organisations.

The WRC team ultimately decided that it was not the WRC's task to craft a highly specific interpretation of the Indonesian labour code's mandate of pluralist bargaining. In the team's view, it was up to the PT Dada workers themselves to decide whether they wished to bargain through three separate unions or instead to engage in single-channel collective bargaining through a coordinated or unified bargaining structure. The team did conclude, however, that a robust conception of free association required the PT Dada management to not 'freeze out' any significant minority representative. That is, PT Dada should in fact bargain or consult with all three unions, whether separately or together as the workers might choose.[34]

By the spring of 2003, the three unions at PT Dada had in fact created a coordinated bargaining committee and were making substantial gains in collective bargaining, as described further in the next section.

Remediation—Promoting Private and Public Capacity.

Adidas noted that '[f]rom the outset [of the WRC Assessment] it was agreed that there was a need for constructive dialogue between the WRC, factory management, and adidas-Soloman'.[35] After the WRC team's on-site mission, the WRC also worked closely with American Needle and Top of the World to ensure that they pressured, encouraged, and assisted PT Dada managers to implement the recommendations for remediation.

At a three hour meeting during the WRC team's on-site investigation, the Adidas compliance team made available its Action Plans for PT Dada and subsequently forwarded updated reports to the WRC team. The WRC team made findings of serious non-compliance that the Adidas monitors had simply missed: (1) mandatory homework, often underpaid or nonpaid (a violation of Adidas' Code sufficient to require Adidas to end its relationship with PT Dada if not immediately redressed), (2) solitary confinement of union supporters; (3) abusive criminal-law charges and surveillance by rogue police officers against union leaders; and (4) several other impairments of freedom of association, including physical threats and other intimidation in support of the management-favoured union.

In April, 2002, the WRC's accountability team was created. At a three-way meeting among the WRC, PT Dada, and Adidas, it was agreed that the accountability team would have access to the factory every two weeks for one full day. The

[34] The impending collective bargaining inflected the WRC's recommendations for remediation outside the area of freedom of association as well. In areas ranging from grievance procedures to worker training, the WRC team thought it was neither legitimate nor effective for the WRC to try to anticipate or displace workers' own preferences, expressed through their chosen bargaining representatives. In these subject areas, therefore, the Report urged that PT Dada remedy the problems in such manner as the collective bargaining process might determine.

[35] Adidas-Soloman, 'Annual Report' (2002).

accountability team consisted of three Indonesians—a human rights lawyer, a worker/researcher affiliated with a labour-education NGO, and a professor of industrial relations. The accountability team conducted ongoing worker interviews, visited the factory on a regular basis, and reported to the WRC's Washington office. The WRC discussed the accountability team's findings in four-corner deliberations among WRC staff, the licensees producing collegiate merchandise, PT Dada's Seoul headquarters, and PT Dada managers in Indonesia. These deliberations were occasions for collaborative problem-solving to implement and further specify the WRC's recommended remedies.

On September 29, 2002, the WRC published a Second Report, describing substantial progress on compliance with freedom of association (as well as other crucial workplace conditions[36]). PT Dada reinstated a leader of one of the two rank-and-file unions, who had been held in solitary confinement and subsequently discharged. The company also withdrew criminal complaints against other union leaders, who were able to return to work without sanction. These reinstatements were facilitated by the regional Ministry of Manpower.

All three unions were given equal access to office facilities and to workers to communicate about union activities. PT Dada managers made factory-wide announcements and postings stating their commitment to respect the workers' freedom of association, and communicated to all supervisors that intimidation or favouritism on behalf of any union was unacceptable. Managers and representatives of all three unions participated in an ILO training on collective bargaining, supported by both the WRC and Adidas. Workers confirmed that the shop floor atmosphere had changed considerably.

As predicted by the 'elder strategists', workers at PT Dada began to hold unified rank and file meetings among themselves and thereby strengthened bonds that stretched across the three union organisations. The leaders of the three unions also engaged in intensified, albeit difficult, efforts to form a coordinated negotiating position and, in early 2003, created a unified bargaining committee. PT Dada managers agreed to negotiate with whomever the unions chose to serve on a negotiating committee. In late March, the negotiations committee and the PT Dada management completed a first phase of negotiations that achieved substantial improvements in the company's policy on annual leave and monthly leaves.[37]

Through its remedial activities, the WRC catalysed private and public actors to strengthen their capacities for long-term monitoring. In the face of in-depth,

[36] According to workers interviewed by the WRC accountability team, PT Dada had ceased punishing workers for taking sick leave and had ceased the practice of requiring homework. On the question of heat stress, PT Dada had installed air-conditioning in the factory clinic where workers took respite from excessive heat; had begun to provide filtered and cooled drinking water rather than heated water; and had installed fans and rearranged production layout to move hot production processes closer to doors and windows. On the question of structural hazards, PT Dada had replaced the factory's asbestos roof, and was in the process of replacing the unsafe cable lift.

[37] As of this writing, the workers' negotiating representatives are completing surveys of local wages and benefits and 'minimum living expenses' in preparation for the second phase of negotiations which will address monetary issues.

transparent reporting by the WRC and the latent threat of damage to brand reputation, the manufacturers sourcing from PT Dada felt little choice but to support aggressive remediation at the factory. The WRC's fact-finding placed pressure even on brands that sourced non-university merchandise at PT Dada.

Because the WRC had quickly established a reputation as the most competent, transparent monitor of labour rights, the brands believed it in their interest to ensure that the public understood that their compliance staff was cooperating with the WRC. Although the WRC found that Adidas' internal monitors had failed to identify several blatant violations of worker rights, Adidas capitalised on the WRC's subsequent praise for Adidas' participation in remediation efforts. In its 2002 Annual Report, Adidas highlighted that the WRC Remediation Report had acknowledged 'the very significant changes that have taken place at PT Dada and adidas-Soloman's "heavy efforts on issue-by-issue remediation work."' Adidas' managers, like Disney's, had considered taking the path of least resistance—namely, exit from the factory altogether—but chose instead to follow the universities' urgings to increase its purchase orders.[38]

The WRC's intervention also appears to have incrementally strengthened the authority of the Purwakarta Ministry of Manpower, Parliamentarians, and Development Officers—newly elected or appointed in the post-Suharto period—relative to the brands, the factory, and local rogue police and paramilitaries (holdovers from the Suharto regime). In meetings between the Purwakarta officials and the WRC team, the former indicated that, in the face of local police corruption and paramilitary thugs working for managers, they were unable to remedy the abusive firings that the team had uncovered in its fact-finding.[39] Local workers confirmed that PT Dada and other export factories in Purwakarta had simply stymied the Minister of Manpower's efforts to engage managers and aggrieved workers in mediation clearly mandated by law. Immediately after meeting with the WRC team, PT Dada agreed to mediation by the Ministry, which resulted in the factory's agreement to reinstate discharged union activists.

A similar pattern emerged in the remediation of abusive criminal charges filed by the factory. Factory managers had filed charges of criminal defamation against a worker on the ground that she had handed the managers a letter stating simply that 'PT Dada has violated worker rights'. After the filing of charges, two police officers began menacing surveillance of the worker. She and other witnesses—

[38] The WRC also agreed to appear alongside Adidas in an ILO video on successful factory monitoring—a media project that further raised Adidas' stake in continuing improvement of labour conditions at the factory. Although, as explained above, the WRC's policy is not to formally certify factories or brands, Adidas sought to give the appearance that the WRC had de facto affirmed its labour policies, at least in one factory.

[39] In a lengthy meeting between the WRC team and the newly installed officials, the latter expressed concern that the WRC would call for a boycott of PT Dada and damage local economic development. The team gave reassurances that the WRC would work actively to maintain and increase investment by the brands. The team also assured the officials that the WRC did not wish to intrude on their sovereign authority but instead stood ready to use whatever transnational power might aid the Ministry, the Parliament, and the Development Office in their public functions.

including a second group of Purwakarta police officers—identified the surveillants as police who free-lanced as violent enforcers for factories and others in the Purwakarta region.[40]

In the WRC team's interview with the Minister of Manpower, he stated that abusive criminal investigations against union activists were a significant problem in Indonesia. He concluded that the surveillance against the PT Dada worker constituted a violation of the worker's right of association, but said he lacked the power to intervene against the unjustified police investigation. However, after the WRC team's on-site investigation—during the worker-manager mediation made possible by the WRC's scrutiny—the Minister in fact won PT Dada's agreement to withdraw the criminal charges. The WRC investigation had made it politically feasible for him to challenge the rogue police.

The Purwakarta Minister of Manpower and his staff—in sharp contrast to the Puebla Conciliation and Arbitration Board in the Kukdong case—were impressive in their knowledge of domestic and international labour law and in their desire to implement the law. The Puebla CAB was captured by the state ruling party and its corrupt union affiliate. In contrast, the post-Suharto Minister and his Parliamentary supporters were sufficiently independent of the local police, paramilitary, and corporate elite to serve as a change agent within the political space opened by the WRC investigation. In Puebla, the WRC had to place sufficient pressure on Nike to ensure that local political elites acquiesced in the ouster of the CROC. In Purwakarta, the WRC's exposure of non-compliance was sufficient to tip the balance of political forces in favour of public authorities committed to democracy and the rule of law, without requiring direct political intermediation by the brand.[41]

Conclusion

One of the chief criticisms of private monitoring is that it may displace collective bargaining and public authorities as vehicles for vindicating worker rights. The cases presented in this Chapter suggest that, at least in some circumstances, private

[40] The team scheduled an interview with the second group of police officers. They arrived in the company of the two officers who had been following the worker. Visibly agitated, they announced that they were no longer willing to speak with the team. The team took the opportunity to question the two officers who had been following the worker. In the tense interview that ensued, they denied engaging in any improper surveillance; stated that they had merely interviewed PT Dada managers to confirm that the allegedly defamatory letter had caused injury; stated that they had made no inquiry into whether PT Dada had in fact violated worker rights (a point confirmed by the PT Dada managers' testimony to the team); and yet conceded that under Indonesian law the truth of a statement was a defence to a charge of defamation. The interview ended when the police officers threatened the WRC team with physical violence and expulsion from Indonesia.

[41] Throughout these interactions, the inclusion of local, independent actors on the WRC team was crucial to the team's capacity to understand and navigate the local political constellation.

monitoring may open 'social and political space' that enables rather than displaces workers' exercise of rights of association. The cases also indicate that in order to play that role effectively, private monitors may be drawn into evaluation of local political structures and may countermand local political elites that support corrupt unions or labour-repressive managers. Private monitors may incrementally strengthen the capacity of those local actors, including democratic public agencies, that seek to enforce the rule of law. In playing this role, however, private monitors' legitimacy and accountability may be stretched to the limit.

In these cases, a private monitor acted as a lever to open space for legitimate collective actors in two major ways: First, the ultimate purchasers or licensors—United States universities—used their latent economic power, by communicating their concern about repression of labour rights to licensees that produced in the factories in question. Second, media reports of the monitor's findings heightened the urgency of corrective action by the licensees and vendors and, concurrently, shined an international spotlight that protected workers against immediate reprisal for their union activities and impelled local public agencies to enforce labour rights.

The monitoring instrument created by universities was relatively *effective* for several reasons. First, the WRC teams are supervised by a governance structure that is neither funded nor controlled by corporations or labour unions. The teams therefore do not face the conflicts of interest that are built into management compliance systems and consortia in which corporations have controlling blocs. Those conflicts disable managerialist monitors from conducting robust investigation of rights of association and other complex labour rights, and from engaging in sustained, transparent remediation in the absence of strong external incentives to do so. Ensuring that several hundred strikers return to a factory from their home villages, after they have been assaulted by riot police, managers, and corrupt union officials, cannot be accomplished by a corporate compliance officer sending a confidential letter of recommendation to factory managers. Nor can it be accomplished by a confidential audit that occurs weeks or months after the event. It requires immediate, continuous, and transparent on-site monitoring and sustained remediation; and it likely requires continuous pressure from monitoring organisations, unions, brands, consumers, or public bodies empowered to allocate incentives—in addition, of course, to the primary effort of the workers themselves.

For observers outside of the United States, it may seem curious that any participation in labour-rights reporting by the predominant organisations representing workers' rights (labour unions) is thought to illegitimate those reports. But in the United States, labour unions are widely viewed as 'special interest groups' and carry negative connotations for much of the mass media and the public. The WRC's organisational independence from both for-profit corporations and labour unions is therefore a foundation of the credibility and perceived objectivity of its reporting. This is especially true when the WRC is investigating factories where workers are currently involved in unionisation efforts, as in the two cases presented in this chapter.

Second, the monitoring organisation created by the universities is itself subject to second-order 'monitoring' and sustained pressure by USAS—a highly motivated and well-organised group of activists committed to ensuring that the universities implement the recommendations of WRC assessment teams. By contrast, managerial monitors face only the diffuse and erratic check of unorganised consumers.

Third, because the WRC is lodged in the university communities, it is able to draw on the expertise and resources of its faculties. Managerial monitors conduct audits through personnel who are generally not professionally trained in compliance with labour rights and standards. While the frontline auditors of corporate brands, for-profit auditing firms, and NGOs may in some instances have professional training in occupational hygiene and safety, they generally have no professional education whatsoever in the complex jurisprudence of freedom of association, collective bargaining, and employment discrimination. The WRC, by contrast, has ready access to the *pro bono* services of professors of labour law, comparative labour law, international labour law, and occupational safety.

This point should not be taken as a fetishisation of professionalism. The question, rather, is one of minimal competence to inquire into complex, multidimensional norm-systems and, in the process, to help build the capacity of local actors to engage effectively with discourses about such systems. In the Kukdong case, for-profit auditors overlooked one of the most basic and pervasive problems of free association—namely, the entrenchment of a company-dominated union by subtle and not-so-subtle interactions among factory managers, union officials, and local labour administrators. In that case as well, Nike's auditor made gross errors of Mexican law that might have undermined remediation altogether if not corrected by the specialists on the WRC team. In the PT Dada case, inexperienced Adidas auditors were unable to effectively address a complex problem of labour-union pluralism.

Fourth, the WRC investigations are resource-intensive, compared to managerialist monitoring. The WRC devotes ten or twenty times the person-days to on-site interviews, compared to corporate audits. The WRC develops high-trust relationships with workers in their home villages and neighbourhoods, compared to the brief worker interviews conducted on factory property by managerialist auditors. The WRC gives continuous, detailed attention to remediation by factory managers, unlike the spot checks used by managerialist monitors. After deliberation within WRC teams, the labour-law specialists on the team write highly detailed reports in the style of objective judicial opinions. University administrators are willing to act on the basis of such reports, drafted by members of the universities' own law faculties, and cannot easily dismiss student groups that launch activist campaigns in support of the reports' recommendation for remediation. At the same time, elite newspapers and broadcasters treat the university reports as especially credible.

Fifth, by virtue of the comprehensive participation of local actors in WRC assessments, the teams are able to extend their remediation efforts into rural villages and urban neighbourhoods—as required by labour markets that span factories, villages, and urban informal sectors. Local actors also enable the teams to understand and negotiate the complex political environment that influences the success or failure of remediation. The WRC would not have achieved remediation in the Kukdong case without the assistance of village networks that reached hundreds of wrongfully discharged workers, and without local advocates' understanding of political clientelism in Puebla. In the PT Dada case, the team could not have successfully extracted vital information from the violent factions within the Purwakarta police department, without the detailed knowledge of local team members.

In addition to their relative effectiveness, the WRC assessments aspire to be relatively democratic, in three senses. First, the assessment teams include local representatives of workers, rights-advocates, and experts. The local team members participate as equals with WRC staff and university specialists in the team's deliberations over findings of fact, interpretation and application of labour rights to specific contexts, findings of legal compliance or non-compliance, and recommendations for remediation and organisational restructuring. The WRC personnel enter the local situation with explicit attention to power disparities among themselves and local participants, and attempt to construct processes that equalise those relationships. The WRC views each investigation as an experiment that yields 'learning' about best practices in symmetricising power.

Second, the monitoring teams conduct structured and unstructured interviews with workers, managers, public officials, and other interested local actors in social settings that evoke high trust. The teams are conceived as the point of encounter between 'central' norms—whether international, domestic, or private codes—and the 'local' normative worlds of the factory and its community. In the interview process, local workforces, managers, and communities contribute to the specification of relatively abstract, 'universal' labour rights. As a consequence, the specifications of rights that emerge from deliberations both within the team and between the team and local workers and managers are likelier to be autonomously shaped and well-suited to local production systems and local preferences. This is illustrated by the WRC's response to complex problems of labour pluralism in the PT Dada case.

Third, the monitoring process is designed to concurrently investigate immediate grievances and to build the capacity of a broad spectrum of local actors—private and public—to conduct long-term monitoring and remediation, as the presence of the WRC team diminishes. This long-term role is played in the Kukdong case by the independent Mexmode union, the Huarez research team, and Nike's strengthened managerial compliance effort. In the PT Dada case, the invigorated regional Ministry of Manpower, the WRC accountability team, the 'elder strategists', and the unified collective bargaining committee play this role.

There is warranted concern among labour unionists about whether any private monitor—no matter how participatory its methodology—can legitimately decide the question whether particular labour unions and particular collective-bargaining relationships are validly established. That question will arise with great frequency whenever workers are attempting to unionise in low-wage countries, in light of the common practice by companies and governments of attempting to create or support protection unions.

In the cases reported here, the WRC recognised the sensitivity of the question of union legitimacy and tried to act accordingly. The different conclusions reached by the WRC in the two cases are instructive. In the Kukdong case, based on the overwhelming evidence that the incumbent union was a corrupt, violent, and unauthorised organisation, the WRC concluded that it was not the legitimate representative of the factory workforce. In the end, the factory terminated its relationship with that union, and the workforce resoundingly gave its support to a new, democratically constituted union. In the PT Dada case, one of the three unions at the factory was supported by managers, but the WRC concluded that that union had sufficient potential to evolve into a more independent bargaining representative to preclude any judgment about its legitimacy by a private monitor—especially in the new Indonesian legal environment that validated pluralist bargaining between management and multiple unions. The WRC therefore deferred to processes of union competition. Even in that case, of course, the WRC recommended that general principles of free association—including guarantees that all workers could communicate freely about union affairs and affiliate with the union of their choice without coercion—be honoured.

Both the relative effectiveness and relatively democratic nature of the private-monitoring interventions in these cases depended in large part on the resource-intensive methodology of the WRC. Whether this methodology can promise improved compliance not just in individual factories but across entire brands, export sectors, or country-wide labour markets depends on either of two developments: the provision of enormously increased resources to monitors, or the implementation of higher-powered incentives sufficient to cause brands, vendors, and local labour boards and inspectorates to implement aggressive remediation in anticipation of monitoring.

Just as pressing as the challenge of 'scaling up' the participatory, resource-intensive model is the question whether its democratic foundations can be deepened. The model's three participatory aspirations, of course, will be unevenly achieved in practice. Beyond that, the model persistently requires the private monitor to influence local political structures, both to succeed pragmatically in improving workplace conditions and to implement the participatory process itself. In each of the cases, the WRC team ran up against local political hierarchies that were coupled with labour-repressive managerial corps. In the Kukdong case, the WRC teams placed sufficient pressure on multinational brands to, in turn, actively challenge authoritarian political structures. In the PT Dada case, the WRC team enabled certain local authorities legitimated by democracy or the rule of law to out-manoeuvre or countermand authoritarian, corrupt, or incompetent public actors that were allies of factory managers.

Such political intervention calls for strengthening the legitimacy and accountability of monitoring teams presently constructed by well-intentioned representatives of collective consumers such as US universities. Many aspects of monitoring—the selection of team members; the choice of fact-finding methods; the deliberative processes for interpreting domestic and international codes; the design of remedial programs, including the new structures of accountability to be embedded in factory organisations—raise familiar questions of democratic governance, the rule of law, and administrative effectiveness. And the monitoring teams' interventions into local political and economic life raise even more pressing questions of accountability. The point may seem obvious to many readers; but it is suppressed in the daily practice of private monitoring, a field that continues to grow exponentially and haphazardly. If a political opportunity arises to integrate participatory modes of monitoring into higher-level democratic bodies, at the national or regional levels, the opportunity should be seized.

4

Timing is Everything: Industrialization, Legal Origin and the Evolution of the Contract of Employment in Britain and Continental Europe

SIMON DEAKIN*

Abstract

The timing and nature of industrialization in Britain and continental Europe had significant consequences for the growth and development of labour market institutions, effects which are still felt today and which are visible in the conceptual structure of labour law in different countries. Contrary to the claims of the 'legal origin' hypothesis, a liberal model of contract was more influential in the civilian systems of the continent than in the English common law, where the consequences of early industrialization included the lingering influence of master-servant legislation and weak institutionalization of the juridical form of the contract of employment.

JEL Codes: J53, J83, K31.

Introduction

The aim of this paper is to explore aspects of the relationship between law and industrialization, by examining the development of the juridical forms which

* Professor of Law, University of Cambridge. This paper builds on my collaboration with Frank Wilkinson (*The Law of the Labour Market: Industrialisation, Employment and Legal Evolution* (Oxford, Oxford University Press, 2005) and on my contribution to the conference on *The Scope of Labour Law: Redrawing the Boundaries of Protection*, Bellagio, 23–27 May 2005 organised by Guy Davidov and Brian Langille ('The comparative evolution of the employment relationship', in G Davidov and B Langille, *Boundaries and Frontiers of Labour Law* (Oxford, Hart Publishing, 2006). I am grateful to Frank, Guy and Brian for their comments on this line of work, and to participants at the joint IALS-Columbia Workshop on Labour Law held in London in July 2004 and the Workshop on *Making Markets Through the Law: Legal Claim and Economic Possibility* held in Paris, June 2005 for discussion of earlier drafts of this paper.

accompanied the emergence of labour markets in Britain and continental Europe. Labour lawyers, taking their lead from Kahn-Freund,[1] have generally assumed that the legal institution of the 'contract of employment' or 'employment relationship' was a product of the legal changes accompanying the industrial revolution, principally the break-up of the guilds and the ending of statutory wage fixing in Britain, and the adoption of the post-revolutionary codes in continental Europe. By these means, all systems supposedly underwent a general movement from 'status to contract'. Yet, studies of the English legislation and case law of this period, including Kahn-Freund's own,[2] indicate that the courts did not use the term 'contract of employment' during this period, and that, instead, a multiplicity of other concepts was in use. The master-servant model was the main point of reference for work relations in emerging industries, while 'employment' was a status reserved, until the late nineteenth century, for professional and managerial workers who were beyond the disciplinary reach of the master-servant code.[3] The modern contract of employment, a category used to describe the situation of all wage-dependent workers subject to the coordinating power of an employer, and sharply differentiated for that reason from the concept of the independent contractor or self-employed worker, was an invention of the late nineteenth and early twentieth centuries.[4] As in other European systems around this time,[5] it crystallized around the notion that in return for 'subordination' to managerial 'control', the waged worker or employee obtained a degree of protection against the risks inherent in an industrialised economy, beginning with accidents at work and extending to sickness, unemployment and old age to incorporate, finally, the idea of a 'living' or 'breadwinner' wage. Fiscal legislation, social insurance and collective bargaining provided the occasion for the emergence of the modern employment relationship.

[1] O Kahn-Freund, 'Blackstone's neglected child: the contract of employment' (1978) 93 *Law Quarterly Review* 508–28.

[2] *Ibid.*

[3] A Merritt, 'The historical role of the law in the regulation of employment—abstentionist or interventionist?' (1982) 1 *Australian Journal of Law and Society* 56–86; K Foster, 'The legal form of work in the nineteenth century: the myth of contract?', paper presented to the conference on *The History of Law, Labour and Crime*, University of Warwick, 1983.

[4] See generally S Deakin and F Wilkinson, *The Law of the Labour Market: Industrialisation, Employment and Legal Evolution* (Oxford, Oxford University Press, 2005).

[5] See B Veneziani, 'The evolution of the contract of employment', in B Hepple (ed) *The Making of Labour Law in Europe* 31–72 (London, Mansell, 1986); M Mansfield, R Salais and N Whiteside (eds) *Aux sources du chômage 1880–1914* (Paris, Belin, 1994); R Castels, *Les métamorphoses de la question sociale: une chronique du salariat* (Paris, Fayard, 1995); R Biernacki, *The Fabrication of Labour: Britain and Germany, 1640–1914* (Berkeley, CA, University of California Press, 1995); C Didry, *Naissance de la convention collective. Débats juridiques et luttes sociales en France au début du XXe siècle* (Paris, Éditions de l'EHESS, 2002); A Cottereau, 'Industrial tribunals and the establishment of a kind of common law of labour in nineteenth century France', in W Steinmetz (ed) *Private Law and Social Inequality in the Industrial Age. Comparing Legal Cultures in Britain, France, Germany and the United States*, 203–26 (Oxford, Oxford University Press, 2000); S Simitis, 'The case of the employment relationship: elements of a comparison', in W Steinmetz (ed) *Private Law and Social Inequality in the Industrial Age, op cit*, 181–202 (Oxford, Oxford University Press, 2000).

The 'revisionist' hypothesis which has just been outlined could well be regarded as being of antiquarian interest only. Practising labour lawyers and labour court judges, who are used to regarding the employment contract as a fixed point in their conceptual universe, might conceivably gain some insights from a fresh interpretation of its origins. However, for this group, the genealogy of employment is likely to be less important than an understanding of the uses to which the idea can be put at the present time. The juridical history of the idea of the contract of employment is one of continual reinvention and adaptation, that is to say, a constant covering up and reinterpretation of the past. In the 1950s British judges and drafters of legislation elided the previously separate categories of 'servant' and 'employee', thereby giving a false impression of their historical meaning.[6] In the same way, French jurists of the late nineteenth century, in attempting to legitimise the then relatively new concept of the *contrat de travail*, 'pretended to themselves and to others that "service hiring" was a category of the Civil Code that had applied to the employment of workers from the outset', a move which was to lead to a 'profound comparative misunderstanding'.[7] Confusing as the results of this technique may be, it is very widely practised. In both common law and civil law systems, successful conceptual innovations tend to be those which refer back to existing forms: 'it is because law has to present the appearance of continuity that change comes about behind such screens as unchanging worlds'.[8] For this reason, labour lawyers may have limited interest in the claim that concepts now used for one purpose originated by way of response to another, quite different one. However, it is also arguable that a deeper understanding of such origins may help to clarify why it is that conceptual constructs such as the employment contract so often appear ill-suited to present-day conditions.

Can a revisionist account of the evolution of the contract of employment be shown to be of concern to the work of social and economic historians? Perhaps not, because there is general agreement that the history of a legal idea may actively mislead if it is taken at face value. The link between legal change and the emergence of new forms of production, and of new types of social or economic relation, is likely to be far from straightforward. Hence according to Douglas Hay (2000: 230–2), 'local, often highly specific legal cultures' mediated the enforcement and operation of master and servant law: 'how both statute and case law were enforced depended on the structure of local industry and indeed on "the custom of the trade"'. Historians therefore have to 'look in the jails and the justices' hearings, to see who the servants and masters were, and the use they made of this distinctive body of law'. The law reports, by contrast, contain decisions that 'are highly unrepresentative, in many ways, and especially as guides to enforcement'. To focus

[6] Deakin and Wilkinson, *The Law of the Labour Market*, *op cit*, at p 107.

[7] Cottereau, 'Industrial tribunals and the establishment of a kind of common law of labour in nineteenth century France', *op cit*, at p 220.

[8] SFC Milsom, *A Natural History of the Common Law* (New York, Columbia University Press, 2003), at p 107.

on legal paradigms 'leads easily to the genetic fallacy, the assumption that a putative origin explains the later development'.[9]

It is, indeed, essential to place any discussion of legal forms in the context of what is known about social and economic relationships at or around the time of juridical innovations. In this context, it is doubtful that British labour lawyers and legal historians would have paid quite so much attention as they have recently done to the evolution of the employment relationship, had it not been for the considerable historiography over the past two decades on numerous aspects of the poor law and master-servant legislation. But it may also be argued that the accounts of economic and social historians have left untouched many issues surrounding the internal development of the law—that is to say, its internal procedures, modes of thought and conceptual foundations—during the period of industrialisation.

From the point when the legal system achieves a sufficient degree of autonomy from political and administrative processes to have developed a language and procedure of its own, it acquires the features of what systems theory calls 'self-referentiality' and 'self-reproduction'.[10] This implies a radical separation between the internal communications of the legal system—in particular, the 'conceptual' or 'dogmatic' forms of legal doctrine—and the 'material' relations to which they (superficially) correspond. Terms such as 'employee', 'servant' and 'workman'—even the term 'contract'—assume a juridical meaning which cannot be taken to be synonymous with the meanings attached even to the same terms when they are used beyond the legal system. For the legal system to hold together, internal congruence and consistency of concepts is more important than making a good 'fit' with social and economic relations. This by no means rules out the possibility of legal innovation of the kind which can trigger, or be triggered by, changes in the wider economic and social environment, but it does mean that the 'coevolution' of law and the economy may be discontinuous, incomplete and asynchronic at best. If there is a functional response from the law to social change, any 'fit' is likely to be contingent on the preservation of somewhat arbitrary 'initial conditions'.[11]

From this perspective, legal texts, in particular public-official documents in the form of codes (where applicable), statutes, judgments and related materials such as governmental papers, as well as doctrinal treatises which form a commentary on the body of the law, form a unique dataset. These texts can be used to trace the evolution of legal ideas over long periods of time. Points of mutation and innovation can be identified, along with the continuing influence of juridical forms whose original rationale has been displaced by new ones. To understand the history of the contract of employment as a legal idea, is therefore to understand something of the movement of the structural forces underlying the wider phenomenon of industrialization. The effect is not unlike the 'decoding' of a complex genetic 'text'—with

[9] D Hay, 'Master and servant in England: using the law in the eighteenth and nineteenth centuries', in W Steinmetz (ed) *Private Law and Social Inequality in the Industrial Age*, *op cit*, 227–64, at p 232.

[10] G Teubner, *Law as an Autopoietic System* (Oxford, Blackwell, 1993).

[11] MT Fögen, 'Legal history—history of the evolution of a social system. A proposal' *Rechtsgeschichte* (2002) September, English language version on line at: http://www.mpier.uni-frankfurt.de/Forschung/Mitarbeiter_Forschung/foegen-legal-history.htm.

one major difference. In genetic analysis, the past environments whose effects are still embedded in the 'code' cannot be directly observed. Their features have to be imputed or assumed, a process which does not have to, but which often does, lead to excessively functionalist and teleological accounts—'just-so' stories. In legal-historical analysis, by contrast, the original conditions under which particular variations first emerged, and were then selected, can often be quite precisely identified and studied. Of course, there will be room for doubt and for discussion, not least because of the scope for divergence in doctrinal interpretation, and because of gaps in the historical record. However, legal genealogies arguably offer us a means to understand the influence of the past on present-day juridical forms, and thereby to appreciate both their capabilities and their limits, in a way which overcomes the limitations of 'just-so' stories and teleologies.

The more specific claim which this paper will seek to develop is that the timing and nature of industrialization in Britain and continental Europe had significant consequences for the growth and development of labour market institutions, effects which are still felt today and which are visible in the conceptual structure of labour law in different countries. The following section outlines the argument for linking certain long-standing features of the British model of the employment relationship to its historical evolution in this sense. Then the discussion turns to the different historical trajectory of legal change and industrialisation in continental European jurisdictions. The concluding section uses this account to assess two currently influential claims, to the effect that legal change is 'functional' with regard to the process of industrialization, and that labour laws and other laws affecting the business enterprise are shaped by the common law or civil law origin of particular national systems.

The British Case: Early Industrialization, Institutional Turbulence, and Legal Innovation in Labour Market Relations

The industrial revolution has, with justification, been called 'the centrepiece of world history over recent centuries, and *a fortiori* of the country in which it began'.[12] Yet the role which legal and institutional factors might have played in paving the way for industrialization in Britain is by no means clear. That England had a relatively advanced and integrated national legal system at a critical point in the development of the early industrial economy does not lead at all straightforwardly to the conclusion that the law made a difference to economic development. It is necessary to identify with some precision the mechanisms by which this could have occurred.

[12] EA Wrigley, *Continuity, Chance and Change: The Character of the Industrial Revolution in England* (Cambridge, Cambridge University Press, 1988), at p 8.

A persistent strand in this debate is Arnold Toynbee's observation, made in the 1880s at the inception of modern historical analysis of the subject, that 'the essence of the Industrial Revolution is the substitution of competition for the medieval regulations which had previously controlled the production and distribution of wealth'.[13] This view explicitly associated industrialisation with liberalization of legal and law-related institutions which occurred between 1750 and 1830. However, the British experience of industrialization is now no longer viewed in terms of the rapid 'take off' into economic growth in the decades after 1750 which is implied by the 'liberalisation' thesis. Revisions to estimates of growth rates have shown that economic development was not especially rapid during this period.[14] The attention of economic historians has turned to the century prior to 1750, during which there was a sustained rise in agricultural productivity, enabling labour to move from the countryside to the towns and industrial employment to grow.[15] Wage labour was already widespread by 1750, as was the nuclear family; but factory employment was comparatively rare, and was to remain so until the middle of the nineteenth century. Thus there was no simple transition from a predominantly agricultural and subsistence-based economy to an industrialised and urban one. What are now understood to be the characteristic features of the industrialised economy emerged in stages, separated by intervals of several decades.

As attention has shifted to the seventeenth and early eighteenth centuries, it has come to focus on the principal economic institutions of that period, namely the guild system and the poor law. The guilds have come to be regarded not simply as barriers or obstructions to commerce, as Adam Smith described them[16] (although this view is by no means absent from contemporary historical analysis), but as constituting a framework of governance for the emerging industrial trades by regulating quality, controlling entry, establishing minimum conditions for competition in labour and product markets, and stabilising the flow of labour from agriculture to industry.[17] The poor law, by providing for outdoor relief in the parish of settlement in return for service under an annual hiring, is now seen as offering incentives for labour migration by the young and unmarried, and compensation for the decline of traditional forms of subsistence via the family and access to land. This is the context in which it has been suggested that 'the creation and elaboration of the poor law system from the reign of Elizabeth onwards was an important reason for the development of a capitalist system in England'.[18]

[13] A Toynbee, *Lectures on the Industrial Revolution in England*, ed with an introduction by TS Ashton (Newton Abbott, AM Kelley, 1969) (originally published 1884), at p 92.

[14] NFR Crafts, *British Economic Growth During the Industrial Revolution* (Oxford, Clarendon Press, 1985).

[15] See Wrigley, *Continuity, Chance and Change, op cit.*

[16] A Smith, *An Inquiry into the Nature and Causes of the Wealth of Nations*, ed with an introduction by JS Nicholson (London, T Nelson and Sons, 1886) (originally published 1776), vol I, ch 10, at p 50.

[17] See generally M Daunton, *Progress and Poverty: An Economic and Social History of Britain 1700–1850* (Oxford, Oxford University Press, 1995), ch 6.

[18] Wrigley, *Continuity, Chance and Change, op cit*, at p 21.

Both the guilds and the poor law were underpinned by legislation and case law whose evolution contains pointers to the role which the legal system might have been playing in the economy during the transition to an industrialised economy. The Elizabethan Statute of Artificers of 1562, largely codifying earlier laws dating back to the fourteenth century, made it an offence punishable by repeated fines of forty shillings per month for any person to 'set up, occupy, use or exercise any craft, mystery or occupation now used or occupied within the realm of England and Wales, except he shall have been brought up therein seven years at the least as an apprentice'.[19] It was also an offence for masters to employ persons who had not been properly apprenticed in the specified occupations; nor could they take on more than three apprentices for each journeyman.[20] In effect, these laws prohibited hierarchical forms of economic organization and preserved the knowledge of the trade against external interference at the expense of limiting the scope of the division of labour and of managerial coordination. This was because no employer could operate in a trade for which he himself had not served an apprenticeship, a restriction which some courts extended to a case in which workmen from different trades were hired to work alongside each other.[21]

From the middle of the seventeenth century the courts used the common law doctrine of restraint of trade to give the Act a narrow interpretation which limited its application, but the case law indicates that the process was not a straightforward one and that rival conceptions of political economy were being played out in litigation during this period. In *Hobbs v Young* (1689)[22] a merchant-capitalist who had employed journeymen clothworkers in his house for a month to make goods up for export was successfully prosecuted for a breach of the Act. Prosecuting Counsel argued that 'he who cannot use a mystery himself, is prohibited to employ any other men in that trade; for if this should be allowed, then the care which has been taken to keep up mysteries, by erecting guilds or fraternities, would signify little'. The majority of the Court of King's Bench agreed, on the grounds that 'the exercise of [the trade] by journeymen and master workmen, or an overseer for hire, is not an exercise of it by them, but by him that employs them; he provided them materials and tools, and paid them wages: by law, he is esteemed the trader who is to run the loss and hazard; the whole managery was to be for his profit, and the workmen are to have no advantage but their wages'. However, a dissenting opinion was already of the view that 'no encouragement was ever given to prosecutions upon this Statute . . . it would be for the common good if it were repealed, for no greater punishment can be to the seller than to expose goods for sale, ill wrought, for by such means he will never sell more'.

[19] 5 Eliz. I, *c* 4, s 21.

[20] *Ibid*, ss 21, 23.

[21] See *re Statute of 5 Eliz, Apprentices* (1591) 4 Leon 9, and the discussion of this case law by Lord Mansfield CJ in *Raynard v Chase* (1756) 1 Burr 6.

[22] 1 Show KB 266.

Hobbs v Young remained good law until 1756 when it was circumvented by the ruling of Lord Mansfield CJ in *Raynard v Chase.*[23] This held that a non-apprenticed merchant or financier could act as an employer in one of the regulated trades if he entered into a partnership with a person who was so qualified. Mansfield's ruling also made it possible to get round the prohibition on workers from different trades being employed in the same business.[24] The courts subsequently found ways to dilute entry requirements. in *Smith v Company of Armourers* (1792)[25] the Court of King's Bench ordered the admission to the guild of the manager of an iron foundry, on the grounds that, although he had not served an apprenticeship and 'did not know how to manufacture the commodity by his own personal labour', he had been employed in the business for seven years 'during the greatest part of which time he conducted the whole of their extensive works, received all the orders, gave directions to the workmen etc . . . he knew how to conduct the business as well as any master in London'. In *Kent v Dormay* (1811)[26] Lord Ellenborough CJ declined to convict a mill owner who had not served an apprenticeship, noting that 'the valuable mills at Wakefield, Leeds etc, [are] the property of several persons of the first families in this kingdom; but who would be liable to informations, or would be required to serve regular apprenticeships as millers, if the defendant could be considered as within the meaning of the Statute'.

In 1814 Parliament repealed altogether the apprenticeship controls of the 1562 Statute. This was not a purely symbolic act; concerted efforts were being made to at this time to enforce entry requirements and to preserve guild structures more generally. Before removing the protective elements of the 1562 Act, successive Parliaments had strengthened those parts of the apprenticeship laws which made it unlawful for workers to take steps on their own behalf to enforce entry restrictions. Proponents of these reforms saw them an expression of the 'natural reason' of the market, since competition, rather than guild controls, provided the appropriate solution for the manufacture of poor quality goods: '[t]he reason for making [the Act] was that bad commodities might not be spread abroad; but natural reason tells us, that if the manufacture is not good, there is no danger of its having a favourable reception in the world, or answering the tradesman's purpose'.[27] Supporters of the guild, on the other hand, saw themselves as defending property rights in the shared skills and know-how of the trade. As Martin Daunton has recently suggested, 'the response of workers should not be interpreted in terms of disorder and ineffectuality, but as part of a well-developed and articulate "corporate discourse" which stressed stability, regulation, and the need to observe strict limits to innovation which threatened independence and accountability'; the

[23] 1 Burr. 6.

[24] *Coward v Maberly* (1809) 2 Camp 127.

[25] Peake 199.

[26] Kingston Assizes, August 14, 1811; see J Chitty, *A Practical Treatise on the Law Relating to Apprentices and Journeymen, and to Exercising Trades* (W Clarke & Sons, London, 1812) at p 122.

[27] *Smith v Company of Armourers* (1799) Peake 199, 201.

guilds looked to the legal system 'to protect their property in skill in the same way as other property, and to recognise their social value'.[28] This was not a straightforward conflict between market-driven and protectionist versions of political economy, but rather a contest between rival conceptions of property within an emerging market order.

The development of the poor law during the same period indicates similar tensions. It is possible to see in the 'old' or pre-1834 poor law a relatively sophisticated framework of taxation and mutual insurance for its time and by comparison to western European countries at a comparable stage of economic development. Via a poor law 'settlement', annual service provided an entitlement to relief in the event of a loss of income through sickness or old age. The system was administered at parish level, but it was national legislation which required each of the fifteen thousand English parishes to raise local taxes for the purpose of supporting the poor, and to suppress indiscriminate charitable giving. Thus the system was both publicly instituted and legally mandated.[29] There were disciplinary elements. Migrating workers could be characterised as 'vagrants' or 'wandering poor', and in common with 'masterless men', who refused to work for customary wages or quit their employment without permission, made liable to punishments which included branding and imprisonment.[30] Migrant workers could be forcibly removed to their original parishes of settlement if they were liable to become a charge to poor relief in the host parish. However, recipients of relief were not regularly confined to workhouses, as was increasingly to be the case in the decades after the passage of the Poor Law Amendment Act 1834. A mid-eighteenth century edition of the leading treatise for justices of the peace informed its readers that the 'poor' were 'here to be understood not vagabond beggars and rogues, but those who labour to live, and such as are old and decrepit, unable to work, poor widows, and fatherless children, and tenants driven to poverty; not by riot, expense and carelessness, but by mischance'.[31]

The poor law also saw the emergence of a body of case law defining the contents of the service relationship.[32] The occasion for this was the rising number of disputes between parishes over the allocation of responsibility for poor relief under the provisions of the Settlement Acts of the seventeenth and early eighteenth centuries. The Court of King's Bench attempted to impose a degree of order on local practice, using the newly-developed prerogative writs. In the process, the juridical concept of service began to take shape as a relationship based on reciprocity, founded on contract but also incorporating status-based obligations on both sides. These included the servant's open-ended duty to obey orders but also the master's

[28] *Progress and Poverty*, op cit, n 26, at p 499.

[29] See generally P Slack, *The English Poor Law 1531–1782* (London, Macmillan, 1990).

[30] A Beier, *Masterless Men. The Vagrancy Problem in England 1560–1640* (London, Methuen, 1985).

[31] M Dalton, *The Country Justice: Containing the Practice, Duty and Power of the Justices of the Peace, as Well in as Out of their Sessions* (London, Lintot, 1746), at p 164.

[32] See generally K Snell, *Annals of the Labouring Poor: Social Change and Agrarian England 1660–1900* (Cambridge, Cambridge University Press, 1985).

obligation, as Blackstone put it, to maintain the servant 'throughout the revolution of the respective seasons, as well when there is work to be done as when there is not'.[33] The courts had to deal with numerous cases of what labour lawyers would now call 'task' or 'fixed-term' contracts' and casual working arrangements, along with attempts by employers to avoid the implication of a settlement by dismissing servants a few days or weeks before they completed a full year's service (also a practice with which contemporary labour lawyers are familiar, in the context of employment protection legislation[34]).

Significantly, the case law was not static.[35] In early decisions, the courts were able to find settlements in cases of service affected by minor interruptions on account of illness or unemployment; they also decided that a contract for yearly service fell under the Acts even if it contained provision for termination on either side by monthly notice, since 'if this should be determined not to gain a settlement, it would overturn great numbers of settlements that subsist on such things'.[36] They also ignored a clear indication in the Settlement Act of 1697 to the effect that the contract for a year's employment and the actual period of service should be precisely conterminous.[37] However, the tide began to turn by the middle of the eighteenth century, which was also the period when rising rural unemployment, casualisation of working conditions, falling wage rates and the rising food prices were putting the settlement system under unprecedented strain. Outflanking an earlier case law which had allowed for the existence of a settlement in cases where the employer 'dispensed' with the worker's services for a limited period of time, the courts now developed the notion that an 'exceptive' hiring, in which the employer granted the servant a period of rest or leave outside formal working hours, was not within the Settlement Acts.[38] This had the effect of considerably reducing the legal incidents of the service relationship, at a time when larger numbers of both workers in both agriculture and industry were entering into contracts which stipulated regular hours of work. By the early years of the nineteenth century Ellenborough could reject as outmoded the concept of the 'dispensation', on the grounds that in the old case law it had 'been stretched as far as ingenuity could go, upon the false idea that the servant had a right to acquire in gaining a settlement'.[39] The category of settlement by hiring was abolished altogether by the Act of 1834; but judicial interpretation had long before ensured that its practical significance, as a route to poor relief, was minimal.

[33] W Blackstone, W *Commentaries on the Laws of England. A Fascimile of the First Edition of 1765–69*, edited with an introduction by SN Katz (Chicago, IL, University of Chicago Press, 1979), at p 413.

[34] See eg *Booth v USA* [1999] IRLR 16.

[35] The relevant decisions are discussed by Deakin and Wilkinson, *The Law of the Labour Market*, *op cit*, at pp 118–24.

[36] *Atherton v Barton* (1743) 2 Str 1142.

[37] *Brightwell v Westhallam* (1714) Foley 143.

[38] *R v Macclesfield* (1758) Burr SC 458; *R v Buckland Derham* Burr SC 694; *R v Kingswinford* (1791) 4 Term. Rep 219; *R v North Tibley* (1792) 5 Term Rep 21.

[39] *R v King's Pyon* (1803) 4 East 351, 354.

The wider move brought about by the Act of 1834 was the instantiation of the principle of 'less eligibility' as the guiding principle of the poor law, which it was to remain up to the national insurance reforms of the early twentieth century. The introduction of less eligibility can be understood in terms of an intensification of competition in the labour market. It was a response to the practice of wage supplementation, under the so-called Speenhamland system, which had been widely applied in parts of the country, in particular the south and east, from the 1790s onwards, from around the point when the system of poor law settlements began to break up. The political economists of that time attacked the old poor law on the grounds that it distorted the working of the market. As Bentham observed, the problem was that 'if the conditions of individuals, maintained without property of their own, by the labour of others, were rendered more eligible than that of persons maintained by their own labour, then, in proportion as this state of things were ascertained, individuals destitute of property would be continually withdrawing themselves from the class of persons maintained by their own labour, to the class of persons maintained by the labour of others'; if this went on, 'at last there would be nobody left to labour at all, for anybody'.[40] The solution, enshrined in the Act of 1834, was the principle that no person in receipt of poor relief should be better off than the least well-off 'independent' workers and households. Confinement in the workhouse for the able-bodied poor was the practical consequence of this. But even this posed a difficulty. As the 1839 report on the continuation of the Poor Law Commission put it, since 'humanity demands that all the bodily wants of the inmates of a public establishment should be provided for', in circumstances where the market could not provide this, it was vital 'to submit the pauper inmate of a public establishment to such a system of labour discipline and restraint as shall be sufficient to outweigh, in his estimation, the advantages which he derives from the bodily comforts which he enjoys'.[41] The result was the conscious use of the administrative apparatus of the poor law to attach demeaning and physically punishing conditions to the receipt of indoor relief, a policy which was periodically renewed and applied with increasing vigour throughout the nineteenth century, almost up to the point when the first statutory schemes of unemployment compensation and old age pension provision were introduced in the early 1900s.

The abolition of legislative support for the guilds and the ending of the old poor law in the first decades of the nineteenth century were viewed at the time, and have been viewed since, as steps in the removal of distortions and interferences in the working of the labour market. However, the legal record shows that, in the juridical sphere at least, and arguably beyond it, these processes led neither to the contractualisation of work relations, nor to the adoption by the courts of the contract

[40] J Bentham, 'Essay II. Fundamental positions in regard to the making of provision for the indigent poor', in *Essays on the Subject of the Poor Laws* (1796), reproduced in M Quinn (ed) *The Collected Works of Jeremy Bentham. Writings on the Poor Laws* Volume I (Oxford, Clarendon Press, 2001), at p 39.

[41] *Report on the Continuance of the Poor Law Commission* (1839), reproduced in HR Jenner-Fust, *Poor Law Orders* (London, PS King, 1907), at p 4.

of employment as the paradigm legal form of the work relationship. If there was a 'contract of employment' in the mid nineteenth century, it described the situation of occupational groups, such as managers, lawyers and clerks, with a high-level status or professional background, a stable relationship with their employer, and a degree of protection against interruptions to income by virtue of sickness on the one hand and temporary fluctuations in demand on the other. By contrast, manual workers in both industry and agriculture, a category which included skilled artisans, were covered by the Master and Servant Acts, under which breach of contract by the workers carried with it the possibility of fines or imprisonment. Thousands of prosecutions took place each year under the master-servant code up to its repeal in 1875.[42] This punitive regime had roots in the Statute of Artificers, but was not simply a hold-over from medieval or pre-modern legislation. The disciplinary powers of the magistrates had been strengthened by statute in successive Acts of Parliament between the 1740s and the 1820s. Nor did the influence of the master-servant model end with the repeals of the 1870s. The magistrates and county counts continued to have a quasi-disciplinary power to award damages to employer whose workers quit without notice or refused to obey orders under the Employers and Workmen Act 1875, a power which was regularly in use up to the 1940s, and the hierarchical model of service still permeates the common law of employment, although to a gradually decreasing extent.[43]

In modern labour law, the category of the contract of employment has expanded to cover almost all wage-dependent workers, with the category of the 'contract for services' describing independent contractors and the self-employed. This 'binary divide' entered British labour law at a late stage, in the 1950s and 1960s.[44] This was a reflection of the persistence of the master-servant model in labour law, and the lingering influence of less eligibility in social security law. The post-1945 welfare state saw the completion of a system of state-run social insurance which was intended to be 'comprehensive' in the sense of protecting against a wide-range of work-related risks, and the introduction of employment protection legislation stabilising the individual work relationship; it was in the context of this legislation that the courts began to apply the model of the contract of employment as a unitary category covering all forms of wage-dependent labour. The labour law model of the contract of employment was essentially borrowed from concepts which had already developed in fiscal law and social security law.[45] Almost from the outset, the labour law version was criticised for being an unrealistic and archaic account of work relations.[46]

[42] See generally Deakin and Wilkinson, *The Law of the Labour Market, op cit*, pp 61–74.

[43] *Ibid* see also the comprehensive survey of master-servant laws in the British Empire, D Hay and P Craven (eds) *Masters, Servants and Magistrates in Britain and the Empire* (Chapel Hill, NC, University of North Carolina Press, 2004).

[44] See MR Freedland, *The Personal Employment Contract* (Oxford, Oxford University Press, 2003), chs 1 and 2.

[45] See Deakin and Wilkinson, *The Law of the Labour Market, op cit*, at pp 86–100.

[46] RW Rideout, 'The contract of employment' (1966) 19 *Current Legal Problems* 111.

Thus the British case is one in which the contractualisation of work relations occurred relatively late in the process of legal development following industrialisation, and in which the employment model was only weakly institutionalised even then. Why did contract in general and the employment model in particular play a relatively insignificant role in defining work relations in the nineteenth century? The answer, perhaps paradoxically, lies in the phenomenon of Britain's early industrialization. Britain's path to industrialization was assisted by the development of institutions which were complementary to the emergence of wage labour, namely the guild system and the poor law. These institutions grew up alongside the development of the 'advanced organic economy' of the seventeenth and eighteenth centuries, during a period when advanced techniques in agriculture and a relatively fluid labour market assisted the movement of a majority of the working population from agriculture to industry. However, this was an economy still constrained by limited access to the resources needed for development: as EA Wrigley puts it, 'an organic economy, however advanced, was subject to negative feedback in the sense that the very process of growth set in train changes that made further growth additionally difficult because of the operation of declining marginal returns in production from the land'. By contrast, in the 'mineral energy economy' based on the exploitation of coal and steam power, and so 'freed from dependence on the land for raw materials', sustained growth in real wages was possible.[47] But in the process of moving from one paradigm of economic development to the other, the institutions of the organic economy came under unprecedented strain, to the extent that, in the end, they proved ill-fitted to the demands placed upon them. Britain entered the industrial age in a period of institutional turbulence, when traditional forms of collective solidarity were disintegrating, but before the point at which new mechanisms of economic coordination and risk-distribution, appropriate for a market-based economy, had had time to develop. On the continent of Europe, by contrast, this process was reversed: many of the relevant institutional mechanisms were already in place, or had developed to a significant degree, when the transition to an industrial economy occurred in the mid-nineteenth century. This comparison between Britain and the continent will now be explored in more detail.

The British Case in Comparative Perspective: Industrialization and the Emergence of the Contract of Employment in Continental Europe

Industrialization in France and Germany began several decades after it had commenced in Britain, and after the point at which continental legal institutions

[47] Wrigley, *Continuity, Chance and Change*, *op cit*, at pp 29–30.

and doctrine had already been liberalised under the influence of the post-revolutionary codes. The codes formalised the shift towards a market-based conception of legal relations, structured around notions of contract and of property rights. Labour relations were not unaffected by this process. As in Britain, the transition from pre-modern legal forms to the concept of the contract of employment was not straightforward; however, thanks to the influence of the codes, contractual concepts shaped the response of the continental systems to the growth of industrial enterprise at an earlier stage and more explicitly than they did in Britain. As the nineteenth century progressed, this liberal contractual model was adjusted to the conditions of industrialization in ways which reflected the legal, cultural and economic influences of different systems. The result was a juridical model of the employment relationship which was more deeply embedded, both socially and juridically, than its British counterpart.

On the face of it, at least, the French Revolution was the occasion for a fundamental break with pre-modern economic institutions; guilds and their equivalents were peremptorily 'abolished' by the décret d'Allarde and loi Le Chapelier of 1791 (the latter also made workers' combinations and strikes illegal). The French Civil Code of 1804 then classified the work relationship as contractual in nature, placing it, moreover, in the category of the law of things rather than the law of persons. This gave expression to the idea that the labour contract, just like sale or lease, was a relationship of exchange between juridical equals, in sharp contrast to Blackstone's treatment, half a century earlier, of the personal relation of master and servant in English law. The two types of work relationship set out in the French Civil Code were the *louage d'ouvrage* and the *louage de services.* The *louage d'ouvrage* or hire of work was modelled on the Roman law concept of the *locatio conductio operarum*, which referred to a contract for a finished job of work or completed task. The *louage de services*, on the other hand, bore a resemblance to the Roman law *locatio conductio operis*, or hire of services. In both cases, the link to Roman law concepts was more a matter of rhetoric than substance. The concepts used in the Civil Code were adaptations which were 'the same as the old *locatio conductio* in name only'.[48] This was because the Roman law notion of the *locatio conductio* was understood at this point to have been a form which implied the subordination of the worker, a notion regarded as incompatible with the liberal idea of formal equality between contracting parties. Thus even in the case of the *louage de services*, the form which superficially bore the closest resemblance to an open-ended agreement to serve, services could only be provided for a certain purpose or for a limited period of time. A commitment to lifelong service would be struck down as a nullity.

The concept of the worker's subordination to the employer did not, however, disappear. It was obliquely acknowledged in the rule of the French Civil Code which stipulated that, in the event of a dispute over wages between employer and

[48] B Veneziani, 'The evolution of the contract of employment', in B Hepple (ed) *The Making of Labour Law in Europe*, *op cit*, 31–72, at p 32.

worker, only the word of the former was to be believed. This provision was carried over into the other continental codes and remained in force for most of the nineteenth century. In addition, in the same period as the post-revolutionary codes were being adopted, continental systems preserved and in certain respects strengthened the punitive, pre-modern system of the workbook or *livret*. This gave state authorities powers to regulate labour mobility and punish breaches of discipline through the use of criminal sanctions. The distinction between the *louage d'ouvrage* and the *louage de services* needs to be understood in this context. Workers in both categories might come under the regulatory jurisdiction associated with the *livret*, which, just before the adoption of the Civil Code, was strengthened by legislation (the law of 12 germinal An 11, or 12 April 1803). Thus the emerging forms of wage labour, rather than being confined to the superficially service-like *louage de services*, were to be found in both categories, and in each case were subject to a disciplinary legal régime?[49]

For the same reason, the idea that there is a direct line of descent between the *louage de services* and the notion of the contract of employment or *contrat de travail* should be resisted. Although the existence of such a link was posited at the end of the nineteenth century by a number of labour law jurists, this was, it has been more recently claimed, a 'mystification' of the process involved.[50] This was done to lend the appearance of continuity to the law at a time when the concept of the *contrat de travail* was still relatively novel. The term *contrat de travail* appears not to have been in widespread use in France before the mid-1880s.[51] The main impetus for its adoption was an argument by employers in larger enterprises that the general duty of obedience should be read into all industrial hirings. However, once the term became established, it was used in turn of the century legislation on industrial accidents[52] and its adoption was promoted and systematised by commissions of jurists charged with developing a conceptual framework for collective bargaining and worker protection.[53] At the core of the concept was an adaptation of the notion of 'subordination': an open-ended duty of obedience was accepted, and, indeed, extended to all wage-dependent and salaried workers; but it was now traded off in return for the absorption by the enterprise and by the state of social risks covering the range from health and safety to income and job security. It was also at this point that the French legislation on the workbook was revised so that its punitive elements fell away, to be replaced by an obligation on the employer to record and abide by the details of the employment contract.[54]

[49] See H Petit and D Sauze, 'Une lecture historique du relation salariale comme structure de répartition des aléas: en partant du travail de Salais', in F Eymard-Duvernay (ed) *L'économie des conventions: méthodes et resultants. Tome II Développements*, 303–16 (Paris, La Découverte, 2006).

[50] Cottereau, 'Industrial tribunals and the establishment of a kind of common law of labour in nineteenth century France' *op cit*, at p 220.

[51] *Ibid.*

[52] Veneziani, 'The evolution of the contract of employment', *op cit*, at p 64.

[53] *Ibid*, at p 68.

[54] *Ibid*, at p 43.

The terminology used in the German Civil Code, the BGB, adopted in 1896, appears to be the same as used in the French Civil Code at the beginning of the nineteenth century, but this appearance is deceptive. The BGB formally distinguished the *Dienstvertrag*, literally the 'contract for service', from the *Werkvertrag*, the contract for work or sub-contract. The BGB nevertheless broke with the Roman law model of the *locatio*. The two categories of the *Dienstvertrag* and *Werkvertrag* were placed in separate volumes of the code, signifying the fragmentation of the *locatio* concept. In terms of substance, too, there was a difference; the *Dienstvertrag* came to embody the idea of the employer's duty of care (*Fürsorgepflicht*), the counterpoint to the duty of loyalty (*Treuepflicht*) owed by the worker. This reflected the influence of Otto von Gierke who argued for the integration into the Code of the principles of social solidarity which, he argued, were to be found in the historical antecedents of the *Dienstvertrag*. In this way, the emerging employment law was realigned with the law of persons and with a communitarian notion of the enterprise (Veneziani, 1986: 59; Sims, 2002: 85–6).[55]

Nor is there a clear reference in the BGB to the binary divide between employees and the self-employed: 'at the time the BGB was drafted . . . the distinction between employment and services had not been established, so the term *Dienstvertrag* . . . covered both types of agreement. This means that in the context of Art 611 [BGB], *Dienstvertrag* refers both to the contract for service . . . and the contract of employment' (Sims, 2002: 83). The modern notion of the employment relationship or *Arbeitsverhältnis* came later, as in France, with the adoption of protective social legislation, legalization of trade unions, recognition of the right to strike, and legal acknowledgement of the practice of collective bargaining.

Alain Supiot[56] has developed a wide-ranging argument which crystallizes the differences in the French and German experiences of adjusting the contractual model to labour market conditions in course of industrialisation. In French-influenced systems, the state assumed a power to regulate basic conditions of work, a power which was given doctrinal expression in the concept of *ordre public social*. This signified a set of minimum, binding conditions which applied as a matter of general law to the employment relationship. The logic of this idea was that the legal system acknowledged the contractual equality of the parties to the employment relationship, but in doing so also assumed, in a symmetrical fashion, the responsibility for protecting the individual worker, who was thereby put in a position of 'juridical subordination'. In German-influenced systems, by contrast, the individual contract of employment was qualified by a 'communitarian' conception of the enterprise. At the point when the German Civil Code was drafted, in the 1890s, the communitarian response to industrialization was sufficiently strong for Gierke to be able to argue that the French Civil Code, in attempting to produce a modernised version of the 'eternal juridical truths' of the Roman law

[55] Veneziani, 'The evolution of the contract of employment', *op cit*, at p 59; V Sims, *Good Faith in Contract Law: A Comparative Analysis of English and German Law*. PhD Thesis, University of Cambridge, 2002, at pp 85–6.

[56] A Supiot, *Critique du droit du travail* (Paris, PUF).

tradition, had merely served to conceal 'formulas expressing individualistic and capitalistic assumptions'.[57] Under Gierke's influence, the provisions of the BGB governing the employment relationship were orientated away from the law of obligations and towards the law of persons. By these means, German law came to recognise the 'personal subordination' of the worker in the form of 'factual adhesion to the enterprise' or *Tatbestand*, a process conferring upon the individual 'a status equivalent to membership of a community'.[58] At the same time, Supiot also emphasises that the distinction between what he calls the 'Romanist' and 'Germanic' traditions in labour law is one which affected all continental European systems to some degree. The 'synthesis' of contractual and communitarian elements became a source of 'structural ambivalence' in the conceptual framework of continental labour law:

> The law of obligations takes as its reference point an individualist and liberal ideology, which asserts the liberty and equality of individuals and affirms the primacy of the individual over the group, and of the sphere of the economic over that of the social. The law of persons (exemplified above all by the model of family law) is aligned with a communitarian ideology, which asserts the hierarchy of parent over child and affirms the primacy of the group over the individual and of the sphere of the social over that of the economic. This is the source of the point-by-point opposition of such concepts as equality and hierarchy, *societas* and *universitas*, association and corporation, contract and status, *Gesellschaft* and *Gemeinschaft*, individualism and holism, and so on.[59]

Thus the French and German experiences can be seen as illustrating different ways in which the liberal model of contract was accommodated to the growth of industrial and labour legislation in the course of the nineteenth century. The forms of adjustment may have varied, but by comparison to the British case there was a more explicit recognition of the role of the contract of employment as a mechanism of economic integration within the enterprise and of social cohesion beyond it. The result has been, historically, a more complete institutionalization of the employment model within juridical doctrines and legal norms, and, more recently, greater resistance to its fragmentation in the face of demands for increased 'flexibility' in the labour market.

Why did continental labour law take a different path from the British case, leading to the more complete institutionalization of the contract of employment? Part of the answer may lie in the different economic and cultural conditions under which industrialization took place on the continent. According to DS Landes, 'the continental entrepreneur' of the nineteenth century 'had a different conception of his role from the British'. Landes ascribes this to 'a strong feudal and manorial tradition' in which factory owners saw themselves as having 'duties as well as the

[57] O von Gierke, *Das Deutsches Privatrecht. Systematisches Handbuch der deutschen Rechtswissenschaft* (Leipzig, Duncker & Humblot, 1895), at p 32.
[58] Supiot, *Critique du droit du travail*, *op cit*, at p 18.
[59] *Ibid*, at p 32.

privileges that such a position entails'.[60] More prosaically, industrial paternalism on the continent owed much to 'the danger and inconvenience of losing a working force collected with difficulty and only too easily dispersed'. In comparing Britain and France, Patrick O'Brien likewise points to the processes which ensured that the rural population in France continued to have access to the land, and hence to alternatives to waged employment, long after this had ceased to be the case in Britain.[61] In addition, attitudes on the continent were reinforced by what Landes refers to as 'public and official opinion': 'in [nineteenth-century] France, the government was sensitive to factory unemployment, keeping watch on hiring and firing and utilizing political pressure when necessary to limit the number of jobless, even in—or rather especially in—severe crises'.[62]

Britain was insulated from a revolutionary political tradition which, while it may have helped to pave the way for economic liberalization in the 1790s and 1800s, had by 1848 placed the issue of social protection at the forefront of the political agenda. As Bruno Veneziani argues, 'the authors of the French Constitution around the middle of the nineteenth century came close to granting constitutional recognition of the right to work'.[63] The concept was debated by the 1848 National Assembly and, although transformed into a right to public assistance in the Constitution of the Second Republic, that text also included reference not just to the right to engage in industry and enterprise, but also to constitutional protection for the opportunity to work in the form of provision for primary education and job training: 'France in 1848 represents the country most committed, at least on the constitutional level, to transforming the labour market'. Although few other continental systems went this far, the tradition of constitutionalising the right to work was carried over into the post-1918 Weimar Constitution in Germany, and to the post-1945 constitutions in France, Italy, Germany, Denmark and the Netherlands.[64]

That no similar tradition emerged in Britain has been attributed to the absence of a working class political party during the period, in the late 1860s, when the first significant steps were taken towards the removal of legal impediments to collective bargaining. As Lord Wedderburn puts it, this 'formative period saw a unique conjunction of three elements in Britain: (i) a relatively strong but wholly industrial labour movement; (ii) the absence of a working class political party, with the political ideology of which the unions might have been associated; and (iii) the first, but gradual extensions to men of the political franchise'.[65] It was this conjunction, he suggests, which gave rise to 'the strange base of British labour law', the system of trade dispute immunities which provided the foundation for trade union organi-

[60] DS Landes, *Unbound Prometheus: Technological Change and Industrial Development in Western Europe from 1750 to the Present* (Cambridge, Cambridge University Press, 1969), at p 191.

[61] P O'Brien, 'Path dependency, or why Britain became an industrialized and urbanized economy long before France' (1996) 52 *Economic History Review* 213–49.

[62] Landes, *Unbound Prometheus, op cit*, at p 192.

[63] 'The evolution of the contract of employment', *op cit*, at p 36.

[64] *Ibid*, at pp 36–7.

[65] Lord Wedderburn, 'Industrial relations and the courts' (1980) 9 *Industrial Law Journal* 65–94.

zation and the right to strike and which came into being in two major waves of legislation in the 1870s and 1900s. Far from seeing the legal system as a guarantor of social rights, the British trade union movement was content to see the courts excluded as far as possible from involvement in the emerging system of collective bargaining. This had implications for the contract of employment: in order to preserve the right to strike as far as possible from judicial interference, unions in the final decades of the nineteenth century were willing to argue in favour of a basic model of employment, similar to the US employment at will, under which contracts could be terminated by either party on at most a day's notice.

If the emergence of voluntarism as the characteristic British response to the rise of collective bargaining owed much to a particular conjunction of economic and political circumstances, the same point can be applied to the wider role played by British industrialisation in shaping labour law institutions in the nineteenth century. The under-development of the contract of employment in the period between 1750 and 1850 was in part the consequence of an industrial structure dominated by small-scale enterprises with limited managerial capabilities. Company law did not develop mechanisms for the concentration of capital, in the form of limited liability for shareholders, until the 1850s; aside from statutory corporations such as railway and canal companies, most enterprises took the legal form of partnerships, which placed a limit on their growth and also on the exercise of centralised managerial coordination.[66] Complete vertical integration of production was rare; sub-contracting or the 'internal contract' system was the norm in many industries well into the twentieth century.[67] The disciplinary force of master and servant legislation provided employers with legal support for managerial prerogative at a point when organizational forms of coordination had yet to develop. Even after changes to company law and the repeal of master and servant legislation had created a context more conducive to the modernization of organizational forms, most British manufacturing enterprises remained small scale, and did not make much use of limited liability or even of separate corporate personality until the 1890s and 1900s, when a wave of mergers and acquisitions led to greater industrial concentration.[68] Thus the slow emergence of modern managerial practice in the second half of the nineteenth century and in particular the persistence of forms of sub-contracting within the enterprise provides a further explanation for the late development of the contract of employment in Britain. Vertical integration was more advanced in France and Germany during this period.[69]

[66] J Saville, 'Sleeping partnership and limited liability, 1850–1856' (1956) *Economic History Review* 418–33.

[67] L Hannah, *The Rise of the Corporate Economy* (London, Methuen, 2nd edn, 1983).

[68] *Ibid* M Holbrook-Jones, *Supremacy and Subordination of Labour: The Hierarchy of Work in the Early Labour Movement* (London, Heinemann Educational Books, 1982).

[69] See Biernacki, *The Fabrication of Labour*, *op cit*; Didry, *Naissance de la convention collective*, *op cit*.

Conclusions: Legal Origin, Institutional Change and Functionalism in Labour Law

From even this brief overview, it will be clear that the origins of the legal institution of the contract of employment law were highly complex, in all systems. In particular, the interpretation offered above does not map on to the over-simplified distinction between legal systems according to whether their origin lies in the common law or the civil law. The currently influential idea that, in respect of labour market regulation, 'common law countries tend to rely more on markets and contracts, and civil law (and socialist) countries on regulation (and state ownership)',[70] finds no support at all in the historical analysis which has been presented here. On the contrary: it would be highly misleading to characterise the civilian approach as necessarily more regulatory than that of the common law. Thanks to the liberalizing influence of the post-revolutionary codes, nearly all the continental systems, including those influenced by the German tradition, acquired a liberal-contractual model of the employment relationship well in advance of the English common law. In contrast, again, to the British experience, the continental systems accepted the application of contractual concepts to work relations before the point at which wage labour in its modern form became widespread. As industrialization advanced, the continental legal systems responded to the wave of labour regulation in ways which incorporated and acknowledged the principle of protection of the worker against economic and social risks (accidents at work, occupational disease, loss of income through sickness, unemployment and old age). However, the same process implied the recognition by the legal system of the primacy and legitimacy of capitalist modes of economic organization. The juridical form of the contract of employment symbolised this fusion of the 'social' and the 'economic': at one and the same time it underpinned the managerial power of coordination within the enterprise, while providing mechanisms for shifting and spreading the risks of wage dependence in a market economy, a task shared with the state as systems of employment taxation and social insurance became more widely adopted at the turn of the twentieth century.

The British experience is the inverse of that just described: by virtue of early industrialization, wage labour was widespread before contractual concepts had been applied on a systematic basis to the labour market relations. Far from contract determining the rights and obligations of the parties, the disciplinary master-servant code and an increasingly punitive poor law system provided the

[70] J Botero, S Djankov, R La Porta, F Lopez de Silanes and A Shleifer, 'The regulation of labor' (2004) 119 *Quarterly Journal of Economics* 1340–82, at p 1345. For a more complete review and critique of the 'legal origin' hypothesis in the context of labour law, see B Ahlering and S Deakin, 'Labour regulation, corporate governance and legal origin: a case of institutional complementarity?' (2007) 41 *Law & Society Review*, forthcoming.

institutional setting for the work relationship in the transition to an industrial economy. The influence of these institutions, which looked back to pre-modern forms of labour market governance, was slow to fade, just as collective bargaining and social insurance were slow to have an impact on the juridical structure of labour law. It is no accident that as late as the 1950s, the juridical form of the contract of employment is only barely discernible in British labour law, while its French equivalent, the *contrat de travail*, can be clearly identified in the 1880s. In one particular respect, the legal origin hypothesis does find some support from this analysis: the influence of British practice on the common law world in general, and in particular on certain British colonies, is clear. However, it was not the liberal-contractual model which was disseminated via British colonisation, but rather the master-servant regime and the associated use of criminal sanctions to discipline workers; these became omnipresent features of colonial legal development in the common law world.[71]

What of the claim that certain juridical forms have a functional relationship to economic development? This argument has reached its height in recent accounts of the evolution of company law: on the basis that the institutions of limited liability and separate corporate personality, among others, are 'induced by the economic exigencies of the large modern business enterprise', it is suggested that 'corporate law everywhere must, of necessity, provide for them'.[72] It could equally well be argued that the emergence of a 'labour market' based on the separation of the mass of the population from traditional forms of subsistence and the integration of work relations into the organizational structure of the capitalist enterprise requires a range of complementary institutions, the foremost of is the contract of employment. Yet the analysis presented in this paper suggests that the process of industrialization is compatible with a wide range of such forms. There has been considerable variety in the evolution of the contract of employment even within the context of the relatively homogeneous societies of western Europe. On this basis it would seem difficult to argue that there is a single set of legal institutions which is uniquely well fitted to the conditions of a market economy. Those forms which have survived may have done so not because they were better than the alternatives, but because of chance conjunctions and the arbitrary effects of timing. The institutional underpinnings of capitalism are perhaps more diverse, and more contingent, than some current theories allow.

[71] D Hay and P Craven (eds) *Masters, Servants and Magistrates in Britain and the Empire* (Chapel Hill, NC, University of North Carolina Press, 2004).

[72] H Hansmann and R Kraakman, 'What is corporate law?', in R Kraakman, P Davies, H Hansmann, G Hertig, H Kanda, K Hopt and E Rock (eds) *The Anatomy of Corporate Law: A Comparative and Functional Approach* 1–19 (Oxford, Oxford University Press, 2004), at p 2; *cf* R Harris, *Industrializing English Law: Entrepreneurship and Business Organization 1720–1844* (Cambridge, Cambridge University Press, 2000), at p 291: '[t]here is no reason to assume that the new framework of 1844–1856 was evolutionarily selected for the industrial economy because it better defined and enforced property rights, minimized transaction costs, or maximized efficiency in any other strong sense. One can conceive a slightly different historical path in earlier periods that would have led to a different outcome that cannot be readily evaluated as less efficient'.

5

Rebuilding the Law of the Workplace in an Era of Self-Regulation

CYNTHIA ESTLUND*

As the New Deal model of industrial self governance in the United States has grown old and ossified, the problems to which collective bargaining was to be the answer have not disappeared.[1] Nor has the law ceased to grapple with them. On the contrary, the role of external law—of courts, of legislation, and of regulatory bodies—has burgeoned as the New Deal system of internalised lawmaking and dispute resolution has shrunk. Since the 1960s, the New Deal collective bargaining system has been supplemented, and largely supplanted, by other models of workplace governance: a regulatory model of minimum standards enforceable mainly by administrative agencies (think of OSHA and the minimum wage laws) and a rights model of judicially enforceable individual rights (think especially of anti discrimination law). These two bodies of law, which make up much of what we in the US call 'employment law', each mobilised institutions and resources that were not central to the collective bargaining model constituted by 'labour law'. The regulatory model harnessed the coercive power and comprehensive reach of the government, while the rights model made courts central to the articulation and enforcement of employee rights, and tapped into the self interest and indignation of aggrieved individuals and the professional and entrepreneurial energies of their attorneys.

Much as they resisted the constraints of collective bargaining, employers have fought back against the burdens of regulatory compliance and of litigation; they have proclaimed the virtues of deregulation and decried the 'litigation crisis'. But challenges to the efficacy of regulation and litigation of workplace rights and standards have come not only from employers but from scholars and employee advocates as well. Observers from a range of perspectives have argued that the post war regime of command and control regulation is losing its grip in the face of rapidly changing markets, technology, and firm structures; that civil litigation is a costly, slow, and unwieldy mechanism for securing employee rights.

* CA Rein Professor, New York University School of Law.

[1] By 'ossified', I mean entrenched against reform by a variety of mechanisms. See Cynthia Estlund, 'The Ossification of American Labor Law' (2002) 102 *Columbia Law Review* 1527 at 1530 [hereinafter Estlund, Ossification].

These critiques have begun to converge on the concept of self-regulation, and to make their mark on the external law of the workplace. Agencies responsible for enforcing labour standards have experimented with cooperative programs designed to bring about self-regulation and voluntary compliance. Courts responsible for enforcing employee rights have begun to formalise the role of internal compliance procedures, and to defer to private dispute resolution schemes, according employers a partial shield against litigation and liability based on those schemes. These developments bring the locus of enforcement of both rights and regulations inside the firm or under the firm's control, and to confer a partial shield against regulatory and judicial intervention on the basis of self-regulatory programs.

Detractors see in these moves toward self-regulation a disguised form of deregulation. Proponents see the evolution of more efficient and effective systems for enforcing legal norms. Much turns on how self-regulation works—what standards of efficacy and what institutional safeguards regulators require of self-regulating firms. In the workplace setting in particular, much turns on whether employees themselves play an effective part in firms' self-regulation of their labour practices. Regulatory theory and experience in a range of settings around the world teach that effective self-regulation in the workplace should be 'tripartite' in structure: It requires the participation of the state, the regulated firm, *and* the workers for whose benefit the relevant legal norms exist. Self-regulatory processes in which workers participate can introduce flexibility and responsiveness into the regulatory regime, and can reduce the costs and contentiousness associated with litigation, while promoting the internalisation of public law norms into the workplace itself.

The problem, of course, is that the move toward self-regulation has coincided with a drastic decline in unionisation, the only legally-sanctioned vehicle in the US for employee representation within the firm. Even apart from the trend toward self-regulation, both employee rights and workplace regulations are often under enforced in the absence of union representation, especially where employers are committed to competing through the minimisation of labour costs. The movement toward self-regulation, and the attendant retreat of public agencies and of courts from the front lines of enforcement, exacerbates this vulnerability.

To my mind, the movement of employment law and its enforcement inside firms creates not only the need, but also the opportunity, to revive employees' voice inside firms. That is because the law can and does impose conditions on firms' ability to secure the legal advantages of self-regulation—conditions that aim to ensure the efficacy of self-regulation. Among those conditions should be some form of tripartism, and in particular the effective involvement of the employees whose rights and working conditions are at stake. The challenge is to reconfigure tripartism for the overwhelmingly non union environment that exists, and is likely to persist, in the United States.

My aim here is to chart a strategy for reforming the law of the workplace that straddles the conventional divide between labour law and employment law—one that finds footholds within employment law for the pursuit of the core normative commitment of New Deal labour law to workplace democracy. It is grounded in the observation that workers' freedom of association and self-determination are not only of intrinsic value in a democratic society but of instrumental value in realising the rights and the regulatory norms governing the workplace. That is especially true in an era of self-regulation, in which the locus of enforcement is moving inside the workplace and away from direct public oversight. Giving employees an institutionalised role in self-regulatory processes will help both to make rights more real and regulatory standards more effective, and also to rebuild mechanisms for effective worker participation in self-governance. In other words, the models of workplace governance that have emerged in the wake of the decline of the collective bargaining model can be both improved by *and turned to the cause of* promoting democratic self-governance within the workplace.

The Rise of Regulation, and of Self-Regulation, in the Law of the Workplace

The New Deal, in which the template for the modern regulatory state was forged, was founded on the conviction that market mechanisms for the organisation of the economy, albeit superior to the alternatives, were intrinsically flawed and prone to failure. Regulatory agencies were established to protect the public interest against market malfunctions through the enactment and centralised enforcement of uniform rules and standards, later denominated 'command and control'. Alongside the NLRA's reconstitution of the framework for private bargaining, command and control mechanisms gained a foothold in the New Deal workplace with the Fair Labor Standards Act of 1938 (FLSA), which provided for a nationwide minimum wage and an overtime premium for leading sectors of the private labour market. Later the Occupational Safety and Health Act of 1970 (OSHA) established minimum health and safety standards through regulation. Congress went on to regulate employee pension and benefit plans with the Employee Retirement Income Security Act of 1974; to require advance notice of plant closings and mass layoffs in the Worker Adjustment and Retraining Notification Act of 1988; and to expand and regulate (unpaid) parental and medical leave policies with the Family and Medical Leave Act of 1993.

Even as this web of regulations was under construction, however, the viability of command and control regulatory schemes has come under challenge from many directions. Many employee advocates depict the main problem as one of under enforcement: not enough inspectors, not enough penalties, not enough deterrence or compliance.[2] But the opposite critique—decrying regulators'

[2] See T McGarity and S Shapiro, *Workers at Risk: The Failed Promise of the Occupational Safety and Health Administration* 26–8 (1993).

excessive zeal, rigidity, and adversarialism—has been at least as voluble.[3] Business interests in particular pleaded for deregulation in the interest of competitiveness and flexibility. Even for proponents of public intervention, however, the reigning regime of centrally administered uniform standards, and the lengthy process for developing those standards, appeared increasingly out of step with ever more agile forms of production, porous product markets, and trans-national corporate structures.

Alongside growing doubts about the viability of command and control, we have seen growing corporate capabilities, and apparent commitment, to comply with legal standards. Larger firms in particular have invested heavily in internal compliance machinery. Procedures vary, but they typically involve charging one or more employees with overseeing compliance with legal requirements (as part or all of their job), and establishing procedures for other employees to report apparent violations. The existence of these structures has, in turn, enhanced the credibility of firms' demands for more cooperative regulatory approaches and for more latitude to self-regulate their labour practices. These developments converged to yield a growing conviction that traditional command and control regulatory approaches are anachronistic—ineffectual at best, counterproductive at worst—and that the law must be reconfigured to promote self-regulation.

The move toward self-regulation has not yet made major inroads on the basic federal labour standards statutes themselves. Still, state and federal regulatory agencies have begun to experiment with forms of self-regulation within the confines of these command and control statutes. These experiments in regulated self-regulation—a few of which I will discuss below—still occupy only a very small part of the larger scheme of labour standards regulation in the United States. Yet the decline of command and control and the rise of employer self-regulation—more or less well monitored and enforced—seem inexorable. It converges with the development and legal encouragement of corporate compliance programs across a range of regulatory arenas. The rise of self-regulation is also in keeping with regulatory trends, both in theory and in practice, across many areas of regulation and many countries across the globe.[4] And it parallels emerging efforts to gain regulatory traction over manufacturing workplaces outside the developed world, where a growing share of the world's goods are produced.[5]

There is much scepticism from organised labour and worker advocates about the efficacy of corporate codes of conduct and other forms of self-regulation. And there is too little research that rigorously evaluates the efficacy of the internal com-

[3] See E Bardach and R Kagan, *Going by the Book: The Problem of Regulatory Unreasonableness* 32 (1982).

[4] See J Braithwaite and P Drahos, *Global Business Regulation* (Cambridge, Cambridge University Press, 2000) at 28.

[5] For a discussion of those efforts, see KA Elliott and RB Freeman, *Can Labor Standards Improve Under Globalisation?* (Washington, DC, Institute for International Economics, 2003) at 49–72; M Barenberg, 'Law and Labor in the New Global Economy: Through the Lens of United States Federalism' (1995) 33 *Columbia Journal of Transnational Law* 445, at 447–8.

pliance regimes that are gaining legal recognition.[6] But a preference by many employee advocates for stronger adversarial enforcement is tempered by a growing realisation that workplaces are too numerous and too varied, and production is too mobile and too global, to hope for traditional regulatory methods to do the whole job. There will simply never be enough inspectors to rely on public enforcement alone. The question is no longer whether to invest in self-regulatory mechanisms but how to make those mechanisms effective in improving labour standards. It is to that question that I now turn.

Elements of Effective Self-Regulation in the Workplace: Tripartism, Monitoring, Whistle-blowing, and Private Enforcement

Among the analytical frameworks that have been put forward to illuminate and shape the mega trend toward self-regulation, that of Responsive Regulation, elucidated by Professors Ayres and Braithwaite, is particularly well suited to the problem of labour regulation.[7] But the tenets of Responsive Regulation prove to be at variance with regulatory reality in the US labour standards arena. Responsive Regulation will thus be our starting point but not our ending point.

Responsive Regulation and US Regulatory Reality

A wide range of regulatory experience in many different national regimes and many different regulatory domains has shown that one basic problem for regulators is the variety and complexity of human motivations among regulated actors.[8] In short, there are both 'good guys' and 'bad guys', and there are many who could go either way depending partly on the workings of the regulatory scheme. This heterogeneity poses a challenge for regulators, particularly in a world of scarce enforcement resources. A system of regulation that assumes that all regulated actors are self-interested opportunists who will respond only to carrots and sticks will waste enforcement resources on those who seek to do the right thing and will squander the goodwill and the vast regulatory resources within those actors. Yet a system that assumes instead that regulated actors are well intentioned and seek to abide by the law—such as a system of wholesale self-regulation—invites the more

[6] See K Krawiec, Cosmetic Compliance and the Failure of Negotiated Governance, 81 *Wash UL Q* 487, 510–1543 (2003).

[7] See I Ayres and J Braithwaite, *Responsive Regulation: Transcending the Deregulation Debate* 4–6 (1992).

[8] *Ibid* at 22–7.

opportunistic actors to cheat, puts competitive pressure on the would-be law abiders, erodes trust and norms of good citizenship, and breeds resentment.[9]

Ayres and Braithwaite propose a pyramid of enforcement mechanisms, from the least interventionist form of self-regulation and reporting at the bottom of the pyramid to highly punitive (but hopefully rare) sanctions—what they call 'the benign big gun'—at the top. Compliance is rewarded with more cooperative, less adversarial, firm-centred enforcement strategies; non compliance is met with the escalation of regulatory scrutiny and sanctions, coupled with a willingness either to escalate further in response to chronic non compliance or to return to cooperative strategies in response to improved compliance.[10]

A system that relies heavily on self-regulation and that encourages cooperation between regulators and regulated actors seeks to tap into a wealth of knowledge, experience, creativity, goodwill, and organisational efficacy within firms. If those resources can be brought to bear on the enforcement of legal norms, then scarce public regulatory resources can be targeted at bad actors and leveraged into more thorough accomplishment of the public's regulatory aims. But such a system is also vulnerable both to cheating by reputedly compliant actors and to capture of the regulators, who may indulge a preference for cooperation when it is not warranted.[11]

Responsive Regulation seeks to guard against both cheating and capture in part by empowering third party watchdogs that are independent of both regulators and the regulated and that represent the interests that the particular regulatory scheme seeks to advance. It is a 'tripartite' model of regulation. 'The simplest arena to understand how tripartite regulation would work is with occupational health and safety', say Ayres and Braithwaite.[12] In that setting, a union and its 'elected union health and safety representatives' would participate in inspections, receive information, and initiate enforcement.[13] They suggest that elected safety representatives might play the same role at a non union workplace, provided that one could ensure access to technical and legal assistance; for '[w]here there is no power base and no information base for the weaker party, tripartism will not work'.[14]

The reason occupational safety (and indeed workplace regulation generally) provides such a nice illustration of tripartism is that, unlike many regulatory regimes, workplace regulations operate for the benefit of fully competent adults who work inside the regulated entity, and are potentially capable of speaking for

[9] See I Ayres and J Braithwaite, *Responsive Regulation: Transcending the Deregulation Debate* 4–6 (1992) at 51–3.

[10] Ayres and Braithwaite describe the appropriate regulatory strategy as a version of the 'tit-for-tat' strategy that game theorists have found to produce a cooperative equilibrium among repeat players in prisoners' dilemma type games. Above n 9 at 60–8.

[11] *Ibid* at 54–7.

[12] *Ibid* at 59. For a simplified two-track version of this regulatory approach to occupational safety and health, see Neil A Gunningham, 'Towards Effective and Efficient Enforcement of Occupational Health and Safety Regulation: Two Paths to Enlightenment' (1998) 19 *Comparative Labor Law and Policy Journal* 547 at 549–56.

[13] Ayres and Braithwaite at 59. See also *ibid* at 106, 126.

[14] *Ibid* at 59.

themselves and playing a part in the internal regulatory regime. Workers are on the scene, informed about workplace conditions, and motivated to represent their interests within the firm. Employee representatives not only monitor self-regulation; they participate directly within the self-regulatory process, helping to devise and implement rules and standards, take complaints, train employees, and the like.[15] Within the internal self-regulatory regime, a union—or any other representative of employees—functions not only as an independent third party but as an integral constituent of the 'self' that is charged with self-regulation.

Self-regulation as it is conceived in Responsive Regulation is not a substitute for public regulation. It bears little resemblance to the bland invocations of 'voluntary compliance' of some employer advocates and allies. Rather, it embeds self-regulation in a system of external and internal accountability—external accountability to public regulators with the power to impose coercive sanctions and internal accountability to the workers whose interests are at issue. And it situates self-regulation in a broader scheme in which traditional inspections, enforcement, and punitive sanctions continue to operate for the low road or less capable actors at the bottom of the labour market.

The application of Responsive Regulation to US labour regulation faces several hurdles, however: Can Responsive Regulation work in an environment of chronic under investment in the enforcement of labour standards? Can tripartism work in the overwhelmingly non union American workplace, and in the face of the vehement anti unionism of most American employers? Or would an effort to apply Responsive Regulation to US reality founder on the shoals of under enforcement, union decline, and anti union animus?

While Responsive Regulation aims to make more efficient use of scarce enforcement resources, it still demands greater regulatory oversight and resources, and more potent sanctions, than are available to labour regulatory agencies in the US.[16] For many employers who are tempted to violate these laws, the risk and cost of detection by public agencies is much too low to induce compliance when market conditions encourage defection, producing compliance rates of less than 50 per cent in some low wage industries.[17] The low rate of enforcement defies one of the key prescriptions of Responsive Regulation: The cost of non cooperation or 'defection', primarily in the form of enforcement and sanctions, must be great enough to deter wilful defectors and to protect co-operators against demoralising and injurious competition from defectors. Absent a serious escalation in labour standards enforcement generally, an effort to apply the tenets of Responsive Regulation might end up masking what amounts to a process of deregulation.

[15] On the role of union representation in the workplace health and safety group, see *ibid* at 106, 126.

[16] On the chronic shortage of OSHA inspectors and resources, see McGarity and Shapiro, Workers at Risk, above n 2, at 41–2; TO McGarity, 'Reforming OSHA: Some Thoughts for the Current Legislative Agenda' (1994) 1 *Houston Law Review* 99 at 101–2.

[17] See David Weil, Compliance with the Minimum Wage: Can Government Make a Difference? at 9–13, 45.

Another challenge is how to adapt tripartism to predominantly non union American workplaces. Union participation in self-regulatory programs is both predicted by theory and shown by experience to make such programs more effective.[18] Unfortunately, unions exist inside too few workplaces in the US to serve as the only vehicle of employee representation. Unfortunately, too, the apparent solution—the creation and participation of non union employee committees—confronts several hurdles in the US context. The first lies in the peculiarities of US labour law, which prohibits employers from dominating, interfering with, *or supporting* a labour organisation, which is defined to include any employee committee that deals with an employer on work-related matters.[19] The law's chief target was 'company unions', whose subservience to employers and potency as a union avoidance device made them anathema to New Deal reformers.[20] But the law reaches many forms of interaction between employee committees and employers that may seem innocuous to the uninitiated. In effect, the NLRA rules out a range of intermediate options between purely individual bargaining and full-fledged union-like representation, and limits the range of potential experimentation with alternative forms of employee representation within a tripartite scheme for labour standards regulation.

It is tempting to regard this peculiar legal constraint as an anachronistic vestige of New Deal preoccupations. But the labour law's wariness toward non union institutions of employee representation counsels scepticism toward those institutions' ability to perform their part in a tripartite scheme for workplace standards enforcement. Employee committees that exist only inside firms—that have no outside power base or organisational structure—may be too vulnerable to capture or intimidation by employers to serve as the chief guardians against both employer cheating and agency capture. That is especially true for employees who are terminable at will, as most non union employees are in the US, and even more true among immigrant workers—often undocumented immigrants—who occupy many of the worst jobs, and who fear not only discharge but deportation. An organisational existence outside as well as inside the workplace may be essential for an employee representative to serve as the third leg of a tripartite system of regulated self-regulation.[21]

A third impediment to non union forms of employee representation lies in the deep-seated employer opposition to unions and, by extension, to any kind of

[18] See, eg Weil, Enforcing OSHA, above n 194, at 30.

[19] See NLRA, 29 USC § 152(5) (2000) (defining 'labor organisation'); § 158(a)(2) (prohibiting employer assistance, interference in, or domination of labour organisations).

[20] See M Barenberg, 'The Political Economy of the Wagner Act: Power, Symbol, and Workplace Cooperation' (1993) 106 *Harvard Law Review* 1379 at 1385–6.

[21] Indeed, unions might help supply independence and expertise to employee committees—such as the health and safety committees that are mandatory in some states—even in workplaces in which they do not represent the majority of employees. See MW Finkin, 'Employee Representation Outside the Labor Act: Thoughts on Arbitral Representation, Group Arbitration, and Workplace Committees' (2002) 5 *University of Pennsylvania Journal of Labor and Employment Law* 75 at 99.

independent employee representation.[22] Even if legal hurdles were surmounted and concerns about efficacy addressed, any proposal to mandate 'works councils' or the like would be vehemently opposed by anti union employers, who would see such an entity as a proto-union, the risks of which outweigh the benefits of a more cooperative and less adversarial enforcement regime. (Ironically, some union adherents would see those same employee bodies as proto-*company* unions, and as posing risks of capture and cooptation that negate or outweigh the potential benefits of organised employee participation.) If employers' participation in a system of self-regulation were conditioned on the existence of a structured, elected, and independent employee council or committee, the system would have few takers among employers in non union workplaces.

Where it is possible, full-blown tripartism—in which strong and independent labour organisations represent employees vis-à-vis both their employers and regulatory agencies—is a worthy aspiration for an effective system of self-regulation. But it is an elusive aspiration in the current political and labour relations climate in the US. Self-regulation has too much momentum and too much potential to be confined to the eight per cent or so of the private sector workforce that is unionised. Unless we find ways to make self-regulation effective beyond the small union sector, we are more likely to end up with *ineffective* forms of self-regulation than to halt the spread of self-regulation altogether. The challenge is to find alternative mechanisms of effective self-regulation for the non union workplace that leave open the road toward true tripartism, or even take a few steps down that road, without depending on its fulfillment.

'Ratcheting Labour Standards' and the Role of Monitoring

In light of the problems of under enforcement and under representation, it may be useful to consider models of regulation that rely less on intensive state engagement with regulated actors and independent union-like employee representation. Indeed, we should take a close look at efforts to gain regulatory traction over workplaces and working conditions in countries without effective regulatory agencies or viable independent labour unions. Those efforts began with a highly decentralised movement among labour and consumer groups in developed countries to pressure large multinational corporations—almost exclusively in garment manufacturing and retailing—to adopt voluntary 'codes of conduct' for their own and their contractors' and suppliers' operations, and to submit to outside monitoring of those operations.[23] These early private, voluntary schemes varied greatly, both

[22] On the depth and breadth of employer resistance to unions, see RB Freeman and MM Kleiner, 'Employer Behavior in the Face of Union Organising Drives' (1990) 43 *Industrial and Labor Relations Review* 351.

[23] For an overview of such efforts, see KA Elliott and R Freeman, above n 5, at 49–69. For critiques, see HW Arthurs, 'Private Ordering and Workers' Rights in the Global Economy: Corporate Codes of Conduct as a Regime of Labour Market Regulation' in J Conaghan *et al* (eds), *Labour Law in an Era of Globalisation* (Oxford, Oxford University Press, 2001) at 485–7; Blackett, above n 13, at 411–17. For a

in the content of corporate codes and in the nature and quality of outside monitoring; critics pointed to inspection protocols that allowed cheating to go undetected, and reporting practices that indulged firms' taste for secrecy, thus blocking the crucial flow of information to advocates and consumers.[24] Codes and monitoring regimes have evolved in recent years toward greater consistency, transparency, and accountability.[25] Advocacy groups and other observers remain sceptical.[26]

Ratcheting Labour Standards

Based on those emerging practices, Charles Sabel, Archon Fung, and Dara O'Rourke have put forward a radically new approach to regulation of labour standards that they call 'Ratcheting Labour Standards' (RLS).[27] Like Responsive Regulation, RLS deploys third party nongovernmental organisations (NGOs) and seeks to activate the internal regulatory capacity of firms themselves. But RLS does not depend on the state to monitor, inspect, or sanction employers, and does not depend on independent representation of the employees whose working conditions are at stake. RLS may thus suggest ways to improve domestic enforcement of employee rights and labour standards in the low wage non union workplace in the face of chronically inadequate regulatory oversight.

The basic idea behind RLS is that the large trans-national enterprises at the top of the manufacturing pyramid have enormous untapped regulatory capabilities with regard to their chain of suppliers, including those at the lower rungs of the

discussion of the ineffective state of international standards and suggested responses to deal with an increasingly global business environment, see B Hepple, 'A Race to the Top? International Investment Guidelines and Corporate Codes of Conduct' (1999) 20 *Comparative Labor Law and Policy Journal* 347.

[24] For thoughtful assessments of corporate codes in practice, see Barenberg, above n 26; Blackett, above n 13, at 416–17; D O'Rourke, 'Outsourcing Regulation: Analyzing Nongovernmental Systems of Labor Standards and Monitoring' (2003) 31 *Policy Studies Journal* 1 at 20–5. For a highly revealing report on the practices of one prominent monitoring organisation, see D O'Rourke, 'Monitoring the Monitors: A Critique of Corporate Third-Party Labour Monitoring' in R Jenkins, R Pearson and G Seyfang (eds), *Corporate Responsibility and Labour Rights: Codes of Conduct in the Global Economy* (London, Earthscan, 2002) at 196–207.

[25] See Elliott and Freeman, above n 5, at 63–4.

[26] See below pp 101, 108. Some of those critics convened to establish an alternative model of monitoring that was more participatory and more engaged with local governmental authorities. For a description of the resulting Workers Rights Consortium (WRC) model, with case studies, see M Barenberg, 'Toward a Democratic Model of Transnational Labor Monitoring?' (Chapter 9 herein). The WRC model is a major, though still experimental, innovation that responds to leading critiques of the major private monitoring regimes. At the same time, it is so resource intensive—investigators conduct up to 200 interviews over a week-long period, *ibid* at 7, 28—and so context-specific—interventions take place when 'local workforces are "in motion" [and] in fact attempting to address factory non-compliance through their own associational activities', *ibid* at 8—that it is very hard to envision replicating it on a large scale. The WRC may serve more as an exceptionally useful, if still exceptional, supplement and spur to large-scale reform than as a template for such reform.

[27] Charles Sabel *et al*, 'Ratcheting Labor Standards: Regulating for Continuous Improvement in the Global Workplace' 1–3 (John F Kennedy School of Government, Harvard University, Faculty Research Working Paper Series, KSG Working Paper No 00-010, May 2 2000), available at http://papers.ssrn.com/sol3/papers.cfm?abstract_id=253833.

global production hierarchy. Those corporations have, by necessity, developed effective ways to monitor and coordinate the activities of far-flung contractors and subcontractors. These capabilities can be tapped, and harnessed to the goal of improving labour standards, by creating mechanisms of transparency and exploiting the large enterprises' vulnerability to public and consumer pressure. Firms can be induced to compete with each other on the basis of their labour standards, while monitoring organisations compete with each other on the basis of the quality of their monitoring. Moreover, to the extent that improved labour standards go hand in hand with higher quality, greater agility, and ultimately productivity, the same competitive imperatives can help generate a race to the top.

A crucial part of the equation is consumer solidarity with workers and repugnance toward exploitative practices. Trans-national corporations' enormous investment in their brands makes them sensitive to the consumer pressure and negative publicity that can attend the exposure of exploitive labour practices among the corporations' suppliers.[28] To brand-conscious corporations, bad publicity, and the loss of sales, of prestige, and even of share price that can follow, can be an even more potent sanction than those wielded by regulatory agencies. These pressures can induce the firms to enter into codes of conduct that commit them to compliance with international and domestic labour rights and 'continuous improvement' in labour standards, and to a system of outside monitoring that both verifies progress and permits comparison of labour standards with the highest performing firms operating under similar conditions.[29]

A central element of RLS is thus transparency—that is, the transmission of reliable information about labour practices and conditions from the bottom layers of the supply chain, located mostly in remote, poor, developing nations with no effective regulatory apparatus, to the public and the customers of the multinational corporation in the developed world. The reliability of that information depends, in turn, on the transparency of monitoring regimes and protocols, so that consumers and watchdog organisations can compare the performance of monitors. Transparency enables comparison, and comparison engenders competition and improvement.

So the crucial actors in RLS, apart from the multinational firms themselves, are consumers, a critical mass of whom can be counted on to prefer brands associated with fair labour practices; and NGOs, which serve both as monitors, inspecting and certifying labour conditions with the cooperation of firms, and as advocates, publicising good and especially bad labour practices. The prodigious internal resources of the multinationals, together with the power of publicity and consumer pressure, largely supplant governmental oversight and compulsion in an economy that moves faster and reaches farther than any government can.

RLS has powerful virtues. It explicitly engages the complexities of modern global manufacturing supply chains. It seeks to harness the resources of the largest,

[28] *Ibid* at 7. On evidence of consumer 'demand for labor standards', see Elliott and Freeman, above n 5, at 28–45.

[29] Sabel *et al*, above n 27, at 16–18.

most visible, and most competent corporate actors not so much to regulate themselves as to regulate the less competent and less visible entities through which they get most of the labour that goes into their products. It is a scheme of self-regulation in which the 'self' encompasses the entire network of firms that make up the supply chain in much of the manufacturing sector. That redefinition allows for the expansion of self-regulation from the good corporate citizens (who qualify for self-regulation under Responsive Regulation) to the near-outlaw firms at the bottom of the labour market.

The vulnerability of the scheme lies in its dependence on the potentially fickle sympathies of comparatively rich consumers, many of whom may prefer to remain ignorant of the conditions under which their sneakers are produced. That dependence is due in turn to the lack of coercive state authority to reliably discipline the outlaws and opportunists, and to the virtual absence of independent union representation in the producer countries themselves. Of course, where there is no viable regulatory alternative—no state apparatus with effective enforcement capacity—RLS-like systems may not have to work very well to be worth supporting. But where there is a potentially competent regulatory regime—as is the case within the United States—it may not make sense to sidestep it altogether in favour of a private monitoring regime.

Responsive Regulation and RLS: Points of Convergence and Divergence

Both Responsive Regulation and RLS seek to mobilise the vast regulatory resources that lie within the modern firm. Both abjure 'command and control' in favour of a quasi-contractual approach to regulation in which firms agree, under certain constraints, to submit to self-regulatory protocols. Both designate non-governmental actors to play crucial roles safeguarding the interests of workers and the public. The two models diverge, however, on the roles of the state, of worker representation, and of outside monitors.

First, government coercion—rarely used but always on call—plays a pivotal role in Responsive Regulation, while it is almost entirely absent from RLS. Indeed, critics charge that the private (and stateless) code of conduct approach to regulating working conditions in developing countries not only ignores but circumvents and potentially undermines local governmental powers.[30] At a minimum, pragmatists on both sides would recognise that governmental powers and institutions, where they exist, can be brought into the RLS equation in helpful ways, while NGOs might help to fill the partial regulatory vacuum that frustrates the full implementation of Responsive Regulation in the US (and elsewhere). A hybrid approach might expand the role of nongovernmental actors to the extent that both the role and efficacy of government diminish.

Second: Responsive Regulation is a full fledged tripartite regime; it insists on empowering representatives of the primary regulatory beneficiaries, particularly

[30] See Barenberg, above n 26, at 8; Blackett, above n 13, at 427–9.

when those beneficiaries are situated within the regulated organisation. The proponents of RLS are rather hazier and less insistent about the role of the workers themselves and their organisations. Trade unions figure among possible advocates of RLS, monitors and proponents of improvement, and beneficiaries of its regime of transparency. But the workers whose working conditions are at stake play no real role in the scheme. The absence of worker involvement is a weakness of RLS, and it is another ground upon which private code of conduct schemes like RLS are criticised by some global anti sweatshop activists.[31] A consensus is emerging among participants in global anti sweatshop schemes that monitoring is not a substitute for employee voice, for it can only work effectively if employees can speak for themselves, not only during but in between monitoring inspections. Increasingly, these regimes seek to incorporate workers' voice and freedom of association into codes of conduct and monitoring protocols.[32]

Third, and relatedly: Responsive Regulation would have employee representatives such as unions monitor the firm's self-regulation, while RLS assumes employees have no collective representation, and inserts outside entities to do the monitoring. We have observed that effective monitoring requires the participation of workers. But the converse may also be true: Participation of workers, in the non union setting, may require the support of outside monitors. Outside monitors may supply some of the independence and expertise that unions supply within Responsive Regulation's tripartism, but that are missing from the non union and anti union workplaces that predominate within the US The use of outside monitoring can also help to liberate individual employee voice and to give voice to outside worker advocates, thus enhancing the prospects for more robust forms of tripartism in the future.

Monitoring works in rather diffuse ways to advance workers' freedom of association and expression. For the presence of outside monitors opens the doors of the workplace to a degree of outside scrutiny beyond what occasional governmental inspections could do; they demonstrate tangibly to employees that their rights matter and that someone is watching out for them. An employer's agreement to submit to monitoring represents the negotiated surrender of part of the sovereignty that employers—at least in the US—still claim over the workplace and that has always operated to frustrate the realisation of workers' rights. Moreover, effective outside monitoring both depends on and helps to protect employees' ability to speak up for themselves without fear of reprisals. It does so in part by providing a conduit through which workers can speak anonymously and in part by supplying a watchdog to whom workers can turn if they do suffer reprisals. The problem of employee fear in the non union setting is an enormous hurdle both to self-organisation and to employee participation in enforcement. But if a system of outside monitoring contains effective assurances of non retaliation for employees

[31] See, eg Barenberg, above n 26, at 7–8; Blackett, above n 13, at 436; Elliott and Freeman, above n 5, at 69–72; L Shaw and A Hale, 'The Emperor's New Clothes: What Codes Mean for Workers in the Garment Industry' in Jenkins, *et al*, above n 24, at 101, 104–5.

[32] See Elliott and Freeman, above n 5, at 71–2.

who speak up—and it must do so to work at all—then it may help to lay the groundwork for employees to speak to each other as well and to associate for other shared workplace goals.

Policing Monitors, Empowering Whistle-blowers: A Sarbanes-Oxley for the Workplace?

Both Responsive Regulation and RLS offer models of workplace regulation based on well-developed general theories of regulation. But the importance of employee 'whistle-blowers' and of monitor independence and accountability in a monitoring regime suggests that we might draw lessons from a third source of a rather different sort: the theories and institutions that seek to ensure corporate integrity and accountability. The twentieth century US model for avoiding corporate misconduct and fraud couples a mandatory regime of disclosure with a system of audited self-regulation.[33] Recent corporate scandals dealt a blow to the proponents of self-regulation, but the most tangible legal response to those scandals, the Sarbanes-Oxley Act, relies less on new forms of regulatory oversight than on shoring up and revitalising self-regulation: The law seeks to ensure the independence and public accountability of the outside monitors or auditors, and to formalise and protect employee whistle-blowing.

The problem underlying recent corporate scandals is analogous to the problem of widespread disregard of labour standards: The pressure to maximise profits (or apparent returns) generates a tremendous temptation on the part of managers to cut corners and to disregard the constraints of external law. Knowledge of legal transgressions is mostly confined to insiders within complex organisations and is hidden from public view and public enforcement. And the individual employees who do have that knowledge—who might be moved to expose the illegal conduct—are often economically dependent on the transgressors at the top of the organisation and vulnerable to reprisals.

In the corporate governance context, the traditional solution to the problem of hidden corporate self-dealing has been to mandate the use of independent, publicly licensed auditors—themselves subject to a system of professional self-regulation—who must certify a firm's compliance with relevant standards of accounting and disclosure.[34] Sarbanes-Oxley sought to buttress that system of outside auditing and to combat the capture of auditors by insuring the indepen-

[33] For criticisms of the reliance on self-regulation, see WW Bratton, 'Enron and the Dark Side of Shareholder Value' (2002) 76 *Tulane Law Review* 1275 at 1282–8; WW Bratton and JA McCahery, 'Regulatory Competition, Regulatory Capture, and Corporate Self-Regulation' (1995) 73 *North Carolina Law Review* 1861 at 1892–8. For a more favourable view, see HL Pitt and KA Groskaufmanis, 'Minimizing Corporate Civil and Criminal Liability: A Second Look at Corporate Codes of Conduct' (1990) 78 *Georgia Law Journal* 1559 at 1647.

[34] On the centrality of these outside monitors or 'gatekeepers' in guarding against corporate misconduct, see JC Coffee Jr, 'Gatekeeper Failure and Reform: The Challenge of Fashioning Relevant Reforms' (2004) 84 *Boston University Law Review* 301 at 308 [hereinafter Coffee, Gatekeeper Failure].

dence of auditors from regulated firms, strengthening the self-regulatory oversight of auditors, and imposing new liabilities on those auditors.[35] At the same time, legislators sought to tap into the enormous regulatory potential within corporations themselves by encouraging employees to disclose wrongdoing. To that end, the law prohibited reprisals against employee whistle-blowers, and backed that prohibition with both criminal and civil sanctions, including private rights of action with compensatory damages, back pay, reinstatement, attorneys' fees, and litigation costs.

Sarbanes-Oxley thus fortifies an existing system of monitored self-regulation by combating the capture of monitors and by protecting and institutionalising employee whistle-blowing—that is, by ensuring the independence and accountability of the outsiders looking in and by encouraging insiders to speak out. Congress backed up its new mandates with new criminal and civil penalties administered by the Securities and Exchange Commission (SEC). But much as in the labour standards context, the mismatch between agency resources and the number and complexity of the regulated actors ensures that the SEC and public prosecutors can play only an episodic role in enforcement. Enforcement is assumed to come primarily from private securities litigation.

These lessons are directly relevant to the development of an effective system of monitored self-regulation of workplace rights and standards. Given the importance of independent outside monitoring in both settings, Sarbanes-Oxley counsels the adoption of safeguards against the capture of monitors by the monitored firm. In the labour standards context, that might mean certification and selection of monitors by a tripartite oversight group, the use of approved and well-publicised inspection protocols, and implementation of conflict-of-interest prohibitions. Given the importance of protecting individual employees who speak up, Sarbanes-Oxley's whistle-blower protection provisions, which include both criminal sanctions and fully compensatory private civil remedies against reprisals, represent a 'gold standard' worthy of emulation. And given the shortfall in public regulatory oversight both in the securities context and in labour standards, Sarbanes-Oxley and the regime that it reforms reminds us that private litigation can supply some of the coercive pressure that is supposed to emanate from the state in Responsive Regulation and that is elusive within RLS.

The division of employment law into employee rights enforceable through litigation and workplace standards enforced by regulatory agencies turns out to be somewhat artificial, for employee rights and private rights of action are embedded within many labour standards regimes, and offer potential leverage to private sector worker advocates. Private lawsuits can potentially help to fill the enforcement gap, and can sometimes supply a big gun where public enforcement has none to wield. They can also provide a check on public agencies' failure to enforce the laws,

[35] For a summary of major provisions of Sarbanes-Oxley, see JC Coffee Jr, 'A Brief Tour of the Major Reforms in the Sarbanes-Oxley Act' *ALI-ABA Continuing Legal Education*, 5 December 2002 [hereinafter Coffee, Brief Tour].

mobilising or simply bypassing regulators that become captured, hamstrung, sclerotic, or ideologically resistant to enforcing statutory labour standards.[36]

Litigation by private parties has proven to be a potent stimulus to workplace reform. We in the US do not do regulation especially well, but we do litigation better than any society in the world. This hardly calls for celebration, but it does call for exploration. For litigation has effectively become our primary mode of workplace regulation in some areas, especially under the civil rights laws; and it has had a dramatic impact on employer practices and workplace culture. When patterns of conduct that were endemic to many workplaces began to produce costly judgments, employers responded with an arsenal of anti discrimination and anti harassment policies and procedures and 'diversity initiatives'. While some of this may be window dressing, these practices have genuinely transformed the working environment for many women and minorities. That is an important lesson to remember as we consider how to extend and improve self-regulatory institutions in other areas of workplace law.

Toward Monitored Self-Regulation of Labour Standards: A Hybrid Model and Some Examples

The US regime of workplace regulation is neither the comprehensive and fully staffed regulatory regime that Responsive Regulation assumes as its starting point, nor is it the regulatory vacuum assumed by RLS. Nor, finally, is it precisely analogous to the regime of corporate securities regulation that Sarbanes-Oxley reforms. But all three of these approaches to regulation of organisations teach useful lessons—lessons that can inform the evaluation of several recent self-regulatory experiments in the field of wage and hour regulation.

A Hybrid Model of Monitored Self-Regulation

Let me begin with one feature that unites all three approaches to self-regulation from which I have drawn: All of them recognise that, for a system of self-regulation to be effective, it needs to be open to observation and criticism from without. At the heart of all three systems is one or more mechanisms for gathering credible information relevant to compliance—not just what the firm chooses to reveal—and for conveying that information, not merely to regulatory agencies, but also to members of the public with an interest in the information: workers and their organisational advocates, pro worker consumers, or, in the case of Sarbanes-Oxley, shareholders and securities analysts. While employers' interest in

[36] See C Sabel and W Simon, 'Destabilisation Rights: How Public Law Litigation Succeeds' (2004) 117 *Harvard Law Review* 1015.

self-regulation may often be driven by a desire to insulate themselves from outside scrutiny, the key to making self-regulation effective is to resist that insulation.

Beyond this common core, the three approaches each supply distinct elements to the emerging model. The Responsive Regulation model supplies the fundamental logic of encouraging self-regulation within a system of public regulation—of tapping into the pro compliance capabilities and impulses within the firm, largely through a judicious combination of inducements and threats emanating from public institutions—while conditioning the privilege of self-regulation on the presence of safeguards against cheating by firms and capture of regulators. Also drawn from Responsive Regulation is the commitment to tripartism—to institutionalising and fortifying the role of the workers whose interests are most immediately at stake as a check against laxity by both the self-regulating firm and the public regulators.

RLS, and the global labour standards regimes that it both elucidates and seeks to refine, teach the crucial lesson that a good deal of regulation is possible without state regulators (and therefore, it seems fair to assume, with only episodic interventions by state regulators). It also suggests an architecture, and an innovative constellation of actors, for gaining regulatory traction over the worst performing workplaces. RLS does this by leveraging the regulatory resources within larger and more advanced firms to reach the smaller, less visible, and less competent firms that supply them with goods and labour. RLS begins with codes of conduct—quasi-contractual commitments that include but frequently extend the requirements of public law. It introduces the crucial mechanism of independent monitoring as a partial substitute for state enforcement (and union representation). It recognises the need for standards of accountability and performance for monitors (though it declines to proffer any particular standards, trusting instead in the dynamics of transparency and competition). And it demonstrates that external actors other than unions and professional monitors—for example, independent worker advocacy organisations—can play important roles, especially in publicising good and bad practices and 'monitoring the monitors'.

Finally, from the recent response to corporate scandals, and from scholarly and legislative assessments of the strengths and vulnerabilities of a system of self-regulation, I draw three elements: close attention to the prerequisites for vigorous and independent monitoring; strong and privately enforceable protection of employee whistle-blowers against reprisals; and the value of private litigation on behalf of those who are injured by misconduct as a supplemental form of enforcement and deterrence where public enforcement falls short.

The net result is a hybrid model that uses targeted public enforcement and private litigation to back up, and to induce entry into, a system of monitored, quasi-tripartite self-regulation. The basic template for effective self-regulation would be based on an explicit code of conduct encompassing employers' substantive obligations. The agreement or 'code' should promise not simply compliance with substantive legal standards—for example, wage and hour laws or lawful standards of health and safety—but also adherence to the institutional requisites of effective self-regulation that have emerged from the foregoing. In particular, it must promise the institution of independent monitoring; assurances of no reprisals against employees who communicate with monitors, public agencies, or the public; and workers' freedom, individually and collectively, to speak for themselves, both during and in between monitoring visits that will necessarily be occasional.

Code compliance would be monitored by outside entities that are independent of the employer and accountable to workers and the public. Both independence and accountability should be secured by tripartite oversight of the monitors: Monitors could report to and operate under the oversight of a body with union or other worker representation as well as representation of the public and of employers. This oversight, or monitoring of the monitors, aims to ensure that the monitors follow inspection protocols and standards of good practice that include confidential communication with employees as well as inspection of employer records and of the workplace itself. To that end too, the composition, manner of compensation, and inspection protocols of monitors should be transparent and open to public scrutiny.

Crucial to the efficacy of this system of monitored self-regulation—both to firms' willingness to enter into it and to their good faith participation in the system—is that it is not wholly voluntary. It must be backed by public and private enforcement mechanisms—targeted public enforcement and the threat of potent sanctions against the worst lawbreakers, and private rights of action on behalf of aggrieved employees, including whistle-blowers—the full force of which would be mitigated or held in abeyance for employers engaged in a system of effective self-regulation. So firms might enter into the system in pursuit of a prospective partial shield against targeted prosecution, criminal liability, excess fines, or punitive damages, or in pursuit of a reputation as a good corporate citizen. Alternatively, monitored self-regulation might be negotiated between targeted violators and public or private enforcers as the condition for abating potent and potentially ruinous sanctions. In either case, the shield that firms gain by entering into monitoring should be partial, not total, lest there be too great a gain from successful cheating and too little chance of uncovering it.

Monitored self-regulation may thus serve both as a high-road strategy by actors wishing to demonstrate their consummate compliance with public norms and as a remedial response to chronic defectors. High-road actors would be in a position to exert greater discretion over both the content of the code and the monitoring arrangements, subject to potential post hoc scrutiny of those arrangements in the event they were found to have nonetheless run afoul of external law. Low-road employers who are compelled to adopt these arrangements under the gun of threatened sanctions would obviously have less discretion over these arrangements; moreover, monitors would report to government agencies, not just to the firm and to the worker advocacy organisations overseeing them.

Assessing Recent Experiments in Self-Regulation of Labour Standards

The idea of private monitoring has begun to catch on in some corners of the US labour standards landscape. Let us apply some of the lessons just learned to several recent forays into monitored self-regulation in the arena of wage and hour laws.

Monitoring in Garment Manufacturing

The garment industry is a low wage sector with notoriously high rates of non compliance with minimum wage and overtime pay requirements, as well as with health and safety laws and other labour laws. Larger and more visible manufacturers, or sometimes very large and visible retailers themselves, contract out garment production to a network of smaller, low visibility, and often transient contractors. Enforcement is further impeded by contractors' widespread reliance on undocumented immigrant labour, among whom fear of deportation exacerbates the usual fear of reprisals that silences many low-wage employees.

In an effort to improve FLSA compliance in the garment sector, the Department of Labor (DOL) in the 1990s turned to the largely-neglected 'hot-goods' provision of the FLSA, which allows the Secretary of Labor to petition to embargo goods produced in violation of the law. The interdiction of goods has two major advantages over traditional sanctions: First, it hurts large manufacturers a lot, especially in a retail market such as fashion apparel that puts a high premium on speed of delivery. Second, by targeting the goods themselves, the remedy cuts through contracting arrangements that may insulate manufacturers from liability for the substandard wages of workers at the bottom of the production chain. The threat of an embargo can induce manufacturers to discover and fix compliance problems among their contractors at lower levels of the production chain. The manufacturers' *capacity* to discover and fix such problems grows out of developments in production itself, which bound manufacturers and contractors or 'jobbers' closer together to the end of producing high quality goods in very short and fast production runs.[37] Capitalising on these features of the apparel industry, DOL deployed the threat of a hot-goods embargo to induce manufacturers to agree to monitor the wage and hour practices of their own contractors.[38] The manufacturers in turn entered into agreements with their own contractors to abide by wage and hour laws, keep records, and submit to inspections by representatives of the manufacturers or by outside monitors.

[37] For a description of these arrangements in apparel, see Weil, Labor Standards, above n 17, at 34–6. For an account of how similar dynamics have come to characterise much of global manufacturing, see Sabel, above n 27, at 9–13.

[38] See Weil, Compliance, above n 17, at 18. For an excellent history and critique of the garment industry monitoring program, see Jill Esbenshade, Monitoring *Sweatshops: Workers, Consumers, and the Global Apparel Industry* (2004).

The program leverages limited public enforcement powers to generate a system of private enforcement that is more vigilant than a public agency could possibly be. The jury is still out, however, as to whether it is an effective system of self-regulation. Empirical evidence presents a glass half-full at best: compliance has improved, yet non compliance remains high in some areas, even among monitored contractors.[39] Critics of the program have questioned the independence and inspection protocols of the monitors employed under this program—typically, private profit making entities chosen and paid by the manufacturers.[40] Our foray into regulatory theory suggests that the program could be improved by strengthening assurances of monitor independence and responsiveness to worker interests (perhaps through tripartite oversight); formalising confidential and protected channels of employee communication with monitors; and incorporating assurances of worker freedom of communication and association among themselves.

The Greengrocer Code of Conduct

A striking example of creative state enforcement of wage and hour laws can be found in New York City's greengrocer markets, small retail produce markets that sprang up in the city in the 1980s.[41] Several years ago, unions and other worker advocates discovered rampant wage and hour violations, and started bringing cases to the Labor Bureau of the New York State Attorney General (AG). State investigations showed a recurring pattern of workers being paid $200 to $300 a week for as much as 72-hour weeks. Cases were nearly open-and-shut, and produced back pay liability that was often ruinous for these small businesses. But case-by-case investigations and settlements proved unsatisfactory, given the AG's limited resources and the large number of green grocers in the city. So once having gained the attention of employers, the AG brought representatives of employers and of labour to the bargaining table. Together they devised a Greengrocer Code of Conduct (GGCC).[42]

The GGCC binds signatory employers to comply with wage and hour laws (as well as with other labour and employment laws), to keep payroll records, to undergo training and to allow their employees to do so, to post notices advising employees of their rights, and, crucially, to submit to regular inspections by

[39] Weil, Compliance, above n 17, at 22. Weil found that minimum wage compliance levels rose from 63% (with no monitoring) to 74% (with low monitoring) to 79% (with high monitoring) in New York City; from 33% to 56% to 72% respectively in Los Angeles; and from 71% to 94% to 95% respectively in San Francisco. *Ibid.*

[40] See Esbenshade, above n 38; Laura Dubinsky, 'The Fox Guarding the Chicken Coop: Garment Industry Monitoring in Los Angeles' in Jenkins, *et al*, above n 24, at 161.

[41] See MT Bodie, 'The Potential for State Labor Law: The New York Greengrocer Code of Conduct' (2004) 21 Hofstra Labor and Employment Law Journal 183 [hereinafter Bodie, State Labor Law]). For a first hand account of the negotiation of the agreement, see generally MT Bodie, 'The Story Behind the New York City Greengrocer Code of Conduct: A Conversation with Patricia Smith' (2004) 6 Regional Labor Review 19 [hereinafter Bodie, Smith Interview].

[42] The text of the GGCC is available at http://www.oag.state.ny.us/labor/final_ggcode_english_long.pdf (last visited 27 October 2004). For a more detailed description of its provisions, see Bodie, State Labor Law, *ibid*, at 194–9.

independent labour standards monitors appointed by the AG. Monitors make unannounced visits to the workplaces, inspect employers' payroll records, speak privately with employees about these issues, assist employers in compliance, and report on violations to the AG's office and to a Code of Conduct Committee. The Committee, which oversees the GGCC, deals with disputes, and certifies new signatories, consists of three members representing workers, employers, and the AG. A merchant's submission to and compliance with the GGCC secures a kind of provisional amnesty with respect to past violations of wage and hour laws.[43]

The GGCC follows many of the principles of effective self-regulation identified here. In particular, it contains elements of employee representation. Representatives of the state AFL-CIO, as well as Casa Mexico, an advocacy group for Mexican-American workers, who make up most of the affected labour force, participated in its creation. One of the three members of the Code of Conduct Committee is appointed by Casa Mexico. And for shops with more than ten employees, the GGCC provides for appointment of an employee spokesperson by the monitor, after consultation with employees. The last innovation appears to be largely symbolic, unfortunately, as few green grocers employ that many workers.

The GGCC has, by all accounts, significantly improved rates of compliance with wage and hour laws, especially among the 20 per cent of merchants who are signatories, but even among those who are not.[44] Unfortunately, the agreement expired in February 2005, and renewal is uncertain.[45] The GGCC meets most of the basic requisites of effective monitored self-regulation. Its weakness—and one that deserves greater attention—lies in the need for continuing pressure in the form of threatened enforcement or consumer mobilisation. Given the paucity of public enforcement resources (which have been remarkably well-leveraged through the GGCC), private advocacy organisations may need to explore the possibilities for private litigation to keep up the pressure.

Monitoring in Janitorial Services

Janitorial services is another chronically low wage sector that, in many parts of the country, operates as a virtual outlaw in violation of immigration laws, tax laws, wage and hour laws, and other labour protections.[46] Much as garment workers supply goods, through contractors, to large and publicly visible manufacturers (and eventually to retailers), janitors perform essential maintenance services, through contractors, to large firms—retailers, banks, office buildings. By contracting out janitorial services to low wage contractors, larger and more publicly accountable firms may lower their costs without directly violating the law.

[43] See Bodie, Smith Interview, above n 138, at 91; S Greenhouse and S Kugel, 'Labor Truce Wearing Thin for Koreans and Mexicans' *New York Times*, 27 September 2004, at B3.

[44] See Greenhouse, above n 43.

[45] Greenhouse and Kugel, above n 43.

[46] S Greenhouse, 'Illegally in the US, and Never A Day Off at Wal-Mart' *New York Times*, 5 November 2003, at A1 [hereinafter Greenhouse, Illegally].

Not all janitorial contractors are outlaws, however. Indeed, as a result of organising campaigns in the past decade by the Service Employees International Union (SEIU), the sector is partially unionised, especially in California. Unionised janitors receive at least minimum wages and overtime in accordance with the law, and usually health and other benefits, the total cost of which can exceed by at least 40 per cent the labour costs of the worst outlaws among non union contractors.[47] Recognising that the non union, low-wage sector threatened to undercut them both, the SEIU and the unionised employers created and funded, through collective bargaining, a non profit watchdog organisation, the Maintenance Cooperation Trust Fund (MCTF), to identify and investigate labour standards violations among janitorial contractors. The MCTF sometimes helps to initiate private lawsuits on behalf of workers; often it seeks to spur enforcement by state or federal regulators.[48]

The MCTF took the latter course upon discovering rampant wage and hour violations on the part of Global Building Services, which performed maintenance services for Target Stores in California and much of the West. The case was complicated by the fact that most of the workers were undocumented immigrants—many of them no longer employed by Global, hard to locate, and reluctant to speak—and by the fact that Global had itself contracted out much of the janitorial work to smaller contractors who often paid in cash and kept no payroll or time records. But investigations revealed widespread violations for which Global was clearly liable. The DOL sued Global and secured a settlement in which Global agreed to pay $1.9 million in back wages to 775 employees.[49]

In the view of MCTF, however, the settlement did not exhaust Global's past liabilities, nor did it ensure future compliance or improved conditions for Global's workers. Global, for its part, recognised that its wage and hour practices, and those of their subcontractors, were 'out of control', and a continuing source of potential liability. Aiming to avoid further costly litigation and publicity at the hands of MCTF, Global entered into a separate agreement with the MCTF to clean up its payroll practices and to submit to monitoring (by MCTF itself) of future compliance with wage and hour laws. Under the agreement, the MCTF inspected records and job sites and met with workers to determine employer compliance with labour standards. As long as MCTF played this monitoring role, and had access to Global's records, it agreed to file no complaints against Global, though it did file reports on compliance or non compliance with the DOL and state labour officials. Early experience under the MCTF/Global agreement was promising; unfortunately, the agreement lapsed in 2006 when Global lost a major chunk of its business.

The MCTF/Global agreement exemplified several of the principles of effective self-regulation outlined here. The Global agreement embodied an unusually

[47] Greenhouse, Illegally, *ibid.*

[48] Interview with Lilia Garcia, Executive Director, MCTF, (14 September, 2004) [hereinafter Garcia Interview] (on file with the *Columbia Law Review*).

[49] See Steven Greenhouse, 'Labor Department Wins $1.9 Million in Back Pay for Janitors' New York Times, 26 August, 2004, at A16.

robust form of tripartism given the non union status of the monitored employers. The collectively-bargained creation and oversight of the MCTF, and the MCTF's grassroots approach to its watchdog role, made it an almost ideal monitor of workplace standards. But the monitoring agreement might not have been concluded without the joint leverage that MCTF and the DOL were able to exert. The Global agreement thus illustrates the potential synergies of a hybrid public-private approach to enforcement: The MCTF was able to exercise considerable leverage on its own by credibly identifying violations and threatening (if only implicitly) costly litigation and publicity against violators; yet the DOL wielded public resources and powers of investigation beyond those available to a private entity like MCTF.

Conclusion

The National Labor Relations Act of 1935 recognised the value, both intrinsic and instrumental, of industrial democracy when it sought to secure workers' ability to participate in workplace decisions that vitally affect them. But the US. Congress has not seriously revisited the issue of workplace democracy since the New Deal. In the meantime, the system of collective bargaining has become distorted and dysfunctional, if not irrelevant, for most employees, while employment law has mushroomed into a fearsome hydra head of liability for employers and a font of rights and entitlements, real or illusory, for employees.

Employment law is in many ways a poor substitute for the system of self-governance envisioned by the labour laws. Indeed, it is not really a substitute at all, for the rights and regulations that make up employment law inevitably will be incomplete and under enforced without a complementary system of collective representation to back them up. But the solution to the representation gap may lie partly within employment law rather than solely within the traditional realm of labour law. Employment law has a broader political constituency, and more points of entry for reform efforts, than does labour law. It encompasses diverse institutional energies and sources of leverage that might be turned to the cause of workplace democracy. Employment law—especially in the form of costly and embarrassing litigation—has led to some dramatic reforms in how workplaces are organised, on the part of both employers who have experienced litigation and those who have observed its traumatic effect on others. Partly as a result of these developments, employment law itself has circled back, as if inevitably, to the realisation that 'employers' are organisations with a vast potential for self-governance and self-regulation.

The movement toward self-regulation—toward encouraging and channelling the impulses and resources that lie within and among private firms toward public-regarding ends—is here to stay in some form or another. It extends beyond the law of the workplace, beyond the United States, and beyond the domain of domestic law. Its proponents are found among the most stalwart proponents of workers' rights and of public regulation. For there are undoubtedly vast regulatory resources—knowledge, expertise, and even some goodwill—within firms; a regulatory framework that activates and leverages those resources promises to be far more effective than one that relies solely on traditional mechanisms of adversarial inspections and enforcement. On the other hand, the movement threatens to justify regulatory disengagement and to disguise a process of deregulation. A system of privatised enforcement that is detached from public oversight and the prospect of serious coercive sanctions for non compliance may simply obscure the unleashing of market forces and of a race to the bottom to compete with domestic and foreign low-wage competition.

The movement toward self-regulation also casts a prismatic light on the representation gap in the workplace. On the one hand, it magnifies the dangers of still-declining levels of unionisation. If responsibility for ensuring compliance with rights and labour standards is increasingly to be pushed inside the regulated firm itself, then it is deeply troubling that the employees whose rights and interests are at stake are increasingly unlikely to have an organised voice within the firm. At the very least, the movement toward self-regulation has the makings of a new argument for labour law reform that makes unionisation possible. But even if a worker-friendly constellation of political forces managed to produce real labour law reform for the first time in over a half century, it is unlikely to lead to widespread collective worker representation, at least for decades. So the problem of the non union workplace in an era of self-regulation must be reckoned with.

Fortunately, the movement toward self-regulation provides not only a justification for promoting employee representation but potential leverage to that end. If the movement toward self-regulation is, as it should be, part of a regulatory scheme in which serious sanctions also play a role, then both good corporate citizens and bad actors may be induced to accept conditions—including some form of employee representation within a scheme of outside monitoring—either as a prerequisite of responsible self-regulation or as part of a remedy for chronic non compliance. To be sure, full-fledged tripartism is not imaginable within the existing landscape of labour relations and politics, given the adamant opposition of most American employers to unionisation and other forms of independent representation of employees, and the resulting political deadlock over anything that smacks of labour law reform. But a system of independently monitored self-regulation can provide footholds for employee participation as well as improving compliance with employee rights and labour standards. That participation represents a modest step toward democratisation of the workplace, and one that may enable further steps in that direction.

Rejuvenating the idea of workplace democracy, and of the worker as a citizen of the workplace, aims to make better workplaces and a better democracy. But the path to workplace democracy in the United States is at best a long one, and its direction is uncertain and likely to change in coming decades as transformations in the economy and the organisation of work continue to race ahead. For pragmatic proponents of workplace democracy, the best hope in these circumstances may be to take a few steps in the right direction, advancing important instrumental goals to which the public is more clearly committed while opening a bit of space for workers to decided for themselves what forms of self-organisation and participation will best serve their particular needs within the workplace and the labour market.

6

Flexibilization, Globalization, and Privatization: Three Challenges to Labour Rights in Our Time*

KATHERINE VW STONE**

Flexibilization, globalization, and privatization are three dynamics that are coalescing to reshape labour relations in the twenty-first century in the United States. *Flexibilization* refers to the changing work practices by which firms no longer use internal labour markets or implicitly promise employees lifetime job security, but instead seek flexible employment relations that permit them to increase or diminish their workforce and reassign and redeploy employees with ease. *Globalization* refers to the increase in cross-border transactions in the production and marketing of goods and services that facilitate firm relocation to countries that have low labour costs. And *privatization* refers to the rise of neo-liberal ideology, the attack on big government, and the dismantling of the social safety net that has dominated public policy in the United States in recent years. All three of these dynamics have been detrimental to US employment standards and union strength. They are like Fluffy in the first Harry Potter book, the vicious three-headed dog that guards the Philosopher's Stone.

This article describes how each of these dynamics has undermined labour rights. It then asks, what prospects are there for protecting employment rights, re-invigorating unions, and securing a social safety net? The answer lies in the proposition that the spread of the global leads to the re-emergence of the local. We see this in the area of culture, where the threat of global homogenization has spawned movements to preserve indigenous cultures and revive near-extinct languages all over the world. The revival of near-extinct languages is a testament to the will of many to retain their local individualities, cultures, and histories in the face of pressures for global convergence. Similarly the renaissance of indigenous people's art, music, and culture shows local spirit resisting global uniformity. So too, in the area of labour relations, the global begets the local. The response to the global threat to labour standards lies in a revival of collective action at the local

* 2006, KVW Stone. This article was first published in 44 Osgoode Hall LJ 77 (2005).

** Professor, UCLA School of Law, Los Angeles, California.

level. Further, the combined forces of flexibilization, globalization, and privatization make collective action at the local level not only necessary, but also possible.

This article begins with a brief description of the three-sided onslaught on labour rights. It then shows how the three dynamics are interrelated in a way that raises new possibilities for effective action at the local level. The final section provides some examples of local initiatives that have emerged in response to Fluffy. These initiatives might point the way towards taming, if not slaying, the three-headed beast.

Pressures Shaping the Employment Relationship

Flexibilization

In the twentieth century, most large corporations organised their workforces into what have been termed 'internal labour markets'.[1] In internal labour markets, jobs were arranged into hierarchical ladders and each job provided the training for the job on the next rung up. Employers who used internal labour markets hired only at the entry level, and then used internal promotion to fill all the higher rungs. Employers wanted employees to stay a long time, so they gave them an implicit promise of long-term employment and of orderly and predictable patterns of promotion. Consistent with internal labour market job structures, employers structured pay and benefit systems so that wages and benefits rose as length of service increased.[2]

Recently, employers have dismantled their internal labour market job structures and abandoned the implicit promises that went along with them. They now create new types of employment relationships that do not depend upon, or encourage, longevity. This gives employers flexibility to cross-utilise employees. It also allows for quick adjustments in production methods as firms confront increasingly competitive product markets. Work has thus become contingent, not only in the sense that it is formally defined as short-term or episodic, but also in the sense that the attachment between the firm and the worker has been loosened. The 'recasualization of work' has reportedly become a fact of life all along the employment spectrum, from blue-collar workers to high-end professionals and managers.[3]

[1] See KVW Stone, *From Widgets to Digits: Employment Regulation for the Changing Workplace* (New York, Cambridge University Press, 2004) [Stone, *From Widgets to Digits*]. See also, P Doeriner and M Piore, *Internal Labor Markets and Manpower Analysis* (New York, DC Heath & Co. 1971); P Osterman, ed, *Internal Labor Markets* (Cambridge, MIT Press, 1984).

[2] See KVW Stone, 'Policing Employment Contracts Within the Nexus-of-Contracts Firm' (1993) 43 UTLJ 353, 363–9.

[3] See eg 'The Future of Work: Career Evolution' *The Economist* 354:8155 (29 January 2000) at 89. See also PF Drucker, *Managing in a Time of Great Change* (Oxford, Butterworth Heinemann, 1995); R Kanter, *On the Frontiers of Management* (Cambridge: Harvard Business School Press, 1997) at 190; and R Sennett, *The Corrosion of Character* (New York, WW Norton and Company, 1998) at 23. See generally Stone, *From Widgets to Digits*, *supra* note 1.

Changes in the employment relationship are reflected in the government employment data on job tenure and turnover. According to the Current Population Survey of the US Bureau of Labor Statistics, there have been dramatic declines in job tenure between 1983 and 2002 among all men over the age of twenty, with the most significant declines among men in the age groups over forty-five. Between 1983 and 2002 there was a significant decline in the proportion of men who have been with their current employer for ten years or more. For men ages forty to forty-four, the percentage declined from 51 per cent in 1983 to less than 38 per cent in 2002. Similar large declines occurred for men in every age group over forty-five.[4] These changes were largely among blue-collar males who had a high school education or less.[5] That is, the internal job structures that characterised the labour market experiences of the US blue-collar male work force are fading.[6]

In addition to the empirical data, we know about the contemporary labour market from the accounts of journalists, scholars, and corporate executives. These informants report that there is a fundamental change in the implicit, psychological contract under which most Americans are now employed. For example, the sociologist Richard Sennett interviewed a number of younger employees about their experiences in the labour market, and reports:

> The most tangible sign of that change might be the motto "No long term". In work, the traditional career progressing step by step through the corridors of one or two institutions is withering: so is the deployment of a single set of skills through the course of a working life.[7]

The changing employment patterns result from a series of new work practices that employers have instituted over the past decade. They include innovations such as broadbanding, designed to give employers flexibility to cross-utilise employees across job titles and departmental lines. They also include compensation practices such as pay-for-performance and benchmarking that attempt to match each employee's pay to their individual contribution and to their value in the external labour market. Other features of the new employment relationship are flattening the job hierarchy and increasing the discretion of lower ranks of employees. The latter trend is the result of a new appreciation of the role played by employee knowledge, skills, and imagination in firm success. Firms have designed various types of workforce empowerment programs to give bounded discretion to

[4] US, Department of Labour, Bureau of Labour Statistics, News Release, 'Employee Tenure in 2002' (19 September 2002), online: BLS News Releases <ftp://ftp.bls.gov/pub/news.release/History/tenure.09192002.news>.

[5] Henry Farber, *Are Lifetime Jobs Disappearing? Job Duration in the United States: 1973–1993, National Bureau of Economic Research Working Paper Series No 5014* (Cambridge, MA, National Bureau of Economic Research, 1995) at 16–20.

[6] For women, there was not such a marked decline, and in some cases there was even a modest rise, because women have not traditionally been part of the long-term employment system. However, the overall percentage of women working for ten years or more is significantly lower than men in any event. See *ibid.*

[7] Sennett, *supra* note 3 at 22.

relatively low-level employees in order to cultivate and capture employee knowledge, skills, and imagination.[8]

The new employment relationship also involves a change in the implicit contract between the employee and the firm. Instead of giving employees an implicit promise of employment security, today's employers implicitly promise employability security—the ability to acquire skills that will enhance their opportunities in the labour market. Employers also no longer implicitly promise their employees orderly promotional opportunities. Rather, they promise opportunities for employees to network and gain skills that will prepare them for other jobs outside the firm. In the new 'boundaryless' employment relationship, employees are expected to manage their own careers, rather than to expect long-term employment from a single firm.[9]

In many respects, unions in the United States are ill-suited to the emerging workplace. Many of the traditional practices of American labour are antithetical to the core ideas of the boundaryless workplace. For example, unions insist on using seniority to define promotional rights, and seek narrow definitions of job duties. Both of these practices are flatly inconsistent with the new employment practices. Seniority encourages and rewards longevity and worker-firm attachment rather than mobile, multi-employer careers. The new employment relationship de-emphasises attachment, and instead stresses flexibility and cross-utilization, features that are the very opposite of narrow job classifications and seniority-based work assignments. Unions also seek to obtain uniform standards for compensation and promotion. They seek to establish systems for job bidding that require employers to rely on internal promotion to fill openings and bumping rights along pre-specified demotion paths during downsizing. These practices, like seniority, discourage cross-utilization within firms or divisions. Other union bargaining demands that are antithetical to the boundaryless workplace are scope clauses that keep work inside the bargaining unit and no-subcontracting clauses that keep work inside the plant. Unions attempt to draw tight jurisdictional lines around their certified bargaining-unit work by bargaining for provisions that require supervisors to refrain from performing unit work. These practices seek to prohibit the very blurring of departmental and firm boundaries that characterises the boundaryless workplace.[10]

The mismatch between today's flexible work relations and conventional union practices has led companies to resist unions more fiercely than ever. Indeed, unions have had a difficult time gaining a foothold in companies, such as TRW and Hewlett Packard, that have been at the vanguard of the new human resource revolution. Some companies, such as General Electric, engaged in an aggressive practice to deunionise first in order to restructure their labour relations. The move

[8] See generally Stone, *From Widgets to Digits, supra* note 1 at 87–113.

[9] See generally MB Arthur and DM Rousseau, *The Boundaryless Career: A New Employment Principle for a New Organizational Era* (New York, Oxford Univerity Press, 1996).

[10] See Stone, *From Widgets to Digits, supra* note 1 at 203–6.

to flexible employment practices has thus been one of the factors feeding management's assault on unions.

At the same time, the new work practices have drained workplace-centred unions of much of their effectiveness. Under the present labour laws, unions represent a group of workers in a specifically defined bargaining unit.[11] The terms and conditions they negotiate apply to jobs in the defined unit rather than to the individuals who hold the jobs. Yet, as discussed above, the new workplace is not job-centred nor is it made up of separable bounded departments. It involves cross-utilization, broadbanding, and other features of boundarylessness. Collective bargaining based on bargaining units means that as individual workers move between departments, units, or firms, their labour contracts do not follow them. In today's world of frequent movement, unionism based on bargaining units means that union gains are increasingly ephemeral from the individual's point of view.

Globalization

Globalization is the cross-border interpenetration of economic life. While we cannot see globalization directly, its imprint is evident in the spread of foreign plants across domestic landscapes, the telecommunications and computer technologies that enable firms to produce, distribute, and market all over the world, falling trade barriers, and the fading foreign exchange restrictions. National borders are becoming permeable to products made all around the globe and to global capital flows.

Trade unionists and progressive policy-makers have long warned that the spread of globalization will mean the demise of hard-won labour standards and workplace rights in the Western world.[12] There are considerable data that indicate that these fears are well founded. William Cooke analysed data on foreign direct investment by US multinational firms within the nineteen OECD countries between 1982–1993. He found that one of the most important factors in firm locational decisions within the developed world was that investment was negatively correlated with levels of unionization and protective labour legislation.[13] In a similar vein, Richard Freeman and Ana Reganga found that increased trade between the United States and less developed countries between 1970–1992 led to significant reduction both in employment levels and wages for low-skilled workers in the United States.[14] Further, Laura Tyson and Bill Cline have concluded that trade is

[11] 29 USC § 159(a) (2000).

[12] See KVW Stone, 'Labour and the Global Economy: Four Approaches to Transnational Labour Regulation' (1995) 16 Mich J Int'l L 987 (citing sources) Stone, 'Labour and the Global Economy'.

[13] WN Cooke, 'The Influence of Industrial Relations Factors on US Foreign Direct Investment Abroad' (1997) 51 Indus & Lab Rel Rev 3.

[14] R Freeman and A Reganga, 'How Much Has LDC Trade Affected Western Job Markets?' (Paper presented to the ECARE/CPEII Conference on International Trade and Employment, Paris, 25 September 1995) in M Dewatripont, A Sapir and K Sekkat, eds, *Trade and Jobs in Europe: Much Ado about Nothing?* (London, Oxford University Press, 1999).

responsible for somewhere between 20 and 53 per cent of the increase in income inequality in the United States.[15] These findings are powerful evidence that companies are moving low-skilled jobs to low-wage, low union density countries, thereby depressing wages and increasing unemployment in their wake.

Some transnational institutions have been constructed to harmonise labour standards across borders, but they operate only in limited geographic areas and deal with only limited subjects. For example, the European Union has a complex multi-tier system for the harmonization of certain employment standards among its member countries. EU Directives address many issues of concern in the employment relationship, such as equal pay for part-time work, protections for workers during corporate insolvency, and health and safety standards. However, the current EU regulations do not cover most issues of collective labour rights nor do they set specific labour standards in most areas.[16] The Labour Side Agreement in the North American Free Trade Agreement (NAFTA) creates a system of cross-border monitoring that does not require countries to enforce any particular labour standard. It does, however, attempt to ensure that each country enforce whatever its domestic law happens to be. Some predict that this may become a widespread model for transnational labour governance.[17]

Globalization directly undermines domestic labour standards. It also does so indirectly by undermining the strength of domestic labour organizations. The specific ways in which globalization threatens labour are well known but worth restating briefly.[18]

First, globalization diminishes labour's bargaining power. As capital mobility increases, businesses tend to relocate to countries with lower labour standards. Further, when firms can relocate easily, unions have less power at the bargaining table in their home countries because they are always bargaining against the threat of relocation. This means that companies will be less likely to yield to union demands, and unions will not make demands out of fear of triggering business flight.

Second, globalization diminishes the level of domestic labour-protective regulations. Companies prefer to produce in legal environments that offer the least protections for labour and, when feasible, they shift production to capture the resultant lower labour costs. Thus, they engage in a labour standards 'race-to-the-bottom'. The prospect of races to the bottom places organised labour in a prisoners' dilemma: it wants domestic protective legislation to improve labour standards but is acutely vulnerable to the capital flight that increased labour standards can

[15] These studies are summarised in Robert Scott, 'Alternatives to the Neo-Liberal Model that Address Differences Between North and South, and Labour and the Environment' (1998) Economic Policy Institute at 3–4.

[16] KVW Stone, 'To the Yukon and Beyond: Local Labourers in a Global Labour Market' (1999) 3 J Small & Emerging Bus L 93 at 108–11.

[17] B Hepple, *Labour Laws and Global Trade* (Oxford: Hart, 2005).

[18] For further development of each of these issues see Stone, 'Labour and the Global Economy', *supra* note 12 at 990–7.

trigger. This dilemma is intensified as economic life becomes more global, rendering labour less effective as a political actor.

Third, globalization encourages regulatory competition. Regulatory competition occurs when nations compete for business using lower labour standards to attract businesses. It leads non-labour groups to oppose labour regulation on the ground that business flight hurts them. Thus regulatory competition could trigger a downward spiral in which nations compete with each other for lower labour standards, and labour loses its historical allies at the domestic level, rendering it powerless to resist.

Fourth, runaway shops, races-to-the-bottom, and regulatory competition pit labour organizations in one country against those in another. Thus, while globalization could be an impetus toward international labour solidarity and cooperation, it can also lead to organizational fragmentation and dissension. One strategy unions in developed countries (DCs) have used to diminish the possibilities of domestic runaway shops and races-to-the-bottom is to advocate supranational legislation that would equalise labour standards. But unions in less developed countries (LDCs) have resisted these measures and attacked them as protectionist.[19] Another possible union strategy is to attempt to organise workers across national and regional borders and bargain for parity. However, while such a strategy has succeeded at times within a single country, it is a problematic approach when corporations move beyond national boundaries. Countries have labour laws and collective bargaining systems that differ markedly from each other, even within the Western world. Thus it is difficult for unions in one country to collabourate with unions in other countries in a way that jointly harnesses their economic weapons and furthers their common bargaining goals.

Finally, globalization can lead to the deterioration of labour's political power. National labour movements operate in the context of a particular regulatory environment. Labour's political power is undermined when the locus of labour regulation moves from a national to an international arena.

Privatization

A third trend that is reshaping labour relations is privatization, broadly defined. The term 'privatization' is generally used to refer to policies that shift responsibilities and resources from the public sphere to the private sector. But it is useful to understand privatization as not merely the shift from the public to the private sector, but also the free market ideology that underlies the shift, in particular the neo-liberal assault on the New Deal social welfare state.

In the United States, the neoliberal assault on New Deal social policies has had two dimensions. First, it attempts to shift responsibility for social welfare out of the public domain and into the arena of private contract. Second, it attempts to

[19] See Louise D Williams, 'Who Pays For Free Trade—The Dilemma of Free Trade and International Labour Standards' (1996) 22 NCJ Int'l L & Com Reg 181 at 215–16.

move responsibility for social welfare away from the federal government and to the states. Both of these intellectual and political attacks on the New Deal have been garnering strength over the past twenty years.

Beginning around 1980, as the National Labor Board retreated from protecting union organizing, the core of social regulation devolved more and more to the states that had recently enacted a number of state employment laws protecting individual employees.[20] At the same time, changes in the pre-emption rules of labour law had the effect of undermining unions' contractual protections while strengthening protection for individual workers.[21] The new era corresponded to a decline in labour's political power. In the 1990s, the trend continued with the rise of the 'new federalism' in constitutional law and the continued dismantlement of the social welfare state of the New Deal. For example, in *United States v Morrison*, the Court struck down the *Violence Against Women Act* on the grounds that it was not a valid regulation of interstate commerce.[22]

The devolution of the site of regulation from the federal to the state level was accompanied by other neo-liberal policies. For example, the shifting in the responsibility for social welfare to the states and localities occurred at the same time that local anti-tax movements succeeded in enacting tax cuts and defeating local bond initiatives. This fiscal austerity constrained local governments' capacity to fund many social programs. As a result, social welfare programs have moved from the federal level to the states and localities where there are less resources to pay for them. This shift is in keeping with the neo-liberal agenda of shrinking the public sector. With increased responsibility for social welfare, state and local governments have to make hard choices between education and welfare, between street repairs and public health. All of these trends are a result of the neo-liberal ideological attack on the policies of the New Deal and the idea of a redistributive role for government.[23]

The shift from federal to state regulation and the rise of neo-liberal ideology also involves shifting responsibilities and resources from the public sphere to the private sector. The impulse to move regulation from the public to the private domain is justified by a free market ideology that celebrates contract over regulation. One area where this has occurred is in the adjudication of violations of labour rights. Increasingly, employers are requiring employees to waive their rights to a public

[20] KVW Stone, 'The Legacy of Industrial Pluralism: The Tension Between Individual Employment Rights and the New Deal Collective Bargaining System' (1992) 59 U Chicago L Rev 575.

[21] For a detailed discussion of the changes in the pre-emption rules and their detrimental impact on union strength see *ibid.*

[22] 529 US 598 (2000). There have also been a number of recent cases cutting back on federal power to impose anti-discrimination measures on the states. See *eg Kimel v Florida Board of Regents*, 120 S Ct 631 (2002). On the nature of the 'new federalism' in the area of social regulation, see RC Post and RB Siegel, 'Equal Protection by Law: Federal Antidiscrimination Legislation After *Morrison and Kimel*' (2000) 110 Yale LJ 441.

[23] These attacks are embodied in the current 'constitution-in-exile' view of constitutional law. See eg MJ Gerhardt, 'On Revolution and Wetlands Regulations' (2002) 90 Geo LJ 2143 at 2144–5; 'Special Symposium Issue: The Constitution in Exile' (2001) 51 Duke LJ 1 (containing articles for and against this view of the Constitution).

forum and agree instead to bring any claims of violations of labour rights to a private forum, a forum that is crafted and often controlled by the employer. The US Supreme Court has upheld the use of private arbitration tribunals for adjudicating claims under the discrimination laws, and lower courts have upheld them for many other types of employment claims.[24] Employment law is thus becoming a body of law that is interpreted by private arbitrators outside of the public eye. As employers move more and more disputes about labour rights out of public fora, the resolution of employment disputes becomes invisible and the decision makers become unaccountable. There also fails to develop a body of publicly-known jurisprudence that can provide a normative basis for the assertion of labour rights by others.[25]

In the United States the ascendancy of neo-liberal public policies has had many ramifications, including dismantling welfare, easing environmental regulations, diminishing worker health and safety protections, diluting the right to organise unions, weakening the strike weapon, and reducing the funding for public education and health programs, to name just a few. One result is that regulatory competition has again become a serious concern. States aggressively compete for businesses by touting their low labour costs and union-free environment, thereby pressuring other states to lower their labour protections. For example, we are in the early phases of a movement sweeping the states to revise workers' compensation laws to reduce protection and compensation for injured workers.

The Three-Headed Beast

The triple onslaught of flexibilization, which has rendered many of the old labour market skills and institutions obsolete, globalization, with its propensity for geographic dispersion, and privatization under neo-liberal ideology, with its repudiation of social legislation at the national level, all contribute to union decline and a diminishment of labour rights. Flexibilization increases employers' incentive to avoid unions because they perceive unions as promoting rigidity, uniformity, job security protections, and narrow job definitions. Globalization increases employers' opportunities to avoid unions and labour regulations in their quest for lower labour costs. In addition, global production chains, enhanced transportation and communication, and lower trade barriers give employers considerable leverage to avoid unions or limit their effectiveness. The development of transnational global governance institutions also undermines the political strength of unions at the national level. Privatization fosters policies that diminish legal protection for labour rights and collective bargaining, and contribute to rapidly growing income inequality.

[24] *Gilmer v Interstate/Johnson Lane Corp*, 500 US 20 (1991); *Circuit City Stores, Inc v Adams*, 535 US 1112 (2002).

[25] For critiques of the use of private dispute resolution in employment relations, see KVW Stone, 'Mandatory Arbitration of Individual Employment Rights: The Yellow Dog Contract of the 1990s' (1996) 73 Denv UL Rev 1017.

The Local as a Counterweight to the Global

How can progressives and union groups respond to the three-pronged onslaught caused by flexibilization, globalization, and privatization? Are there prospects for social progress in the midst of the above-described trends? Social progress can be defined as improvement in income distribution and provision of reasonable income and livelihood security for all members of our society. This is a minimalist vision—it does not describe complete equality nor total welfare support and insurance against all adversity. Rather, social progress means progress toward reasonable equality and a reasonably functioning social safety net to provide individual dignity, social justice, and a humane society.

If social progress is the goal, the question is, how can it be achieved? As stated earlier, globalization begets localization. The more homogeneous and cosmopolitan the world, the more some groups embrace and assert their local particularities and distinctive cultures. Globalization not only breeds a desire for localization, it also breeds new means to accomplish it. For example, the Internet is a rich terrain for local groups to keep their cultures alive and build new networks and connections that reflect their own particular shared values. A simple Google search for the term 'Gaelic' revealed over three million Web sites brimming with information about Gaelic societies, Gaelic schools, Gaelic dictionaries, Gaelic music groups, Gaelic Bibles, as well as many sub-languages such as Scottish Gaelic, Manx Gaelic, Irish Gaelic, Cymraec, and others. These sites give individuals of Gaelic origin the ability to connect, network, learn about their ethnic past, build on shared interests, and develop programs to keep their cultures alive. Similarly, while the dynamics of flexibilization, globalization, and privatization weaken labour rights, they also contain features that could make a revitalised progressive movement possible.

Globalization Versus Agglomeration: The Gravitational Pull of the Local

While corporations have a tendency to leapfrog across the globe, jumping over any country that imposes burdensome labour regulations, some corporations have a gravitational pull toward a particular place. Regional economists and economic geographers have found that certain types of firms want to locate near others that produce in their same field in order to take advantage of what they call 'agglomeration economies' that exist in specific regional locales.[26] These findings suggest that there might be a pull toward staying in place that is in tension with globalization's pull toward dispersion. If so, it might be possible for local policy-makers to develop local and regional institutions that facilitate the development of good jobs

[26] See generally EL Glaeser, 'Are Cities Dying?' (1998) 12:2 J of Econ Persp 139.

and sustainable economic growth. That is, globalization is not a one-way juggernaut, but rather it is a process that exists in tension with local embeddedness.

Economists became interested in the effect of agglomeration on economic growth in the 1980s. It had long been noted that firms producing certain types of goods and services were likely to locate near others of their type, such as the diamond district on 47th Street in New York City or the clusters of used car lots found in most small cities.[27] Paul Krugman observed that 80 per cent of the industrial carpet in the United States was produced in Dalton County, Georgia. That and similar producer clusters, he said, could not be explained by neoclassical economic theory.[28] This led economists to hypothesize that when certain types of firms were located in proximity to one another, they all received value from agglomeration that was independent of any single firm's contribution. A great deal of empirical work has since confirmed the existence of agglomeration economies that play a powerful role in the locational choices of firms.[29] One well-known study is Anna Lee Saxenian's description of the dramatic effects of agglomeration in the Silicon Valley computer industry.[30] Other examples of successful localised agglomeration economies are the clusters of biotechnology firms around Princeton, New Jersey, of banking and financial firms in New York City, and of computer hardware manufacturing firms around Austin, Texas.

Regional economists attribute many of the positive effects of agglomeration economies to the skills and knowledge that are concentrated in, and shared among, the locality's work force.[31] Through networks built in informal gatherings in bars and coffee houses, workers share information about jobs, firms, and the specifics of their work. This 'job talk' enables them to increase their knowledge about their work and enhance their own labour market prospects. The knowledge-sharing means that new ideas are constantly transmitted through the local 'job talk' grapevine, eventually ending up informing the work itself. Also, each time workers change jobs, they broaden their knowledge of work techniques and practices in their field. Knowledge-sharing leads to innovation and to more highly trained workers. Thus, in an agglomeration economy, the availability of a trained, knowledgeable work force generates a culture that continually and seamlessly trains new employees, updates existing employees' skills, and provides firms with innovative ideas.[32]

[27] See generally JM Quigley, 'Urban Diversity and Economic Growth' (1998) 11:4 J Econ Persp 127 at 132 (describing studies).

[28] P Krugman, *Geography and Trade* (Cambridge, MA, MIT Press, 1991) at 59.

[29] See eg MP Drennan, 'National Structural Change and Metropolitan Specialization in the United States' (1999) 78 Papers in Regional Sci 297 at 314–15 (describes an empirical study finding agglomeration economy in information-intensive industries in urban areas). See generally Glaeser, supra note 26 at 148–50 (citing studies).

[30] AL Saxenian, *Regional Advantage: Culture and Competition in Silicon Valley and Route 128* (Cambridge, MA, Harvard University Press, 1994).

[31] See generally J McDonald, *Fundamentals of Urban Economics* (Upper Saddle River, NJ, Prentice Hall, 1998).

[32] See eg R Batt *et al*, *Net Working: Work Patterns and Workforce Policies for the New Media Industry* (Washington, Economic Policy Institute, 2001); Saxenian, *supra* note 30 at 150.

The significance of agglomeration effects for firms and for local economic development has been a fertile subject of discussion amongst planners, regional economists, and economic geographers in recent years. What has eluded attention to date is the significance of agglomeration economies for labour. Yet to the extent that the choice of location of firms is influenced by the prospects of valuable agglomeration effects, firms will be less likely to move overseas, or across the country, to escape rising labour costs. Because the fuel on which agglomeration economies run is the store of knowledge residing in the local workforce, the workers in the locality have considerable leverage to pressure firms at the local and regional level.

The Cult and Cultivation of Human Capital

Firms today operate on the basis of a belief that the knowledge possessed by their employees is one of their major assets and a primary source of competitive advantage. In the words of Fortune magazine editor Thomas Stewart, 'Information and knowledge are the thermonuclear competitive weapons of our time'.[33] The new flexible work practices are designed, in large part, to cultivate the intellectual engagement and abilities of employees and harness them on behalf of the firm. Employers' reliance on employees' knowledge and skill gives employees renewed leverage.

Firms want to enhance and utilize their employees' human capital, but they face a difficulty. Because they no longer use promises of job security as an inducement for employees to develop their skills, they need to find another way to align their employees' interests with their own. They do so by promising employees the opportunity to learn skills that can be used outside the firm, to build the employee's own career. Today's employees have a great interest in gaining human capital, not merely, or even primarily, to assist in their firm's success, but to enhance their own labour market opportunities. Employees, therefore, want to gain the kinds of general knowledge and expertise that they can take with them as they move from firm to firm in their own boundaryless careers.

Despite their reliance on employee knowledge, firms are reluctant to provide general training, at least on company time, because they cannot ensure that their employees stay in their employ indefinitely.[34] Some companies provide training, but insist that new hires take the training on their own time, before they start work. Others rely on the outside market for training. Indeed, there has been an explosion of private training programs, many of which train in areas, such as airline reservation skills, that were previously taught on-the-job. There has also been an explosion in publicly funded job training through vocational education, community colleges, and other lifetime learning programs.

[33] TA Stewart, *Intellectual Capital: The New Wealth of Organizations* (New York, Currency/Doubleday, 1997) at ix.

[34] See P Cappelli, *The New Deal at Work: Managing the Market-Driven Workforce* (Boston, Harvard Business School Press, 1999).

Firms also attempt to ensure that any knowledge an employee gains in the course of their employ is not utilized to the benefit of a competitor. Thus employers increasingly seek to impose post-employment restraints by insisting on covenants not to compete and bringing actions to protect trade secrets. As a result, there has been a growing number of lawsuits over the enforceability of post-employment restrictive covenants and over the definition of trade secrets.[35] The issue of who owns the employees' human capital is shaping up to be one of the most contentious in the field of employment law.

Employees and businesses have a shared interest in training a local labour force in the skills needed by local firms. Businesses need training to generate the human capital essential to the development of an agglomeration economy. Employees need training to retool and reposition themselves as they move in and out of jobs in a fluid labour market. For employees, training and retraining are key to enabling them to operate in the new flexible work environment. The central role of training for both firms and employees opens up opportunities for local activism and the development of local unions. Thus we might expect local unions to pressure businesses to contribute to public adult education and training programs. Already, the *Workplace Investment Act* attempts to foster local and regional training programs tailored to the needs of a locality's businesses.[36]

Community and worker groups can play a leading role in securing training and job opportunities. Collective action by grassroots groups to secure adult education and skills training could both expand employment opportunities for, and provide assistance to, those caught in the interstices of the boundaryless workplace. Training is an issue for which collective action can succeed and might make a difference. Training can help make a locality's workforce more flexible and skilled. But no individual employer has an incentive to establish such programs unilaterally because it cannot capture all the benefits for itself or prevent their capture by a competitor. However, if a group of workers, organised as a citizens' association or a local union, pressures firms in an area to contribute to a job training program, they would create a benefit in which all would share. Similarly, if enough corporations were induced to contribute to a locality's social infrastructure—its school system, hospitals, parks, cultural activities, and child care—this would help attract a highly skilled workforce who want quality educational opportunities for their children. Such community investment would benefit all firms in a locality. Thus the prospects of agglomeration economies combined with increased reliance by corporations on human capital could provide the glue to keep corporations in place. This could prevent them from bolting each time a citizen union demands that local firms adopt good corporate-citizen behaviour.

[35] KVW Stone, 'The New Psychological Contract: Implications of the Changing Workplace for Labor and Employment Law' (2001) 48 UCLA L Rev 519.

[36] See N Ellis, 'Individual Training Accounts Under the Workforce Investment Act of 1998' (2001) 8 Geo J on Poverty L & Pol'y 235; see also Susan Saulny, 'New Jobless Centers Offer More than a Benefit Check' *New York Times* (5 September 2001) A1. See generally Stone, *From Widgets to Digits*, *supra* note 1.

Shifting Social Policy From the National to the Local

The ascendancy of neo-liberal public policies has had many ramifications, including dismantling welfare, easing environmental regulations, diminishing worker health and safety protections, diluting the right to organise unions, weakening the strike weapon, and reducing funding for public education and health programs. One aspect of neo-liberalism is the dismantling of the public sphere and the shifting of resources to the private sphere. In the private arena, actors lack accountability and decision-making processes lack transparency. However, as Ronen Shamir says, 'When the public milieu becomes privatized, the private becomes a matter of public concern'.[37] Hence, as more and more important issues are handled in the private domain, we are seeing emerging movements to monitor the deeds, and misdeeds, of the private sector. The public outcry over the Enron and other corporate scandals of the early 2000s could be a harbinger of a new form of social awareness.

Privatization does not eliminate the role of the public sphere, but it changes its source and nature. Retrenchment in the public sector has entailed pushing governmental responsibilities onto the states and localities. Federal aid to localities is vanishing, and as a result, localities are being crushed by the weight of their obligations to provide education, health care, social welfare benefits, policing, and infrastructure. Local politics has become the terrain upon which social welfare battles must be fought. For this reason as well, it is imperative that there be organizations at the local level that represent the local working and non-working population in local political arenas. Those arenas are increasingly becoming the place where economic and social policy is made.

Collective Action at the Local Level Around Issues of Work and Social Citizenship

If there are agglomeration economies to be had, it should be possible for unions and community organizations to capture some of the added value for the benefit of the community. The types of organizations that could most effectively achieve this are local and regional, cross-industry, cross-firm, labour, and community organizations. These organizations, which I call citizen unions, could bargain with employers in a geographic area for higher local minimum wages, uniform and portable benefits, child care, and job training and retraining programs. They could also serve as a political force to press for changes in labour and employment laws to provide higher levels of employment protection more generally. One sees the

[37] 'Between Self-Regulation and the Alien Tort Claims Act: On the Contested Concept of Corporate Social Responsibility' (2004) 38 Law & Soc'y Rev. 635 at 635.

germs of such citizen union organizations in many places, including contingent worker groups and living wage campaigns that have emerged in many states, such as the Justice for Janitors organization in California and the Industrial Area Foundation in Texas.

Citizen unions could act at the local and regional level to pressure corporations to become good corporate citizens. Citizen unionism is animated by the proposition that because employers in a boundaryless workplace draw on the collective skills, knowledge, experience, and expertise of the local workforce, they should contribute to the welfare of that workforce generally. Employers should contribute to the local school systems, libraries, museums, cultural programs, sporting events, and hospitals. They should also fund educational programs for children. Corporate contributions of this sort would benefit all working people in the communities in which they operate.

A citizen union could be a potent force in the local political process. On the local level it could run candidates and push for legislation to provide some of the measures mentioned above, including portability of benefits, a local minimum wage, publicly funded wage supplements, publicly funded child care, and job training programs.

On the national level, a federation of citizen unions could lobby for measures that promote equality and justice in the workplace and in society more generally. It could press for anti-discrimination legislation, occupational safety and health protection, minimum wage increases, universal health insurance, and other worker protection measures. In addition, because a citizen union defines its members both as workers and as citizens of their locality, state, and nation, it can go beyond traditional labour issues and address issues of concern to working people more generally.

A number of local organizations have emerged in the United States in the past decade that embody some of the features described as citizen unionism. Here I will describe just a few, so that we can begin to see that the vision is not utterly fanciful.

Examples of Citizen Unions in the United States

Contingent Worker Groups and the National Federation for Fair Employment

In many cities, groups have organized to press for rights for contingent workers in all types of workplaces. The Boston Center for Contingent Work (CCW) is one example. With support from Boston area unions and foundation grants, CCW uses media and other mechanisms to pressure companies that hire contingent workers to adopt codes of conduct that specify minimum rights and benefits. It has waged successful campaigns at trucking warehouses, retail stores, and tugboat operations. CCW is also active in lobbying the Massachusetts state legislature to enact a Workplace Equity Bill that would end discrimination in wages and benefits for contingent workers. To date, the bill has garnered significant support.[38] CCW also works with Boston area labour unions to encourage them to provide for wage and benefit parity for contingent workers in their collective bargaining agreements.[39] In 2000, CCW joined with contingent worker organizations from more than twenty-five cities to form the National Alliance for Fair Employment (NAFFE). NAFFE is lobbying to get temporary workers the same rights under the labour and employment laws as permanent employees. NAFFE has also proposed a *Temporary Industry Code of Conduct*, which would require temporary employment agencies to provide to workers written job descriptions, adequate safety equipment, on-site orientation, training, sick pay, holiday pay, health insurance rates, and transportation to work sites that are not publicly accessible.[40] This Code further specifies that temporary workers may join unions at client employers if the existing collective agreement so permits.[41] It also provides that '[t]he agency will pay welfare-to-work participants a living wage consistent with local standards and benefits'.[42]

Local Living Wage Campaigns

In 1994, in Baltimore, members of the clergy joined members of the American Federation of State, County, and Municipal Employees (AFSCME) to do something about the problem of the working poor. Despite local economic development, there was a lot of poverty in the city. So they began to pressure the city to pay its employees higher wages. Ultimately they got the city to agree to require construction contractors who did business with the city to pay their workers a minimum wage sufficient to bring a family of four up to the federal poverty line. This entailed an increase in the minimum wage for those workers from $4.35 to $7.70.[43]

Since then, 'living wage' campaigns have been mounted in many cities. Los Angeles passed an ordinance in 1997 that included more categories of workers and provided not only higher wages but also higher benefits. According to historian Stephanie Luce, 'as of early 2002, 82 living wage ordinances are on the books, and approximately 70 campaigns are ongoing'.[44]

The Baltimore living ordinance only applied to city construction workers, but over time other cities have expanded their scope to cover more types of workers.

[38] US, H Res 2105, *The Workplace Equity Bill—An Act Regarding Workers in Contingent and Part-time Work*, 2000. This bill was referred to the Committee on Public Safety, and hearings were held on 6 May 2005.

[39] See interviews of T Costello and G Nicholson, Director and Associate Director of Center for Contingent Work in Boston, Mass. (May 2000) [on file with author].

[40] See National Alliance for Fair Employment, 'Contingent Workers Fight for Fairness' (May 2000), online: <http:// www.fairjobs.org/fairjobs/contingent/cwffe.php>.

[41] *Ibid.*

[42] *Ibid.*

[43] S Luce, 'The Full Fruits of Our Labor: The Rebirth of the Living Wage Movement' (2002) 43 Labor History 401 at 402–3.

[44] *Ibid* at 403.

Some ordinances apply to firms that receive tax breaks as part of economic development strategies and firms that hold leases on city-owned properties. Some also cover direct city employees. And some cities have expanded the concept to impose a living wage on all private sector employers in a particular locality. For example, in Santa Monica, all large employers in the city's tourist zone are subject to the living wage ordinance. In 2002, New Orleans enacted a citywide minimum wage, set at a level that is considerably higher than the federal minimum.[45] In 2003, San Francisco adopted a living wage ordinance, followed by the state of Nevada in 2004. In 2006, the minimum wage in Santa Fe went up to $9.50 an hour.[46]

The movements to achieve city living wage laws are broad, geographically-based movements focused on issues of work. They are comprised of unions together with community organizations, church groups, organizations helping the homeless, women's groups, and other activists. The living wage campaigns often expand beyond the single issue of wages to require cities to pay for holidays and benefits, and to hire through community-operated hiring halls. Some also require the city to remain neutral in the case of a union organizing campaign.[47]

The Industrial Areas Foundation and Project Quest

The Industrial Areas Foundation (IAF) is a multi-issue organization that works at the grassroots level on local issues concerning social services, education, and employment. It has established organizations in a number of cities, including Chicago, Baltimore, Los Angeles, New York, and Boston, and has been particularly active in the Southwest. For example, in Texas, it has chapters in Dallas, Houston, Fort Worth, El Paso, San Antonio, and the Rio Grande Valley. The IAF's goal is to build broad-based coalitions that can exert pressure at the local and state level on issues such as job training, living wages, education, local economic development, health care, social services, and housing. Its members are not individuals, but rather churches, schools, unions, community groups, health centres, and other local organizations. It attempts to integrate concerns at the neighbourhood, family, and workplace level. The IAF organizing style is to identify leaders within existing organizations and teach them to mobilize others and exert political power. It has had a number of successes and has become a-potent political force in many cities.[48]

The IAF is involved in so many types of activities that it is impossible to catalogue them fully. Of particular interest for present purposes are the IAF activities in the labour market. In the early 1990s in San Antonio, the IAF developed an innovative job training program called Project QUEST. The program enrolled trainees in an eighteen-month intensive skill-training course. It utilised local

[45] *Ibid* at 404.

[46] J Gertner, 'What Is a Living Wage?' *New York Times Magazine* (15 January 2006) 38 at 40.

[47] *Supra* note 43 at 404–7.

[48] For a thorough and insightful description of the history and current operation of the Industrial Areas Foundation, see P Osterman, *Gathering Power: The Future of Progressive Politics in America* (Boston, Beacon Press, 2002).

community colleges to provide the classroom instruction. It also secured commitments from 650 local businesses to provide jobs to the QUEST graduates. According to Paul Osterman, who evaluated Project QUEST for the Ford Foundation, the program 'led to substantial gains for its participants, gains that far exceed that of typical training efforts'.[49] Osterman found that the program's graduates saw substantial enhancement in their earning power, and that the program provided other tangible benefits to the community. It led firms to raise their wage levels generally because QUEST insisted that participating employers pay trainees a living wage. The program also improved the community colleges because by working with QUEST, they were persuaded to revise their curriculum in a way that better reflected the needs of the labour market, in turn giving their students more marketable skills.[50]

The IAF has also been involved in workplace safety campaigns and living wage campaigns in numerous cities. In the Rio Grande Valley, it is currently attempting to build an employee association, which according to Osterman, will be a broad-based employee organization including all types of workers—low-wage workers, contingent workers, unemployed workers, public employees, semi-self employed, and full-time workers. It plans a living wage campaign for health care workers, and hopes that the campaign will affect wage levels throughout the community. The association plans to offer training programs, job placement assistance, or other services to its members. However, it will not engage in collective bargaining.[51]

Justice for Janitors

The Service Employees International Union (SEIU) has been involved in innovative organizing drives in the building service area in several large cities since 1985. The first was in Los Angeles. Due to the unusual three-cornered employment relationship in which janitors work for building service companies that are themselves hired by building managers, economic pressure by janitors runs the risk of violating the secondary boycott laws. Instead of relying exclusively on economic weapons, the SEIU organised a direct appeal to the public for support. It marched in parades and participated in church events. It organised large public protests near, but not at, the buildings it was seeking to organise. In one case, the union staged a protest against the building used for the television show *L.A. Law* because the show used a non-union cleaning service. It also emphasised that one goal of the organizing drive was to gain health care coverage for janitors. In this way, it portrayed the organizing drive as a social justice movement in order to form alliances with other progressive elements in the community. The union also enlisted the help of community leaders to pressure the building owners by opposing permits for building projects. While the janitors were not strongly attached to

[49] P Osterman, *Gathering Power: The Future of Progressive Politics in America* (Boston, Beacon Press, 2002) at 163.

[50] *Ibid* at 163–4.

[51] *Ibid* at 167–8.

any particular workplace, they were deeply embedded in the community and were able to use their community connections to assist in their organizing drives.[52]

WashTech and the Community Workers Association in Seattle

The Washington Alliance for Technology Workers (WashTech) is an example of a cross-workplace organization that involves workers with different types of skills within the same general industry. WashTech is a community-based membership organization that was founded in 1998. It was formed by a group of temporary workers at Microsoft, but has since expanded to include workers from Amazon.com and other high-tech companies. It currently includes lower- to middle-skilled technical workers in high-tech industries in the Seattle area. It has a Web page, a listserv, and a staff to address the labour-related issues of high-tech firms.

The WashTech Mission Statement states:

> WashTech/CWA is an innovative and influential union whose members advocate for all technology workers in Washington State and beyond. We are a visionary community of activists and a leading voice for our members in the global economy. We help build economic security and fair working conditions through collective action, bargaining and legislative advocacy.[53]

Its goals are to address issues related to benefit portability, training, assistance with networking, concerns about non-compete covenants, and the problems of temporary work—many of the issues raised by the new employment relationship.

WashTech has attempted to engage in collective bargaining on two occasions, but each time the units it was seeking to organise were sold or moved overseas. As a result, the organization primarily focuses on two other features of unionism—providing mutual aid, and political action. For example, WashTech has set up a regional training centre in Seattle for high-tech workers that offers courses in many different programming techniques and web design skills. It also participates in a national training program that its affiliated union, the Communications Workers of America, has established with Cicso Systems. WashTech uses publicity to help high-tech workers resist non-compete clauses and helps them challenge the use of restrictive covenants.[54] It also offers its members job listing services and training classes.

WashTech engages in extensive publicity and lobbying on behalf of temporary workers' interests. For example, it helped defeat a proposed law that would have eliminated overtime for computer professionals. It also lobbied successfully for a

[52] CL Erickson, *et al*, 'Justice for Janitors in Los Angeles: Lessons from Three Rounds of Negotiations' (2002) 40 Brit J of Indus Rel 543.

[53] For information about WashTech see online: WashTech: A Voice of the Digital Workforce <http://www.washtech.org> [WashTech]; see also DD van Jaarsveld, 'Collective Representation Among High-Tech Workers at Microsoft and Beyond: Lessons from WashTech/CWA' (2004) 43 Indus Rel 364.

[54] WashTech, *ibid.*

law to protect temporary workers in the public sector from misclassification or other attempts to deny them benefits they are entitled to under state law or collective bargaining agreements. Currently they are attempting to get legislation enacted that would force temporary employment agencies to inform their employees of their pay, work schedules, and other conditions of employment.[55]

Experiments in Regional Institutions in Europe

The European Union has also been engaged in experimentation with local solutions to global problems. In the past fifteen years, local and regional institutions have developed in Europe that are dedicated to protecting labour rights and at the same time to strengthening local economic opportunities. In some areas of Italy, Spain, the United Kingdom, and other countries, local and regional social pacts have been negotiated among tripartite institutions at the local level, empowering these areas to set labour-market policy. The pacts are typically negotiated not only by the traditional social partners—employer associations and trade unions—but also by civic groups and other organised local constituencies. They receive funding from the European Union structural funds as well as their national governments to invest in infrastructure and regional economic development.[56] As Bruno Caruso writes, territorial employment pacts in Italy have fostered:

> territorial bargaining in the so-called economy of 'districts' . . . which often correspond to sectors traditionally featuring small firms or craftsmen (textiles, furniture, building, tourism). . . . [Territorial bargaining has involved a] bilateral partnership but at a territorial rather than industry or plant level, to support the competitiveness of micro firms by injecting a heavy dose of flexibility (as regards working hours, wages and geographic location) into both the internal and external labour market. These measures are almost always accompanied by others supporting income levels if not permanent employment security.[57]

There is considerable debate about the effectiveness of these local forms of bargaining. However, many observers acknowledge that these forms of bargaining could improve local economic performance and provide employment protection to local populations.[58]

[55] WashTech, *ibid.*

[56] For a detailed description of local social pacts in Europe see Ida Regalia, 'Decentralizing Employment Protection in Europe: Territorial Pacts and Beyond' in J Zeitlin and DM Trubek, eds, *Governing Work and Welfare in the New Economy: European and American Experiments* (Oxford, Oxford University Press, 2003) 158 at 163–70.

[57] 'Decentralised Social Pacts, Trade Unions and Collective Bargaining—How Labour Law is Changing' in Marco Biagi, ed, *Towards a European Model of Industrial Relations? Building on the First Report of the European Commission* (Great Britain: Kluwer Law International, 2001) 193 at 210.

[58] *Supra* note 56.

Conclusion

The US organizations described above have all emerged independently over the past decade or two. Each focuses on making improvements for workers and communities at the local level. While they differ as to their tactics and organizational design, they all share some attributes of the proposed citizen union model. They demonstrate the truth of the observation that the best response to globalization is localization. Further, these organizations promote civic engagement, countering the isolation and invisibility that result from privatization. And they are making serious efforts to build social safety nets to help individuals weather transitions they encounter in the new flexible labour market.

None of the activities of citizen union organizations described above depends upon the National Labor Relations Board to certify the organization as a majority representative. Rather, the organizations function as hybrids of local-improvement civic associations and citizens' lobbying groups, emphasizing issues emanating from the workplace. Citizen unionism could supplement and support plant-level collective bargaining by individual unions in settings in which they exist. However, to truly facilitate the development of citizen unions in the United States, there would have to be many changes in the labour bargaining laws. These changes can only come about from a social movement that is informed by a vision of the possibilities for social justice in the new economy.[59] There remains a question of whether local organization can transform national politics and transnational institutions. We do not yet have any empirical evidence that this can occur, but on the other hand, the localised forms of citizen bargaining described above are new and still quite small. It is thus too soon to know whether these and other experiments at the local level can devise a strategy and coalesce into an organization on the national or even transnational level that can slay the three-headed beast.

[59] For a more detailed discussion of changes to labour law that would facilitate the development of citizen unions, see Stone, *From Widgets to Digits*, *supra* n 1.

7

Law, Norms, and Complex Discrimination

SUSAN STURM*

For years, scholars have challenged the dominant legal paradigm for addressing employment discrimination. They have criticised its formalistic, intent-based doctrinal framework as insufficiently descriptive of the dynamics that produce inequality; insufficiently explanatory of what judges actually do; and insufficiently robust as a normative theory of equality. Viewed in the light of recent interdisciplinary scholarship, the formal equality account—its prime protagonists, its plot, its problematic, and its prognosis—is an easy target.

Recent interdisciplinary scholarship shows that workplace bias often operates as a set of social practices, a dynamic interaction among culture, cognition, and context.[1] For example, Charles Lawrence, Linda Krieger, and others have drawn on cognitive and Freudian psychology to debunk conscious intent as an adequate explanation of racial and gender influence on employment decision making.[2] Vicki Schultz has criticised courts' failure to consider how organisational and cultural factors, often sustained by employers, shape employees' interest and success in non-traditional jobs.[3] David Charny, Mitu Gulati, and David Wilkins have shown that the dearth of black corporate lawyers results not primarily from overt racism or the lack of qualified candidates. Instead, the interaction of the tournament system of advancement, cognitive bias, and group interaction cause much of the underparticipation by black lawyers in firms.[4] Martha Minow has exposed the

* Professor of Law, Columbia Law School

[1] D Charny and GM Gulati, 'Efficiency Wages, Tournaments, and Discrimination: A Theory of Employment Discrimination Law for "High-Level" Jobs', (1998) 33 *Harvard CRC L Rev* 57; LH Krieger, 'The Content of Our Categories: A Cognitive Bias Approach to Discrimination and Equal Employment Opportunity', (1995) 47 *Stanford L Rev* 1761; C Lawrence, 'The Id, the Ego, and Equal Protection: Reckoning with Unconscious Racism', in *Foundations of Employment Discrimination Law* 122 (J Donahue ed, 1997); R Post, 'Prejudicial Appearances: The Logic of American Antidiscrimination Law', (2000) 88 *California L Rev* 1, 30; S Sturm, 'Second Generation Employment Discrimination: A Structural Approach', (2001) 101 *Columbia L Rev* 458.

[2] Krieger, above n 1, at 1161, 1217; Lawrence, above n 1, at 122; C Freshman, 'Whatever Happened to Anti-Semitism? How Social Science Theories Identify Discrimination and Promote Coalitions Between "Different" Minorities', (2000) 85 *Cornell L Rev* 313.

[3] V Schultz, 'Reconceptualizing Sexual Harassment', (1998) 107 *Yale L J* 1683.

[4] DB Wilkins and GM Gulati, 'Why Are There So Few Black Lawyers in Corporate Law Firms? An Institutional Analysis', (1996) 84 *California L Rev* 496; Charny & Gulati, above n 1, at 57.

implicit, baseline assumptions that normalise a world organised around the values and practices of dominant groups.[5]

The inequality stories anchoring these rich accounts convey a flavour of complexity and, to varying degrees, uncertainty. They are descriptively and normatively far more complicated than the stock story of deliberate discrimination. The problematic activities they target are embedded in institutional structures, group interactions, and cultural stereotypes. Their exclusionary character is not intuitively obvious, and sometimes emerges only from analyzing problematic patterns and their potential causes in particular contexts. These dynamics implicate equality principles, although the precise character of the harm and the contours of the particular norm can be hard to pin down.

What is law's role in addressing these complex problems? How do and should courts elaborate and enforce ambiguous norms? What legitimate repertoires are available to courts for addressing complex discrimination consistent with the rule of law? How do they construct the relationship between the articulation of rights and the enforcement of remedies? What is and should be the nature of judicial interaction with other normative actors? Generally stated, what are the implications of the sociological/institutional/contextual/interdisciplinary analysis of legal problems for judicial participation in the reconstruction of institutional practices?

The answers to these questions are often taken for granted in the discussions about legal doctrine and remedies for workplace discrimination. When grappling with law's response to complex and subtle discrimination, many employment scholars fall back on a surprisingly formalistic conception of law. Their punch line is often a new legal rule that better reflects current understandings of the problem. Some scholars propose doctrinal standards that reflect more complex and dynamic accounts of workplace inequality.[6] Yet another approach offers a different cognitive or decisional framework to shape judges' reasoning process as courts address cases involving discrimination.[7] A final set of responses considers the implications of this complexity for courts' capacity to address the problem at all. Some scholars advocate private or market solutions as better suited to this type of complex, interactive problem.[8] Others counsel against any judicial intervention until sufficient evidence develops to permit articulation of a clear and workable rule.[9]

These responses take for granted a formalistic conception of legal norm elaboration. This conception presumes that 'law' emerges from formal adversary process producing post-liability judicial decisions that interpret loosely worded civil rights statutes. It assumes that legal rules dictate the boundaries between legal and illegal conduct. Courts affect informal workplace norms by the 'shadow' their

[5] Schultz, above n 3, at 1683; Lawrence, above n 1, at 122; D Oppenheimer, 'Negligent Discrimination', (1993) 141 *University of Pennsylvania L Rev* 899; M Minow, 'Justice Engendered', (1987) 101 *Harvard L Rev* 10. K Yoshino, 'Covering', (2002) 111 *Yale L J* 769, 781; Post, above n 1, at 30.

[6] Schultz, above n 3, at 1683; Lawrence, above n 1, at 122; Oppenheimer, above n 4, at 899.

[7] Minow, above n 5, at 88–9.

[8] A Wax, 'Discrimination as Accident', (1999) 74 *Indiana L Rev* 1129.

[9] *Ibid.*

outputs (and the costs of generating them) cast over informal decision making.[10] Law and legal process operate as a decontextualised process detached from the dynamics by which norms develop and influence practice. This formalistic judicial conception shapes and constrains scholars' substantive responses to complex discrimination. It influences the proposed content of legal norms, the judicial strategies chosen to address complex problems, and the perceived legitimacy of these choices. The rule-enforcement conception of law and courts is, however, vastly over-simplified, as both a descriptive and normative matter. Its legal formalism, clashes with the rich, interdisciplinary, and structural analyses that characterise scholars' critique of formal equality doctrine. Indeed, public law scholars' blanket commitment to a rule-enforcement conception of law and law-making seems surprising when compared to the more dynamic and reflexive accounts in human rights scholarship[11] and in the commercial and business domain.[12]

As a descriptive matter, the judiciary's current dispute processing repertoire includes a much richer set of legal norm elaboration practices than the dominant narrative acknowledges. Within the context of judicial decision making, norm elaboration occurs in less formal settings that more directly facilitate data gathering and deliberations by relevant stakeholders and experts. These processes generate learning and outcomes that are more generally applicable, even if they have less formally binding effect than a formal adjudication. These settings include determinations of the scope of and participants in resolving the legal conflict, as well as proceedings about settlement and remedy. Outside the formal law-making and enforcement process, actors participate in norm elaboration that directly contributes to the content of formal legal norms, and courts sometimes actively shape the contours of that informal norm elaboration process.

As a normative matter, the facilitative position that courts, sometimes apologetically, occupy is in fact an important, legitimate, and under-theorised aspect of judicial participation in norm elaboration and implementation. It connects the use of coercive state power to providing significant, legally mandated occasions for those directly affected by or responsible for the conduct at issue to participate in evaluating the relationship between current and desired practice. This role encourages a collaborative, deliberative, and accountable problem solving process that can be linked to collective learning and norm generation. It permits legitimate judicial involvement in addressing problems for which some state intervention is needed because the problems might otherwise remain unidentified, under-analysed, or insufficiently linked to collective understandings, but coercion through rule enforcement may not be justified or workable. I take the less familiar position of advocating greater use of the nonformal or interactive—within courts

[10] RH Mnookin and L Kornhauser, 'Bargaining in the Shadow of the Law: The Case of Divorce', (1979) 88 *Yale L J* 950.

[11] K Rustiala and AM Slaughter, 'International Law, International Relations, and Compliance', in *Handbook of International Relations* 538 (Carlsnaes, *et al* ed, 2002).

[12] M Cain, 'The Symbol Traders', in *Lawyers in a Postmodern World* 15 (M Cain and C Harrington, ed); D Sugarman, 'Blurred Boundaries: The Overlapping Worlds of Law, Business, and Politics', in *Lawyers in a Post-Modern World* 115 (1994).

and outside—to develop norms specifically to deal with a problem that otherwise resists redress: complex discrimination.

I am not suggesting that courts give up their formal rule elaboration role under the right circumstances. The hammer of rule enforcement is a necessary backdrop, both substantively and procedurally, for the judiciary's facilitative role. I instead suggest that scholars and judges explicitly tailor the relationship between dispute processing institutions and the development of substantive norms. The overarching insistence on judicial imposition of the 'right' legal rule places considerable strain on both the law and the courts. As I have discussed elsewhere,[13] the complex problems revealed by institutional and behavioural analysis of discrimination resist resolution by either generally applicable rules or private, decentralised norms. Relying on purely private solutions suffers from the mirror image of these problems.

This seemingly intractable dilemma—legal intervention as both necessary and problematic—hinges on shared premises about law and judicial role. I want to step back from the substantive equality debate to examine these unarticulated yet foundational conceptions of the law and the judiciary. This analysis builds on the observation that a significant portion of legitimate 'law-making' results from much more dynamic and judicially de-centred interactions than accounted for by the conventional account, both within the workplace context and between formal and informal legal actors.[14] Moreover, I argue that law's role should include creating occasions and incentives for non-state actors to deliberate about norms in context, and to construct conditions of permeability between legal and non-legal actors so that formal law can legitimately and effectively take account of informal normative activity and vice versa. This expansion in conceptions of law's role holds considerable promise in resolving the regulatory dilemma posed by complex discrimination.

This chapter begins by identifying the conception of judicial process and role that recurs in discrimination scholarship drawing on organisational, sociological, psychological, and economic knowledge to critique doctrinal approaches to workplace equality. It then briefly discusses the limitations of this conception of the judiciary, drawing on the interdisciplinary insights used by scholars to critique anti-discrimination doctrine. Finally, building on earlier work, it suggests a conception of the judiciary role that emphasises creating spaces for normative engagement and acting as a catalyst for effective norm elaboration and remediation.

[13] Sturm, above n 1, at 458; and Wisconsin Law Review 2002.

[14] Suchman and L Edelman, 'Legal Rational Myths: The New Institutionalism and the Law and Society Tradition', (1996) 21 *Law & Soc Inquiry* 903.

Unpacking the Implicit Assumptions About Law and Legal Process

The Form and Function of Equality Norms

Scholars disagree about the judiciary's proper response to complex and structural discrimination. Their proposals run the gamut, from assuming direct managerial responsibility[15] to reformulating legal rules[16] to refraining from ruling at all.[17] Despite these profound differences, many intellectual adversaries become fellow travellers when it comes to their implicit view of a legal equality norm's form and function. They agree that legal equality norms are, or at least should be, rules that establish boundaries between lawful and unlawful conduct. These rules must be sufficiently clear, consistent, and general to justify attaching coercive consequences to the rule's violation.

An example demonstrates the rule-enforcement conception's centrality in equality scholarship. In her important article, *The Content of Our Categories*, Linda Krieger embraces a rule-enforcement/boundary-setting definition of legal equality norms. She expresses scepticism about proposals that would impose a duty upon employers to reduce 'cognitively based judgment errors'. Her reservations stem from the current lack of certainty or clarity about how to understand and remediate the problem. Krieger concludes that courts should not intervene until 'we know enough about how to reduce cognition-based judgment errors to enable us to translate such a duty into workable legal rules. . . . If our goal is to reduce race, gender, and ethnicity-based categorical responses, the imposition of a duty of care without defining what specific actions an employer should undertake to fulfil that duty could prove counterproductive'.[18]

Even scholars analyzing legal equality norms operating outside of courts and inside organisations employ a formalistic conception of legal norms. For example, *Internal Dispute Resolution: The Transformation of Civil Rights in the Workplace*, explores the tension between legal and organisational norms and practices in complaint handlers' approaches to resolving discrimination complaints.[19] The authors conclude that law plays a very peripheral role in complaint handlers' orientation toward discrimination. The formalistic conception of law they apply in evaluating complaint handlers' approaches plays a critical role in reaching their conclusion. For them, 'a major goal of legal forums is to define and announce the boundaries

[15] ML Selmi (2003) 'The Price of Discrimination: The Nature of Class Action Employment Discrimination and its Effects', (2003) Texas L Rev MORE INFO.

[16] Oppenheimer, above n 5, at 899; and Schultz, above n 3, at 1693.

[17] Wax, above n 8, at 1129.

[18] Krieger, above n 1, at 1245, 1247. For other examples, see Schultz, above n 3, at 1683 and Post, above n 1, at 1, 17, 30.

[19] L Edelman, C Uggan, and H Erlanger, 'Internal Dispute Resolution: The Transformation of Civil Rights in the Workplace', (1993) 27 *Law & Soc Rev* 497.

of compliance'.[20] They posit that 'claims framed in terms of rights are often absolute'.[21] If law is ambiguous or procedurally oriented, it departs from the ideal of 'law'. Moreover, formal legal standards constitute key measures of law's presence.[22] When complaint handlers construe anti-discrimination law as requiring fair, unbiased treatment, rather than 'adopting the calculus of the courts and EEO agencies'. the authors interpret their conduct to signal a shift from law to management.[23]

A legal norm thus operates under this view as a code of conduct that gives rise to clear obligations to address well-understood problems with clear normative implications. Legal pronouncements should settle disagreements or uncertainties about the nature and scope of problematic activity and its relationship to the generally articulated constitutional or statutory principles calling for judicial interpretation. Less formal and definitive norms, such as those produced through judicially accountable agreements or emerging from administrative—or expert—facilitated problem solving, do not count as legal norms. Nor do the processes requiring parties to generate information and engage in self-assessment about whether legal norms have been violated. Legal norms are the substantive product of post-adjudicatory deliberation by a court, adoption of enforceable regulations by an administrative agency, or statutory enactment by the legislature. Given the EEOC's current inability to promulgate binding regulations and the legislature's enactment of predominantly open-ended statutes, development of legal equality norms for many scholars thus depends on judicial elaboration.

This type of equality norm presupposes the judiciary's capacity to define and redress the problem through centralised articulation of an appropriate legal rule. Complex, poorly understood or normatively uncertain problems strain judicial capacity to craft and justify robust legal rules. These attributes underlie the queasiness apparent in many scholars' efforts to craft rule-based solutions for complex discrimination. The worry is that courts will get it wrong or, in getting it right, compromise their legitimacy as principled elaborators of public norms.

The Role of the Judiciary

The picture of a court that emerges from the anti-discrimination literature is that of a unilateral norm elaborator and enforcer. The judicial task is to figure out what abstract legal norms mean in particular contexts, and then to determine what to order others to do to comply with those more fully elaborated norms (and compensate those injured by non-compliance). The judge's defining role is to produce certain and specific outcomes that will differentiate lawful from unlawful conduct

[20] L Edelman, C Uggan, and H Erlanger, 'Internal Dispute Resolution: The Transformation of Civil Rights in the Workplace', (1993) 27 *Law & Soc Rev*, at 511.
[21] *Ibid*, at 505.
[22] *Ibid*, at 513.
[23] *Ibid*, at 513.

and dictate effective remedies for the latter. Through adjudication, judicial participation in law-making achieves legitimacy: it is public, norm- or precedent-generating, and accountable. Settlement necessarily removes a dispute from the realm of public law and potential norm generation. Underlying much scholarship is the assumption that, when courts deviate from formal adjudication of liability (which they do frequently), they no longer engage in norm elaboration and they depart from their core competency.[24] For courts to consider the adequacy of the institutional architecture that produced the current level of understanding and practice, the processes used to address problems with legal implications, or the subsystems' engagement with those legal norms would be to stray beyond this core function of specifying the governing code of conduct.

Judicial pronouncements resulting from formal adversary process are the hallmark of legitimate and effective judicial intervention. Judges react to factual evidence and legal argument presented through formal proof in court. They receive inputs (evidence and arguments) and produce outputs (legal rules, judgments, and sanctions for non-compliance). Paradigmatic judicial involvement takes place in the courtroom through receiving evidence and argument, and in chambers through detached deliberation and unilateral judgment. The judicial role in discovery and pre-trial motion practice is to narrow and properly frame the issues requiring judicial decision through adjudication and to eliminate issues for which adversary process is unnecessary or inappropriate. Remedial determinations are subsidiary to and in service of the core function of liability determination. Experts and affected stakeholders do not participate in elaborating norms; their role is to supply facts, interpretations, and legal arguments, which are then processed by the judicial decision maker. Interactions outside of those stylised spaces and forms lack the imprimatur of the adversary process, and thus adjudication's presumption of accountability, transparency, and legitimacy.

Owen Fiss has perhaps the most romantic articulation of this directorial conception of judicial role. The central task of the judiciary is to give operative meaning to constitutional values by searching for 'what is true, right or just'.[25] Although Fiss' faith in judicial truth-telling makes him somewhat of an outlier, his basic conception of the judge as unilateral decision maker is more widely shared. Often, this conception operates implicitly, cropping up in the section of the article that proposes doctrinal reform. This scholarship does not necessarily focus on the court's role in addressing discrimination. Its emphasis, instead, is on demonstrating (quite effectively, I might add) that prevailing doctrinal categories distort or misdirect judges' analyses of employers' decision making processes,[26] or that unstated norms and empirical assumptions dictate judicial outcomes in discrimination cases.[27] Relying on insights drawn from psychology, organisational theory, sociology, and critical theory, these scholars show how prevailing doctrinal fails to

[24] J Molot, 'An Old Judicial Role for a New Litigation Era', (2003) 113 *Yale L J* PAGE?.
[25] O Fiss, 'The Forms of Justice', (1979) 93 *Harvard L Rev* 1, 9.
[26] Krieger, above n 1; Schultz, above n 3, at 1683; Oppenheimer, above n 5, at 899.
[27] Minow, above n 5, at 88–9; Post, above n 1, at 1, 17, 30.

account for the role of cognitive bias, dominant value structures, and the practices of racial and gender conventions. When it comes to proposing remedies for these empirical and conceptual blind spots, all eyes turn to the judge, or more precisely, to the judge's capacity to craft new rules or frameworks that are adequately sensitive to the complexities of race, gender, and other 'practices' of difference. Does the court have the right operative framework for understanding and explaining the social practices of gender and race?[28] Do 'we know enough about how to reduce cognition-based judgment errors to enable us to translate such a duty into workable legal rules'?[29]

These questions lead one to ask how courts goes about elaborating specific standards, particularly when they are interpreting ambiguous legal texts. Again, Fiss is perhaps the most didactic in his discussion of method.[30] Particularly in cases involving injunctive relief, judges use intuition, logic, and analogy to apply general law to specific facts and then to issue pronouncements. 'The text clothes the court with the authority to give specific meaning to the ideal of equity—to choose among the various subgoals contained within the ideal'.[31] What is needed is just the right rule. If judges get good enough information through the adjudicative process, processed through the right cognitive frame, they can provide just that.

Other scholars have taken a less sanguine view of purely intuitive, logical and textual methods for developing and applying discrimination doctrine. They challenge the capacity of judges to stand outside the practices they must assess, showing instead that 'anti-discrimination law always begins and ends in history, which means that it must participate in the very practices that it seeks to alter and to regulate'.[32] They strive to expand judges' capacities to identify their own preconceptions and stereotypes, and to learn from experts presenting current empirical understandings of discrimination and from those with unfamiliar and suppressed perspectives. Acknowledging that judges, as humans, cannot self-identify the range of perspectives that they are failing to see or the preconceptions that are influencing their decision making, these scholars gesture toward expanding participation by experts,[33] amici, and parties in the adjudicative process.[34]

Yet, these scholars seem to accept the hegemony of a rule-elaboration and enforcement regime, with judges developing norms exclusively by imposing a decision, after full consideration of competing perspectives and data. According to this conception, judges dictate to other actors about the details of legal norms as they apply to new circumstances. For norm elaboration to occur, they assume that the judiciary must choose among competing views about how to give concrete meaning to ambiguous standards, rather than to facilitate a participatory process

[28] Post, above n 1, at 1, 17, 30; Shultz, above n 3, at 1683.
[29] Krieger, above n 1, at 1245.
[30] JL Cohen, *Regulating Intimacy: A New Legal Paradigm* 143 (2002).
[31] Fiss, above n 25, at 173.
[32] Post, above n 1, at 17.
[33] Krieger, unpublished, at 7.
[34] Minow, above n 5, at 88–9.

of public, accountable, informed, and principled norm elaboration.[35] Even in cases involving other public bodies involved in some norm-generating role, such as administrative agencies, the focus is primarily on evaluating whether the agency got it right, or at least whether they acted within their authority in interpreting and enforcing the applicable norm. Once a court rules on the applicability of legal norms in a particular case, extended interaction (either with the court or within the relevant institution) questioning the meaning and implementation of the legal norm suggests failure—failure to articulate a precise enough rule, failure to embody the ideal of dispassionate adjudication, or failure to achieve compliance with the applicable rule.

This formalistic conception of law may explain why some discrimination scholars question the legitimacy and desirability of more interactive, consent-based resolutions of conflicts involving public norms. Scholars like Fiss are 'against settlement' because they assumes that resolution by agreement necessarily detracts from the judiciary's core function of articulating public values.[36] Conflict resolution that takes place outside of formal adjudication is 'bargaining in the shadow of the law'—at best a distant and non-binding approximation of public values and more likely a product of personal preferences discounted by bargaining power. Settlement and internal dispute resolution are taken necessarily to mean the inevitable privatisation and managerialisation of law, thereby undermining its normative force.[37]

This view of judicial role, method, and relationship places employment discrimination remedies involving institutional redesign in an uneasy relationship to the articulation of rights. Remedies for complex discrimination often involve redesigning systems, transforming institutional culture, and realigning incentives—practices that connect to but extend beyond the conduct constituting the legal violation. The liability norm does not provide criteria for choosing among those values unrelated to the legal violation itself, although it does shape the definition of the problem to be remedied. For example, a legal violation may consist of maintaining an arbitrary selection system that fosters decision making biased against women. A non-arbitrary system could take a variety of forms, depending on considerations unrelated to bias minimisation (such as efficiency and consistency with organisational culture). Why should judges make these decisions, if judicial legitimacy depends upon adversary process designed to interpret

[35] For example, Linda Krieger's remedy for the current gap between Title VII doctrine and current psychological theory is to have legal actors 'accurately and completely specify the various ways in which race can adversely skew an employment decision maker's perception and judgment of a particular applicant or employee and adversely affect his or her employment opportunities'. The adversarial, jurocentric method for revising legal norms remains uninterrogated, but the substance of current doctrine is 'naturalised' to reflect developments in empirical social science. Krieger acknowledges the promise of soft law such as jury instructions and advocate argumentation, but seems to value these legal forms as avenues leading to a fully elaborated, judicially imposed specification of desired norms, behaviors, levers, and doctrinal models, rather than as appropriate sites for ongoing and contingent norm elaboration.

[36] O Fiss, 'Against Settlement', (1984) 93 *Yale L J* 1073.

[37] Edelman, Uggen, and Erlanger, above n 19, at 406, 442.

constitutional or statutory principle, and these principles do not govern remedial decision making? The judiciary as rule-elaborator and enforcer thus faces a legitimacy deficit when it unilaterally imposes remedial choices.[38]

Remedial solutions developed by intermediaries, such as monitors, masters, and experts employed by the judiciary to shore up their remedial design capacity, are similarly suspect. Intermediaries who facilitate the participatory formulation of remedies by affected parties do not invite the same legitimacy problems, but their role tends to be viewed as expedient rather than principled, designed to settle particular disputes and not to generate public norms.

The relationship between legal and workplace norms

How does (and should) law interact with organisational and cultural norms to reshape the conditions and practices constituting complex discrimination? This law/norm interaction is quite important to the identification and remediation of complex discrimination. The question, for example, of whether reasonable people would experience conduct as hostile and abusive involves an inquiry into the relevant expectations, power relationships, and gender patterns.[39] Professional norms about effective management and grievance processing may affect judicial allocation of legal responsibility for detecting and responding to exclusionary practices.[40] Effective remedial decision making also depends on successfully negotiating the relationship between law and norms. Complex bias reflects and is sustained by informal and organisational norms, incentives, and practices. Changing exclusionary practices requires addressing the interaction of identities such as gender and race with power, merit, and status within particular normative communities.[41]

Scholars (and courts) have long recognised law's influence, as well as its dependence upon norms.[42] Indeed, employment discrimination law's paramount aim has often been described as fostering informal norms of equal participation in the workplace, and its primary obstacle as the resistance of informal normative systems to formal legal intervention. The thumbprint of formalism is detectible in this scholarship nonetheless. Formal conceptions of law permeate the analysis of *how* law influences norms: the stock story emphasises the output of formal legal process determined by judges. Law influences norms, if at all, by judicial calibration of the rules and the remedial consequences of their violation. Law is produced in the courthouse and the legislature by formal state actors with official power to generate and enforce law. Non-judicial actors operate in the world of norms, and as consumers, manipulators, or resistors of these legal products. The impact of the

[38] Fiss, above n 36, at 1073.

[39] *Harris v Forklift Systems, Inc*, 510 US 17 (1993).

[40] *Farragher v City of Boca Rotan*, 524 US 775 (1998); Edelman, Uggen and Erlanger, above n 19.

[41] Minow, above n 5, at 88–9; Post, above n 1, at 17; Sturm, above n 1 at 478.

[42] Engel and Munger, CITATION 1996; Yngvesson, CITATION 1988; and Merry CITATION)

processes producing legal outcomes, and of the interactions of formal legal actors with stakeholders outside the domains producing formal legal outputs, does not figure into the law/norm relationship.

In the 'law and norms' literature, for example, the law/norm relationship has often been posed as a choice: are the courts (through the imposition of legal rules) better at formulating the appropriate across-the-board norm, or are private actors operating through market interactions, custom and practice more able to develop workable norms?[43] Will coercive enforcement disrupt prevailing norms and incentives of non-legal actors or simply underscore their legitimacy?[44] Depending upon the answer to these questions, many scholars recommend a legal outcome: the law should incorporate, supplant, or defer to informal norms. Thus the question of whether courts should intervene to address complex discrimination would be cast in terms of whether courts have the capacity to figure out what informal norms or processes are and should be. If so, the courts will tailor a legal rule based on that correct understanding. If not, they will stay out.

The concept of 'bargaining in the shadow of the law', coined by Robert Mnookin and Louis Kornhauser in a much-cited article,[45] acknowledges that law and norms interact, but their analysis focuses on law's formalistic aspects. Law casts a shadow on negotiations and decisions that take place outside of formal legal process. Legal rules establish the range within which informal settlements operate, and can even influence the terms governing informal agreements by legitimating particular principles dictating how the case would come out in court. Non-legal actors take law into account as the fixed outer boundary of their private conflict resolution. If law does migrate into the language of organisational culture, some commentators treat this translation process as necessarily denoting privatisation and managerialisation (not internalisation or elaboration).[46] Nor does the 'shadow of the law' metaphor take account of any impact that non-legal norms have on the development of the legal principles.

As Lauren Edelman, Christopher Uggan, and Howard Erlanger have shown, the causal arrows can go in both directions: the results of the norm generation process in each domain influence the substantive calculus in the other.[47] Edelman and her co-authors point out the 'endogeneity' of legal norms: courts sometimes incorporate the norms of regulated groups into the judicial formulation of the legal rules. This work also documents the important role of norm intermediaries—lawyers, human resource administrators, organisational consultants—in transporting norms between legal and organisational domains.[48] Their account, however, emphasises law's formal dimensions—adversary process and the legal

[43] EB Rock and ML Wachter, 'The Enforceability of Norms and the Employment Relationship', (1996) 144 *University of Pennsylvania L Rev* 1913.

[44] Bernstein CITATION; D Charny, 'Illusions of a Spontaneous Order, "Norms" in Contractual Relationships', (1996) 144 *University of Pennsylvania L Rev* 1841, 1852.

[45] Mnookin and Kornhauser, above n 10, at 950.

[46] Edelman, Uggen, and Erlanger, above n 19, at 406, 442.

[47] *Ibid*, at 406.

[48] *Ibid*.

rules it produces. Intermediation of formal law takes place outside legal process, in informal, professional or managerial networks. In this narrative, courts act as passive consumers of normative outputs produced by non-legal actors outside of the legal domain. The judiciary does not actively shape how local or professional norms take account of existing legal norms, or the circumstances under these informal norms will influence public and enforceable legal norms.

The Value of Bridging Law and Norms

It is striking to contrast scholars' static paradigm of judicial role with their dynamic analysis of discrimination that drives the critique of the dominant doctrinal paradigm. Formalism is problematic as a unitary method of norm elaboration for complex discrimination. General rules don't really tell you much about how structural bias operates in particular settings, or why challenged decisions or processes are exclusionary. Detailed prescriptions are problematic because, as detached, centralised adjudicators, the judiciary lacks the deep knowledge of local circumstance or the occasions for ongoing adaptation to context needed to solve local problems. Judicial mastery of a particular workplace dynamic does not get around the dilemma of generalisability; moreover, it will likely trigger concerns about judicial legitimacy and competence, not to mention questions about judicial resources.

Yet, complete privatisation abandons the law's role in generating public norms. It would also relegate the intended beneficiaries of employment discrimination laws to the informal norms, power dynamics, and problem solving capacities of their particular workplace. For this reason, many scholars worry about the trend to encourage informal resolution of employment discrimination disputes.[49] Insistence on rule elaboration and enforcement as the preferred mode of judicial interaction thus disables courts in responding to conditions that implicate publicly articulated values.

Situated knowledge generated through reflective interaction may be more productive than detached logical consideration in identifying the normative significance of challenged practices, what sustains them, and how they can be changed. It may be important to know how particular practices affect members of identified groups, how and why those patterns persist over time, what they mean for the status of group members, and whether alternatives exist that could minimise exclusion. Identification, definition, and remediation of group based inequality requires a process of problem solving. That process identifies the structural dimensions of a problem through an insistent inquiry of tracing back to root causes. It enables participants to articulate norms in context as part of the process

[49] CITATAION (Silbey and Sarat 1989; CITATION Delgado 1985; T Grillo, 'The Mediation Alternative: Process Dangers for Women' (1991) 100 *Yale L Rev* 6.

of determining why particular circumstances pose a problem requiring remediation. It encourages organisations to gather and share information enabling that analysis to proceed. It emphasises developing individual and institutional capacity and incentives to respond to problems thus revealed. It fosters the design, evaluation, and comparison of solutions that involve the stakeholders who participate in the day-to-day patterns that produce bias and exclusion. It also entails reframing the aspirations motivating change to reflect these interlocking problems and constituencies. Legal rules resulting from logical analysis do not elucidate the aims, scope and strategies of this essential problem solving.

As a practical matter, judges and litigants resist participation in rule-enforcement type judicial regulation of complex discrimination. Courts have been extremely reluctant to assume direct responsibility for constructing managerial solutions for subtle bias, based on concerns about institutional competence, resource constraints, and uncertainty about the problem itself. Employees are reluctant to utilise formal process to complain about practices that they are not sure count as discrimination. Employers resist identifying problems within their workplace if they perceive that doing so will essentially do plaintiffs' counsel's work for them. In fact, the formalistic, adjudicatory, rule-enforcement paradigm does not fully describe how judges in fact fulfil their norm elaboration function. The prospect of continued judicial involvement in addressing complex discrimination thus necessitates surfacing these less formal judicial modes and thus expanding law beyond the model of judiciary as rule-enforcer.

Law as Catalyst of Normative Elaboration and Problem Solving

Expanding the Form and Function of Equality Norms

Rules enforced by sanctions remain an important backstop and platform for normative elaboration in the area of equality jurisprudence. Some conduct violates clear and well-understood principles. At this point in our history, deliberate exclusion based on race, sex, religion, age is a normatively easy case, as is quid pro quo sexual harassment.[50] Rules solidify and preserve well-established baseline norms and aspirations. They also legitimate normative discourse about the domains they regulate. Rules dictating that defendants 'stop doing that!' can effectively remedy deliberate discrimination. Compensation to those harmed by intentional discrimination seems directly connected to the wrongful conduct and important to law's purpose and legitimacy. Moreover, the hammer of substantial compensatory damages and coercive sanctions may be necessary as a first step to 'destabilise the

[50] *Burlington Industries, Inc v Ellerth*, 524 US 742 (1998).

status quo' and open up institutions to an effective problem solving approach.[51] This approach depends on the presence of some company insiders who assume responsibility for interpreting law to prompt internal norm elaboration and implementation. Coercion is sometimes needed to bring companies to the point where they take equity problems seriously, particularly in organisations that have resisted addressing pervasive discrimination. The 'complex discrimination' discussion assumes the continued operation of legal rules backed by coercive sanctions in areas of normative simplicity.

What about the role of equality norms in addressing more complicated, less well understood bias—problems that cannot be isolated to a particular act or actor, that involve dynamics of interaction and evaluation producing marginalisation or exclusion, that are inextricably linked with activities that we actually value? Is there any way for courts to particulate in the elaboration of norms for problems that resist resolution through rules? Can equality norms be dynamic, responsive, and contextually contingent and still robust, in the sense of influencing private actors to engage in normatively desirable conduct?

A more dynamic and expansive conception of law's form and function (building on such conceptions developed in international human rights and corporate governance domains) offers a way forward. In areas of (normative and remedial) uncertainty and complexity, the function of judicially articulated legal norms is not to establish definitive boundaries of acceptable conduct which, if violated, warrant sanction. It is instead to prompt—and create occasions for—normatively motivated inquiry and remediation by non-legal actors in response to signals of problematic conditions or practices. This legal equality norm is one of inquiry, analysis, reflection and remediation. Law imposes an obligation to inquire upon a showing of an unexplained pattern of bias. The legal consequence of exposing a discrimination problem through this normative inquiry is not the imposition of a sanction; it is instead the imposition of a legally enforceable obligation to correct the problem. This attenuation (but not elimination) of coercion relieves the pressure for a clear, before-the-fact rule (which is needed to justify sanctions for failure to comply) and still maintains incentives and opportunities to elaborate robust norms in context.[52]

Law's involvement sustains the normative dimension as a relevant and legitimate part of the problem solving process. It creates occasions and incentives for parties to convene, thereby solving collective action problems. It introduces 'rule of law' values (such as participation, transparency, and reasoned decision making) to deliberations by non-judicial actors. Courts and other public institutions also provide the architecture to compare and build on the outcomes of this contextual problem solving. Over time, this process promotes the development new legal norms when clear, recurring patterns and normative consensus emerge.

[51] Liebman and Sabel, above.

[52] In a similar vein, Silbey and Sarat show that because informal conflict resolution doesn't require violation of the law to trigger action and does not stigmatise participants, intervention can be earlier and unconstrained by jurisdictional boundaries (Silbey and Sarat, 1989).

There is a procedural dimension to this substantive responsibility to inquire about identified and unexplained problems. What if we think about the exercise of judicial power to prompt inquiry as on a continuum? Each phase of the conflict resolution process offers an occasion for bringing together affected and potentially responsible stakeholders to deliberate, albeit with different levels of legal obligation to take action on what is learned from that inquiry.

What makes a condition or practice sufficiently 'problematic' to trigger an obligation to correct? This would require a prima facia showing that a condition or practice causes unexplained and unjustified exclusion or marginalisation. Congress has articulated general, ambiguous equality norms that potentially comprise a variety of equality theories, or mediating principles, such as anti-subordination, equal access, or equal treatment. Individuals or groups must show how a condition or practice raises concerns under one or more of these mediating principles. Courts and administrative agencies can and indeed have begun to identify indicators of potentially discriminatory conditions or practices. Enduring and unexplained patterns of lower promotion rates by members of particular groups are one such signal. Unequal participation by the targeted group in informal networks or access to mentors and training are another. Conduct or comments of a sexual or gendered nature, but that are susceptible of multiple interpretations are a third. These practices alone may not signify gender or racial bias. But in some contexts and circumstances, they do, particularly in the absence of investigation and institutional response. When the problem is complex and contextually contingent, the court lacks an adequate basis for imposing a unitary, overarching mediating principle. It is in a position, however, to trigger attention to a potential problem, and to stimulate problem solving that engages with the normative significance of this potentially problematic activity.

One interesting aspect of these signals is that they demonstrate the link between 'right' and 'remedy' in defining the normative significance of complex bias. An uninterrogated pattern of exclusion or subtle harassment often looms larger and in fact may produce greater inequality than the same conduct that prompts analysis and change. The institution's failure to respond contributes to, and indeed, can become a crucial element of the discrimination experience. This is in part because of the incremental, cumulative, and systemic causes of much complex discrimination.[53] In these areas, inequality can result from the interaction of micro-level interactions and inadequate structural responses capable of interrupting these cumulative patterns. Conversely, prompt inquiry into and remediation of problematic conditions or practices can affect whether that pattern ultimately produces, and is experienced as producing, discrimination. The capacity to identify and respond to problems is thus integrally related to the normative significance of the underlying conditions. Process becomes part of the substantive meaning of equality. Elaborating a general norm in context is crucial to formulating a

[53] J Cole, 'A Theory of Limited Differences: Explaining the Productivity Puzzle in Science', in *Women in the Scientific Community* (Zuckerman and Cole, 1991).

remedial response, which in turns deepens and even alters the understanding of the aspirational norm. This dynamic relationship between problem identification and remediation provides further support for expanding beyond rules for complex discrimination.

The Role of the Judiciary

How does the judiciary participate in this norm elaboration and capacity building process? More precisely, is there a role for the judiciary that is consistent with the judiciary's practices, competencies, self-conceptions, and institutional role? Are there ways, in addition to formal adjudication, for courts to participate in public, accountable norm elaboration? How can they engage in a less directorial relationship to non-legal actors in the norm generation process and still act like judges?

Crafting a workable judicial role is doable. But it requires expanding our analytical lens beyond liability decisions and examining actual judicial practices that intervene in and influence workplace norms. This inquiry moves beyond formalistic notions of law and judicial role, just as more nuanced understandings of discrimination resulted from a functional and institutional methodology. By this, I mean examining the full range of normative activity in which the courts and the law participates, as well as the array of actual and potential channels for making that normative activity transparent, public, and precedential.

This pragmatist analysis also takes seriously the impact of courts' concurrent and, for many judges, core function as adjudicators on their non-adjudicatory activities, and how that identity constrains judicial role development. In this sense, this approach differs from the position articulated by Malcolm Feeley and Ed Rubin that judges are just like other public actors in their role as implementers of public policy. Feeley and Rubin 'assign the judge the same range of tasks that are assigned to other administrators'.[54] They pay little attention to the 'how' question—how judges participate in public problem solving. Their analysis of judicial legitimacy and efficacy lumps together distinct forms of judicial problem solving activity, from director to broker to catalyst.[55] This blanket acceptance glosses over valid concerns about certain types of judicial intervention. The legitimacy (and, in my view, long term efficacy) of a judicial actor who assumes direct responsibility for institutional redesign differs markedly from that of a judge who uses the tools and processes of the judiciary to prompt responsible actors to engage in effective problem solving. Judges' willingness to participate in problem solving under conditions of complexity turns on the availability of a role that is consistent with their tools, practices, and relationships.

[54] M Feeley and E Rubin, 'Responsive Law and the Judicial Process: Implications for the Judicial Function', in *Legality and Community: On the Intellectual Legacy of Philip Selznick* 249, 262 (R Kagan, M Krieger, and K Winston, eds, 2002).

[55] S Sturm, 'Resolving the Remedial Dilemma: Strategies of Judicial Intervention in Prisons', (1990) 138 University of Pennsylvania L Rev 305.

I have identified three related judicial roles that operate in this intersection of efficacy and legitimacy:

1. Structuring occasions for collective norm development and problem solving in the penumbra of formal judicial process;
2. Increasing non-legal actors' capacity to conduct conflict resolution and problem solving that generates and institutionalises efficient, fair, and workable norms; and
3. Developing the capacity of mediating actors, such as experts and administrative agencies, to connect the domains of law and norms.

Legal norms thus develop not only through liability determinations, but also through legally structured occasions for deliberating about the relationship between norms and practice. These practices cast courts in a crucial but limited role in addressing problems that implicate public norms but are insufficiently understood and/or resistant to centralised rule enforcement. They emphasise law's role in structuring focal points of intra- and inter-institutional normative activity.[56] Each of these roles could be (and will be) the subject of its own article. I undertake here only to give enough concrete meaning to these roles to allow a discussion about their viability and desirability as role conception for addressing complex discrimination.

Norm Generation in the Penumbra of Formal Adjudication

Discussions of courts' role in elaborating equality norms typically involve liability determinations (or, in the critiques of alternative dispute resolution, the absence thereof): Have courts rendered a published opinion determining whether liability does or could flow from the application of legal norm to a particular set of facts?[57] This focus on liability determinations and rule making as the location of normative elaboration is understandable. These determinations produce a public normative outcome in the form of a published opinion, which is widely available and serves as a guide or binding precedent for future decisions. They result from a formal process designed to enable participation and principled decision making. This process also incorporates caution, certainty, and predictability that justify the state's imposition of coercive authority.

Liability determinations are not, however, the most frequent or necessarily the preferred occasions for judicial participation in norm elaboration about complex discrimination. Courts regularly participate in deliberations about the meaning and scope of norms as a necessary part of reaching other decisions that are less directly tied to coercive imposition of rules or liability. They do this both by assessing the potential viability of discrimination theories in pre-liability (and sometimes post-liability) type decisions and, importantly, by structuring occasions for parties to deliberate about the normative implications of complex discrimination

[56] Charney, above n 44, at 1841.
[57] CITATATION (Albiston 1999:869)

and strategies for its remediation as part of moving a case forward. In both of these roles, courts can participate in and foster normative development in a more open-ended and exploratory posture. Judicial involvement can also influence the way non-legal actors negotiate and deliberate, by paying attention to the methods of inquiry and governance structures that produce informal norms and agreements and weighting more heavily the outcomes that result from principled, accountable, and participatory practices. Courts could also encourage and facilitate sharing of the results of less formal norm elaboration in its penumbra to encourage public norm development.

It is important to emphasise that this does not mean necessarily requiring processes that mirror the features of formal adjudication. As Kenneth Winston has argued, 'the form [due process] should take depends crucially on the setting in which it finds its application. Specific norms or rules should depend on the purpose of the enterprise and even its stage of development'.[58] Indeed, under some circumstances, insisting on adversary process as the measure of fair and effective process would defeat the values motivating due process, such as participation, information generation, and effective problem solving, by importing the previously discussed limitations of a rule enforcement approach into the informal arena. Courts would instead encourage parties to develop (and the court would then assess the adequacy of) criteria of adequate process in light of the purposes and attributes of the particular project. Processes or outcomes could be precedential (in the sense of providing a normative or remedial solution that others can learn from) even if they are not formally binding. Parties' full and fair participation could be achieved through creative institutional design and governance, even if they are not represented by counsel. Decisions could be public and norm generating, even if they are not published by Westlaw and Lexis. Courts could develop standards for evaluating informal agreements and expert opinions and reward those that that give general legal norms concrete meaning in the particular context, articulate criteria by which their agreements can be evaluated, and generate the information needed to evaluate resulting normative assessments and agreements.

The judicial process builds in a variety of decision points that invite less binding norm elaboration. Norm elaboration occurs as part of a decision about whether to keep the judicial machinery open as a public forum for engaging with a particular type of problem. One could look at decisions denying summary judgment in the same light.[59] The decision at stake may also involve the question of who can legitimately participate in the problem solving process. It sometimes entails assessments of the type and quality of information needed to participate in the problem solving process or to justify reaching a particular outcome. These types of questions cast the court in a role beyond determining whether to impose liability for violation of a rule. Courts either consciously or unwittingly craft

[58] K Winston, 'Lessons from the Right of Silence', in *Legality and Community: On the Intellectual Legacy of Philip Selznick* 389, 392 (R Kagan, M Krieger, and K Winston, eds, 2002).

[59] Albiston, above n 57, at 869.

process frameworks that potentially shape the capacity and incentives of non-legal actors to engage in effective problem solving and accountable norm elaboration. These non-binding occasions for normative elaboration have the potential to be public, norm generating, accountable, and precedential, if these terms are given operative rather than formalistic meaning. If, for example, consent decrees are published and used as benchmarks of new normative understandings and remedial responses, they can have general and precedential value even if they are not binding.[60] Web publication and developing professional practice networks make possible the dissemination of informal normative activity.

A few examples might help clarify the meaning of norm elaboration in the penumbra of judicial rule-enforcement. Class certification decisions require courts to assess plaintiffs' theory of discrimination in deciding that there are questions of law and fact common to the class, that the representative claims are typical, and that remediation would warrant an injunction affecting the class as a whole (Rule 23, FRCP) Class certification decisions frequently discuss in some detail the types of problems asserted as discriminatory by plaintiffs and whether they are sufficient systemic to warrant class treatment.[61] This is not a determination of the likelihood of success at trial,[62] but rather one of whether the case is in a posture to warrant group-based resolution. Class certification also can create a framework for assessing whether participants engage in legitimate and effective norm generation if a class is certified.[63] They function as a focal point for defining the contours of a conflict, identifying the participants (including employees, key company officials, and outside experts) who should be involved, developing the data needed to understand if and why systemic problems persist, and creating ground rules for effective and accountable participation. Class certification is thus an occasion to establish a governance structure that can produce fair, effective, and principled norm generation.[64] They are particularly important because most cases settle following class certification.

Similarly, the decision to approve a class action settlement, if taken seriously by the court, involves an assessment of the adequacy of the process that produces the settlement as well as the reasonableness of the settlement itself. Judicial opinions evaluating the adequacy of settlements also address the plaintiffs' theories of discrimination and remediation as part of the process of determining whether the proposed settlement is reasonable. Although this inquiry is too often a judicial rubber stamp, it need not be. It does offer an occasion for the court, which some

[60] M Galanter, The Quality of Settlements, (1988) J Dispute Res 55.

[61] *Latino Officers Association City of New York v City of New York*, 209 FRD 79 (SDNY 2002); *Webb v Merck & Co*, 206 FRD 399 (ED Pa 2002); *Beck v Boeing*, 203 FRD 459 (WD Wash. 2001); *Butler v Home Depot, Inc*, 1996 US Dist LEXIS 3370 (ND Cal 1996).

[62] R Bone and D Evans, 'Class Certification and the Substantive Merits', (2002) 51 *Duke L J* 1251.

[63] *Cf* A LaHay, 'Fundamental Principles for Class Action Governance', (2003) 37 *Indiana L Rev* 65 (proposing process requirements that would enable courts to play this role in small claims class actions).

[64] S Issacharoff, 'Governance and Legitimacy in the Law of Class Actions', (1999) Sup Ct Rev 337, 367.

courts have taken seriously, to review the adequacy of the governance process and the resulting agreement. Courts could develop criteria for evaluating settlements that would take seriously the norm elaboration function of consent decrees, even if the terms of the agreement do not constitute precedent in the formal sense of the word. They could pay attention to the process by which decrees are formulated, the adequacy of participation, and the sufficiency of the information generated through the problem solving process. This type of process review might remedy the legitimacy deficit courts face in monitoring and enforcing consent decrees by offering a process based justification for backing a private agreement with state enforcement resources and authority. The prospect of a robust process evaluation could induce parties to develop meaningful ways of including affected stakeholders, to develop a workable problem solving process as part of the negotiations, and to elaborate the equality theory underlying the settlement, whether it would in fact present a viable claim at trial.[65] They may also spell out the parties' remediation theories and strategies.

Decisions about the admissibility and weight of expert testimony also require courts to assess the adequacy and viability of plaintiffs' discrimination theories.[66] A relevancy determination necessarily involves consideration of the relationship between the expert evidence and an underlying theory of discrimination.[67] For example, as part of its consideration of the admissibility of expert testimony, the court in *Butler v Home Depot* articulated several possible discrimination theories that would support the relevance of expert testimony 'as to the causes, manifestations, and consequences of gender stereotyping as well as the organisational circumstances which allow such stereotypes to flourish'.[68] These included the failure of Home Depot to take steps to correct stereotyped decision making, notwithstanding its awareness that the problem existed and that current practices were inadequate to remedy the resulting gender bias.

Broadening conceptions of judicial role to include prompting and keeping open normative deliberation could provide a workable framework for courts' pre- and post liability involvement with complex discrimination. Decisions about discovery, party and expert participation, settlement, and out-of court problem-solving would be seen as occasions to (1) bring together those with responsibility for, knowledge of, concern about, and expertise in the potentially problematic conditions; (2) establish the heightened authority and validity of non-adjudicatory deliberations that functionally satisfy core legitimacy and accountability concerns, (3) create incentives for non-judicial actors to develop and demonstrate the capacity to solve problems and to identify the norms and criteria by which those

[65] *Molski v Gleich*, 318 F3d 937 (9th Cir. 2002).

[66] *Butler v Home Depot, Inc*, 984 F Supp 1257 (ND Cal. 1997); *Collier v Bradley University*, 113 F Supp 2d 1235 (CD Ill. 2000).

[67] L Walker and J Monahan, 'Social Facts: Scientific Methodology as Legal Precedent', (1988) 76 *California L Rev* 877. T Meares and B Harcourt, 'Foreword: Transparent Adjudication and Social Science Research in Constitutional Criminal Procedure', (2000) 90 *J Crim L & Criminology*, 733, 1264.

[68] Meares and Harcourt, above n 67, at 1264.

problem solving practices should be evaluated; and (4) share and evaluate the results of this problem solving and conflict resolution. Courts would focus less on getting it right all by themselves and more on determining that there is sufficient reason to be concerned about complex discrimination to warrant sustained and publicly accountable problem solving by non-legal actors.

Moreover, there are some potential advantages to norm elaboration in the penumbra of judicial power that critics have not taken into account. Courts are more likely to remain involved in addressing complex discrimination if they are not imposing a general rule or assuming direct responsibility for institutional problem solving. They are also constructing an interactive relationship with those responsible for addressing complex discrimination, without actually administering private institutions. This view of judicial role enables courts to avoid the dilemmas facing courts operating solely within the rule enforcement conception.

Shaping Non-Legal Actors' Participation in Effective Normative Elaboration and Remediation

Courts also can shape norms for addressing complex discrimination by creating the architecture to prompt effective problem solving and conflict resolution by non-legal actors, and then developing points of permeability between legal and non-legal arenas so that public norms can emerge out of that local norm generation process.[69] The judiciary becomes involved in addressing complex discrimination when there is a strong indication that particular systems and practices are failing in ways that fall within the purview of generally articulated equality aspirations. In contexts that resist resolution by a clearly defined rule, judicial intervention supply incentives for employers to implement effective internal problem-solving and conflict resolution mechanisms, to evaluate their effectiveness, and to learn from the efforts of others facing similar problems. Coercion is used to induce employers to develop robust internal problem solving mechanisms to address and prevent structural bias, and to sanction failure to take steps needed to address identified. They do this by insisting that employers, with the help of inside and outside collaborators, develop and justify working criteria for evaluating the effectiveness of informal mechanisms. Courts are then in a position to assess employers' justification for and compliance with their effectiveness criteria. This enables courts to function as a catalyst, rather than as a de facto employment director or a deferrer to employers' unaccountable choices.

This structural role has assumed heightened significance because of the explosion of interest in alternative dispute resolution as a way of resolving employment discrimination disputes. Judicial doctrine has encouraged employers to develop internal dispute resolution and problem solving mechanisms.[70] The EEOC has

[69] Sturm, above n 55, at 305.

[70] *Farragher v City of Boca Rotan*, 524 US 775 (1998); *Burlington Industries v Ellerth*, 524 US 742 (1998); *Gilmer v Interstate/Johnson Lane Corporation*, 500 US 20 (1991).

embraced mediation as a method resolving discrimination charges.[71] Employers have instituted a wide range of dispute resolution processes, including ombuds officers, mediation, peer review, open door policies, and arbitration.[72]

The move to alternative dispute resolution ('ADR') has raised concern among scholars and practitioners who value the judiciary's role in elaborating and holding employers accountable for compliance with public norms. The worry is that ADR (or internal dispute resolution ('IDR') when it takes place inside an organisation) is necessarily private, non-norm generating, and unaccountable.[73] As David Charny put it, reliance on informal systems is problematic 'because one loses the 'public goods' associated with more formal litigation: development of a set of precedents, public revelation about information about important policy matters . . . and the use of judicial decision to propagate and reinforce social norms'.[74] Scholars have also expressed concern that the processes used to produce settlements may be unfair, particularly for addressing zero-sum problems involving disputants with unequal power.[75]

This critique assumes that the move to IDR necessarily displaces judicial involvement in norm generation processes and outcomes. It also assumes that IDR is by definition individualistic (not systemic) in its orientation, private (not transparent) in its operation, instrumental (not normative) in its analysis, *ad hoc* (not precedent-setting) in its results, and unaccountable in its process and implementation.[76] To the extent that informal processes currently fit this description, these concerns are well-founded. Indeed, research shows that these processes are all that employers claim, and are sometimes used to 'bullet-proof' a company rather than remedy problems.[77] However, it is important to separate critiques of current practice from normative theories about the appropriate relationship between courts and informal conflict resolution. The judiciary can and sometimes does play a role in shaping the terms under which informal systems operate to address discrimination. Courts have the opportunity to assess the adequacy of the processes and to consider the normative outcome of the results. When executed in keeping with this role, judicial intervention introduces a level of accountability and genuine participation that is absent from ADR involving purely contractual norms. Judges can evaluate whether a system is sufficiently robust, accountable, and norm generating to justify private involvement in publicly relevant norm elaboration.

[71] McDermott, O'Barr, and Bowers, 'An Evaluation of the Equal Opportunity Commission Mediation Program', http://www.eeoc.gov/mediate/report/index.html. (2000).

[72] KVW Stone, 'Dispute Resolution in the Boundaryless Workplace', (2001) 16 *Ohio S J Dispute Resolution* 467, 480; Sturm, above n 1.

[73] CITATION (Abraham 2003; CITATION Edwards 1986; Fiss, above n 36, at 1073.

[74] Charney, above n 44, at 1852.

[75] Abraham, above n 71; Grillo, above n 49; Van Wezel Stone, above n 70, at 467, 480; and Fiss, above n 36, at 1073.

[76] Edelman, Erlanger, and Lande, above n 19; Grillo, above n 49.

[77] CITATION Bisom-Rapp 1999:959, 967–71; Edelman, Erlanger, and Lande, above n 19.

With judicial involvement in assessing and publicising adequacy criteria, IDR has the potential to be norm generating, transparent, and accountable, at least at the systemic level. These systems build in a process of gathering data about recurring patterns that trigger concern about systemic problems, provide a regular mechanism for reflecting about those patterns, use employee and expert participation in designing and monitoring the system to assure its fairness and legitimacy, and institutionalise opportunities to develop and revise institutional norms and practices that respond to the problems identified through data analysis. Intel's conflict resolution system, described in *Second Generation Employment Discrimination: A Structural Approach*, has built in many of these features.[78] So has the National Institute of Health in designing its Center for Cooperative Resolution, which is the subject of a current study.[79]

Courts could, and in some instances have, evaluated internal dispute resolution systems with criteria that relate to the legitimacy and efficacy of the conflict resolution or problem solving process. Sexual harassment and judicial evaluation of subjective employment systems are two areas where courts have made gestures in this direction. Thus far, the criteria have been unevenly developed, without an explicit emphasis on building the capacity and incentives of non-legal actors to engage in norm elaboration and problem solving. Broadening the court's conception of its role to include this crucial function could shore up the lower courts' spotty performance to date in enforcing the Supreme Court's embrace of a structural role that measures decision making processes in relation to their effectiveness in preventing and addressing problems. This role is also sensitive to judicial competency concerns. Courts are not themselves developing the criteria and architecture for these processes, but rather they are insisting that those who use these processes develop and justify effectiveness criteria.

Promoting Mediating Actors' Capacity to Bridge Legal and Non-Legal Normative Practice

Finally, courts play an important role in influencing how governmental actors (such as the Equal Employment Opportunity Commission) and nongovernmental actors (such as experts and lawyers) mediate the relationship between formal law and informal norms and practices. These mediating actors play a normative role within both the judicial and workplace domains. They translate legal norms to non-legal actors, and they educate courts about non-legal normative activity. These mediating actors can play an ongoing role of: (1) building the capacity and constituencies needed to operate effective, accountable systems within organisations; (2) pooling and critically assessing examples across institutions; (3) generating and revising norms that emerge from that reflective practice; and (4) constructing communities of practice to sustain this ongoing reflective inquiry.

[78] Sturm, above n 1, at 489

[79] Center for Cooperative Resolution/Office of the Ombudsman, *Annual Report* (Washington, DC, Center for Cooperative Resolution, 2001).

Courts review the activities and outcomes of these mediating actors who participate in normative elaboration and capacity building. This review process affords the opportunity to prompt the development of standards and processes of accountability governing the role of these norm intermediaries. An example will help illustrate the idea. I have already discussed evaluations of expert testimony as a site for norm elaboration outside the context of rule enforcement. There is also a structural reason to pay attention to the role of experts as participants in norm elaboration. Experts play a crucial intermediary role in the formation and translation of norms. Many of the experts who appear in employment discrimination litigation also conduct research and consult with organisations about the adequacy of their workplace practices.[80] They play a key role in translating legal principles into organisational norms and vice versa.[81] They are repeat players who work across the boundaries of legal regulation and workplace practice. It is crucial, and not always the case, that these professional intermediaries articulate and satisfy criteria of methodological and process accountability.

Courts can structure processes for the admissibility and evaluation of expert testimony that foster transparency and professional accountability for these norm intermediaries. Courts evaluating expert evidence must assess its persuasiveness, methodological validity, and generalisability.[82] They also consider the degree to which expert evaluation develops replicable methodologies that receive review and validation within the relevant professional community. This review could be conducted with more explicit attention to the crucial intermediary role being played by experts. Ideally, courts could also review administrative agency decision making with this concern about effective norm intermediation and capacity building as a guiding principle.[83]

Conclusion

This paper questions the adequacy of rule enforcement as a unitary theory of law's role in addressing complex discrimination. It also critiques the 'shadow of the law' image as an adequate guide for shaping the relationship between law and norms. The catalyst judicial role developed here requires a new metaphor that captures the dynamic and interactive relationship between informal norms and formal law. Courts can and should actively participate in structuring the relationship between law and norms, between non-legal and legal actors. This role conception also takes account of the crucial connections between regulatory forms and normative possibilities for defining and addressing inequality.

[80] www.bendickegan.com.

[81] Edelman, Uggen, and Erlanger, above n 19.

[82] Walker and Monahan, above n 67, at 877. Meares and Harcourt, above n 67, at 1264.

[83] MC Dorf and CF Sabel, 'A Constitution of Democratic Experimentalism', (1998) 98 *Columbia L Rev* 267, 345.

8

The WTO as a Mechanism for Labour Regulation

BOB HEPPLE*

Introduction

The first theme of this chapter is *institutional design*, that is the efficacy of different regulatory mechanisms/techniques/institutions for the attainment of the objective of real rights and protection for workers. The second theme is the *democratic legitimacy* of techniques of labour regulation, in particular the role of employees and their organisations. In this chapter I argue that the World Trade Organisation (WTO) fails both in terms of institutional design and of democratic legitimacy as a vehicle for labour regulation.[1]

There have been attempts to link trade and labour standards since the late 19th century—in Charnovitz' words, a 'long story of false starts, hollow promises and forgotten laws'.[2] Three broad objectives have been pursued. The first is to encourage labour standards in the exporting country that are comparable with those in the importing country, that is harmonisation or a level playing-field, to prevent 'unfair' competition. The means used are characteristically the imposition of anti-dumping or countervailing duties. This was popular in the 1930s, but has generally fallen into disuse as 'cost equalisation' arguments have been discredited

A second objective has been to ensure compliance with common international labour standards, to which exporting nations must adhere. The means have included the 'stick' of quantitative restrictions on imports (negative conditionality), as well as the 'carrot' of preferential trade benefits (positive conditionality). The international standards to which such measures apply have developed over time starting with the trade in slaves, followed by bans on the importation of the products of prison labour, forced labour and child labour. Other standards sometimes enforced in this way include occupational safety and health (starting with

* Emeritus Professor of Law, University of Cambridge.

[1] This contribution draws heavily on my book *Labour Laws and Global Trade* (Oxford, Hart Publishing, 2005) [hereafter *LLGT*], esp chs 4, 5, 6, with the kind permission of the publishers. The final version of this paper was submitted on 23 May 2005.

[2] S Charnovitz, 'The influence of international labour standards on the world trading system: a historical review' (1987) 126 *International Labour Review* 565 at 580.

the famous Berne Treaty of 1906 between 14 nations to prohibit the importation of matches containing white phosphorous), minimum wages and maximum hours of work. These subjects are today included in the concept of 'internationally recognised worker rights' utilised in US trade legislation. A more widely utilised definition is that of 'core labour standards' corresponding to the four heads of the ILO 1998 Declaration of Fundamental Principles and Rights at Work.[3] These are regarded as essential human rights which should be protected through trade sanctions.

A third objective is to ensure the enforcement of domestic labour laws on defined subjects by the exporting country. Unlike the second objective, this recognises the sovereignty of each country to set its own labour laws, but holds them accountable to ensure compliance with certain basic principles. The most important example is the North American Agreement on Labor Co-operation (NAALC) which contains 11 labour principles including but going beyond the ILO's 'core'. Under NAALC, fines can be levied on countries that persistently fail to enforce domestic laws relating to child labour, minimum wages and occupational health and safety.

Unilateralism

Some of these objectives may be pursued unilaterally, that is by the action of a state or trading bloc without the agreement of the targeted state. The US is the major practitioner of unilateralism, particularly through its Generalised System of Preferences (GSP). Since the 1980s the promotion of labour rights in developing countries has become an increasingly important part of US trade policy. This is the result of pressure from labour and human rights activists in the US and marks a shift from the older purely protectionist campaigns of US unions to 'stop imports' or 'buy American'. The spate of legislation designed to protect the labour rights of workers in foreign countries has been characterised by some critics as 'aggressive unilateralism',[4] global bullying', and disguised protectionism.

The GSP and other measures have had both positive and negative effects. On the positive side, labour rights violations have led to 13 countries being suspended from GSP beneficiary status, and 17 being placed on temporary extension with continuing review. As a result several of the suspended countries have undertaken labour law reforms to regain GSP beneficiary status. A review of the CBI apparel

[3] These are freedom of association and collective bargaining (Conventions 87 and 98); the elimination of forced labour (Conventions 29 and 105); the elimination of the worst forms of child labour and securing a minimum age in employment (Conventions 182 and 138) and the elimination of discrimination in employment (Conventions 100 and 111).

[4] P Alston, 'Labour rights provisions in US Trade Law: "aggressive unilateralism"?' (1993) 15 *Human Rights Quarterly* 1; and see too Alston, ' "Core Labour Standards" and the transformation of the international labour regime' (2004) *European Journal of International Law* 457 at 495–7.

exporting countries in 1998 by the US General Accounting Office concluded that governments had reformed their labour laws to meet international standards and had been making efforts to improve and upgrade their labour departments. The reforms had included strengthening and streamlining procedures to form unions and negotiate collective agreements, establishing labour courts, enhancing labour inspection and enforcement capabilities.[5]

However, despite the progress made, 'allegations of worker rights abuses persists, and enforcement of labour laws generally remains a problem in CBI countries'.[6] A 20-year review of labour rights in the GSP by Compa and Vogt provides detailed case studies of 6 countries (Chile, Guatemala, Malaysia, Indonesia, Pakistan and Belarus). They conclude that 'the merits of a petition have little bearing on the outcome of a case. Geopolitics and foreign policy are the chief considerations for applying the GSP labour rights clause, not the merits of a country's compliance or non-compliance with the law'.[7] But in most cases the dynamics of petition and review led to alliances between unions and human rights groups in the US and those in the developing countries, and resulted in modest but significant changes in labour conditions. Compa and Vogt argue that the criticisms of the labour rights system in US trade law are arguments for improving the system and not renouncing it.

But critics have argued that unilateralism is a fundamentally flawed approach for three principal reasons: first, it undermines the rule of international law by the use or threat of sanctions against a country for failing to adopt international standards which it has not accepted and do not form part of customary international law; secondly, the processes are ineffective; thirdly the motivation for the unilateral measures is primarily protectionist and political; and finally, there exist suitable alternatives.[8]

The US GSP may be compared with the 'soft' unilateralism of the EU's Generalised System of Preferences (EU GSP). The current scheme, embodied in Council Regulation 250/2001 of 10 December 2001, adopts a 'carrot' (positive conditionality) and 'stick'(negative conditionality) approach to core labour standards. The carrot is the 'special incentive arrangements for the protection of labour rights' in Title III, section 1 of the Regulation. A beneficiary country has to request these preferences and must show that its national legislation incorporates the substance of the standards laid down in ILO Conventions Nos 29 and 105 on forced labour, Nos 87 and 98 on the freedom of association and the right to collective bargaining, Nos 100 and 111 on non-discrimination in respect of employment and occupation, and Nos. 138 and 182 on child labour (the core standards).

Both the US and EU GSPs may be described as unilateral because they do not rest on agreement with the targeted countries. However, the EU system may be

[5] United States General Accounting Office, Caribbean Basin, Worker Rights, Progress Made but Enforcement Issues Remain, GAO/NSIAD 98-205, July 1998.

[6] *Ibid*, at 29.

[7] L Compa and JS Vogt, 'Labor rights in the generalised system of preferences: a 20-year review' (2001) 22 *Comparative Labour Law and Policy Journal* 199 at 236.

[8] See *LLGT* at 94–101.

described as 'soft' unilateralism because it avoids most of the criticisms which have been directed at 'aggressive' US unilateralism.[9] First, the EU does not undermine the rule of international law. It applies the ILO 8 core conventions, which all EU Member States have ratified, unlike the US which has ratified only two of these. Compliance with the core standards is a condition of membership of the ILO, even by those countries that have not ratified the core conventions. Unlike the US, the EU does not require compliance with any other unratified conventions. In the EU, unlike the US, a clear link has been established with the various supervisory bodies of the ILO. These are 'the point of departure' for EU action.

Secondly, unlike the US, the EU has to follow transparent and fair procedures before withdrawing or refusing preferences. The European Commission does not have the same ambiguous discretions as the US Trade Representative (USTR); for example, there is no equivalent in the EU to the US criterion of whether a country is 'taking steps' to afford worker rights. In the absence of a full-scale study, it is still too early to say whether the EU procedures have been fully effective, but it is clear that the carrot of preferences has induced countries to ensure that they have, at least, ratified the core conventions. There has thus far been only one case in which temporary withdrawal of GSP has been applied. This was in March 1997 when the Commission found that the Union of Myanmar was involved in the 'routine and widespread' use of forced labour, and the Council temporarily withdrew access to the tariff preferences granted under an earlier GSP regulation. On the other hand, around the same time, the Commission did not seek temporary withdrawal against Pakistan for use of child labour because Pakistan had introduced legislation to outlaw child labour and kept the Commission regularly informed about implementation. At that time the GSP regulation did not refer specifically to child labour, and the Commission was concerned that withdrawal of preferences might increase family poverty unless accompanied by positive measures.

Thirdly, it is far harder to sustain the charge of protectionism against the EU GSP than it is against US trade measures. These preferences are a legacy of the historical relationship with former European colonies and are now part of a larger framework for the integration of developing countries . They appear to fall within the WTO's 'enabling clause' which allows the grant of non-reciprocal trade benefits provided that these benefit all developing countries without discrimination. There is no equivalent in the EU to the labour rights amendment to section 301 of the US Trade Act that permits mandatory retaliatory sanctions, and there is no evidence of preferences being granted or denied by the EU for protectionist or political purposes. This indicates that it is possible to maintain a policy of linking trade preferences with core labour standards. The US is unlikely to modify its approach to one that is more development-friendly without a push from the WTO and also from the developing countries.

[9] See *LLGT* at 105.

Bilateralism and Regional Agreements

The North American Agreement on Labor Co-operation (NAALC), the companion 'side agreement' to the North American Free Trade Agreement (NAFTA), was the first-ever trade agreement to make a significant link between trade and labour rights. The parties to NAFTA and NAALC are the US, Mexico and Canada. The Agreements came into force on 1 January 1994. They have been the model for later Free Trade Agreements (FTA) negotiated by the US with Jordan (2000), Chile and Singapore (2003). The Chile and Singapore agreements in turn are being proposed by the US as models for the sub-regional Central America Free Trade Agreement (CAFTA) between the US, Costa Rica, El Salvador, Guatemala, Honduras and Nicaragua. These models also feature in negotiations for a Free Trade Agreement of the Americas (FTAA), expected to include 34 countries, for a proposed regional free trade agreement with the Southern African Customs Union (SACU), and a bilateral agreement with Australia. A new uniquely American system of cross-border monitoring of the enforcement of domestic labour laws is emerging. This is likely to become much more important than the current unilateral US measures, discussed above.[10]

The core feature of the NAALC is that it requires the enforcement of *domestic* labour law by each of the parties, and not the application of *international* labour standards. The definition of 'labour law' for this purpose consists of 11 principles, which fall into three categories . These categories determine the extent to which enforcement can occur . NAALC does not demand adherence to supranational standards (such as 'internationally recognised worker rights' which are the cornerstone of US unilateral trade measures), nor does it create a supranational enforcement system. Instead, there is a review and dispute resolution procedure aimed at holding countries accountable for enforcement of their own laws and collective agreements. The Preamble affirms the parties' 'continuing respect for each party's constitution and law'. A general commitment in Article 2 by each party to 'ensure that its labour laws and regulations provide for high labour standards, consistent with high quality and productivity workplaces' is preceded by an affirmation of 'respect for each party's constitution', and a recognition of ' the right of each party to establish its own domestic labour standards'.

The first official review of NAALC, covering the first four years, took place in 1997–99, and the second commenced in 2002. In the first review, unions and employers' organisations in the three countries heavily criticised NAALC from different perspectives. Unions thought it had been a failure because the enforcement processes are too weak; employers' groups were worried about the support it gives to labour and human rights activists. The Mexican Government and corporatist unions complained that it had been used for 'Mexico-bashing' and had

[10] *Ibid*, at 108–22.

been captured by protectionist groups in the US. Some academics and independent experts were more willing to see positive results.[11]

The small number of submissions has been explained in terms of the nature of the NAALC process which involves a 'soft law' review of the enforcement of domestic labour laws rather than the 'hard law' of enforcing labour rights which is left to domestic law. The NAALC provides a long-term mechanism for changing the culture of law enforcement and promoting adherence to internationally recognised labour rights. NAALC advocates point out that the process has led to some positive outcomes. There have been conferences, seminars and public reports dealing with issues raised. For example, in response to concerns about gender-based discrimination, the NAFTA governments convened a conference to discuss women's rights at work in all three countries; another conference (arising out of the *Pesca Union* case)[12] dealt with the relationship between national laws and ILO conventions; and another case was resolved by holding three conferences and preparing an experts' study on union representation rights. There have been some cases where settlements have resulted in withdrawal of the submission. Seven ministerial implementation agreements, covering 12 cases, have been reached. In the view of many labour activists, the most important achievement of NAALC has been its contribution to international labour solidarity. The cross-border complaints mechanism provides a platform for the promotion of labour rights, and for labour advocates to seek partners in other countries. Most of the submissions have involved cross-border coalitions of unions and human rights and community groups, but these alliances are still at an early stage and their achievements are modest.

On the other hand, the weaknesses of the NAALC's core obligation—the effective enforcement of domestic labour law—have been revealed. Several submissions have been rejected because the alleged infringement of one of the 11 listed labour principles was in conformity with domestic labour law. Striking flight attendants who accused the Mexican Government of violating the right to strike because they were forced back to work when the Government intervened by executive order to take over the airline and end the strike, were denied a hearing of their case by the US NAO on the ground that the takeover was in accordance with Mexican law. The US NAO also refused to review a complaint by Canadian rural letter carriers that they were excluded from Canadian labour legislation, including the rights to organise and bargain collectively, protection against occupational injuries and employment discrimination. In the *Duro Bag* case,[13] the US NAO refused to hear a case in which it was alleged that the Mexican Government had failed to fulfil a commitment to promote the use inter alia of secret ballots in union elections on the ground that Mexican law did not confer a right to a secret ballot, and more generally because a review would not further the objectives of

[11] See esp L Compa, 'The North America Free Trade Agreement and the North American Agreement on Labor Co-operation' in R Blanpain (ed), *International Encyclopedia for Labour Law and Industrial Relations* (Deventer, Kluwer).

[12] US NAO 9601, see *LLGT* at 112.

[13] US NAO 2001–01, see *LLGT* at 120.

NAALC. What is particularly disturbing about this decision is that Mexico had entered into the commitment in a Ministerial implementation agreement following earlier complaints of violation of union electoral laws. This was not a straightforward case of the absence of an enforceable right in domestic labour law, but raised an issue as to the effectiveness of a Ministerial agreement, which the US NAO was not willing to consider. All of these are cases where the application of ILO core standards on collective labour law would probably have led to a different conclusion. The NAALC core obligation tends to reinforce the status quo in domestic labour law, it lacks mechanisms to raise standards to a 'high level' (ambiguously promised in Article 2), and it does not prevent the relaxation of domestic standards to attract trade or investment. It remains to be seen how far stronger texts of the newer FTAs can overcome these deficiencies.

There is also an institutional problem. Enforcement is dependent upon the action of private parties, and decision-making ultimately rests in the hands of politicians and diplomats. It is not surprising that the majority of submissions have related to collective labour law, because the complainants are usually unions. Marley Weiss argues that issues such as child labour and compensation for injury have rarely been raised because the victims lack an organised constituency.[14] This leads her to propose an independent tri-national entity with prosecutorial authority, and a permanent impartial tribunal to deal with NAALC complaints. There is also a question whether financial sanctions, of the kind found in NAALC and in the US-Chile and US-Singapore agreements are preferable to the open-ended discretion conferred by the US-Jordan agreement to impose trade sanctions. Arguments against the latter are that they can more readily be used for protectionist purposes, and that the more draconian the sanctions the less likely they are to be used in practice. Moreover, trade sanctions may result in those workers who are the subject of abusive working conditions being out of work—a basic dilemma of trade-labour conditionality.

A comparison may be made with the EU's external trade agreements with developing countries.[15] When the fourth Lomé Convention (1989) was revised by the Mauritius Agreement of 1995, a specific commitment to 'human rights, democratic principles and the rule of law' became an 'essential element' in the fourth Lomé Convention. These human rights provisions served as a model for other external EU agreements. They became standard clauses and thus part of the *acquis communautaire.* A new African-Caribbean-Pacific (ACP)-EC Partnership Agreement, signed on 23 June 2000, at Cotonou, Benin, continues (in article 9) the commitment to 'respect for human rights, democratic principles and the rule of law' as 'essential elements' of the Agreement. There is a non-compliance clause (article 96), similar to that in Lomé IV. There must be a 60-day consultation period 'with a view to seeking a solution acceptable to the parties'. These consultations are

[14] 'Two steps forward. One step back or Vice Versa: Labour rights and free trade agreements from NAFTA through Jordan via Chile to Latin America and Beyond' (2003) 37 *University of San Francsco Law Review* 689 at 748.

[15] See *LLGT* at 122–6.

excused in cases of 'special urgency', defined as 'exceptional cases of particularly serious and flagrant violation of one of the essential elements' that 'require an immediate action'.

An innovation in the Cotonou Agreement was the addition of a clause on Trade and Labour Standards (article 50). This states:

1. The Parties reaffirm their commitment to internationally recognised core labour standards, as defined by the relevant International Labour Organisation (ILO) Conventions, and in particular the freedom of association and the right to collective bargaining, the abolition of forced labour, the elimination of the worst forms of child labour and non-discrimination in respect to employment.
2. They agree to enhance co-operation in this area, in particular in the following fields:

   —exchange of information on the respective legislation and work regulation;
   —the formulation of national labour legislation and strengthening of existing legislation;
   —educational and awareness-raising programmes;
   —enforcement of adherence to national legislation and work regulation.

3. The Parties agree that labour standards should not be used for protectionist trade purposes.

The reference to 'internationally recognised core labour standards' was clearly influenced by the 1998 ILO Declaration on Fundamental Principles and Rights at Work. There is room for argument as to whether the list of core standards is exhaustive, but the words 'in particular' suggest that a wider but unspecified list of conventions could be intended. A subsequent co-operation agreement between the EC and Bangladesh, has widened the scope by a clause stating:

> The Parties agree that human resources development constitutes an integral part of both economic and social development.
>
> The Parties acknowledge the necessity of safeguarding the basic rights of workers by taking account of the principles in the relevant International Labour Organisation instruments, including those on the prohibition of forced and child labour, the freedom of association, the right to organise and bargain collectively, and the principle of non-discrimination.
>
> The Parties recognise that both education and skills development as well as improving the living conditions of the disadvantaged sections of the population with special emphasis on women, will contribute to creating a favourable economic and social environment.

This does not limit co-operation to 'core' rights, but widens it to an undefined category of 'basic' rights taking account of 'principles' established by the ILO instruments. The clause may therefore have been intended to focus on compliance with conventions which Bangladesh has ratified or may ratify in future. No such clause is to be found in the agreement with Cambodia. An extensive partnership agreement with Mexico has clauses on human rights and democracy and on 'the need to respect the rights' of 'vulnerable groups, such as indigenous population, the rural poor, women on low incomes and other population groups living in poverty', but makes no specific mention of core labour standards.

The European Parliament has, on a number of occasions, declared itself in favour of a specific social clause. The European Commission, too, has proposed that trade and co-operation agreements should in future include specific provisions on core labour standards. The current practice treats 'human rights'—which appear to include at least the 'core' ILO standards—as an 'essential element' with consequent sanctions for violation. However, other ILO standards are relegated as matters for co-operation, and are not sanction-based. The reason for this is the developing countries' fear of disguised protectionism, a fear expressed in Article 50.3 of the Agreement. The European Council, conscious of this, has decided to focus its strategy on capacity-building and co-operative programmes, rather than negative sanctions. A Council resolution of 21 July 2003 supported all forms of incentives to promote core labour standards, including corporate social responsibility, the generalised system of preferences, more effective dialogue between the ILO and WTO, strengthening the monitoring of the application of labour standards by the ILO, technical assistance to developing countries, programmes with binding deadlines for abolishing all forms of child labour, and incentive measures such as social labelling.

As a matter of theory, all the parties to a trade agreement benefit from the opening of their markets. This encourages each country to produce the goods and services which it can provide most efficiently and to import those which it produces least efficiently, leading to increased profitability, lower consumer prices, and in the long-run more jobs and higher wages in both countries. In developed countries the main gains are for high-skill, high technology exporters, for firms that use cheap imports from developing countries in their production processes, and for transnational corporations (TNCs) who are able to relocate in low-wage developing countries. The losers in developed countries are labour-intensive firms whose products and services compete with imports from developing countries, and the workers in those firms whose jobs and labour standards are placed at risk.

When a social clause is included in a bilateral trade agreement, this may change the equation. Potentially, firms and their workers in the developed country are in a win-win situation. Their products and services have access to the markets of the developing country, but the developing country is excluded from the developed country's market unless the prescribed social standards are met. In reality, however, this protection is likely to be illusory. First, it is only rarely that observance of human rights standards, ILO core labour standards or 'internationally protected worker rights' add significantly to labour costs. Secondly, NAALC and the free trade agreements have had only relatively minor effects on labour standards in developing countries, and have not acted as an effective barrier against products and services produced by workers with low labour standards. US critics of NAFTA can point to the closure of US plants and the shifting of jobs to Mexico. The US-Cambodia textile agreement, while leading to some improvements in working conditions in Cambodia, has not halted the continuing decline of the US textile industry. From the viewpoint of firms and workers in the developed countries, the march of trade liberalisation is relentless and social clauses of the kind found in

NAALC and other American FTAs are powerless to stop it. Supporters of NAALC and other FTAs claim that against the loss of around 500,000 jobs under NAFTA some 14 million new jobs in the US since 1993 owe their existence to trade agreements like NAFTA. It is virtually impossible to evaluate claims of this kind, given other major influences on trade and employment such as the devaluation of the Mexican peso in 1994 and the enormous turnover for many different reasons in the US jobs market

The effect of social clauses on firms and workers in developing countries is equally problematic, but for slightly different reasons. The main winners from free trade agreements in these countries are TNCs and other exporting labour-intensive firms located in these countries. These firms are usually able to increase the number of jobs. Potentially, the pressure of social clauses for improved enforcement of domestic laws can also contribute to better working conditions. But under NAALC there is no incentive to improve the content of domestic laws. Only the newer FTAs provide a limited recognition of higher ILO core standards. Under NAALC there is not even a formal commitment, of the kind in newer FTAs, against lowering labour standards in order to attract trade and investment. To date, the improvements in domestic enforcement have been marginal, but the NAALC procedures have increased international labour solidarity and, in some cases, have enhanced the status and capacity of trade unions in the developing countries. Against this, the imposition of fines or withdrawal of benefits for non-compliance is feared as potentially counter-productive if it causes job losses in the very sectors in which workers are most abused.

The EU's partnership agreements provide a more balanced approach than NAALC and newer FTAs. The EU rewards firms for complying with ILO core standards, and places the emphasis not on possibly destructive sanctions but instead on capacity-building, education and training and other positive co-operative activities that will raise labour standards at the same time as expanding the economies and job markets in developing countries. Conversely, access to the markets of developing countries benefits firms and workers in the EU.

Multilateral Trade-Labour Conditionality

When the ILO was founded, it was suggested that discrimination should be allowed against articles produced under conditions of unfair competition. This was partially reflected in the original article 28 of the ILO Constitution which allowed a government to complain that another government was not observing an ILO convention that both had ratified. The Governing Body could then set up a Commission of Inquiry to investigate the matter and make findings of fact. The Governing Body could indicate 'the measures, if any, of an economic character against a defaulting government which it considers to be appropriate, and which it considers other governments would be justified in adopting'. Either party could then approach the permanent International Court of Justice which was to make the final decision on both the merits and on 'any measures of an economic character'. This provision was dropped in 1946, no such measures ever having been recommended. However, article 33 of the ILO Constitution was amended so as to allow the Governing Body to 'recommend to the Conference such action as it may deem wise and expedient to secure compliance'. This was invoked for the first time in 2000, when the International Labour Conference authorised appropriate measures against Myanmar (Burma) for continued failure to comply with the ILO Forced Labour Convention (No 29).

More ambitious attempts to integrate labour rights into the multilateral world trading and financial systems have so far failed. No specific provision relating to labour standards was made in the General Agreement on Tariffs and Trade (GATT 1947), an inter-governmental treaty incorporating the commercial policy chapter of the failed Havana Charter of 1947. The only exception is Article XX(e) which allows prohibition on the import of products of prison labour. The GATT 1994, updating the 1947 treaty made no changes in this respect. Attempts to interpret the GATT so as to permit trade measures for non-observance of labour standards are likely to collide with the non-discrimination principles on which the GATT is based. Moreover, the general exceptions and safeguards provisions of the GATT do not appear to be apt to allow trade measures for breach of labour standards. An explicit amendment to the GATT would be required, but there is no political consensus to bring this about.

During the Tokyo Round of multilateral trade negotiations (1973–79) the United States raised the issue of labour standards, but failed to gain support. The reciprocal allegations between developed and developing countries of social dumping and protectionism surfaced again during the Uruguay Round (1986–94). The United States requested that a working group be formed to study the issue. Although this had the support of the EU, the Nordic countries, Switzerland, Canada, New Zealand, some Eastern European countries and Japan, no agreement could be reached . The issue was again put on the agenda at the WTO ministerial conference in Singapore in 1996 by the United States, France and Canada. The Ministerial Declaration at the end of that conference, while renewing the commitment 'to observance of internationally recognised core standards', said that the ILO 'is the competent body to set and deal with these standards'. The ministers in effect accepted the position of the developing countries, and rejected 'the use of labour standards for protectionist purposes'. They stated that ' the comparative advantage of countries, particularly low-wage developing countries, must in no way be put into question'. The approach of the WTO ministers was echoed in paragraph 5 of the ILO Declaration of Fundamental Principles and Rights at Work (1998) which states:

> Labour standards should not be used for protectionist purposes, and . . . nothing in this Declaration and its follow-up shall be invoked or otherwise used for such purposes; in addition the comparative advantage of any country should in no way be called into question by the Declaration and its follow-up.

Attempts led by the United States to revive the issue at the Seattle (1999), Doha (2001) and Cancun (2003) ministerial conferences also failed.

Advocates of WTO sanctions for violation of labour standards have made several suggestions for amending the WTO Agreements. One of these[16] would be to interpret Article XX GATT (exceptions) to include measures necessary to enforce core labour standards. There are, however, a number of obstacles to the application of Article XX to labour rights. One is the jurisdictional question whether these exceptions are limited to protecting domestic public morals and life, or can be interpreted to allow measures targeted at violations of labour rights in other countries. Does public morality stop at the border? This is still an open question. In the *Shrimp Turtle I* case,[17] the United States had placed an embargo on certain shrimp or shrimp products for the purpose of protecting endangered sea turtles. The Appellate Body left open the question whether there is an implied jurisdictional limitation in Article XX(g), but found that the migratory nature of sea turtles created a sufficient nexus between the turtles and the United States. The implications of this finding for Article XX(a) and (b) are uncertain. Would it need to be shown that the low labour standards in the targeted country have substantial effects in the importing state? The Appellate Body pointed out that extra-territorial measures were not in themselves ruled out, indeed that interpretation 'would render most, if not all, the specific exceptions inutile'. This is certainly the case with prison labour. The real issue is whether a state can show a legitimate interest in the observance of international labour standards. This raises the question whether these standards are common concerns of the community of nations, and part of customary international law. It is also relevant to know whether there are domestic labour laws which parallel the standards being demanded of the target country.

Another potential obstacle is that Article XX(a) and (b) both require the measures to be 'necessary' to promote public morals or human life. The exception does not apply if there is a reasonably available alternative to trade measures. This has limited the effectiveness of Article XX(b) in relation to environmental protection. For example, US efforts to control smog-causing contamination by gasoline products was held not to justify trade measures because less trade-restrictive alternatives were available and had not been pursued.[18] In relation to human rights Cleveland gives the telling example of a ban on products made with exploitative child labour. 'The targeted state could argue that an available, less trade restrictive

[16] Others include Arts.VI (anti-dumping), XIX(safeguards), XXXV (opt-out) GATT. These and other possibilities are discussed in *LLGT*, ch 6.

[17] *United States—Import Prohibition of Certain Shrimp and Shrimp Turtle Products,* WTO Appellate Body Report, WT/DS58/AB/R, 12 October 1998 (*Shrimp Turtle I*); *United States—Import Prohibitions on Certain Shrimps and Shrimp Products,* WTO Appellate Body, WT/DS58/AB/RW, 22 October 2001 (*Shrimp-Turtle II*).

[18] *United States—Standards for Reformulated and Conventional Gasoline*, WTO Disputes Panel Report, WT/DS2R, 29 January 1996, as modified by Appellate Body in *Reformulated Gasoline*, WT/DS2/9, 20 May 1996.

measure, such as foreign assistance to improve educational opportunities, would be equally, if not more, effective'.[19]

The Article XX(e) prison labour exception is not limited by a necessity requirement. It simply requires the measure to be 'relating to' the products of prison labour. In the *Shrimp/Turtle I* case, the Appellate Body, construing the words 'relating to' in Article XX(g) (conservation), held that the import restriction could not be 'disproportionately wide in its scope in relation to the policy objectives' which in this case was the protection and conservation of sea turtle species. The means used must be reasonably related to the ends. Cleveland argues from this that a 'tailored' sanction, which directly relates the traded product to a human rights abuse (eg carpets made with exploitative child labour) would be permitted, but not a 'semi-tailored' sanction which imposes a ban on goods which do not directly cause the human rights violation (eg a ban on all carpets from a country where child labour is prevalent in the carpet industry).[20]

Even if these obstacles can be surmounted, the trade measure must also satisfy the non-discrimination requirements of the opening paragraph of Article XX (called the *chapeau*). This tries to prevent the use of the exceptions to justify disguised trade protectionism by making them subject to the proviso that 'such measures are not applied in a manner which would constitute a means of arbitrary or unjustifiable discrimination between countries where the same conditions prevail, or a disguised restriction on international trade . . .'. GATT panels and the Appellate Body have applied the *chapeau* stringently, requiring the interference with free trade to be proportional to the legitimate interest being pursued and the benefit likely to result from the measure (eg all imports could not be banned to prevent some products of child labour). The restrictions must not be imposed in a manner which would constitute arbitrary or unjustifiable discrimination between countries where the same conditions prevail. This would involve an evaluation of the labour standards record of all comparable WTO members (including the state imposing the restriction), and there would need to be agreement on the criteria for such an evaluation.

Maupain points out that this would exacerbate fears of protectionism because it would simply leave it to each member state to decide whether to take action.[21] To overcome this objection, use could be made of Article XXIII GATT. This was the centrepiece of the GATT dispute settlement mechanism for obtaining compliance with GATT obligations and is still relevant under the WTO. Article XXIII can be invoked on grounds of 'nullification or impairment' of benefits expected under the agreement. If a 'satisfactory adjustment' is not effected between the parties, then 'the CONTRACTING PARTIES may authorise a complaining country to suspend the application of such concessions or other obligations as the

[19] SH Cleveland, 'Human Rights sanctions and international trade: a theory of compatibility' (2002) 5 *Journal of International Economic Law* 133 at 162.

[20] *Ibid*, at 140–5.

[21] F Maupain', Protection internationale des travailleurs et la libéralisation du commerce mondiale: un lien ou un frein?' (1996) 100 *Revue Générale de Droit International Public* 45 at 81–2.

Contracting parties determine to be appropriate'. The Disputes Settlement Understanding (DSU), adopted as part of the WTO agreements, now provides a stronger framework for multilateral approval of sanctions. The DSU states that, after procedures have been exhausted, the Disputes Settlement Body (DSB) '*shall* grant authorisation to suspend concessions or other obligations'.[22] In contrast to discretionary GATT-authorised retaliation, the WTO-sanctions system for failure to observe recommendations and rulings is mandatory.

WTO-authorised sanctions for failure to observe labour standards would plainly be an improvement on unilateral sanctions. The former ensure that sanctions are rule-based and appropriate, and provide due process for the defendant state. The latter are power-based, subvert the rule of international law, encourage protectionism and discrimination and may lead to unregulated retaliation. The WTO system could also provide a route for consulting the ILO because, under Article XXIII.2 'any appropriate intergovernmental organisation' (such as the ILO) may be consulted. Similarly, Article 13 of the DSU allows dispute panels to seek information and technical advice from 'any individual or body which it deems appropriate'. This has been utilised in intellectual property disputes, and would allow panels to seek advisory opinions in labour matters from the ILO. However, this would leave the ILO in a subsidiary position. At present, the ILO does not even have official observer status at the WTO, although it has a standing invitation to attend ministerial conferences which it did at Doha (2001) and Cancun (2003). (Conversely the WTO has observer status at the International Labour Conference and the ILO Governing Body). Matters would be decided within the inter-governmental structures of the WTO which, unlike the ILO, does not have the benefit of employers' and workers' delegates. It is trade ministers who are in the driving seat and their primary objective is free trade not labour rights. In practice, the WTO always acts by consensus, effectively giving every member a veto, unlike the ILO where conventions can be adopted by a two-thirds majority of delegates but require ratification before they are binding on a member state. Decisions to impose sanctions for labour rights violations would be virtually impossible to achieve in the WTO. In contrast, the International Labour Conference may act by a majority under Article 33 to secure compliance with the recommendations of a Commission of Inquiry, as happened in the case of Myanmar.[23] ILO members are not bound to impose measures, but this is no different from the WTO where a consensus-based decision still leaves members free to decide whether or not take action once authorised by the WTO. Trade diversion to countries which choose not to impose sanctions remains a distinct risk.

The crucial question is whether WTO-authorised sanctions would be more effective than action under Article 33 of the ILO Constitution. Charnovitz has pointed out that the WTO has now achieved a sanctions-based dispute settlement system substantially similar to the one intended for the ILO in 1919 (described

[22] DSU, art 22.6 (emphasis added).
[23] See *LLGT* at 51–2.

above), 'but never embraced because of its poor fit to the ILO's mission'.[24] If the earlier ILO system failed to achieve its purpose, the institutional features of the WTO make it an even worse fit for the enforcement of international labour standards.

The WTO as a Threat to Bilateral and Regional Agreements

The real impact of the WTO is its potential for undermining such positive developments as the EU GSP and some of the bilateral trade agreements made by the US. One example must suffice. The non-discrimination principles in the WTO agreements are facially neutral, but their impact can be indirectly discriminatory on weak non-industrial economies. This concern was first expressed in a demand for better than Most Favoured Nation (MFN) access to the markets of rich countries. Such preferences were recognised by the imperial powers, in particular, the United Kingdom and France, in respect of their colonies and dependencies. As developing countries won independence they sought exemptions from GATT rules. They argued that they should be allowed to impose trade barriers in order to improve their terms of trade, and to protect their infant industries, so that they could develop rapidly.

Article XVIII of GATT 1947 recognised the need of developing countries for infant industry protection, and in 1954–55 it was modified to allow some restrictive measures to protect their balance of payments. However, it was not until 1964, following the formation of the UNCTAD, and a committee on Trade and Development in the GATT, that the demand backed by a bloc of developing countries in the UN for 'special and differential treatment' (S & D) for developing countries came to the fore. A new Part IV of the GATT on Trade and Development was adopted in 1965, recognising the notion of non-reciprocity for developing countries. In 1971, GATT granted a ten-year waiver allowing industrial countries to establish their own discretionary Generalised Systems of Preferences (GSP) to grant trade preferences on a non-reciprocal basis, provided that these benefited all 'developing countries'. In 1979, the GATT Contracting Parties adopted a decision, known as the Enabling Clause, which allowed the indefinite continuation of GSP.[25] This Decision has been carried over into the WTO as part of GATT 1994. Although the requirements to qualify as a 'developing country' were not defined, the Enabling Clause appears to sanction a 'graduation' principle. This in effect

[24] S Charnovitz, 'Should the teeth be pulled? An analysis of WTO sanctions' in DLM Kennedy and JD Southwick (eds), *The Political Economy of International Trade Law* (Cambridge, Cambridge University Press) at 614.

[25] Declaration on Differential and More Favourable Treatment. Reciprocity and Fuller Participation of Developing Countries. Decision of 28 November 1979, L4901 of 3 December 1979, GATT BISD Supp 203 (1980). The scope and nature of the Declaration is controversial.

allows unilateral or bilateral measures to differentiate between countries based on their levels of development, as is the case in EC Council Regulation 2501/2001. The aim is that the more successful developing countries should lose their preferences and be integrated back into the WTO/GATT system with reciprocal obligations.

The extent to which the Enabling Clause permits preferences for observing core labour standards is an open question. In 2003, India complained under the disputes settlement procedures against the special incentive arrangements in EC Council Regulation 2501/2001.[26] The complaint was primarily directed at the Regulation's special arrangements to combat drug production and drug trafficking. Initially, India also complained about the special incentive arrangements relating to protection of the environment and labour rights. The last two complaints were withdrawn, but India reserved its right to raise them in the future should the EC apply them in a manner detrimental to India's interests. The decision of the Appellate Body (AB) in relation to the validity of the drugs arrangements gives some pointers as to how a WTO disputes panel might approach the protection of core labour rights in future.

The drugs arrangements give preferences to products being developed in substitution for drugs by listed countries in the Andean region. The gist of India's complaint was that this preferential treatment violated the Most Favoured Nation principle contained in Art.1.1 of the GATT 1994, and was not justified under the Enabling Clause, para.1 of which states:

> Notwithstanding the provisions of Art.1 of the General Agreement, contracting parties may accord differential treatment and more favourable treatment to developing countries, without according such treatment to other contracting parties.

The main issue was whether the drug arrangements are consistent with paragraph 2(a) of the Enabling Clause, which reads:

> The provisions of paragraph 1 apply to the following:
>
> (a) Preferential tariff treatment accorded by developed contracting parties to products originating in developing countries in accordance with the Generalised System of Preferences [(3)]
>
> ---
>
> 3. As described in the Decision of the CONTRACTING PARTIES of 25 June 1971, relating to the establishment of "generalised, non-reciprocal and non-discriminatory preferences beneficial to the developing countries . . .".

The Appellate Body (AB) upheld findings by the Disputes Panel, that the Enabling Clause is an exception to Art 1.1 GATT, and that it does not exclude the applicability of that Article. The AB held, further, that it is incumbent on the complainant to raise the Enabling Clause in making its claim of inconsistency with Art 1.1 GATT, but that the respondent (in this case the EC) then bears the burden of proving that the arrangements satisfy the requirements of the Enabling Clause.

[26] See *LLGT* at 148.

However, the AB went on to decide, contrary to the Disputes Panel, that the term 'non-discriminatory' in footnote 3 of paragraph 2(a) of the Enabling Clause does not require identical tariff preferences under GSP schemes to be provided to all developing countries (apart from Least Developed Nations). The AB also reversed the Dispute Panel's ruling that 'developing countries' means *all* such countries. India's submission that there must be identical treatment for all developing countries was rejected, and the AB accepted the EC's argument that treating objectively different situations differently is not discriminatory. So long as the GSP is 'generalised' (ie generally applicable) it need not apply to all developing countries, but can refer to individual countries in response to their 'needs'. Responding to these 'needs' may entail treating different beneficiaries differently. Sub-categories of developing countries, according to need (eg Least Developed Nations) are permissible. It is only when similarly situated countries are treated differently that the non-discrimination principle is violated; where they are in the same situation then they must be afforded the same treatment. The AB held that the drug arrangements were inconsistent with the non-discrimination requirement, because they had no objective criteria for adding countries to or removing them from the list of beneficiaries.

It is significant that the AB favourably contrasted the labour rights provisions (Art 8) of the EC Regulation with the drug arrangements. The labour rights clause has substantive criteria and a detailed procedure for dealing with applications for beneficiary status. The standards are applied to all developing countries, and they are objective. Their point of departure is the 8 core ILO conventions, and the available assessments, comments, decisions, recommendations and conclusions of the various supervisory bodies of the ILO. This gives grounds for believing that the EC's labour rights clause would survive challenge in the WTO disputes procedures.

The position is far less certain in regard to the US GSP. The USTR has wide and subjective discretions in deciding whether a country is 'taking steps' to achieve internationally recognised worker rights, and whether conditions of work are 'acceptable'. Some of the interpretations adopted by the USTR (eg in regard to freedom of association) are inconsistent with the interpretations by ILO supervisory bodies, and there are examples of blatant political judgments (eg in relation to Pakistan). It would also be difficult to justify other unilateral US measures (eg under section 301 of the Trade Act) under the Enabling Clause.

Although there are some useful pointers in the *India-GSP* decision, a number of key questions remain. How are the 'needs' of developing countries to be defined in labour matters? One approach would be to say that since the International Labour Conference unanimously declared in 1998 that all members of the ILO should comply with ILO core conventions, there is an existing standard of 'need' reflected in these conventions. But what of a Muslim country that does not ratify or comply with the ILO non-discrimination conventions for cultural or religious reasons? Is such a country 'similarly situated' to a secular developing country? All developing countries need to improve working conditions and to enforce their labour laws effectively. The objective criteria of ILO conventions provides an incentive for them to do so, but the requirement that countries must be 'similarly situated' is likely to be a source of continuing controversy.

Conclusion

The conclusion is that multilateral trade-labour conditionality is politically unlikely, and that the WTO would be an unsuitable mechanism for ensuring observance of international labour standards and for achieving democratic legitimacy.

In terms of institutional design, the WTO agreements do not lend themselves to the enforcement of international labour standards. They lack democratic legitimacy because of the absence of tripartism of the kind found in the ILO, and the failure to accord any role to the ILO within the WTO framework.

Although the recent *India-GSP* ruling gives some grounds for optimism, WTO agreements continue to pose a threat to the EU GSP mechanisms which provide balanced incentives for the observance of core labour standards, and involve the ILO. It is time for the US to move away from the unilateralism of US GSP, which not only violates the principle of non-discrimination, but also undermines the rule of international law, adopts unfair processes, and is primarily protectionist. The future surely lies in the development of bilateral and regional trade agreements which include a social dimension, and focus on capacity-building and positive incentives for the promotion of 'decent work'—the ILO's guiding vision of employment promotion, social protection, social dialogue and rights at work.

9

A Changing Institutional Architecture of the European Social Model?

BRIAN BERCUSSON*

Introduction

This paper explores and illustrates the two general substantive themes of this Columbia-London workshop which are of considerable contemporary concern in European labour law.

The first is *institutional design*: the efficacy of different regulatory mechanisms/techniques/institutions for the attainment of the objective of real rights and protections for workers. The European Union has recently produced 'soft law' mechanisms of formulation, implementation and enforcement of norms in the area of employment and industrial relations which contrast with more traditional forms of 'hard' regulation. The emergence of new regulatory techniques raise general and complex questions of the appropriate level of regulation for different mechanisms, specifically, the relation between EU supra-national, sectoral supra-national, national, sectoral and sub-national levels.

A second theme is the wider question of *democratic legitimacy* of techniques of labour regulation: the role of employees and their organisations in whatever institutional designs are put forward. This can be illustrated by the practical workings of the revolutionary new mechanism introduced by the Treaty on European Union (the Maastricht Treaty) of 1991: European social dialogue. More recently, the proposed Treaty establishing a Constitution for Europe[1] raises many issues concerning the role of labour in the overall institutional design of a European Union. Alongside this 'formal constitution' there also appear signs of an 'informal constitution', which also addresses questions of regulatory technique (legislation or social dialogue) in the sphere of employment and industrial relations.

* Professor of Law, Kings College, London.

[1] Produced on 18 July 2003 by the Convention on the Future of Europe chaired by V Giscard d'Estaing proposed for ratification by the EU Member States, but rejected by referenda in France and the Netherlands in 2005. Draft Constitution proposed by the Convention on the Future of Europe, Draft Treaty establishing a Constitution for Europe, CONV 850/03, Brussels, 18 July 2003. Treaty establishing a Constitution for Europe adopted by the Member States in the Intergovernmental Conference meeting in Brussels 17–18 June 2004, OJ C 310/1 of 16 December 2004.

This paper comprises five sections. Recent research is highlighted to illustrate the interaction of different techniques of enforcement of labour law at different levels, primarily the national and the transnational EU levels (I). The emergence of new techniques of labour regulation at EU level is explored, as they appear to engage a combination of the open method of coordination (OMC) with the European social dialogue (II). The practical operation of one of these new techniques, the European social dialogue, is analysed through the experience of negotiation of the Framework Agreement on Fixed-Term Work concluded by ETUC, UNICE and CEEP (respectively, the organisations of workers and employers at the EU level). This illustrates the interaction of representative organisations of workers at transnational, national and sectoral levels, in order to highlight issues of the democratic legitimacy of mechanisms of labour regulation (III). The proposed Constitutional Treaty reflects the role of social dialogue in the institutional design of the EU (IV). Finally, the institutional design of this 'formal' constitution is contrasted with institutional practices at EU level which indicate the parallel existence of an 'informal' constitution with quite different implications for the role of social dialogue (V).

Levels of Regulation: Interaction of Enforcement of Labour Law at National and Transnational EU Levels

An earlier account of application of labour law in national jurisdictions, identified three principal mechanisms of application in the national context: through the administration, through the courts and through the social partners (administrative, judicial and industrial relations enforcement).[2] A similar framework has been applied to enforcement of transnational EU labour law,[3] and questions of the effectiveness of different mechanisms arise also in the enforcement of EU labour law.

The increasing prominence of EU labour law in national systems raises complex issues of the *interaction* of national enforcement mechanisms and enforcement of EU labour laws in the EU Member States.[4] Broadly speaking, EU law determines substantive rules, but domestic law determines remedies and procedures. There is an important distinction between the full *effectiveness* of rights deriving from EU law and the *formal* remedies for breach of EU law. Analysis of the case law of the European Court of Justice (ECJ) elucidates subtle and important qualities

[2] B Bercusson, U Mückenberger, A Supiot, '*L'application du droit du travail en Europe*', *Travail et Emploi*, 1991, no 41.

[3] B Bercusson, *European Labour Law* (Sweet & Maxwell, London, 1996), Part III, chs 7–11, 'Enforcement of European Labour Law'.

[4] For example, one UK source estimates that 40% of UK employment law derives from EU requirements. Better Regulation Taskforce, *Employment Regulation: Striking a Balance*, May 2002, cited in C Kilpatrick, 'Has New Labour Reconfigured Employment Legislation?', (2003) 32 *Industrial Law Journal* 135 at p 141.

distinguishing the enforcement of EU labour law. The outcome of the cumulation of three principles: equivalence, effectiveness and proportionality is the emergence of 'the principle of effective enforcement'.[5] This principle can be applied to cover not only judicial, but also administrative and industrial relations processes of enforcement of EU labour law.

For example, the incorporation of rules of transnational EU labour law into collective agreements implies the commitment of the negotiating parties to enforcement, and may both promote compliance and lessen the need for administrative or judicial enforcement.[6] The obvious fact, sometimes overlooked by lawyers, is that when a worker or a workers' representative is confronted with an employer's violation of his or her rights, the first step is not to go to court but to seek to resolve the conflict through discussion. Judicial processes are thus preceded by negotiations engaged in the similar exercise of assessing facts and interpreting rules, including formal legal rules. Collective bargaining, including information and consultation, is an integral process of enforcement of rules in conflicts also over EU labour law, in particular where they are embodied in an EU social dialogue agreement.

Hence, for EU labour lawyers, the rules on industrial relations processes may be of equal significance to the question of the requirements which Member States must meet with respect to access to a court and *locus standi* in order correctly to implement transnational EU labour law directives. The complementary areas of enforcement overlap in the major problem of the *locus standi* of workers' representatives in labour law litigation, and the issue of securing the interests of the individual worker where these diverge from those of the collective representative. The use of collective actors in judicial enforcement procedures of EU labour law is underdeveloped compared with its relatively widespread use in the Member States, at least until recent EU initiatives attributing *locus standi* to interest groups, as in Article 9(2) of the Framework Employment Equality Directive[7] and Article 6(3) in the amended Equal Treatment Directive.[8]

The incorporation into the proposed EU Constitution or Reform Treaty of the EU Charter of Fundamental Rights, including many labour law rights and principles, means that questions of the enforcement, and not only the justiciability, of rights and principles of labour law will become a focus of attention. Alternatives

[5] B Fitzpatrick provides a closely argued analysis of the ebb and flow of the ECJ's doctrine on effective judicial protection based on principles of equivalence, effectiveness and proportionality. See his contribution to the Introduction to J Malmberg (ed), *Effective Enforcement of EC Labour Law*, Iustus Forlag (Uppsala, 2003), at pp 43–58. The following section draws on my Foreword to this book.

[6] In a chapter on industrial relations processes T van Piejpe investigates the extent to which the combination of EC labour law and the respective systems of national labour law contribute to the use of negotiations as a means of enforcement in the respective fields of restructuring, working time and equal treatment; Malmberg (ed), *op cit*, pp 77–108.

[7] Council Directive 2000/78 establishing a general framework for equal treatment in employment and occupation. OJ 2000, L303/16.

[8] Council Directive 76/207/EEC of 9 February 1976 on the implementation of the principle of equal treatment for men and women as regards access to employment, vocational training and promotion, and working conditions, OJ 1976, No L39/40, as revised by Council Directive 2002/73/EC, OJ 2002 No L269/15.

to judicial processes of effective enforcement of the social and labour rights in the EU Charter may become a central element in this debate. Jonas Malmberg points out that it 'might it be argued that the more fundamental the Community right which is infringed, the more intrusive should be the remedial structure'. He contrasts 'ordinary' labour rights, with 'fundamental social rights': equality, health and safety and even information and consultation of workers, and asks 'Should it be a factor in Community law enforcement that the level of scrutiny of national remedies, and wider judicial process, should be stricter where fundamental social rights are at issue?'

This argument is particularly timely in the aftermath of the struggle over the issue of sanctions in the recent directive on information and consultation at national level.[9] The incorporation in the final directive of the traditional formula regarding judicial sanctions was a retreat from the Commission's approach in its initial draft proposal seeking more targeted remedies for specific and serious breaches.[10] However, as Article 27 of the EU Charter makes workers' right to information and consultation a fundamental right, the question of what sanctions are required for its effective enforcement, especially if integrated into an EU Constitution, may now perhaps be revived.

As regards administrative processes of enforcement, it is argued that, historically, these were established in national labour laws because workers were unable in practice to enforce their rights through judicial processes.[11] There is an apparent paradox that EU labour law has failed to recognise this feature of labour law and failed to develop specific instruments of administrative enforcement.[12] It is not so much that the pendulum has to switch to the other direction, for administrative processes alone may not be sufficient for effective enforcement of the directives concerned. Rather, it is that effective enforcement of the directives may require some administrative intervention to reinforce individual or collective action.[13]

[9] Council Directive No 2002/14 establishing a framework for informing and consulting employees in the European Community. OJ 2002, L80/29.

[10] For a detailed account, see B Bercusson, 'The European Social Model Comes to Britain', (2002) 31 *Industrial Law Journal* (September) pp 209–44.

[11] S Laulom, in Malmberg (ed), *op cit*, pp 109–35.

[12] Laulom points to some indicators in the form of requirements of administrative intervention in EC laws on collective redundancies (informing public authorities; Council Directive 75/129 of February 17, 1975 on the approximation of the laws of the Member States relating to collective dismissals, OJ L 48/29, as amended by Directive 92/56 of 24 June 1992, OJ L 245/92; consolidated in Council Directive 98/59/EC of 20 July 1998, OJ L 225/16) and the new Race Directive (designation of special bodies to promote equal treatment; Council Directive 2000/43 implementing the principle of equal treatment between persons irrespective of racial or ethnic origin, OJ 2000, L/180/22).

[13] Laulom demonstrates that the nature of administrative intervention is dependent on the area concerned, looking at the three areas of working time, equal treatment at work and restructuring of the enterprise: 'The administrative processes and the industrial relations processes or judicial processes are strongly interrelated in all the three fields of labour law under study and in all the Member States investigated. But these interrelations are slightly different in the three areas. The task of administrative authorities in the field of working time has a traditional foundation due to the established link between working time and health and safety. Nevertheless, the rising importance of collective bargaining in the regulation of working time can imply some modifications to the functions of administrative bodies . . .

An example of exceptional practical significance, though often ignored in labour law, concerns the issue of interim decision-making powers in questions of enforcement of EU labour law. This is a particularly Swedish concern, manifested in the Co-Determination Act of 1976.[14]

Jonas Malmberg points out that though labour disputes may be resolved through legal proceedings, these normally take considerable time and, given the practical continuity of employment relationships: 'it is of great importance to establish which of the parties' interpretation of their duties applies until the dispute is finally solved'. In particular: 'The first question is to what extent one of the parties has the power to enforce his interpretation without awaiting a decision of a court', or in the Swedish terminology, which party has the 'priority of interpretation'. There are also other related questions, such as which of the parties has the consequent burden of bringing the dispute to court to enforce his or her interpretation, and, subsequently, in what circumstances may the court make an interim decision. Comparative analysis provides a number of important indicators. For example, 'the rules on priority of interpretation and burden of litigation differ largely depend on whom the enforcing party is . . . an administrative authority . . . the workers' representatives . . . or individual employees . . . there are examples where the workers' representatives are given a priority of interpretation, with the rules in the Swedish Co-Determination Act as the most striking example'.

Interim measures largely depend on the ultimate sanctions available. Where the sanction is pecuniary compensation, a claim for an interim decision on payment will normally be turned down, since such a claim can usually be subsequently satisfied. The significance of this is particularly poignant in light of the Commission's initial proposal for a specific penalty, that of retaining the *status quo* of employment for employees affected, for serious breach of an employer's duty in Article 7(3) of the proposed draft directive on information and consultation. Sadly, this provision for a special sanction was eventually deleted following pressure from certain Member State governments when the final Directive was adopted in 2002. The consequences for interim remedies may be significant, for as Jonas Malmberg points out, 'The availability of interim measures seems to be most important in dismissal cases . . .'.

Different processes of enforcement of labour rights through administrative, industrial relations and judicial mechanisms may have different impacts at individual and collective levels, and can be mutually beneficial. For example, it may be that collective methods of enforcement of labour law are stronger and individual enforcement mechanisms relatively weaker at Member State level, but the reverse is true at transnational EU level. If so, this may offer a positive prospect of the European Court of Justice reinforcing the micro level of national judicial

[C]oncerning equality, the Member States, where a labour inspectorate has specialized powers, have provided for independent authorities to ensure observance of equality principles. This shows the need for some form of control auxiliary to the collective and judicial enforcement of equality rights'. In Malmberg (ed), *op cit*, pp 109–35.

[14] See J Malmberg in Malmberg (ed), *op cit*, pp 159–90.

procedures. Decisions of the ECJ have had an impact on national enforcement of employment rights through judicial processes.[15] Conversely, national industrial relations systems could contribute to supporting effective enforcement of transnational EU labour rights at the collective level.[16] The objective is mutual reinforcement of transnational and national systems of labour law.

Institutional Design: New Techniques of Labour Regulation at EU Level

Throughout its history of almost half a century, the European Community has experienced a variety of legal strategies for the formulation and implementation of transnational labour law and social policy. The past decade has witnessed dramatic changes in the EU's methods of labour regulation. The traditional approach of *judicial enforcement* of labour standards laid down in EU legislation (directives) is constantly under the pressure of new doctrinal developments. In addition, there has emerged a new *industrial relations* mechanism, the process of social dialogue and European framework agreements between the social partners (Maastricht Treaty, now Articles 138–139 of the EC Treaty). There is also a new *administrative* mechanism, the 'open method of coordination' (OMC), applied to the European Employment Strategy (EES) (Treaty of Amsterdam, now Articles 125–130 of the EC Treaty). These new developments have produced new approaches to application and enforcement of transnational labour law. Of particular interest are the evolution at EU level of *hybrid methods of enforcement and application of transnational labour law*, merging administrative, judicial and industrial relations processes.

The context of these changes is the so-called 'Lisbon Strategy', but the Treaty of Nice provided the *legal* framework for the changes on labour policy signalled by

[15] An example is provided by three time-related questions: (i) how much time is allowed to claim a right before a court; (ii) when does time begin to run; and (iii) what are the possible retroactive effects of a claim. A close analysis of the ECJ's case law reveals that '. . . in some cases national time limits to challenge before a court the validity of a dismissal have somehow been 'communitarised' by national judges. In Germany and the Netherlands, for example, the *Bundesarbeitsgericht* and the *Hoge Raad* have been ready to extend the time limits laid down in ordinary dismissal cases, when the contested dismissal is allegedly grounded on a transfer of undertaking, contrary to what Community law prescribes'. Antonio Lo Faro characterises this as a sort of ' "procedural added value" which can sometimes be found when a Community right is claimed before a national court'. Indeed, 'In a burst of Europeanism probably unparalleled in any other Member State, the German legislation excludes whatsoever limitations on the retroactivity of claims brought for the application of Community legislation on equal treatment'. See A Lo Faro in Malmberg (ed), *op cit*, pp 190–214.

[16] Research at the Swedish National Institute for Working Life aims to contribute to addressing the latter issue by examining the role of European social dialogue agreements in EC labour law K Ahlberg, B Bercusson, N Bruun, C Vigneau, *Fixed-term Work in the EU: A European agreement against discrimination and abuse*, National Institute for Working Life (Stockholm, 1999).

the Lisbon Strategy, which took shape in the Commission's Social Policy Agenda 2001–2005.

The context: the Lisbon Strategy

The Lisbon European Council of 23–24 March 2000 articulated a new strategic goal for the EU: 'to become the most competitive and dynamic knowledge-based economy in the world capable of sustainable economic growth with more and better jobs and greater social cohesion'.[17] As well as a new strategic goal, the Lisbon Council highlighted the 'open method of coordination' as a principal process through which this goal was to be achieved.

In its Social Policy Agenda 2001–2005, the Commission confirmed the Lisbon Strategy.[18] Reflecting the approach favoured by the Lisbon Council, the Commission stated: (p 7)

> This new Social Policy Agenda does *not seek to harmonise social policies.* It seeks to work towards common European objectives and increase *co-ordination of social policies* in the context of the internal market and the single currency.

The Treaty of Nice: from judicial enforcement to administrative process

The approach emphasising *coordination* is reflected in the changes to the Social Chapter of the EC Treaty adopted by the Treaty of Nice in December 2000. Article 137(2) EC was amended by the Treaty of Nice in two apparently minor ways. First, it *added* to Article 138(2)'s provision encouraging cooperation between Member States the phrase '*excluding any harmonisation of the laws and regulations of the Member States*'. Secondly, this phrase *replaced* the former Article 137(2)'s provision limiting cooperation measures solely '*in order to combat social exclusion*'. Instead, the reference to 'combating of social exclusion' is inserted into the Treaty of Nice's new Article 137(1)(j) EC.

The replacement in Article 137(2) of the phrase 'in order to combat social exclusion' by the insertion of the new phrase 'excluding any harmonisation of the laws and regulations of the Member States' has two very significant implications. The first is that *coordination/cooperation* is an approach which may henceforth be applied to *all* the social policy areas listed in the revised Article 137(1) EC (not only 'in order to combat social exclusion'). Secondly, in social policy generally, as in the case of employment policy (Article 129 EC), the process of cooperation/coordination *excludes* 'any harmonisation of the laws and regulations of the Member States'.

[17] Lisbon Presidency Conclusions, paragraph 5.
[18] COM(2000) 379 final, Brussels, 28 June 2000, s 1.2, p 5.

These amendments to Article 137 EC by the Treaty of Nice mark the new departure in EU social policy signalled by the Lisbon Strategy. EU social policy is *not* primarily to be implemented through the adoption by means of *directives of minimum requirements* (Article 137(2)(b) EC, formerly 137(2)) in the fields listed in Article 137(1).

Rather, in all these fields there is the *alternative* of measures designed to encourage *cooperation* between Member States in all social policy fields (Article 137(2)(a)), no longer restricted to combating social exclusion (ex Article 137(2) EC), and explicitly '*excluding* any harmonisation of the laws and regulations of the Member States'.

The Social Policy Agenda 2001–2005: legislation, social dialogue and administrative processes

The European Council at Nice in December 2000, in adopting the Commission's Social Policy Agenda 2001–2005 of 28 June 2000, declared that in its implementation 'all existing Community instruments bar none must be used; the open method of co-ordination, legislation, the social dialogue, the Structural Funds, the support programmes, the integrated policy approach, analysis and research'.[19] The Commission's Social Policy Agenda 2001–2005 also stated that 'To achieve these priorities, an adequate combination of all existing means will be required' (p 14). Although a *variety* of means were listed, the *scope* of application allocated to each was significant.

The *first* was 'The open method of co-ordination, inspired by the Luxembourg Employment Process and developed by the Lisbon and Feira Councils'. There was *no limit* specified to the scope of matters suitable for the application of this method.

In contrast, the *second* means listed was: 'Legislation: Standards should be developed or adapted, *where appropriate*, to ensure the respect of *fundamental social rights* and to respond to *new challenges*. Such standards can also result from agreements between the social partners at European level'. The scope of legislation required to achieve the European social model is here *limited* to fundamental social rights and new challenges.

Thirdly: 'The Social Dialogue as the most effective way of modernising contractual relations, adapting work organisation and developing adequate balance between flexibility and security'. The role of social dialogue is *even more limited* to work relationships within the enterprise.

The unlimited scope of the open method of coordination as an instrument for achieving the Lisbon strategy is in clear contrast with the restricted scope of legislation and social dialogue. The emphasis is on the open method of coordination as the instrument for achieving the Lisbon strategy. The Lisbon strategy, and the

[19] Nice European Council, 7–9 December 2000, Annex 1, para 28.

Social Policy Agenda 2001–2005, would succeed or fail depending on the efficacy of its chosen instrument.

Merging industrial relations and administrative mechanisms (social dialogue and the OMC)

In its Communication of 26 June 2002 on the role of social dialogue in European labour law, entitled 'The European social dialogue, a force for innovation and change',[20] the Commission noted, under the heading 'Improving monitoring and implementation', that:

> The European social partners have adopted joint opinions, statements and declarations on numerous occasions. More than 230 such joint sectoral texts have been issued and some 40 cross-industry texts . . . However, in most cases, these texts did not include any provision for implementation and monitoring: they were responses to short-term concerns. They are not well known and their dissemination at national level has been limited. Their effectiveness can thus be called into question.

On the question of the perceived lack of effectiveness, the Commission noted that:[21]

> Special consideration must be given to the question of how to implement the texts adopted by the European social partners. The recommendations of the High-Level Group on Industrial Relations and Change see the use of machinery based on the open method of coordination as an extremely promising way forward.
>
> The social partners could apply some of their agreements (where not regulatory) by establishing goals or guidelines at European level, through regular national implementation reports and regular, systematic assessment of progress achieved.

To that end, the Commission recommended:

> The social partners are requested to:
>
> —adapt the open method of coordination to their relations in all appropriate areas;
> —prepare monitoring reports on implementation in the Member States of these frameworks for action;
> —introduce peer review machinery appropriate to the social dialogue.

The significance of this recommendation is highlighted by the Work Programme of the European Social Partners 2003–2005. For example, of the twelve items in the Social Partners' Work Programme under the Employment Heading, only three refer to 'agreements', while nine appear to be eligible for the Commission's recommendation on application of the open method of coordination.[22]

[20] COM(2002) 341 final, 26 June 2002.

[21] *Ibid*, s 2.4.1, p 18.

[22] The three appear only in proposals for a 'seminar in view to negotiate a voluntary agreement' on stress at work (2003) and a 'seminar to explore possibility of negotiating a voluntary agreement' on harassment (2004–2005). An additional item refers to the framework agreement on telework signed on 16 July 2002.

Given the nature of the Social Partners' Work Programme, therefore, the Commission questions the ineffectiveness in implementation and monitoring of texts other than agreements. Its solution is, first, to clearly identify those areas where 'regulatory agreements' are the chosen instrument. Secondly, where other instruments are proposed (frameworks of actions, declarations, orientations, joint opinions) the OMC method may be adapted as appropriate; in particular, 'monitoring reports on implementation' and 'peer review machinery appropriate to the social dialogue': a new *hybrid form of implementation and enforcement.*

It remains to be seen whether the OMC, hitherto often criticised as to its effectiveness when implemented by Member States' administrations in the field of employment policy, is appropriate for the Work Programme of the Social Partners on Employment. If joint opinions and other non-regulatory instruments continue to be ineffective, their failure may imply other, more rigorous steps towards effectiveness, including regulatory agreements and/or legislation.

Legitimacy: The Interaction of Transnational and National Levels of Industrial Relations in Negotiating the Framework Agreement on Fixed-Term Work

A case study in the European social dialogue: the experience of negotiation of the Framework Agreement on Fixed-Term Work,[23] illuminates the two issues which are the focus of attention: the democratic legitimacy of mechanisms of labour regulation, and the interaction of representative organisations of workers at various levels: transnational EU, national and sectoral.[24]

The case study analyses the way in which the social partners, in particular, the European Trade Union Confederation (ETUC) and its affiliates have undertaken the EU social dialogue. The report analyses the process of EU social dialogue not only in terms of the interactions between the EU social partners, but also in terms of the engagement in the EU social dialogue process of representatives of the EU social partners' affiliates in the Member States.[25]

The EU social dialogue engages the social partners in the Member States which are affiliated to the EU-level organisations: ETUC, UNICE and CEEP (respectively, the EU-level organisations of trade unions and of private and public

[23] See Council Directive 1999/70/EC of 28 June 1999 concerning the framework agreement on fixed-term work concluded by ETUC, UNICE and CEEP; OJ 175/43 of 10.7.1999.

[24] The following draws on the report of a research project supported by the European Trade Union Institute, B Bercusson, *The Role of the Social Partners in the Member States in Labour Regulation through the EU Social Dialogue*, Brussels, 2004. See also K Ahlberg, 'The negotiations on fixed-term work', in C Vigneau, K Ahlberg, B Bercusson and N Bruun, *Fixed-term Work in the EU*, National Institute for Working Life, Stockholm, 1999, pp 13–38.

[25] The report focuses on the trade union side of the dialogue simply because more material was available which illuminated that side of the social dialogue.

employers). The relationship between these EU intersectoral organisations and their national affiliates affects crucial aspects of the social dialogue. For example, the decisions to undertake the social dialogue on a particular subject, to define the negotiating mandate, to decide whether to approve the agreement reached and to resolve disputes over interpretation of the agreement. The report describes how the arrangements *within* the national social partners, and *between* them and the central organisations at EU level, operated in the EU-level social dialogue which produced the framework agreement on fixed-term work.

Three distinct phases were analysed in the study of the EU social dialogue on fixed-term work: (i) formulation of the mandate, (ii) negotiations, and (iii) ratification of the agreement.

In the *mandate* stage (between mid-November 1997 to mid-March 1998), the following 3 phases were identified: (a) providing information on the national position: affiliates from ten Member States provided written information prior to the technical meeting; (b) participating in a 'technical' meeting aiming to elucidate issues (12 January 1998); confederations from eleven Member States participated in this meeting; (c) providing further comments and views; correspondence indicates a number of national confederations taking an active and detailed interest in the content of the mandate, as well as expressing views as to the subsequent process of negotiations prior to its being initiated.

In the *negotiations* stage (mid-March 1998 to mid-January 1999), the following 3 phases were identified: (a) the ten Negotiations Group meetings, in which all Member States had an affiliate represented, interspersed with the Drafting Group meetings, which included representatives of three national affiliates, two European industry federations (EIFs) and two representatives of the ETUC; (b) the critical pre-final session vote on 8 January 1999 and (c) the vote on the final agreement on 14 January 1999.[26]

In the *ratification* stage (between mid-January 1999 and mid-March 1999), the following 3 phases were identified: (a) reference back to affiliates for their consideration through their internal constitutional processes; (b) meetings of ETUC bodies, the Industrial Relations Committee (26 February 1999), and the Women's Committee (2 March 1999); (c) approval by the ETUC Executive Committee (15–16 March 1999). The vote at the ETUC Executive Committee meeting on 15 March 1999 indicates how different affiliates decided. In some cases, all we have is an indication as to how the affiliate voted. However, some insights are provided into the different types of responses of the ETUC affiliates between the approval of the agreement by the Negotiating Committee on 14 January 1999 and the vote on ratification of the agreement by the ETUC Executive Committee on 15 March 1999.

The experience of the EU social dialogue which produced the framework agreement on fixed-term work leads to the identification of a number of issues relevant to transnational labour regulation.

[26] The report summarises the involvement of confederations from each of the fifteen Member States and six EU industry federations and provides a detailed account of the substantive content of the type of interventions.

The EU 'bargaining order': internal constitutional arrangements of the EU social partners

The three successful EU social dialogues at intersectoral level which have produced directives provide some basis for establishing an EU 'bargaining order': the procedure to be followed by the social partners in conducting the transnational social dialogue. Articles 138–139 of the EC Treaty, which provide the legal basis for the EU social dialogue, are notoriously inadequate as a framework. The absence of an established and structured bargaining order is a serious defect in terms of the legitimacy, transparency and efficacy of the EU social dialogue.

The aspect of the EU bargaining order of concern is not so much that *between* the social partners, though this is of primary importance. The concern here is with that part of the bargaining order which regulates the relationship between the EU social partners and their *affiliates* in the Member States.

In anticipation of the negotiations on fixed-term work, the meeting of the ETUC's Industrial Relations Committee held on 28 October 1997 prepared proposals to supplement the rules of procedure on the application of Article 13 of the ETUC Statutes by specifying the tasks allotted to, respectively, (a) the Secretariat; (b) the Executive Committee; (c) the Steering Committee; (d) the Industrial Relations Committee; (e) the negotiating delegation and (f) the drafting group. Four stages were envisaged: (1) preparing the mandate, (2) conducting the negotiations, (3) decision-making procedure on the results of the negotiations, (4) follow-up of the framework agreement in the legislative procedure.

The assumption appears to have been that the representatives of the affiliates on these various committees, bodies and delegations are responsible for ensuring that the information is channelled through to the affiliates in a timely and effective manner. This seems to be emphasised through the injunction calling for the commitment of representatives appointed to participate in the negotiating delegation to ensuring their availability throughout the negotiations and also calls to strengthen the logistical support for the negotiating delegation and the drafting group.

However, the extent to which representatives of the affiliates in the various bodies engaged in negotiations did in practice inform and consult their organisations was very uneven. It is questionable whether this situation, whereby some affiliates are continuously well-informed and others much less so, is sustainable. It undermines both the effectiveness of negotiators, denied information, ideas and proposals coming up from the affiliates, and the legitimacy, and indeed the successful adoption of the outcome of negotiations, when affiliates are not regularly informed and consulted. The great diversity of organisations of workers in the different Member States and their different traditions of collective bargaining may make it difficult to find a common solution to this problem.

Adapting information and consultation mechanisms to negotiations

In the course of the transnational EU social dialogue there are particular points in time which are of maximum concern to affiliates and which may require them to engage more actively.

For example, the proposed ETUC bargaining order implied that certain moments in the bargaining process required particularly close attention on the part of affiliates. For example, the point of *determining the negotiating mandate.* An ETUC memo to affiliates on 4–5 December 1997 fixed a deadline of 24 February 1998. There was a flurry of activity and replies from some affiliates indicating consultation of their affiliates. The mandate was finally fixed by the ETUC Executive Committee meeting on 4–5 March 1998. A memorandum dated 27 February 1998 described the proposals for the mandate and included a Table (7 pages) with 3 columns indicating proposed text, amendments/comments from affiliates and the Secretariat's response. Each amendment in the second column has attached the national confederation or sectoral federation proposing it.

Some ETUC affiliates stated explicitly they had consulted their affiliates. Some had formally adopted a resolution approving the mandate and/or commenting on it with amendments. But, for example, one EU sectoral federation stated this had been done only for the first time. And from some it was not clear whether there had been any detailed consideration of the mandate.

It may not be feasible to have maximum engagement of all affiliates throughout the transnational social dialogue process. This will reflect the nature of internal procedures within different national confederations and EU sectoral federations. It is a question whether these points in time can be identified in advance, and whether the mechanisms can be put in place which will enable affiliates to engage more closely without compromising the effectiveness of the social dialogue process at these critical moments.

Negotiations Group and Drafting Group: composition and competences

In general, the issue is how to define the composition, and deal with the respective roles of the Negotiations and Drafting Groups. The primary issue is that of the roles of each Group and their interaction. As to their respective roles, the borderline between drafting and negotiating is not always clear.

It seems inevitable that there will be a need for a Committee with restricted numbers to undertake some negotiations, which will leave outside the representatives of many affiliates. This makes the reporting back procedure between a restricted membership Drafting Group and a fully representative Negotiations Group all the more essential.

In the case of the EU Social Dialogue on fixed-term work, the ETUC's Negotiations Group comprised 29 people, one from each country in the European

Economic Area (EEA), 8 representing European industry federations (EIFs), one from the Women's Committee, one from Eurocadres and 2 from the ETUC Secretariat. The Drafting Group numbered 7: 2 from the ETUC Secretariat, 3 from national affiliates (Belgium, Germany, Sweden) and 2 from EIFs.

The Negotiations Group met prior to each meeting with the employers. Apart from the unwieldy size of the Group, many representatives on the Negotiating Group were usually not based in Brussels, and this reduced their potential as a cohesive negotiating force. In contrast, the Drafting Group was much smaller, and, whether by chance or design, 6 out of the 7 members were based in Brussels: the 2 from the ETUC Secretariat and the 2 from the EIFs, and, of the 3 from national affiliates, the representative of the Belgian trade unions and the representative of the Swedish trade unions, who was on full-time secondment to the ETUC. In effect, the so-called Drafting Group seemed to operate more as an Executive Committee of the Negotiations Group.

Certain factors may be relevant in constructing a relationship between negotiating and drafting bodies, and between them and the organisations represented on them.

First, as well as these bodies, there were other ETUC bodies which received regular reports on the negotiations: the ETUC Executive Committee and the ETUC Industrial Relations Committee. Affiliates could keep track of negotiations through these bodies as well as through their representatives on the Negotiations Group.

Secondly, of course, some affiliates were represented on the Drafting Group itself, and this gave them privileged access to developments. While reports went back from this Group to the Negotiations Group, affiliates whose representatives were on the Drafting Group had some time advantage in consulting their own organisations.

Thirdly there may be scope for horizontal arrangements between groups of national affiliates, which may overcome some of the problems of lack of representatives on the smaller 'Executive Committee' of negotiators (see section below).

Vertical relationships and horizontal alliances among affiliates

The perception of negotiations in each of the social partners is one of purely bilateral and vertical relationships between individual affiliates and the EU level structures. In the case of the ETUC, this means relationships between the individual national confederations on the one hand, and the Drafting and Negotiations Groups and the ETUC Committees (Industrial Relations Committee, Executive Committee, and so on) on the other.

The problem of accommodating the large number of affiliates on negotiating bodies presents problems not only of the practical effectiveness of negotiations, but also of the legitimacy of their outcome. The issue is securing part of that required legitimacy by ensuring that affiliates are informed and consulted adequately about the progress of negotiations and are engaged in the decisions adopted in the course of negotiations.

There are at least two cases where horizontal relationships between affiliates may play a role in transnational EU social dialogue: (i) where individual affiliates communicate directly with each other; and (ii) where European Industry Federations are concerned (see section below).

The problem of engagement of numerous affiliates in negotiations may be ameliorated by formation of horizontal alliances among groups of affiliates, or, at least, facilitating direct communication among them. This could improve the speed with which information was disseminated and enhance the ability of individual affiliates to engage in the process of negotiations. The resulting sharing of information and, perhaps, expertise, could alleviate the position of affiliates with less resources and less direct access to and representation in Brussels. Increased horizontal communications might also lead to the adoption of common positions, which could improve the coherence of each side's negotiating stance. Forming such alliances might suffice to secure representation of the alliance on the 'Executive (Drafting Group) Committee', and offer guarantees of a flow of information and more effective consultation between that representative and the affiliates it represents. Purely hypothetically, it could be that arrangements among affiliates in the Benelux, Nordic, Anglo-Saxon countries would have some such potential, and could even overcome the ever present problem of linguistic diversity.[27]

The sectoral dimension of the intersectoral social dialogue

The European industry federations (EIFs) representing national affiliates provide an alternative to purely national representation in the EU social dialogue. This provides a parallel path to the ETUC in bringing together at sectoral level the common interests of affiliates in different Member States. In sum, the EIFs provide a network of horizontal linkages among national affiliates which can be represented in the EU intersectoral social dialogue. They allow for cohesive presentation of sectoral demands common to affiliates across a range of Member States. The EIFs' presence on the Drafting Group is thus particularly significant.

At the same time, EIFs replace national particularism with sectoral particularism. While overcoming national bias, the EIFs may further complicate negotiations as sectoral demands are added to national demands in an already complex set of issues to be negotiated.

The role of EIFs in intersectoral social dialogue raises in a different forum many of the fundamental questions underlying the transnational EU social dialogue in general. Specifically, what is the relative weight to be attributed to the intersectoral

[27] In the negotiations on fixed term work, the Drafting Group did include representatives from Belgium (Benelux) and Sweden (Nordic affiliates), as well as from 2 EIFs.

and sectoral social dialogues, and the related question of the relative importance and roles of the actors in each: on the trade union side, the ETUC and the EIFs.

On the one hand, there has been no lack of argumentation and evidence as to the importance of the EU sectoral social dialogue, both in the past,[28] and in the present and future.[29] However, the development of the EU sectoral social dialogue has suffered precisely due to the absence of EU sectoral employers' organisations and, where these exist, their reluctance to engage in EU sectoral social dialogue.

Given the current absence of sectoral organisation and initiative on the side of employers, the engagement of EU sectoral organisations in the intersectoral dialogue could stimulate developments in the EU sectoral social dialogue. A striking example of the interaction of intersectoral and sectoral social dialogues at EU level took place in the course of the negotiations over fixed-term work. The EIF sectoral federation, Euro-FIET (now UNI-Europa) agreed with the representative of the employers in the field of temporary agency work (*Confédération Internationale des Entreprises de Travail Temporaire*, CIETT) to exclude this field from the scope of the negotiations in the intersectoral social dialogue on fixed-term work. A letter signed by the Director of Euro-FIET and the first vice president of CIETT, dated 3 July 1998, and addressed to UNICE, CEEP and the ETUC expressed their joint view that it was inappropriate to include temporary work businesses. Significantly, they concluded that it would undermine progress that they were trying to make at sectoral level.

It was stated, therefore, that any EU level agreement on fixed term contracts should exclude agency work's triangular relationships. However, this exclusion should be accompanied by a commitment to negotiate a specific agreement for this type of relationship, at the appropriate EU level. This request was acceded to by the EU intersectoral social partners and temporary agency work was excluded from the scope of the negotiations. The agreement eventually concluded did, however, include the commitment to undertake an EU intersectoral social dialogue on temporary agency work. These negotiations were unsuccessful and on 22 March 2001 the ETUC Executive Committee abandoned negotiations and called on the Commission to propose a directive regulating temporary agency work. The Commission finally adopted such a proposal one year later, on 20 March 2002.[30] In the meanwhile, however, on 11 October 2001, UNI-Europa (formerly Euro-FIET) and CIETT signed a joint declaration on temporary agency workers.[31]

[28] B Bercusson, *European Labour Law*, London, 1996, ch 6, 'The Strategy of European Social Dialogue', p 72, at pp 78–94.

[29] The creation of more than 30 sectoral social dialogue committees under Commission Decision 98/500/EC of 20 May 1998 on the establishment of Sectoral Dialogue Committees promoting the Dialogue between the social partners at European level, OJ L 225/27 of 12.8.98.

[30] Proposal for a Directive of the European Parliament and the Council on working conditions for temporary workers, Brussels, 20.3.2002, COM(2002) 149 final, 2002/0072(COD).

[31] The next day, 12 October 2001, the EU intersectoral social partners opened negotiations on telework, which were this time successful.

Bilateral social dialogue at national level as an aide to successful transnational EU social dialogue

Individual union confederations or employers' organisations at national level may pose problems specific to their national context which threaten to block progress in the transnational EU social dialogue. Contacts between the social partners at national level may attempt to reach compromises where one or more of the national social partners are raising difficulties in the EU negotiations. A dispute could be resolved between the national social partners to avoid it contaminating the EU level negotiations. In the social dialogue on fixed-term work, one such concerned the issue of occupational pensions, which emerged as a problem for the national employers' confederation in one Member State. The ETUC stressed that it was not possible to make a general exclusion for occupational pensions, especially as part of pay. It was suggested that the trade union confederation and employers' organisation from that Member State should discuss this. This was undertaken and appears to have produced the desired interaction and a solution.

Breaking deadlocks in negotiations: the (temporary) role of mini-summits

It is not clear that the transnational EU social dialogue has yet achieved the 'normalisation', the longer term stability, which would ensure that the expectations of the parties are that obstacles encountered in negotiations will eventually be overcome. This apparent fragility may offer the temptation to some participants, national affiliates of the social partners, to perceive breakdowns in negotiations as more than the temporary and 'normal' checks to be encountered in a mature bargaining process, but rather an opportunity to wreck the process in its entirety. It may be necessary to develop mechanisms to avoid this temptation and break deadlocks. It seems that a change in the level of negotiations, in the form of 'mini-summits' between the leaders of the EU social partners, are used to achieve such breakthroughs.

At the penultimate (ninth) meeting of the Negotiations Group on 26–27 November 1998, the employers presented a text and their spokesperson reported on discussion among the employers' side following the blockage encountered in a meeting on 13 November 1998. In the plenary session which followed on 27 November 1998, the employers made a further proposition making a strong plea in favour of maintaining flexibility. The ETUC side could not accept the employers' proposal and decided that there was therefore no point in continuing discussions. The negotiations were then suspended and it was agreed that reports would be made to each respective organisation describing the situation.

UNICE's Council of Presidents met on 3–4 December 1998 and reaffirmed its willingness to continue negotiations by trying to find a solution to the current blockages. The crucial event was a meeting of the Presidents and General Secretaries of ETUC, UNICE and CEEP at the mini-summit on 4 December 1998 in Vienna. On that occasion, the problem of the negotiations was discussed in an informal manner to see if a possible change in the employers' position was still possible. An informal contact took place with the employers' spokesperson on 10 December 1998, at which point a draft compromise was reached on one of the disputed clauses being negotiated.The employers' spokesman was advised that he must inform the ETUC definitively of the possibilities for the employers to change their position by 12.00 hrs on 15 December 1998, just before the ETUC's Executive Committee discussion. Two hours before the ETUC Executive was to consider whether to continue negotiations, UNICE accepted the compromise formula and informed the ETUC Executive. The Executive Committee agreed to continue negotiations by referring the matter to the Negotiations Group and the Drafting Group for them to deal with it.

In a mature process of transnational EU social dialogue, there should be mechanisms of mediation and conciliation which may successfully break deadlocks and achieve the necessary agreement

The Role and Legal Status of the EU Social Dialogue in the Proposed Constitutional Treaty

The institutional position of the social partners and social dialogue

A proposed Treaty Establishing a Constitution for Europe, presented by the Convention on the Future of Europe on 18 July 2003, was adopted at the June 2004 Intergovernmental Conference of the EU Member States.[32] The Constitutional Treaty breaks new ground by acknowledging the social partners among the institutional elements of the EU in Title VI of Part I: 'The Democratic Life of the Union'

Article I-48: The social partners and autonomous social dialogue

The European Union recognises and promotes the role of the social partners at its level, taking into account the diversity of national systems. It shall facilitate dialogue between the social partners, respecting their autonomy.

The Tripartite Social Summit for Growth and Employment shall contribute to social dialogue.

[32] See footnote 1.

The legal status of social dialogue agreements

The Constitutional Treaty, in Title III: Policies and internal action, Chapter III: Policies in Other Areas, Section 2—Social Policy, Articles III-209–219 mostly replicates the 'Social Provisions' of the EC Treaty (Article 136–145), as amended by the Treaty of Nice.

However, there is one significant change which highlights the specific themes of level of regulation and legitimacy of workers' organisations. It illustrates the, perhaps, unintended consequences of constitutional change by characterising social dialogue agreements as *non-legislative* measures.

Article III-212 of the Constitutional Treaty replaces Article 139 EC. In Article III-212(2), instead of Article 139(2)'s reference to a Council '*decision*' implementing the social partners' agreement, it is to be implemented 'by *European regulations or decisions* adopted by the Council':

> Agreements concluded at Union level shall be implemented either in accordance with the procedures and practices specific to management and labour and the Member States or, in matters covered by Article III-210, at the joint request of the signatory parties, by *European regulations or decisions* adopted by the Council on a proposal from the Commission. The European Parliament shall be informed.

At first glance, this seems to dramatically change the legal nature of implementing measures. The earlier debate over what was meant by 'decision' in Article 139 TEC was not resolved, but in practice led to '*directives*'.[33] Under the Constitution, 'directives' become 'European framework laws'. In the future, it is European regulations or decisions, *not* 'European framework laws', which will implement the social partners' agreements.

It might seem that the wording 'European regulations or decisions' simply replicates the present position of implementation by a 'decision', with the added option of a 'European regulation'. But this is not the case. Both 'European regulation' and 'European decision' are given specific meanings in Article I-33 of the Constitutional Treaty.

However, it does not appear that any change is intended. The legal nature of European regulations and European decisions is defined in Article I-33. Though they are deemed to be 'non-legislative acts', their legal effects are described in terms *identical* to those of the 'legislative acts' (European laws and European framework laws).

A *European regulation* may have the legal effect:

> <u>Either</u> of a *European law*: 'binding in its entirety and directly applicable in all Member States';
>
> <u>Or</u> of a *European framework law*: 'binding, as to the result to be achieved, upon each Member State to which it is addressed, but shall leave to the national authorities the choice of form and methods'.

[33] B Bercusson, *European Labour Law*, Butterworths, London, Law-in-Context Series, 1996, at pp 548–50.

A *European decision* seems to have the legal effect of a *European law*: 'binding in its entirety'.

It appears the difference between legislative and non-legislative acts is *not* in terms of legal effects, but in terms of the *procedure* of enactment.

Article I-34: European laws and European framework laws follow from a Commission proposal and engage the European Parliament and the Council.

Article I-35: European regulations and European decisions engage the Council and the Commission, but not the European Parliament.

If so, the implementation of EU social dialogue agreements through European regulations and European decisions should not change the current procedure under Article 139 EC (new Article III-212). The current procedure does not engage the European Parliament.

In sum: the legal effects of European regulations and decisions implementing future agreements should be the same as the directives which implemented past framework agreements.[34] However, the change does have two potentially significant consequences.

Article III-212(2) changes the legal status of EU-level framework agreements by breaking the link with Article III-210(4)

Article III-212(2) provides that framework agreements are to be implemented through the new legal measures of European regulations or decisions, and not European framework laws. The change from 'directives' (which become European framework laws) to European regulations and decisions breaks a crucial link with Article III-210(4), which replaces Article 137(4) EC.

Article 137(4) provides that implementation of directives (to become European framework laws) can be achieved through agreements between management and labour. In a series of decisions, the European Court of Justice made clear that agreements between management and labour implementing directives must have the same legal effects as the directive.[35] This was initially stated in the second paragraph of Article 137(4) (in the initial Article III-104(4), para. 2 of the Draft Constitution):

> In that case, [the Member State] shall ensure that, no later than the date on which a *European framework law* must be transposed, management and labour have introduced the necessary measures by agreement, the Member State concerned being required to take any necessary measures enabling it at any time to be in a position to guarantee the results imposed by that framework law.

Article III-104(4) thus initially provided that agreements between management and labour are a means for implementing only European framework laws, *but not European regulations or decisions.* The result of the change in Article III-106(2)

[34] For example, the effects of the current framework agreements/directives (eg on parental leave, part-time and fixed-term work) should not be different from future framework agreements which take the form of European regulations or European decisions.

[35] B Bercusson, *European Labour Law*, 1996, at pp 121–6.

(now Article III-212(2)) was that the previous link between Article III-104(4) (ex Article 137(4) EC) and Article III-106(2) (ex Article 139(2) EC) was broken.

This change was not intended. It blocks the implementation of EU level framework agreements through agreements between management and labour within Member States. It is vital that national systems of collective bargaining and agreements take the responsibility for the implementation and enforcement of social dialogue agreements concluded at EU level. Preventing articulation between EU level agreements and collective agreements within Member States strikes at the heart of a transnational EU system of industrial relations.

Fortunately, following late representations, the necessary amendments were made to then draft Article III-104(4) allowing Member States to entrust the social partners with the implementation also of regulations and decisions made under then Article III-106(2). The link between the final Constitution's Article III-212(2) and Article III-210(4) is established by the revised wording of Article III-210(4):

> In this case, [the Member State] shall ensure that, no later than the date on which a *European framework law* must be transposed, *or a European regulation or decision implemented*, management and labour have introduced the necessary measures by agreement, the Member State concerned being required to take any necessary measure enabling it at any time to be in a position to guarantee the results imposed by that framework law, *regulation or decision.*

Review of the representativeness of the social partners concluding EU social dialogue agreements

Under the EC Treaty, *equivalence* of legal effects was presumed to exist between the two methods prescribed by Article 139(2): implementing framework agreements through:

(i) 'the procedures and practices specific to management and labour and the Member States', or
(ii) by a 'decision adopted by the Council'.

In practice, framework agreements were implemented through Council decisions in the form of *directives*. These are now characterised in the proposed Constitution as legislative measures: 'European framework laws'.

As noted above, this previous equivalence between the legal effects of directives and EU-level framework agreements is challenged by the new provision in Article III-212(2) of the Constitutional Treaty. This excludes European framework laws (formerly directives) as the means for implementing EU-level framework agreements. Instead, only European regulations or decisions become the means of implementing EU-level framework agreements.

The result is that the *equivalent* legal status of European framework laws (*legislative* acts) and EU-level framework agreements (*non-legislative* acts: regulations or decisions) (despite their later linkage in the amended Article III-210(4)) has been lost.

Again, this may have unforeseen and unintended consequences. The problem may be illustrated by examining the application for judicial review of the Parental Leave Directive, the first product of the EU social dialogue.[36] In litigation before the European Court of First Instance (CFI) the criterion of 'sufficient collective representativity' was put forward to identify the social partners referred to in Articles 138–139 EC as entitled to engage in the European social dialogue and produce *legitimate* EU social dialogue agreements.

UEAPME, an organisation representing artisans and small and medium enterprises, challenged the legality of the Parental Leave Directive.[37] To do so under Article 230 EC, UEAPME had to show, *inter alia*, direct and individual concern. The CFI held that it could do so if it could show that, UEAPME having been excluded from the negotiations, the agreement had not been negotiated by representative social partners. This view was premised on the equation drawn between the *legislative processes involving the social partners* reaching agreements transformed into directives, and the *legislative process* for adopting directives which *engages the European Parliament.* The CFI said: (paragraph 89):

> . . . the principle of democracy on which the Union is founded requires—in the absence of the participation of the European Parliament in the legislative process—that the participation of the people be otherwise assured, in this instance through the parties representative of management and labour who concluded the agreement which is endowed by the Council acting on a qualified majority, on a proposal from the Commission, with a legislative foundation at Community level. In order to make sure that that requirement is complied with, the Commission and the Council are under a duty to verify that the signatories to the agreement are truly representative.

For an agreement to be democratically legitimate, the CFI stipulates that it must be ascertained: (paragraph 90) 'whether, having regard to the content of the agreement in question, the signatories, taken together, are sufficiently representative'.

The Constitution's rejection of equivalence between legislative measures and non-legislative measures, the latter including social dialogue agreements embodied in regulations or decisions adopted *without* the participation of Parliament,[38] undermines the rationale of the decision in *UEAPME.* If the measures concerned are *not* legislative acts engaging Parliament, the requirement of democratic legitimacy in the form of criteria of representativeness is *not* applicable. It will be that much more difficult to establish *locus standi* for the purposes of judicial review of social dialogue agreements.[39]

[36] Council Directive 96/34/EC of 3 June 1996 on the Framework Agreement on parental leave concluded by UNICE, CEEP and the ETUC, OJ L 145/4 of 19.6.96.

[37] *Union Européenne de l'Artisanat et des Petites et Moyennes Entreprises (UEAPME) v Council of the European Union*, Case T-135/96, [1998] ECR II-2335.

[38] Though, note, the Constitution has added a final additional sentence to Article III-212(2): 'The European Parliament shall be informed'. *Cf* the perhaps unintended irony evinced in the final sentence of the second paragraph of Article III-213: 'The European Parliament shall be kept *fully* informed'.

[39] *Quaere* whether they qualify as a 'regulatory act' under Article III-365(4), the replacement for Article 230 EC.

Further, as the CFI in *UEAPME* also insisted that the Commission undertake such review prior to forwarding any agreement, and the Council likewise before making any decision conferring legal status on such an agreement, these institutions would also appear to be precluded from assessing the representativeness of the social partners as a precondition of approval of their agreements—in that sense reflecting the injunction in Article I-48 of the Constitutional Treaty as regards the social partners: 'respecting their autonomy'.

The 'Informal' Constitution: Social Dialogue and Legislation in EU Labour Law

An *Interinstitutional Agreement on Better Law-making*, dated 9 October 2003, was concluded between the European Parliament, the Council and the Commission.[40] It raises important questions about the achievement by the social partners of a regulatory space for the transnational European social dialogue in formulating EU policy in employment and industrial relations, and social policy in general.

The Interinstitutional Agreement deals with two principal issues: (i) the normal EU legislative process, and (ii) 'alternative methods of regulation'. The normal EU legislative process is dealt with in the sections on 'Better coordination of the legislative process' (paragraphs 3–15) and 'Improving the quality of legislation' (paragraphs 25–31). These sections ignore the special role of the social partners in the EU legislative process in the social policy field laid down in Articles 138–139 EC.

The special role of the social partners is referred to in the part on: 'Use of alternative methods of regulation' (paragraphs 16–23), which deals generally with 'co-regulation' and 'self-regulation'. However, the social partners, the social dialogue process and the agreements which result are subjected to conditions which conflict with Articles 138–139 EC.

The normal EU legislative process as presented in the Interinstitutional Agreement

Paragraph 26 on 'Pre-legislative consultation' states:

> During the period preceding the submission of legislative proposals, the Commission will, having informed the European Parliament and the Council, conduct the widest

[40] The Interinstititonal Agreement was signed and ratified by the Council, Commission and the European Parliament on 16 December 2003. It was published in the Official Journal, (OJ No C 321/2003) of 31 December 2003. Note also the Report from the Commission, *Better Lawmaking 2003*, pursuant to Article 9 of the Protocol on the application of the principles of subsidiarity and proportionality (11th Report), COM(2003)770, Brussels, 12 December 2003.

> possible consultations, the results of which will be made public. In certain cases, where the Commission deems it appropriate, the Commission may submit a pre-legislative consultation document on which the European Parliament and the Council may choose to deliver an opinion.

Yet Article 138 EC requires that 'before submitting proposals in the social policy field, the Commission shall consult management and labour on the possible direction of Community action'.

The proposed revision of the Working Time Directive is an illustration of the operation of this new procedure. In the Communication from the Commission to the Council, the European Parliament, the Economic and Social Committee and the Committee of the Regions concerning the re-exam of Directive 93/104/EC concerning certain aspects of the organization of working time,[41] the Commission states that the aim of this Communication is to consult the European Parliament and the Council, but also the ECOSOC, the Committee of the Regions and the social partners on a possible revision of the text: (page 4)

> . . . this communication should be considered as the first phase of consultation pursuant to Article 138(2) of the Treaty. The Commission will of course subsequently consult the social partners on the content of all proposals envisaged (Article 138(3)).

This is repeated on the last page of the Communication (page 24), which adds: 'They are invited to give their *opinion* on the need to amend the Directive on the issues identified in Part Two. They will be consulted subsequently . . .'. However, Article 138(3) EC provides for an opinion to be forwarded *not* after the first, but subsequent to the second consultation.

The preparation of this Communication had been known for a long time. It is questionable whether beginning the social partner consultation required by Article 138 EC only when others are also being consulted is acceptable.

The Commission's past practice has been that there is an 8-week period of consultation envisaged for the first consultation envisaged under Article 138(2) EC. Yet the Communication stipulates: (page 24) 'All interested organisations can send their comments and suggestions by e-mail only . . . [to] reach us no later than 31 March 2004' (ie 12.5 weeks after 5 January 2004).

If this is an Article 138 EC consultation, then it may be subject to the social partners' agreeing to engage in social dialogue. There is no mention of this possibility anywhere in the Communication, even though there have been numerous successful sectoral social dialogues on working time in various transport sectors.

These factors reinforce the case for the Communication not being the consultation required by Article 138(2) EC, despite the Commission's claim. The Commission has failed in its obligation under Article 138 EC.[42]

[41] COM(2003) 843 final, Brussels, 30 December 2003.

[42] Contrast the title of the Commission's publication of 19 May 2004: 'Second Phase of Consultation of the Social Partners at Community Level concerning the revision of Directive 94/104/EC concerning certain aspects of the organization of working time'.

Rather, it is further evidence that the Commission is reducing the involvement of the social partners and the role of the social dialogue to the level of general public consultations on Commission initiatives. This contravenes Articles 138–139 EC.

Alternative methods of regulation: co-regulation and self-regulation

As regards 'co-regulation', which appears to be a form of delegation to the social partners, the third subparagraph of paragraph 20 is the most alarming provision in the Interinstitutional Agreement:

> At the request of inter alia the European Parliament or of the Council, on a case-by-case basis and depending on the subject, the basic legislative act may include a provision for a two-month period of grace following notification of a draft agreement to the European Parliament and the Council. During that period, each Institution may either suggest amendments, if it is considered that the draft agreement does not meet the objectives laid down by the legislative authority, or object to the entry into force of that agreement and, possibly, ask the Commission to submit a proposal for a legislative act.

As presently understood and applied, the position under Articles 138–139 EC is that the European Parliament has no formal power to suggest amendments to an agreement or object to its entry into force, the Commission (a) has no power to refuse to propose the agreement for decision of the Council once there has been a 'joint request of the signatory parties'; (b) may not opt to submit an alternative 'proposal for a legislative act'; (c) or do so on the grounds that it does not 'meet the objectives laid down by the legislative authority', and the Council has no power to amend an agreement submitted by the Commission. It can only decide to adopt or reject it.

Instead, paragraph 20 of the Interinstitutional Agreement proposes that amendments may re-open social dialogue agreements concluded after extensive negotiations; social dialogue agreements may be subordinated to the 'objectives laid down by the legislative authority'; and social dialogue agreements concluded may be subject to the threat that the Commission will reject them and substitute a legislative act. It is not easy to imagine a more serious threat to the European social dialogue.

As regards 'self-regulation', the first part of paragraph 22 refers to 'the possibility for . . . the social partners . . . to adopt common guidelines at European level (particularly codes of practice or sectoral agreements)'. Paragraph 23 provides for the Commission to notify the Parliament and the Council, and to satisfy itself as to: 'the representativeness of the parties concerned, sectoral and geographical cover and the added value of the commitments'. Finally, the Commission 'will, nonetheless, consider the possibility of putting forward a proposal for a legislative act, in particular at the request of the competent legislative authority or in the event of a failure to observe the above practices'. The Commission may intervene to replace the practice or agreement with a substitute legislative act not only when there are failures of representativeness, etc, but simply at the request of the competent legislative authority.

Conclusion

The Interinstitutional Agreement aims to achieve 'Better Law-making'—*without* the social partners. The contradicts the recognition of the transnational EU social dialogue as the mandatory legislative procedure in Articles 138–139 EC, repeated in Article III-212 of the Constitutional Treaty. The Agreement's 'Alternative methods of regulation' include social dialogue, but the social dialogue is subject to the scrutiny and control of the other EU institutions.

This goes against the constitutional guarantee of autonomy in the Constitutional Treaty (Article I-48), though the last Recital of the Agreement emphasises that it 'is concluded without prejudice to the outcome of the IGC'. However, the active constitutional 'practice' proposed in the Agreement may outweigh the passive text of a Constitutional Treaty.

The fundamental strategic question is the role of the transnational EU social partners and the transnational EU social dialogue in the EU constitutional and legal order. Is it a role of autonomous regulation of social policy, and in particular, of the sphere of employment and industrial relations, by constitutionally recognised social partners? Or is the role of the social partners confined to an industrial relations sub-system subordinate to the internal market regulated by the EU institutions?

10

International Regulation of the Global Economy—The Role of Trade Unions

KD EWING*

Introduction

Much of the literature on globalization has been concerned principally with the role of governments and government agencies on the one hand, and with the role of multinational or transnational corporations on the other. The sometimes neglected third and crucial leg of the tripod are the organisations of workers, who it is claimed both benefit from and bear the burdens of globalisation. The pages that follow consider some of the strategies adopted by trade unions to deal with the problems of globalization, and also consider some of the factors that inhibit the trade union response. The particular focus is the emergence of international framework agreements between global union federations and transnational corporations, the agreements being said to be a 'key trade union tool for addressing the growth of corporate power'.[1] These developments are taking place, and these agreements are emerging, despite the failure of traditional international labour law in an era when some write—perhaps hopelessly—about the need to 'globalise resistance to globalisation'. But whether or not it is sensible to 'resist' rather than 'respond' to globalization, there can be no doubt about the power of the argument that 'if the system works at a very high level of internationalisation, and even of transnationalisation, then the answer has to be a very high level of international co-ordination and unity'.[2] Nor can there be any doubt about the need for international labour law to be part of that international co-ordination.

* Professor of Law, King's College, London. My thanks to Daniel Blackburn, Director of the International Centre for Trade Union Rights and Editor of International Union Rights for his invaluable help and advice in preparing this paper.

[1] www.tuc.org.uk/globalisation/tus_in _action.html.

[2] O Martinez, *Neo-Liberalism in Crisis* (1999), p 30.

The Changing Focus of International Labour Law

The case for international action by trade unions is by no means new. At the first annual conference of the British TUC in 1868, it was resolved that:

> As local organisations of labour have almost disappeared before organisations of a national character, so we believe the extension of the principle of free trade, which induces between nations such a competition that the interest of the workman is liable to be lost sight of and sacrificed in the fierce international race between capitalists, demands that such organisations should be still further extended and made international.[3]

The resolution continued by recommending that British trade unions affiliate to the International Working Men's Association (the First International).[4] Great social, economic and political changes have, of course, taken place since these pioneering days. So have great institutional changes, with the creation and development of the ILO as an agency for the setting of international labour standards. But the need for international action to deal with the consequences of globalisation has yet to be fully met, and indeed may never be met. There are in fact two (related) tasks for contemporary international labour law. The first is a traditional task, perhaps presenting more acutely in the modern era—to deal with those governments that still permit the abuse of trade unionists, the abuse taking the form of murder, rape and other criminal conduct.[5] The second is a more contemporary task—to 'restrain the unbridled power of TNCs'.[6] The latter task can be addressed in two ways: the first is by the countervailing power of labour, consumers, and/or political activists; and the second is by accountability to national or international institutions.

But although there are thus two key tasks, contemporary international labour law has traditionally been addressed mainly to governments, and to national labour law systems, for reasons that are perfectly understandable.[7] The core freedom of association and collective bargaining conventions were drafted and agreed in an earlier epoch, when the concern was with the law and practice within—rather than beyond—the nation state. So ILO Conventions and Recommendations impose duties on countries not companies; the ILO supervises the application of standards by countries not companies; and complaints are made to the ILO (where possible under freedom of association obligations) against countries not companies.[8] This is

[3] As quoted by K Marx, Report to the Basle Congress (1869), in D Fernbach (ed), *Karl Marx, The First International and After* (1974), p 91.

[4] On the aims of the First International, see *ibid*, pp 73–84 (Inaugural Address to the First International).

[5] See ILO, *Organising for Social Justice* (2004). Although Colombia is the best known, is not alone.

[6] B Hepple, 'A Race to the Top?' [1999] 20 *Comp Labour Law and Pol'y Jo* 347, at p 362.

[7] Albeit in a manner revolutionary in its day. See EJ Phelan, *Yes and Albert Thomas* (1936), pp 3–5.

[8] This is not to say that there is no scope for making TNCs accountable within the traditional ILO machinery. Here, however, the accountability is confined mainly to freedom of association matters, and is indirect. It takes the form of a complaint to the Freedom of Association Committee about the

not to deny that there is recognition of the possibility of cross border trade union action: ILO Convention 87 for example anticipates at least the possibility of the right to organise at an international level by recognising the right of national trade unions to affiliate to international organisations.[9] These federations and confederations 'should themselves enjoy the various rights accorded to first-level organisations, in particular as regards their freedom of operation, activities and programmes'.[10] But there is no contemplation of the right to bargain collectively at a transnational level.[11] It is also true that there is recognition by the supervisory bodies of the right to take international solidarity action, as part and parcel of the right to strike as read into Convention 87.[12] But there is no contemplation yet of the right to engage in

activities of a foreign-based multinational violating trade union rights in a host country. The complaint is made against the government in whose territory the alleged violations have occurred, but it is in reality a complaint against the company that has exploited weak labour laws. A good example of this is the complaint made by the UFCW in the United States against the US as a result specifically of the activities of Delhaize-Food Lion, 'a transnational enterprise based in Belgium operating food stores in the United States': *Complaint against the Government of the United States presented by the United Food and Commercial Workers International Union (UFCW), the American Federation of Labor and Congress of Industrial Organizations (AFL-CIO) and the International Federation of Commercial, Clerical, Professional and Technical Employees (FIET) Report No 284, Case No 1523.* The complaint was concerned with the unfair labour practices adopted by the company to keep trade unions out, and in particular its strict non solicitation rule. Although the USA has not ratified either Conventions 87 or 98, the complaint was upheld, and the Committee requested: 'the Government to guarantee access of trade union representatives to workplaces, with due respect for the rights of property and management, so that trade unions can communicate with workers, in order to apprise them of the potential advantages of unionisation'. There have also been similar complaints from the United Kingdom about other companies.

[9] The ILO Tripartite Declaration on Multinational Enterprises (Revised, 2006) also acknowledges the right to join international trade union federations (para 45), and provides that governments should not restrict the entry of employers' or workers' organisations 'who come from other countries at the invitation of the local or national organisations concerned for the purpose of consultation on matters of mutual concern' (para 48).

[10] B Gernignon, A Odero and H Guido, 'Freedom of Association', in ILO, *Fundamental Rights at Work and International Labour Standards* (2003), at p 16.

[11] But although the duty to promote collective bargaining in Convention 98 appears to anticipate a duty to promote collective bargaining within the boundaries of the particular ILO member state, there is a recognition in the ILO Tripartite Declaration of the transnational dimension of collective bargaining by multinational corporations. While there is a great emphasis throughout the Tripartite Declaration on national law and practice, it is also provided that:

> Multinational enterprises, in the context of bona fide negotiations with the workers' representatives on conditions of employment, or while workers are exercising the right to organise, should not threaten to utilise a capacity to transfer the whole or part of an operating unit from the country concerned in order to influence unfairly those negotiations or to hinder the exercise of the right to organise; nor should they transfer workers from affiliates in foreign countries with a view to undermining bona fide negotiations with the workers' representatives or the workers' exercise of their right to organise.

[12] The issue arose in the context of the Committee's examination of the restrictive British labour law, the Committee concluding in 1989 that:

> Other changes to the definition of 'trade dispute' in the 1974 Act also appear to impose excessive limitations upon the exercise of the right to strike: . . . (iii) disputes relating to matters outside the United Kingdom can now be protected only where the persons whose actions in the United Kingdom are said to be in contemplation or furtherance of a trade dispute relating to matters occurring outside the United Kingdom are likely be be affected in respect of one or more of the protected matters by the outcome of the dispute. This means that there would be no protection

co-ordinated trans-national industrial action in the ILO jurisprudence, though it is perhaps implicit. However, if it is implicit in international labour law, there are many national labour law systems which have yet to make it explicit.[13]

Although the nation State thus continues to be the main focus of international institutions and international labour law, that is slowly beginning to change, with transnational enterprises increasingly being brought under closer scrutiny. In the case of the ILO, the responsibility of multi-nationals is clearly acknowledged by the ILO Tripartite Declaration on Multinational Enterprises, first produced in 1977 and most recently revised in 2006: this is addressed to governments, employers' and workers' organizations, and to multinational organisations as well.[14] Although there is no formal complaints mechanism whereby concerns can be raised about the breach of the principles contained in the Declaration,[15] it is nevertheless increasingly possible to have complaints about multinationals investigated by the ILO. A good example of this is the complaint by the International Union of Foodworkers about Coca Cola's activities in Colombia, where it is alleged that the company was implicated in the murder of trade union activists at its bottling plants there.[16] However, a better example of transnational corporations being brought within the scope of international labour standards is provided by the OECD Guidelines on Multinational Enterprises of 2000, which deal with a wide range of issues besides labour standards. Unlike the ILO Declaration of 1977 (as revised), however, the OECD guidelines also provide formal machinery for complaints to be made to National Contact Points,[17] which are expected to investigate and seek to resolve complaints.[18] Yet although the OECD's Trade

> for industrial action which was intended to protect or to improve the terms and conditions of employment of workers outside the United Kingdom, or to register disapproval of the social or racial policies of a government with whom the United Kingdom has trading or economic links.

(See KD Ewing, *Britain and the ILO* (2nd edn, 1994), App IV).

This would appear to anticipate the possibility of industrial action to support a group of workers in another country who may be employed by the same corporate group as the workers taking the action, though in fact the boundaries of international solidarity action go much further. The main point, however, is that the right to strike and to take solidarity action is not confined by national borders or by national industrial relations systems. So while multinational companies are urged by the Tripartite Declaration not to transfer work from or workers to a country in order unfairly to undermine the position of labour, there is no objection to trade unions calling for support from colleagues in other parts of a corporate group. Indeed under ILO jurisprudence this ought to be permitted.

[13] Action by British workers would be unlawful unless they were also parties to the dispute. See Trade Union and Labour Relations (Consolidation) Act 1992, ss 219, 224, 244.

[14] ILO Declaration, above, Preamble, which 'invites' multinationals to 'observe' the principles embodied therein.

[15] The Declaration does, however, provide a procedure 'to interpret the provisions of the Declaration when needed to resolve a disagreement on their meaning, arising from an actual situation, between parties to whom the Declaration is commended'. There is also an ILO Multinational Enterprises Programme responsible for the follow up of the Tripartite Declaration.

[16] See War on Want, *Coca-Cola—The Alternative Report* (2005), pp 8–9. For the official response, see www.coca-cola.com.

[17] OECD Guidelines for Multinational Enterprises (2000), ch 1(10).

[18] See J Murray, 'A New Phase in the Regulation of Multinational Enterprises: The Role of the OECD' (2001) 30 ILJ 255.

Union Advisory Committee (TUAC) has reported some success with this mechanism,[19] it has also reported the emergence of some serious problems with the operation of the guidelines in some countries.[20]

GUFs and International Framework Agreements

The challenge for international trade unionism is an awesome one. Following the merger in 2006 of the ICFTU and the WFL, the international trade union movement is dominated now by the International Trade Union Confederation (ITUC), and 10 global union federations (GUFs). The latter are sectoral bodies to which national trade unions affiliate, and include the International Union of Foodworkers (IUF), the International Metalworkers' Federation (IMF), the International Transport Workers Federation (ITF), and the International Federation of Chemical, Energy, Mine and General Workers' (ICEM).[21] Ranged against them are sometimes hostile governments in the developed and the developing world. Even where there are governments sympathetic to the elimination of poverty and other concerns in the developing world, the concern may not extend to a recognition of the role of international trade unions as part of the solution to the problems. Also ranged against them are what are thought now to be 50,000 multinational corporations and their 450,000 'affiliates', employing some 200 million people.[22] These corporations may frequently inhabit very hospitable legal environments in which trade union rights are poorly or inadequately recognised, which host States may be ill equipped to change or improve.

In terms of a trade union response to globalisation, this has emerged rather belatedly, with a number of global union federations enthusiastically embracing the idea of international framework agreements with multinational corporations. Five of the 10 GUFs have adopted the negotiation of these agreements as a central strategy (foodworkers (IUF), building workers (IFBWW),[23] chemical workers (ICEM),[24] metalworkers (IMF), and communications' workers (UNI),[25] with the ITF (transport workers) having voted to do the same in 2003.[26] This is in fact only one of a number of trade union initiatives, though it is one of the most interesting.

[19] On activity under the guidelines, see OECD, *Specific Instances Considered by National Contact Points* (2006).

[20] See V Nilsson, 'The OECD Guidelines for Multinational Enterprises' (2005) 12(1) *International Union Rights* 11 (on the inadequate performance of some National Contact Points).

[21] For a full list, see ICFTU, *A Trade Union Guide to Globalisation* (2nd edn, 2004), pp 127–54.

[22] www.csr.gov.uk/declarationprinciples.

[23] The IFBWW agreements are available at www.ifbww.org/index.

[24] The ICEM agreements are available at www.icem.org/en/69-Global-Framework-Agreements. The 11 agreements (in November 2006) are with Freudenberg, Statoil, Endesa, Norske Skog, Anglogold, ENI, Svenska Cellulosa Aktiebol AB (SCA), Lukoil, EDF, LaFarge and Rhodia.

[25] The UNI agreements are available at www.union-network.org/uniindep.nsf. There were 12 agreements in November 2006.

[26] *Transport International Online*, 12 July 2003; www.itfglobal.org/transport.

It is all the more interesting for taking place in a legal vacuum, though it is designed principally to ensure the application of legal instruments. It is in fact a voluntary initiative to enforce legal standards (though not standards which are directly binding on the companies in question). However, it would be a mistake to overlook the extent to which this process takes place within a legal environment, particularly in view of the fact European Works Councils have been the forum (albeit a controversial one)[27] for negotiating and supervising many of these agreements. In this last case the agreements have emerged from a legal process, to ensure the application of legal standards, in circumstances where the agreement may have legal effects, even though their legal status may be uncertain.[28]

It is important to emphasise that international framework agreements are different from corporate codes of practice,[29] though to some extent their origins lie in exploiting the vulnerability of corporate codes.[30] Key differences are that the IFA will:

—be negotiated with a trade union and will not be simply a unilateral corporate initiative;
—usually include a commitment to ILO core standards, including specifically freedom of association and trade union rights (unlike some codes).[31]

Although unions are keen to emphasise the difference between agreements and codes,[32] it would be a mistake to generalise any further, for the nature of these agreements varies from company to company, and some are stronger than others.[33] But—as already indicated—so far as trade unions are concerned, this is an initiative which at international level is now attracting a great deal of interest, commitment and enthusiasm, there being a number of significant benefits to GUFs and their national affiliates if these agreements can be negotiated, implemented, and made to work. For the GUFs, it gives them an important role as

[27] J Holdcroft, 'International Framework Agreements: A Progress Report' (2006) (3) *Metal World* 18–22: 'UK affiliate Amicus states in its position paper on IFAs that, 'EWCs do not currently have negotiating mandates, their composition can include non-union members whose views may not be supportive, and clearly they only represent those within Europe'. Amicus argues that while EWCs can play an important role it must be the national trade unions and the Global Union Federations (GUFs) who drive the process' (p 19).

[28] On EWC, see B Bercusson, *European Labour Law* (1996), p 10.

[29] For a critique of which see L Compa, 'Trade Unions, NGO's, and Corporate Codes of Conduct' (2001) 8(3) *International Union Rights* 5, and L Yanz and B Jeffcott, 'Bringing Codes Down to Earth' (2001) 8(3) *International Union Rights* 8.

[30] On corporate codes and the weaknesses thereof, see B Hepple, *Labour Laws and Global Trade* (2005), p 73.

[31] Corporate codes which exclude trade union rights include Samsung, while several which do include freedom of association, such as G4 Securicor have had a number of freedom of association problems in a number of countries: see KD Ewing, *Global Rights in Global Companies: Going for Gold at the UK Olympics* (Institute of Employment Rights, 2006).

[32] International Metalworkers' Federation, *The Power of Framework Agreements* (nd), p 4.

[33] It is also the case that some Codes have trade union input and involvement. This is true of the Ethical Trading Initiative Code of Practice developed in the United Kingdom which has 39 employers and 4 trade union organizations involved, as well as 16 NGOs. See J Hawkins, 'Codes of Labour Practice: Revisiting the Debate' (2005) 12 (1) *International Union Rights* 9.

players in the global economy;[34] though as more agreements are concluded, a heavy burden will be placed on these organizations, in terms of monitoring and supervising the agreements, and dealing with complaints about their breach. There is a danger that not all IFAs will be equally monitored and enforced, with the result that they may have little impact. If they are to be effective, IFAs must be more than vanities to trade union ambition. But if they are effective, these agreements may provide another means of encouraging compliance with international labour standards. They may, moreover, help ensure that minimum standards will be obligatory to some extent in some parts of countries even though they are not required by national law, and even though the standards have not been ratified by the national government.

The Nature and Purpose of International Framework Agreements

Before examining the content and scope of international framework agreement, it is important to emphasise their dynamic nature. Here it is necessary to reinforce the point that their origins lie as an alternative to unilateral corporate codes, and as such they are designed principally to ensure compliance by companies with minimum labour standards. So much is acknowledged by Fred Higgs, the General Secretary of ICEM who wrote about these agreements serving the interests of business:

> If they are to convince a sceptical public of their good intentions, the big global corporations will have to put some content into their ethics. They will also have to go beyond self-proclaimed and self-evaluated codes of conduct.[35]

The agreements were thus about corporate ethics and 'credibility', in the sense that they would ensure standards were being complied with as a result of trade union involvement in the monitoring and compliance process.[36] The same vision of international framework agreements as being designed mainly to ensure compliance with international labour standards is to found in the perspective of AMICUS, a large British based private sector union. Here we find an acknowledgement that:

> Global agreements with multinational companies offer a good way of binding them and their subsidiaries to respect labour standards, while at the same time helping to build solid and effective international solidarity by connecting workplaces'.[37]

[34] See IMF, *The Power of Framework Agreements*, above.
[35] F Higgs, 'Global Companies Need Global Unions', *Financial Times*, 3 April 2000.
[36] *Ibid.*
[37] Amicus, *A Guide to Amicus International Work* (2005), p 2.

As a number of unions have made clear, however, international framework agreements may have a purpose beyond compliance with core labour standards, and in some cases may have an emerging social dialogue or collective bargaining purpose. This may not be collective bargaining in the traditional sense, with Fred Higgs pointing out, that 'the agreements will not be about pay'.[38] But as Higgs also points out, the aim is to 'set a framework for global industrial relations in each company and each sector'.[39]

This is a theme developed by UNI, which has drawn attention to the dynamic potential of these agreements, effectively as global procedure agreements in embryo, allowing a wide range of issues to be discussed. Thus, according to UNI:

> For the unions in the home country of the company, it means international questions become a legitimate subject of discussion and negotiation with the management. This can be crucial when, for example, a company wishes to outsource work to another country.[40]

The theme is developed further, it being pointed out that 'some unions have negotiated their own globalisation agreement with companies', these requiring any off-shoring to be the subject of prior discussion with the union; a guarantee of no redundancies; and assurances that the ILO standards, including the right to organise, will be respected in those countries to which work is transferred.[41] UNI also draws attention to the potential of these agreements for dispute resolution, claiming that 'where conflict occurs, the dialogue between unions and company, the mutual confidence built up, can mean that intervention by the global management with the global union can help resolve conflicts more quickly'.[42] However, although international framework agreements may provide a forum for global industrial relations, they are not a precondition of globalization agreements between national trade unions and multinationals for dealing with off-shoring. AMICUS, for example, has negotiated pioneering off-shoring agreements with a number of banks and finance companies, including Barclays, HSBC, and Prudential.[43] A second caveat which is also important—and which is sometimes emphasized by the agreements themselves[44]—is that:

> These international framework agreements do not substitute for or replace collective bargaining at the plant and national levels. Their purpose is to secure the capacities of unions at those levels to confront the concentrated power of global corporations.[45]

[38] F Higgs, above.

[39] *Ibid.*

[40] www.union-network.org/UNIsite/In_Depth/Multinationals/GFAs.

[41] *Ibid.*

[42] *Ibid.*

[43] AMICUS, *A Guide to AMICUS International Work*, above, pp 5–6.

[44] See the agreement between Fonterra and the IUF (discussed below) which states that it is not intended 'to replace or diminish the importance of local employee relations practice, problem solving and bargaining', with recourse to the review committee established to monitor the agreement being restricted to 'alleged serious or systematic violations of the rights contained in this agreement'.

[45] www.tuc.org.uk/globalisation.

Although there is thus a desire and a potential for international framework agreements to evolve into something beyond compliance with core labour standards, it may be premature nevertheless to conclude that we have here a new global industrial relations system in the making. A basic problem which is likely to constrain and contain the ambition of the GUFs is the problem of resources. Dave Spooner has pointed out:

> As the number of companies involved continues to expand, the GUF's face a major expansion of their workload, and rising expectations from their affiliates. The negotiation and subsequent monitoring and servicing of each IFA require considerable effort and expense, yet the financial and human resources of most GUFs are severely limited.[46]

To put the problem in perspective, as we have seen, there are 50,000 TNCs and only 10 GUFs, with each GUF being responsible for an impossible number of TNCs. Although this simple statistic/ratio is itself an indication of the scale of the problem, it is a problem compounded by the capacity of individual GUFs. Although international in operation, and although having large numbers of affiliated organizations, the GUFs also have limited funding, especially when compared with the resources of the TNCs with whom they have to deal. Some GUFs rely on affiliations from the same national organisations, which themselves are under severe financial pressure. In the United Kingdom (where union membership has halved in 20 years), both AMICUS and the Transport and General Workers' Union claim affiliation with eight of the 10 GUFs.[47] These very practical constraints suggest that while mature dialogue may develop in some cases between companies and unions, in the short-term at least it is likely to be selective, and that the core task of ensuring compliance with core standards will itself be enough to stretch resources beyond capacity. There is talk of the monitoring function being devolved from the GUFs to the national affiliates.[48] But while sensible, this adds to the burdens of already stretched national officers, though in the longer term these problems may be alleviated to some extent by the growing internationalization of the trade union movement, of which the work GUFs is an important—but not the only—symptom.

International Framework Agreements: Content and Substance

The first international framework agreement appeared in 1994 with the agreement between Accor and the IUF.[49] This study is based principally on a review of 31

[46] D Spooner, 'International Framework Agreements: Implementing Workers' Rights in Global Corporations', (2003) 53(1) *Federation News* 16, at p 17.

[47] Amicus, *A Guide to Amicus International Work*, above, p 7.

[48] D Spooner, above, p 18.

[49] See J Wills, 'Bargaining for Space to Organise in the Global Economy: A Review of the Accor—IUF Trade Union Rights Agreement' (2002) 9 *Review of International Political Economy* 675—an outstanding study.

agreements which were in place in June 2004.[50] However, given the stategic importance of these agreements to the GUFs, this is a number which has grown, so that by the end of 2006, there were over 50 such agreements posted or referred to on the websites of the different GUFs. On the employer's side most of the parties are European-based multinationals, though there are South African, American, and New Zealand companies as well. The main point of these agreements is to commit the companies in question to core international labour standards throughout their global operations, and as such they have been welcomed by the ILO as one of a number of initiatives designed to guide 'labour practices and labour relations across borders'.[51] A commitment to core labour standards means a commitment to freedom of association, the abolition of child labour, the elimination of discrimination and the abolition of forced labour. In some cases, these commitments are embellished beyond the core ILO Conventions. For example, the commitment to freedom of association sometimes includes a commitment to protect workers' representatives, often with an express reference to ILO Convention 135.[52] In many cases there is also a commitment to fair labour standards on matters such as pay, working time and health and safety. In other words, the agreements may go beyond core labour standards in two ways: first by expanding the content of these standards; and secondly by dealing with additional matters. It should be pointed out, however, that the OECD Guidelines do the same, and that not all international framework agreements go as far as the OECD Guidelines on both or either of these matters.

So far as promoting ILO core standards is concerned, the following provisions are illustrative:

—'The employer shall take a positive attitude to trade union activities, including organising.'

(Norske Skog and ICEM)

—'Statoil . . . agrees not to oppose efforts to unionise its employees.'

(Statoil and ICEM)

—Danone and the IUF undertake to 'Encourage management and trade unions to negotiate agreements concerning trade union rights, where possible for fixed durations, and to seek to publicize these agreements among the workforce to the widest possible extent.'

(IUF and Danone)

—'In the event of the partial or full closing of a facility, delegates of unions representing its employees may be granted time off with pay in order to perform their duties, if applicable regulations or agreement do not already call for it.

[50] For details of these agreements, see www.icftu.org. Many agreements are posted on GUF websites, though this is not true of them all.

[51] ILO, *Reducing the Decent Work Deficit- A Global Challenge* (2001), p 43.

[52] The Workers' Representatives Convention 1971. There are also examples of the Workers' Representatives Recommendation 1971 being adopted in this way. Convention 135 has only 79 ratifications, compared to 156 and 147 for Conventions 98 and 87 respectively.

Extraordinary time off with pay shall be negotiated with management at the local level'.

(IUF and Danone)

—'The Accor Group therefore undertakes not to oppose efforts to unionise its employees. The Accor Group considers respect for union rights to be part of the good reputation of its brand names'.

(IUF and Accor)

—Club Mediterranee, in the countries covered by this agreement, undertakes 'Not to resort to methods designed to deter trade union membership, including anti—union meetings, tracts, or verbal communications'.

(IUF and Club Mediterranee)

—'Chiquita will ensure that representatives of trade unions . . . have access to employees in the workplace'

(Chiquita and IUF)

—'During organising campaigns the company and the executives will remain neutral; the trade unions and the company will comply with basic democratic principles, and thus, they will ensure the employees can make a free decision. DaimlerChrysler respects the right to collective bargaining'.

(DaimlerChrysler and IMF)

—'Where Fonterra is engaged in collective bargaining with unions, Fonterra shall continue sharing with union representatives the information about Fonterra as a whole and its local operations that is reasonably required to bargain effectively.'

(Fonterra and IUF/New Zealand Dairy Workers' Union)

Also interesting in this context are the agreements between the IMF and DaimlerChrysler which provides that 'Freedom of association will be granted even in those countries in which freedom of association is not protected by law'. A similar provision is to be found in the agreement between Leoni and the IMF, though it is to be hoped that this merely makes express that which is implied by the other agreements.

In terms of agreements going beyond the subject matter of the core Conventions, it is to be noted that the OECD Guidelines provide that enterprises should, 'within the framework of applicable law, regulations and prevailing labour relations and employment practices', observe 'standards of employment and industrial relations not less favourable than those observed by comparable employers in the host country'.[53] They should also take adequate steps to ensure occupational health and safety in their operations',[54] as well as 'provide training with a view to improving skill levels' in the local economy.[55] International

[53] OECD Guidelines for Multinational Enterprises (2000), Ch 4(4)(a).

[54] *Ibid*, Ch 4(4)(b).

[55] *Ibid*, Ch 4(5).

framework agreements generally do not go this far. The IMF agreements with Volkswagon, Leoni and DaimlerChrysler typically deal with pay, working time, health and safety, though based on prevailing national standards (which is not the same as the standard of the comparable employer). So far as training is concerned, this entails a commitment only by way of 'support' or 'encouragement'. None of these agreements commits to international standards on these matters where the national legislation is inferior. This contrasts with the IMF agreement with Bosch which provides on working time that:

> The working hours including working time may not permanently exceed the existing statutory and/or collective agreement standards in the respective countries and/or international standards.

ICEM agreements typically deal mainly with health and safety in addition to the core standards. This is generally to be judged by reference to 'best practice standards' (Statoil), 'the application of industry best practice' (AngloGold), or 'the strictest respect of standards and required behaviour' (ENDESA). In the case of Norske Skog in order to achieve 'industry best practice' the company undertakes to 'work with the employees, their representatives and trade unions, to continually improve the company's health and safety performance'.[56] But although there are similar commitments on health and safety in other agreements, nevertheless many of the agreements are weak beyond core labour standards.[57] There are, however, some striking exceptions, including the following provisions of the Triumph agreement with the European Works Council and the ITGLWF:

> Appropriate remuneration and occupational advancement
>
> TRIUMPH INTERNATIONAL grants its employees an earned income that is orientated to comparable standards in the relevant country and is within the general remuneration guidelines of TRIUMPH INTERNATIONAL.
>
> Wages and other performance related payments conform to the legal or, for the industry applicable, minimum wage, which is enough to fulfil the basic needs of the employee and also leaves an amount, for free disposal.
>
> Before taking up employment all employees receive in writing understandable information regarding the wage conditions exact particulars regarding their wages for each period of payment.
>
> Capable employees are supported and whenever possible within the framework of the respective personnel development taken into consideration for future management function.
>
> All employees are offered an up to date working environment, whereby the general working conditions were created under protection of the relevant national standards and rules.

[56] The ICEM agreement with the Russian company Lukoil (12 May 2004) also has interesting provisions relating to advance notice of any restructuring, the professional development of workers, and respect for family values (committing to ILO Convention No 156), as well as respect for religious beliefs and habits of workers and the local population. See www.icem.org/en/69-Global-Framework-Agreements.

[57] For example, the Fonterra and IUF/New Zealand Dairy Workers' Union agreement extends only to 'healthy and safe working conditions'.

Job Security and Health & Safety
A safe and hygienic working environment is guaranteed at the place of work. Health and Safety measures are promoted under consideration of up to date knowledge and possible specific dangers within the industry.

Prohibited are physical mistreatment, threatening and physical force and mistreatment, unusual punishment or disciplinary measures, sexual and other molestation or intimidation.

Regular working hours
Working hours are set according to the current laws and the industry norm. Generally, a working week is not more than 48 hours and all employees receive at least one day off within a period of 7 days. Overtime is voluntary and as a rule restricted to no more than 12 hours per week. Each time this is compensated with an additional overtime payment, provided nothing different is agreed within flexible working arrangements.

International Framework Agreements: Scope of Application

Apart from the content of international framework agreements, an important issue is whether they apply to suppliers and licensees, or other third parties. This varies significantly. In some cases, there is no obligation extended to third parties; whereas in others, the agreement will commit the company to inform contractors and encourage them to apply its terms. In the case of the Fonterra agreement with the IUF, for example, the company undertakes to inform joint venture partners of its obligations under the agreement. There is, however, a third category of agreements which are extended beyond the immediate employer. In the case of the DaimlerChrysler agreement, the company 'supports and encourages its suppliers to introduce and implement equivalent principles in their own companies'. It goes further with an additional *expectation* for 'its suppliers to incorporate these principles as a basis for relations with DaimlerChrysler'. In common with a number of other companies, DaimlerChrysler regards the principles 'as a favorable basis for enduring business relations'. There are, however, a number of agreements which go further still, in the sense that they require the signatory corporations to impose obligations on suppliers of a more unequivocal nature.

In the case of Chiquita, for example, the agreement commits the company to '*require* its suppliers, contract growers and joint venture partners to provide reasonable evidence that they respect national legislation and the minimum labor standards outlined in Part 1 of the agreement' (Emphasis added.) (Part 1 of the agreement covers the core ILO Conventions, as well as health and safety at work.) In extending the principles to third parties in this way, the agreement is subject to the caveat that such extension is 'dependent on a number of factors such as Chiquita's relative degree of influence over its suppliers and the availability of appropriate and commercially viable supply alternatives'. More demanding is the agreement between Triumph International and its EWC and the ITGLWU. This provides:

> TRIUMPH INTERNATIONAL binds contractors, sub-contractors, suppliers and licensees to support and participate in the monitoring of the Code of Conduct; by:
>
> —providing TRIUMPH INTERNATIONAL with the relevant information regarding their activities
> —Allowing the work place and activities to be checked at any time
> —Recording the names, age, working hours and wage level of all the employees and make this documentation available upon request;
> —Informing the employees concerned verbally and in writing regarding the setting up of this Code of Conduct.
> —Apart from disciplinary measures, dismissals or other discrimination of employees; passing on information about the keeping of the Code of Conduct.
>
> If a supplier violates one or more of the regulations contained within this Code of Conduct, the company concerned will be approached to instigate immediate measures to correct this. Should the requested corrective measures not be carried out TRIUMPH INTERNATIONAL can stop the actual production, annul existing orders, suspend future orders or terminate the business relationship.

The Triumph agreement also provides that steps will be taken to 'integrate into all contracts with contractors and suppliers as well as licensees the duty to keep to the Code of Conduct and all its regulations'.

The Triumph agreement appears to be one of the most extensive in terms of scope. It nevertheless falls some way short of the ITGLWF standard agreement. This provides although the IFA would be voluntary in nature, it would give rise to legal duties on the part of contractors. Thus, the ITGLWF model agreement anticipates that the respondent company:

> will place a contractual obligation upon its contractors, their sub—contractors, principal suppliers and licencees (franchise holders) to adhere to the terms of this agreement and will ensure that all contracts allow for the termination of the contract for failure to observe such terms.

But not only does the model agreement anticipate that the company would place a contractual obligation upon its contractors: it also anticipates an obligation on the part of the company to establish and maintain appropriate procedures to evaluate and select its contractors, their sub-contractors, principal suppliers and licencees 'based on their ability to meet the requirements of [the] agreement'. The respondent company would also be required by the model agreement to maintain records about its suppliers' commitment to social accountability, this to include the suppliers' commitment to conform to the labour standards agreement, participate in monitoring activities, promptly remedy any breach of the agreement, promptly and completely inform the company 'of any and all relevant business relationships with other suppliers and subcontractors', and provide a commitment in writing to provide at regular intervals 'independently certified evidence of compliance with the requirements of [the] agreement'. Having secured these commitments, the model agreement anticipates finally that contractors, subcontractors and licencees will provide at regular intervals 'independently certified evidence of compliance with the requirements of [the] agreement'.

International Framework Agreements: Monitoring and Supervision

Apart from questions of content and scope of application, the other critical feature of these agreements relates to their monitoring and supervision. The danger here is that they degenerate into statements of good intent that mean little in practice. The danger for the trade unions is that they are seen to lend legitimacy to poor working practices. It is thus an important feature of these agreements that they should make provision for trade unions to involved in the process of monitoring and supervision. There are in fact a number of preconditions of effective supervision and monitoring. These are:

—Dissemination of the terms of the agreement throughout the enterprise
—Clear identification of who is responsible for the implementation of the agreement
—Procedures for monitoring the application of the agreement at regular fixed periods
—Trade union involvement in the monitoring and enforcement process
—Procedures for raising complaints about breach of the agreement
—Procedures for rectifying any failings where they are identified.

On each of these points practice varies, though there is a greater degree of convergence in relation to the first as opposed to the last of these conditions. So most agreements provide for their dissemination throughout the enterprise, in some cases in the languages of the different countries where the corporation operates. But the nature of the dissemination varies, with problems arising in practice as a result of inadequate dissemination.[58] Some may simply contain a general commitment to 'propagate' the agreement 'by publicising its existence and contents' (Endesa). Others provide that they will be made available 'to all employees and their representatives in an appropriate form' (DaimlerChrysler and IMF), and others still provide for information to be provided by trade unions or elected employee representatives at the workplace (Volkswagen and IMF). In one case, it is provided that the agreement is to be distributed to all the unions that organise employees of the company throughout the world, though several other

[58] See L Riisgaard, *The IUF/COLSIBA—Chiquita Framework Agreement: A Case Study* (ILO Working Paper No 94, nd). Problems have also been identified in the IMF agreements. See J Holdcroft, above.

agreements anticipate that the information will be disseminated to and by the relevant trade unions. Best practice, however, also provides for the agreement to be made available not only at every workplace but also on the company's website and intranet (Norske Skog). Very few expressly deal with the question of responsibility for ensuring compliance with the agreement, though there are a number which do. Again the DaimlerChrysler agreement provides that 'the senior managers of each business unit are responsible for ensuring compliance'. But this is quite unusual, as is the GEA agreement with its EWC, the European Metalworkers' Federation and the International Metalworkers' Federation which obliges 'executives and employees at all levels to observe, accept and promote the agreed objectives'. An important provision of the Fonterra agreement requires both parties to co-operate to give it practical effect, to include training.

In terms of monitoring and compliance, here again the practice varies. In many agreements there is no dedicated monitoring or compliance group. In the case of DaimlerChrysler, it is the responsibility of corporate audit to examine compliance with the agreement: the formal trade union role is limited in the sense that the 'corporate management will regularly report to and consult with the international employee representatives on social responsibility of the company and the implementation of [the agreement]'. In other cases, the operation of the agreement is to be examined by an annual meeting of the parties, and in some cases provision is made for complaints to be made and investigated as necessary (Freudenberg and ICEM; Anglo Gold and ICEM). This compares with agreements such as those signed by Chiquita and Triumph which provide for joint company/union committees to oversee the management of the agreement. In the case of Chiquita, the company and the IUF each appoint up to four members to a review committee that meets periodically to oversee the agreement and discuss other matters of mutual concern. These meetings are to take place twice a year, with an emergency procedure for matters that require urgent discussion. In similar terms the Triumph agreement provides that:

> TRIUMPH INTERNATIONAL, the European Works Council and the EGV/TBL are setting up a committee for the supervision of the regulations of this Code of Conduct. TRIUMPH INTERNATIONAL is sending 2 representatives to this Monitoring Committee, likewise the Euro-Works Council 2 representatives and EGV/TBL 2 representatives. The committee dictates the tasks and authority of the Monitoring Committee according to the principle of unanimity.

Joint monitoring arrangements are thus not universal, an the same is true of express guarantees not to dismiss or discipline union delegates exercising functions under these agreements (Statoil and ICEM).

International Framework Agreements: Trade Union Opportunities

As pointed out above, international framework agreements have the capacity to evolve beyond being instruments to ensure compliance with core labour standards to be instruments for the development of continuing dialogue between employers and trade unions at the highest level. This is a matter to which we return. But quite apart from these questions about the purpose and potential of international framework agreements, at a practical level there is evidence that they provide national trade unions with organizing and bargaining opportunities at local level. This, indeed, is a key motivation in the negotiation of at least some of these agreements. According to the IUF:

> The IUF, as a global federation of unions, believes that international framework agreements on trade union rights can serve as a crucial lever in opening up space for our affiliates to organise. Through this process, international recognition of the IUF by transnational employers can create a structure and agreed procedures to support members organising the company on the ground.[59]

The point is illustrated by the IUF agreement with Accor, which has 'allowed the IUF to open doors for local unions to organise; allowed union affiliates to integrate the international dimension into everyday trade union activities; [and] allowed the IUF to intervene and defend union organising efforts where local managers are violating the [agreement].[60] Indeed Wills shows how 'with regard to developments in North America, Australia, New Zealand and the UK', the agreement between Accor and the IUF 'allows the IUF to get involved in local trade unionism', and that the agreement has 'made a real difference to the outcome of union organizing campaigns', citing the example of hotel disputes in New York and Toronto.[61]

All five GUFs that have negotiated international framework agreements have reported successes of this nature. Thus, in the case of the IFBWW (building workers):

> Some affiliates made some breakthrough in using these agreements. The Polish affiliates were able to organise nine IKEA-owned companies, Swedwood. The Malaysian timber union also organised two IKEA suppliers. North American affiliated have been using these arrangements with SKANSKA and Hochtief to establish unions at construction sites. Workers' representatives were elected in Faber Castell factories in Malaysia and China.[62]

[59] P Rossman, 'The IUF, Chiquita and Union Rights' (2001) 8(3) *International Union Rights* 13.

[60] J Wills, above, at p 685.

[61] *Ibid*, pp 691–2.

[62] IFBWW, *IFBWW Experiences with Global Company Agreements* (Geneva, 2004).

In the case of UNI, there are also reports of discussions between Carrafour and UNI about the latter using an IFA as a basis for organising workers in Colombia, despite claims by local management that:

> as there is no clear legal framework for regulating this activity, domestic and international players compete in unequal conditions against the informal commerce sector—which pays no taxes, is not subject to the same obligations as legally established companies and, therefore, creates unfair competition—seriously affecting the interests of domestic and foreign companies.

Similarly, UNI claims that an affiliate in Brazil used the opportunities provided by an agreement to double its membership.[63] A well-known case involving the International Metalworkers' Federation relates to a DaimlerChrysler supplier in Turkey. In 2002, according to Holdcroft, workers employed by a company called Ditas took industrial action about the anti union conduct of the company, which was alleged to have breached ILO Convention 87. Intervention by DaimlerChrysler's World Employee Committee was said to have 'played a significant role in a negotiated settlement being reached'.[64]

Returning to the experience of the IUF, the example of its agreement with Chiquita reveals that even where other features of an agreement fail, its role as an organizing tool remains constant. The Chiquita agreement with the IUF, for example, provides that:

> In the event of any situation that would seriously affect the volume of employment, working conditions or the type of contracts of work, such as changes or transfers in production or the closure of all or part of a facility, CHIQUITA commits to . . . consult those local trade unions that have been duly appointed as the representatives of the affected workers, which discussions should occur as soon as possible, especially when the change affects a significant number of employees such as in a partial or total closure

As already pointed out, this agreement also provides for the appointment of a joint review committee to oversee its application and to raise other matters of mutual concern. In these ways, there is a potential for 'a continuous and constructive dialogue between unions and employer that could help guarantee core workers' rights'.[65] However, the study by Riisgaard found that these obligations had not always been respected by the company, and that this potential had yet to be realised, due to multiple factors including distrust between unions. Significantly for present purposes, however, it was nevertheless also found that:

> in spite of the poor use of the agreement's potential, it has actually had some very concrete positive consequences. As noted it has been used in Honduras to form new unions. . . . this was in a supplier plantation that before the agreement was very hostile towards attempts at unionising. This seems to indicate that in a context of progressive local organising activity, the agreement can help to enforce local recognition. It has also led to

[63] UNI, above.
[64] Holdcroft, above, p 22.
[65] Riisgaard, above, p 16.

ongoing dialogue between unions and Chiquita in Costa Rica at a national level, resulting in a significant decrease in the number of disputes that end up in the Labour Ministry.[66]

International Framework Agreements: Problems in Practice

For trade unions, IFAs are seen as an important contribution to the problems of globalisation and the power of TNCs. But it would be a mistake to exaggerate their role at this stage or to under-estimate the hurdles that have yet to be encountered. At the present time, most of the agreements are with European-based companies. And though it may be refreshing to see the exporting of European social democracy in this way, this is a strategy which will be weakened without a greater commitment of corporations from other parts of the world. Yet not all employers are sanguine, and the doubts expressed are likely to be contagious. According to Antonio Penalosa, the secretary general of the International Organisation of Employers, companies should have regard to a number of factors when concluding global agreements, these relating to 'legal risk, operational efficiency and reputation'. In his view:

> However general or aspirational these agreements may appear, companies need to carefully consider the implications of anything they sign up to: there have been recent examples of companies having signed such global agreements finding themselves with severe adverse publicity at a time of economic downsizing brought about by the demands of the marketplace.

Mr Penalosa is also reported as being concerned that 'agreements which provide that companies will adhere to ILO core labour standards move responsibility for compliance with ILO Conventions from governments to individual companies, a development that could mean difficulties of interpretation and responsibility at times of conflict'.[67] So although this is an important initiative, it is unclear how far it will travel. But there must at best be scepticism about the likelihood of US based multinationals signing up to these agreements when (a) the principles they contain have not been ratified by their own government, and (b) the company in question may not recognise unions in its own domestic operations. The idea that Wal-mart or McDonald's would sign such an agreement seems remote.

In the context of employer scepticism, a second concern relates to the legal environment in which this initiative is developing. In an ideal world, ILO Conventions 87 and 98 would be modernised and revised to apply to freedom of association and collective bargaining in the international as well as the national arena.[68] States

[66] *Ibid.*

[67] 'Update on Global Agreements', *European Industrial Relations Review*, June 2003 26, at p 30.

[68] KD Ewing, 'Trade Union Rights in the Twenty-first Century' (2001) 5 *Working USA* 19.

would be under a duty to take measures to encourage transnational companies to enter into collective bargaining arrangements with a view to concluding collective agreements with global union federations on matters of international concern. But we do not live in an ideal world. At a time when major developed (USA) and developing (India and China) countries have yet to ratify the existing freedom of association conventions, there seems little prospect of this ever happening. Indeed the forces that make the modernisation of ILO Conventions necessary are the same forces that make such modernisation unattainable. But even if such a modernisation of the Conventions were to be achieved, there is little prospect of their ratification and implementation. There is no reason to believe that the countries which have yet to ratify Conventions 87 and 98 (despite the recent partially successful efforts of the ILO to increase the levels of ratification) would be any more willing to ratify a new Convention designed to impose duties on their transnational companies. The United States, India and China have not ratified existing conventions as a protest against their inadequacy. Yet although legal support is not a precondition for the concluding of an IFA, it is hard to escape the conclusion that such support is helpful. This legal support can take one of two forms: the first would be direct in the sense of a formal obligation to enter into a procedure for the conclusion of such an agreement, an international parallel to a national recognition procedure. The second is indirect in the sense that there is an obligation to establish a forum for dialogue at an international level, such as is provided by the EWC Directive. The existence of such a structured environment allows unions to raise issues of this kind, even if there is no obligation on the part of management to respond, far less conclude an agreement.

The other concern that might be raised here relates to the uncertain legal status of IFAs, which indeed may vary according to the nature and content of the agreement on the one hand and the jurisdiction in which it was concluded on the other. The view has been expressed robustly that the agreements are not legally binding contracts.[69] The very detailed ITGLWF model agreement makes it clear that it is intended to be a 'voluntary' agreement, though this is not reproduced in agreements concluded by the union. The Triumph agreement, for example, is in mandatory terms of 'commits' and 'binds': nothing aspirational there. In agreements concluded by other unions—notably ICEM—there is a degree of formality that we might associate with legally binding contracts. Apart from the ICEM agreements, the Fonterra agreement with the IUF is notable for its solemnity, being signed in New Zealand in the presence of the Minister of Labour (acting on behalf of the Prime Minister who had to travel to London for the Queen Mother's funeral) and the Director General of the ILO.[70] There is also the question about those agreements concluded by EWCs where the status of the agreement may depend on the status and constitution of the EWC itself. At this stage in the development of IFA's, it is probably in no one's interests to exaggerate their legal status,

[69] L Torres and S Gunnes, *Global Framework Agreements: A New Tool for International Labour* (2003), p 9.

[70] www.iuf.org.

and, the view has been expressed forcefully by the International Metalworkers' Federation that 'no legal enforcement mechanisms exist at the global level. This means that any enforcement of IFA provisions relies almost exclusively on the capacity and strength of unions to compel companies to resolve complaints'.[71] In this situation, however, any prospect of transnational industrial action in response to a breach of an international framework agreement seems largely fanciful for a number of reasons, even though such breaches do occur.[72] Just as international and national labour laws have yet to adapt to the possibility of international collective bargaining, so they have to adapt to the possibility of international trade union action against a single corporate entity operating in several countries.[73] It is true that there may be no need for such sanctions, if procedures are developed to resolve disputes by other means. But the fact is that the agreements scarcely recognise that there will be disputes on this scale: they provide an opportunity for trade unions to be heard, but may not provide a detailed procedure for conflict resolution.

Conclusion

International framework agreements are important not so much for what they do as for what they expose. They expose a need for new organisational forms on the part of workers and trade unions to deal with the transnational corporations. Trade unions now recognise that they are ill-equipped to deal with globalization, with one leading General Secretary of one of Britain's largest unions lamenting that:

> In our current condition even AMICUS is ill prepared to fight anything other than a guerilla war on home ground. Individual unions with membership mostly in sectors in terminal decline can offer little resistance against the global giants.[74]

This has led to calls for an 'end game' which will be global trade unions whose aim will be to lift standards for workers everywhere from the UK, to Eastern Europe and the US, to the Far East'.[75] In other cases, it has seen the development of close working relationships between trade unions in different countries and on

[71] J Holdcroft, above, p 21.

[72] Riisgaard, above, p 17 (closure of 4 plantations in Guatemala without prior consultation); Holdcroft, above, p 21.

[73] What is anticipated here is not unilateral action to enforce a model agreement (as in the case of the ITF flag of convenience campaign—on which see H R Northrup and P B Scrase, 'The International Transport Workers' Federation Flag of Convenience Shpping Campaign: 1983–1995' (1996) 23 *Transportation Law Journal* 369; and N Lillie, 'Global Collective Bargaining on Flag of Convenience Shipping' (2004) 42 BJIR 47), nor international solidarity with a group of workers in dispute in another country (as is covered by ILO Convention 87). Rather, what is anticipated as being necessary is the right to take part in coordinated transnational industrial action.

[74] D Simpson, 'One World, One Union', *Amicus—The Magazine*, Winter 2005, p 8.

[75] D Simpson, 'Working Together' *Amicus—The Magazine*, Autumn 2005, p 5.

different continents, as unions in one country take their local concerns to the head office and shareholders of the global companies with which they are in dispute. One of the most interesting consequences of this development has been the end of US isolationism, as American unions have become internationalist in their campaigns against American employers who may be European-based.[76] The most prominent US union of this genre is Service Employees International Union (SEIU), which—to give one example—has taken its campaign for recognition at Wackenhut to its British owner G4S,[77] a multi-national security company recently involved in a high profile dispute in Indonesia.[78]

In the context of these slowly emerging developments (which will help to alleviate if not wholly overcome the problem of resources identified above), international framework agreements also expose the shortcomings of international labour law, which is based on a model of national collective bargaining regimes, and fails adequately to deal with the global context within which that bargaining may take place. We have in fact a very primitive system of international labour law for dealing with an advanced global economy.[79] We have at best a right to organise at an international or transnational level, but not a right to bargain. We have a right to strike in global solidarity (a right typically honoured in the breach by national labour law regimes),[80] but not yet recognition of a right to strike in the form of co-ordinated transnational action. International labour law is at a stage of development not dissimilar to the stage of development of British labour law in 1871: there is a freedom to organise for the purposes of mutual support, but no obligations on employers, and great legal uncertainty about concerted action (even if it were viable). It is difficult to avoid the conclusion that if trade unions are to have a role in transnational labour relations, they too will need the support of transnational government institutions. The EWC Directive provides a possible first faltering step forward, though as has already been pointed out, it provides a controversial basis for a trade union response. But if IFAs are a new phenomenon in embryo, it is difficult to be too optimistic if governments and international institutions refuse to acknowledge the role of law to underpin this new form of trade union activity.

[76] For an account of the US, see WB Gould IV, 'Fundamental Rights at Work and the Law of Nations: An American Lawyer's Perspective' (2005) 23 *Hofstra Labor & Employment Law Journal* 1.

[77] See www.focusongroup4securicor.org.

[78] *Guardian*, 12 August 2006.

[79] See also Judy Scott, SEIU General Counsel—'our current global governance structures are wholly inadequate to protect the fundamental core labor rights of workers employed by multi-national corporations and their supplier chains'—'The Enforcement Challenge of Corporate Social Responsibility: International Codes of Conduct, Global Framework Agreements and Related Strategies', 13 October 2006.

[80] A good example was the move made by the Thatcher government in the Employment Act 1982 against the ITF flag of convenience campaign, with amendments introduced to deny the campaign legality in British law. See HC Debs, Standing Committee G, 29 April 1982, cols 1312–13.

11

Alternative Mechanisms of Voice Representation*

PROF DR ULRICH MÜCKENBERGER**

Introduction

Voice and representation have a twofold impact, a person with voice will be better protected vis-à-vis a given socio-economic environment; and will be better integrated into this environment. The increasing significance of voice within modern society can be observed in the dualism of 'substantive' and 'procedural' rules and the shift from substantive to procedural regulation. Procedural rules 'settle the ways in which substantive rules are made, and the ways in which they can be challenged, changed, interpreted and applied' (Clegg, 1979: pp 1–2). Voice and representation play a decisive role within procedural regulation.

This is particularly so in the field of labour and work where 'reflexive labour law' (Rogowski/Wilthagen, 1994) is said to be characterised by procedural adaptability rather than by rigid substantive standards. There are dangers in the increasing 'flexibilisation' of labour and labour law (*cf* Mückenberger/Deakin, 1989). Proceduralisation must take seriously fundamental rights of citizenship, free collective bargaining, and the legitimacy of public discourse. The role of 'voice' is paramount. A modern discursive society depends on voice and public debate with a view to rational societal decisions—not only in the public sphere of politics and the media, but also in the allegedly 'private' spheres of the work place, the family, the neighbourhood, and in gender and generation relationships. Voice provides both an early-warning system when social risk threatens and a problem-solving capacity with respect to social problems.

This study examines modern socio-economic changes which erode traditional protections of workers, and ways in which voice and representation—in traditional or renewed forms—can help to restore them. The objective of the study is to identify the right questions, not the answers.

* This paper is derived from a study written to provide proposals for further research within the ILO's InFocus Programme on Socio-Economic Security, Ref. TF 61-01-3-D-1-1. I am grateful to Guy Standing for his initiative.

** Professor of Law, University of Hamburg.

Extending the Concept of 'Voice'

The concept 'voice' refers to the book *Exit, Voice, and Loyalty. Responses to Decline in Firms, Organizations, and States* by AO Hirschman (1970). I will briefly summarise what is important in Hirschman's findings to our context. Then I will propose some modifications. Hirschman confines his observations mainly to 'responses' to the behaviour of organisations, leaving aside their development potential. He takes being a member or customer as given—so that only the alternatives of voice or exit exist. Both restrictions seem static. I will try to dynamise Hirschman's model by (i) introducing, as a third category, 'entry' (or the setting-up of an organisation), and (ii) taking into account changes in organisations which are not reactions to the voice or exit of members or customers, and their impact on responsiveness with respect to voice and exit (and entry). This extension of his concepts makes the fruitfulness of Hirschman's approach still more apparent.

Voice, Exit and Loyalty

Voice and exit are the main options for members or clients reacting to organisational decline. Both can induce the organisation to overcome decline (Hirschman, 1970: pp 20–1). Voice and exit are not only in the interest of the members/customers, but also of the organisations/firms, and society as a whole.

The paradigm of exit is the market; a normal economic action. The paradigm of voice is the non-market political arena (*ibid*, pp 15–20). The increase of market forces in modern society promotes a trend toward exit. Which option members/customers choose depends, eg on whether the decline in supply is one of price or of quality and members/customers are low price- or high quality-oriented; whether demand is elastic with respect to time and quality; whether the use of voice appears to be effective or not; whether, in the course of the conflict, the option of voice gets less attractive, etc.

There are a number of factors which affect institutional design promoting choices between voice and exit. For example:

—A certain equilibrium is needed between 'passivity' and 'alertness' vis-à-vis the deterioration of the organisation by the members/customers. On the one hand, the more members/customers are 'passive', the less will they make use of their options and the less their impact on organisational change. As against that, the quicker 'decline-alert' they are and act, the worse for gradual learning-processes and organisational improvement. So only a certain equilibrium between the two will provide an improvement.

—Loyalty can keep members/customers in their roles in order to change 'from within', even in case of discontent. 'As a rule, then, loyalty holds exit at bay and activates voice' (ibid, p 78). However it also can 'overshoot the mark' and neglect the possibility of exit. Then it does not serve organisational change.

—Institutional design affects voice and its effective use. Where the exit option is excluded, is too expensive or is threatened with severe penalties, the voice option equally diminishes. However, when the exit option is too easy, it may be preferred to the sometimes troublesome voice option. A certain institutional equilibrium is needed between incentives to stay 'within' and opportunities to exit to make voice a powerful and effective instrument.

Voice, work and labour

Hirschman was interested in the world of markets and politics, not the world of work and labour. Nevertheless, his observations may be fruitfully applied to the world of labour, particularly his high estimation of 'voice'.

Labour and continuity—preference for voice. At least in modern times, the employment relationship has developed towards stability and continuity. In highly industrialised and service-oriented countries, continuity of production, high-trust relationships, co-operative behaviour have become so important that work inside the organisation has become more important compared to the external labour market. However, the 'standard employment relationship' (SER) is threatened by deregulation trends (*cf* Mückenberger/Deakin, 1989).

Standard employment relationships imply particular patterns of 'voice' and 'exit'. Permanent recourse to 'exit', to the 'external' labour market, is dysfunctional for modern societies requiring change. Rather, 'internal' instruments of adaptation and innovation are needed. Here voice plays a much more important role. And voice will rarely be individual, but rather collective, so that 'voice' goes along with 'representation' (*cf* Supiot 1999, ch IV).

Exit (i): Freedom of contract. Exit is of huge importance. Freedom of workers not to accept certain jobs or to quit (forced labour, slavery) is essential for voice. In this sense, freedom of contract remains indispensable for workers. This freedom is challenged by hidden mechanisms; eg, social security used to regulate the labour market. The option of exit (or the threat of it) is necessary for voice. Institutional design promoting voice must safeguard exit.

Exit (ii): Institutional design. Hirschman explains that satisfactory exit options require an institutional framework, exit must not be too easy or too difficult. In the field of labour, the freedom to dismiss and to quit include sanctions for leaving (on workers) and the duty to pay compensation (for employers). These create 'thresholds' for exit, without excluding it, but barriers against immediate exit lead to stronger voice. Disputes within the employment relationship can contribute to improvement of the firm. But barriers can also threaten exit (free movement of workers (the *Bosman* case in the European Court of Justice (1995)). Institutional frameworks external to the firm can also hinder exit, a lack of social security will constrain the worker from leaving however poor the job, promoting passivity and poor quality work. A good social security system makes labour less dependent on a bad job. A guaranteed basic income would provide a real exit option and could lead to real improvements in working life.

Voice (i): Labour and the asymmetry of the labour market. Exit and voice require some power symmetry between the parties. However, workers dependent on job and income cannot use 'exit' in case of discontent. workers will either not 'exit' at all, or only when other solutions have failed. For workers, therefore, voice is essential to stimulate improvement. Their 'threat of exit' (or temporary exit, a strike) is too weak to cause serious responsiveness from the side of the firms. It can, and will, only function exceptionally, not as a regular means of change.

Voice (ii): Institutional design. Guarantees of free exit indirectly stimulate voice at work. But voice needs to be effective. Workers' representation and co-determination can lead to conflict, but also to innovation within the firm. Voice, Hirschman points out, only has a chance against exit where it provides a certain effectiveness; otherwise the modern trends towards exit will prevail.

Voice (iii): Loyalty, Organisation and Unions. Loyalty, to a certain extent, is a strong support for voice. Particularly highly motivated quality-oriented workers will often refrain from exit (be it from the job, be it from the union) in order to 'change the world of labour' from inside—via voice, representation and organisation. This loyalty, however, is not an endless resource—it needs support in order to persist. This includes encouragement for trade union activity, recognition and bargaining rights, in order to make voice effective. It can also include active provision for the democratisation of unions—loss of loyalty of members is often due to the intransigent and bureaucratic character of union organisations, the results of which are frustration and—exit (or non-entry which is the prevailing West European pattern of decline) of members, ex-members or non-members.

'Entry'

The Hirschman approach appears static insofar as he looks at specific institutional entities with respect to which people already have a relationship of 'member' and/or 'customer' and these institutional entities pursue policies which require, in order to undergo change, external inputs like exit and/or voice.

I propose to add 'entry' to the two Hirschmanian categories. Entry in a larger sense means both entering into an organisation, a union or a firm or so, and establishing, creating, founding new entities, firms, unions, associations. The current crisis of western trade unions and employers' associations is less due to mass exits of former members, but rather to the non-entry of new members—in the case of unions, young workers, self-employed, women, highly-skilled ICT workers etc; in the case of employers' associations, started-up small and medium-sized firms, media and service sector firms, etc

To prevent decline thus will not only require the interaction of exit—threat of exit—voice. It will also need active strategies to make people enter into an organisation, set-up new ones—and then change them, develop them via voice, exit, and the threat of exit. Institutional design must reflect a strategy enabling unions and associations to become attractive and open to people, particularly those who will shape the work life of the future (young, highly skilled, women). It must address barriers to the setting-up and joining of new organisations and associations.

Motivating organisations towards responsiveness with respect to voice, exit and entry

Hirschman focuses upon the 'demand' side vis-à-vis organisational change, less so on the 'supply' side (ie the preparedness or not of organisations to get involved in learning processes), though he does refer to the short-term orientation of managements which affects responsiveness to exit and voice (*ibid*, pp 92–3). A systematic approach towards organisational development, its prerequisites, obstacles, and instruments is today a significant trend (*cf* Osborne/Gaebler 1992; Naschold *et al*, 1997). It can no longer be ignored as an internal factor, apart from the external factors of exit and voice only, that organisations may be structured to be capable of change. Exit and voice encounter, when articulating their demand for change, different organisational 'change cultures'. Responses to decline in organisations depend on successful interaction between *intra-organisational* cultures for change, and *external* demands via exit and voice for change.

Recent political theory (*cf* Cohen/Arato 1992; Habermas 1992) suggests that modern organisations tend to develop 'sensors', 'antenae', 'feelers' vis-à-vis their local and regional environment and its claims and demands. They do not give up their autonomy, but rather make themselves capable of anticipating the demands from outside and to preventively re-act on them. This means that firms are becoming 'learning organisations', which makes them more prepared to respond to external signals via voice or exit.

Old and New Governance

Labour regulation under 'old' governance had consistent points of reference based on the 'normality' of work and labour relations. These points of reference are undergoing radical change. The concept of voice in 'new' governance will have to undergo an equally radical change.

Governance in a given society implies regulation, from both a substantive and procedural point of view, and includes the institutions empowered to regulate. But 'governance' is broader than 'regulation'; it covers whether society regulates an issue or leaves it unregulated. Governance is also broader than substantive rules; it covers the procedures which empower actors or institutions to set rules.

In the present context, governance is given a twofold specification. 'New' governance is broader than the 'old' governance in that it is no longer confined to the boundaries of the nation state. On the contrary, 'new' governance is defined by the crisis, the 'failure', of the 'old' governance of the nation state in Europe (Homann/Suchanek, 2000) and, if under different conditions, the United States (*cf* Dorf/Sabel 1998). The failure of the nation state is the starting-point of the analysis of 'new' governance.

On the other hand, the concept of 'new' governance proposed here is narrower than governance as such in that it covers a sector only, not the whole of the polity. More precisely, it does not cover governance of financial markets, flows of capital and commodities—the whole world of abstract, fluid, and 'homeless' exchange value. Rather, the focus, when dealing with voice, is the 'use value'-oriented sector of governance. Specifically, the focus is on governance of the territory, with its physical and its social components of work, with its relationship to its citizens, their social, economic, and cultural contexts, and their involvement, or non-involvement, in the well-being of the local community.

The points of reference of the old governance of socio-economic security were, above all, the following:

—the nation state as the unchallenged regulating authority, the monopoly of legitimate power, as Max Weber (1974) put it;
—the city as the local and regional environment ('regionalisation' within the meaning of Giddens' theory of structuration (1984)) where work, life, transport, leisure etc take place and have to be made compatible with one another, practically as well as meaningfully;
—collective bargaining as a general collective (self-regulated, hence 'autonomous') labour norm-setting capacity;
—the Standard Employment Relationship as the normal basis of employment and the reference model of social protection;
—the family with built-in gender and generation contracts as a sort of outspoken or hidden prerequisite of gainful work;
—the autonomous individual, knowledgeable and with free will to acquire skills, to take personal and professional decisions, to enter into employment, to make use of voice and exit, capable of rational choice, as the basic resource of economic, social and cultural life.

I take this (largely fictitious[1]) 'normality' as the paradigm of old governance to which I would like to contrast the paradigm of new governance, what I call 'de-centration', with an increase of both globalisation and localisation. Old governance had a model of work and employment, which, if ever valid, no longer

[1] The old paradigm of 'normality' was, from its very beginning, to a large extent ficticious and counter-factual. It held, at least to a high degree, for men but quite frequently less so for women. It held, again at least to a high degree, for the rich industrialised countries of the North quite frequently less so for the rest of the globe. This ficticious bias became obvious only quite recently. The reason for that could be that the allegedly universal normality is now diminishing, even vanishing, within Northern countries and among the male population too. This expresses the paradox that a paradigm becomes visible, not when it is at the peak of its development, but rather when it is in decline and about to be replaced by another one.

corresponds to the present reality of working life. A new governance is inevitable. I concentrate on Europe because this is my main area of work and experience.

Old Governance, Nation State/City—Workplace—Family

The claim is that there are two basic changes in governance which, in their cumulation and interaction, amount to 'paradigm change' (in the sense of TS Kuhn).

Polycentricity, loss of boundaries

Problem-solving capacity and competency, to a certain extent, is shifting away from the nation state and from cities, from collective self-regulation within the productive sector, and from autonomy within the sector of re-production, to new 'polycentric' arenas, actors, and institutions (*cf* Offe 1996).

The latter, despite their diversity, have in common that they lack traditional settings and 'furnitures' of legitimation and legitimised power (in the sense of Max Weber). They indicate a more or less developed 'de-coupling' between factual exercise of power and formal legitimation.

Since the shift is not total, but a partial one, we observe in all these cases a broad variety of 'mixed regimes'—with an equally wide range of new notions such as 'polycentricity' (CRPM 1998), the 'In-between-town' ('*Zwischenstadt*', Sieverts 1997), 'multi-tiered system' (Leibfried/Pierson 1995), 'a regulatory conundrum' (Rhodes 1995), 'variable geometry', 'multi-level', '*à la carte*', '*condominio*', '*consortio*' (Marks *et al*, 1996), 'original construct', '*Staatenverbund besonderer Art*' (German Constitutional Court; *cf* Herdegen 1999) etc.

What is particularly important, within this new regime variety, is the conflict over competencies between actors who have legal, but lack factual power—and *vice versa*—and the emergence of 'legitimation *vacuums*', ie areas where no legitimised power resides, hence where governance obtains a new 'openness'. These *vacuums* seem to be the entry-gates into the game for new players who represent the diffuse 'civil society' (*cf* OECD, 2000) rather than clearly legally defined 'representatives' of, in a clearly legally defined mode of legitimation, an equally legally defined 'constituency'.

Public/Private mix, basic entitlements

Corresponding to this shift, although the theoretical connection has still to be worked out, there is a shift in the basic criteria of 'just' distribution and entitlement with a view to goods and services. The old governance clearly separated the interaction modes of 'markets' and 'hierarchies' (Williamson 1975)—hence of private circulation via the market and public (re-)distribution via the state, of goods and services.

New governance, however, leads to an, if partial, erosion of the separation between the private and the public sphere and between the patterns governing the internal life of these spheres (*cf* Littmann/Jansen, 2000). Entitlement to goods and services partly shifts away from the market and becomes part of social rights to 'basic provision' to be secured by the state or the local authority, hence a shift from autonomy to solidarity (Bercusson *et al*, 1996; Mückenberger *et al*, 1996). State or communal actors—via new public management—begin to apply market principles (Osborne/Gaebler 1992). Market actors shift from competition to co-operation (or 'co-opetition' as limited simultaneous coexistence of both competition and co-operation). Their concern shifts from a merely quantitative exchange value-orientation to a qualitative one integrating, if 'tactically' motivated, ecological, ethical and quality of life perspectives. Quality of everyday-life is safeguarded by an increasingly complex public/private interaction with increasingly converging objectives, instruments, modes of interaction, and methodologies.

The triangle of old governance

Old governance in general, and with respect to work and employment in particular, meant a specific set of regulations and autonomies (ie non- or self-regulation). Three types of actors and agencies were involved.

—The nation-state—and, to a certain extent, local authorities, with their if limited and 'derived' competencies—were the direct or indirect rule-setting authorities.
—There were actors and agencies dealing with the production of goods and services,
—and actors or agencies dealing with the re-production of the human basis of society.

The latter two were addressed in a twofold way by the first, as subjects of regulation and as beneficiaries of autonomies. To simplify[2] and take only the triangle, 'State/city—enterprise—family'. The state has two objectives, to regulate as much as necessary to secure public order and cohesion, and to leave as much autonomy as possible to enterprises and families to enable them to do their work (efficiency and profitability in the case of the enterprise; socialisation and care in the case of the family).

This can be legally constructed. Autonomies are translated into 'Entrepreneurial freedom', 'Freedom of contract' and 'Freedom of trade', on the one hand, 'rights

[2] Leaving aside all other actors and agencies without whom our social systems cannot function—like schools, churches, cultural institutions etc

of privacy', 'parental rights', 'freedom of religion' etc, on the other. Regulation becomes state 'competencies', communal 'autonomy', the 'rule of law', the principle of 'proportionality' etc This is the well-known legal discourse of the old governance.

Instead, the point is to identify the socioeconomic conditions which this mode of governance requires in order to function. These conditions are undergoing fundamental change.

One 'normal' precondition is that the state is capable of both regulating the relevant issues of production and reproduction and guaranteeing autonomy to the actors and agencies involved. This requires sovereignty of the state and complementarity of state sovereignty and subjectivity to state law by the relevant actors and agencies. That both requirements are no longer fully met is one reason for changes in governance.

Another requirement of the old governance model is that the private actors and agencies addressed by regulation and autonomy have to obey, and do obey, regulations, and that they are, where they benefit from autonomy, capable of coping with a situation of non- and/or self-regulation. That, again, both of these requirements are no longer fully met is another reason for changes in governance.

Crisis: Decentration—Individualisation—Dualisation

An earlier project—with Brian Bercusson and Alain Supiot—identified three trends of present European societies which bring about a process of 'de-normalisation' or 'de-standardisation'. One is economic-political (4.1), the second, sociocultural (4.2), and the third, socio-economic (4.3).

Decentration

Decentration (not to be confused with 'decentralisation' or 'deconcentration') means that the three actors/agencies of the model (state, enterprise, family) are about, at least in part, to lose their 'centers', which made them capable of either regulating or, where autonomy prevailed, self-regulating.

Decline of national state power

In the case of the state and the economy, two simultaneous if inverse trends manifest a shift away from the center, as identified in the World Bank's recent World Development Report 1999, a movement to both 'globalisation' and 'localisation' (World Bank 2000).

The powers of the nation state are shifting to supranational agencies, a partial loss of sovereignty. They are also shifting to subnational actors and agencies which, if not a loss of sovereignty, results in a reduction of regulatory (and law-enforcing) power. The law-making monopoly of the centralised nation state is thus, to an increasing extent, under threat. It is being replaced by a plurality of rule-making procedures and rule-makers who, at least in part, compete with one another.

An example from the EU is Article 249(2)–(4) of the EC Treaty, stipulating the legal effects of EC regulations, directives, and decisions made by EU institutions. National law is made subject to a 'secondary' supranational law via the 'primary' law (ie the EC Treaty), a shift to supranational institutions of parts of the EU Member States' sovereignty. Supranational law prevails over all levels of national law, even constitutional law of the Member States. Within the EU Council of Ministers, the heads of the national ministries can make laws with greater legal power than their national constitutions, whereas within the boundaries of their own nation states, as ministers, they are not only subject to their national constitutions and laws, but, as part of the executive branch, not even competent to take legislative action. This paradox is compounded in Germany where, according to Article 23(6) of the post-Amsterdam German *Grundgesetz*, the German *Länder* have the right to participate in EU law-making when its subject-matter is, according to the German constitution, within their jurisdiction. Thus, the *Länder*, when they act at EU level, set norms which are superior to the norms of the federal state to which, according to the German constitution, they are clearly subordinated.

Another example is the norm-setting competence of the European social dialogue, as laid down in Articles 138–139 EC. In the field of social policy, the EU social dialogue is granted a law-making role (Article 138(4) EC). The EU social partners can present their agreements to the Council of Ministers for enactment as EU legislation (Article 139(2) EC). In this way, private parties (the EU social partners) supported by members of the nation states' executives, can make laws which override the constitutional law of the Member States.

From a governance point of view, 'decentration' is reflected in the different forms of federalism[3] in the European Union and how these have recently developed.

First, among the substantial variety of federal regimes in the EU (15), there is a clear majority of centralist, ie non-federalist settings. According to Gary Marks *et al* (1996: p 51) the federalism score (0 to 4) is only fully met by Germany (4), nearly by Belgium (3), Spain (3) and France (1) due to special autonomies, and Italy (1). Taking into account the three parameters of federalism, special territorial autonomy and the role of regions in central government, the summary score (within a range from 0 to 6) is fully met only by Belgium and Germany, followed by Spain (5/4), France (2/1), Italy and the UK (1).

Secondly, and more striking, is the recent trend toward decentralisation, particularly in the more centralised Member States. Nearly all now have regions, provinces or the like, many introduced within the last two decades or so, eg Belgium (1980), France (1982), Spain (1979–83), an indicator of the premise of decentration. Despite their diversity, all EU (15) Member States in 1999 had two subnational electoral levels, an intermediate and a local one (except for Finland and Portugal, with only a local one; Luxembourg is excluded from this compari-

[3] In the continental European meaning of the word.

son) (World Bank 2000, pp 216–7). Decentralisation seems to be a clear point of convergence.

Decentration and cities (sub-/disurbanisation)

As well as the nation-state, the city is a centre of governance. As with the nation-state, however, municipal authority is also experiencing the process of decentration. It is losing its function and significance in two opposite directions—ie centripetal and centrifugal (*cf* Sieverts 1997).

On the one hand, the growth of urban centres and the depopulation of inner-city areas normally attendant on this causes life to shift (at least outside business hours) into sub-centres, which develop their own cultural and gastronomic identities, and so on ('decentralisation'). On the other hand, over-development contributes first to the formation of residential areas (affluent residential belts, dormitory towns), then increasingly to commercial (shopping centres), work and entertainment facilities (science and leisure parks) on the periphery of the cities ('sub-disurbanisation').

The fact that city life is shifting into smaller areas or sub-centres highlights the relationship between work and life, and the transport linking the two. Workers—subordinate as well as self-employed—develop new needs with respect to their life outside work. The transformation of work via new IT facilities allows for a new 're-union' of work and life outside work via telework, neighbourhood work, etc This creates the well-known risks of isolation and gender segregation. But at the same time it allows for new ways to overcome the traditional time-space-separation of work and life. Democratisation is faced with the additional problem of there not yet being any 'sovereign power' involved in the planning—this first has to be constituted or must constitute itself.

The life-situation of working people is becoming more dependent on, and influenced by, local and regional environments. Voice can no longer be restricted to the area of employment and the enterprise/establishment. It has to be extended to living conditions, the infrastructure of health, education and so on. Citizenship, civil as well as political and social (Marshall 1950; Bercusson *et al*, 1996, ch 6; Supiot 1999; p 206), in the sense of being an active member of the 'polis' requires a new type of urban policy ('urban time policies'/'*tempi della città*'), and a new type of local democratic process connected to it. There is an increasing demand for such policies as related to the quality of everyday-life (Bonfiglioli/Mareggi 1997; Boulin/Mückenberger 1999; Supiot 1999; Mückenberger 2000).

What is important is to extend 'voice' to the wider spatial-temporal area of urban life rather than to restrict it to the sphere of gainful work. Citizenship means integrity in the different spheres of life. This also holds for voice and representation as basic elements of democracy. Urban time policies require new forms of involvement of citizens and other parts of the civil society (NGOs etc) who in the past did not take part in decision-making. A concept of 'local social dialogue' includes not only employers and employees, but also others in the territory, a 'societal' or 'civil dialogue'. The relationship between social and civil dialogue is problematic but inescapable for the social partners.

Decentration and problems of legitimacy

These developments and paradoxes, above all the decentration of the nation-state, highlight the extent to which norm-setting competency has already been diversified ('decentrated') within the European Union. Pure nation-state governance has moved towards 'polycentric', multi-tiered or multi-level governance. These shifts place on the agenda the issue of 'legitimation', why can who regulate what? This is one reason why disputes around the principle of subsidiarity have emerged (vertical as well as horizontal subsidiarity, *cf* Bercusson *et al* 1996). But this principle, in Article 5 EC, does not provide any clear guidance to resolve conflicts over competencies. Rather, it asserts a form of economic calculus ('better performance') as a prerequisite for deciding on which level and with which actors the competency for legislation lies.

Decentration and enterprises

The trend towards decentration—in the double sense of globalisation and localisation—holds equally for the level of the enterprise, and still more for individual establishments (*cf* Littmann/Jansen 2000). On the one hand, they are increasingly under the control of, often multinational, conglomerates. Capital export, rather than goods export, constitutes what we call globalisation. On the other hand, within establishments and enterprises, a process of decentralisation takes place. Instead of the traditional Fordist centralised hierarchic structures, project structures, networks, semi-autonomous groups, profit-centres are established. Not, or only indirectly, controlled by central management, they form the basis of new systems of co-operation, communication and bargaining, not only within enterprises, but also between different departments of different enterprises (Sydow/Wirth 1999).

Various consequences follow from this decentration, affecting economic actors both as subjects of regulation and as beneficiaries of autonomy. First, there are tendencies towards an erosion of the capacity of self-regulation, a prerequisite of 'autonomy'. Secondly, nation state regulation fails insofar as the boundaries of state legislation (the state's jurisdiction) differ from the boundaries of the economic actors, the multinational conglomerates (Scharf 1996: pp 16–7). In part, economic activity 'evades' national law, in part globalisation leads to 'regulatory competition' (*ibid*, p 17), in part the fiscal state is blackmailed by capital's exit-options.

Towards 'soft' collective bargaining?

The relative loss of regulatory power by traditional governance may be illustrated by changes, first in collective bargaining, and secondly, in the employment relationship.

The collective bargaining system in Europe in recent decades had certain preconditions which are presently under challenge (Mückenberger 1995):

—The principle of representation and representativeness; the actors on both sides act for their members and are able to bind their members to a decision. Both sides experience problems integrating new members due to differentiation among enterprise structures and social milieus. There is called in question whether employers' organisations can continue to speak effectively for 'the industry' and trade unions for 'the employees'.

—Autonomy of the social partners involved; direct and indirect state intervention challenges the traditional role of the social partners. An example, the impact of the EU monetary convergence criteria on collective wage bargaining.

—Collective bargaining, once highly professional, and allegedly the responsibility of 'neutral' experts, is becoming increasingly re-politicised.

—The collective agreement, regarded as a 'socially guiding agreement', a set of standards beyond the statutory minimum which hinted at future perspectives of social policy, made associations and collective actors attractive for working people. Today collective bargaining is often a zero-sum game of concession bargaining. This weakens the process and makes recruitment more difficult.

—Traditionally trade unions, particularly in Germany, France and Italy were regarded as an 'agent of the general public interest'. At present, they are revealed as ineffective, or as promoting particularistic interests. In the long run, this creates a legitimation crisis not only of the organisations, but of collective interest representation and organisation as such.

—Collective agreements on the European continent (in contrast to the UK) are regarded as legally binding and enforceable agreements. Processes currently challenge even this basic assumption. On the one hand, there are attempts at non-implementation or otherwise avoiding terms of binding agreements (for example, of agreements limiting working hours, or exit of individual employers from employers` federations when, according to German law, the employer continues to be bound by collective agreements). On the other hand, an increasing number of 'agreements' are concluded (for example in the chemical industry) which are no longer legally binding, but rather are 'soft agreements' or 'letters of intent'.

A 'standard', or a variety of employment relationships?

These tendencies indicate a loss of self-regulating capacity in the field of collective bargaining. The basis for this seems to be the 'erosion of the standard employment relationship' (*cf* the various accounts in Standing 1999: ch 8). A leading paradigm within most European individual labour laws is what I called the 'Standard Employment Relationship' (SER). As developed elsewhere (Mückenberger 1985; 1989; 1992; 1996; Supiot 1999: ch III), the rules of the individual employment relationship (via statutory law, collective agreements, and plant agreements) follow a 'hidden regulatory programme' which protects certain employment relationships (the 'standard') more effectively than others ('atypical' or 'non-standard' or 'marginal'). Seven criteria identify the type of employment to which more protection is provided or 'distributed':

(i) seniority within the firm (long-term as opposed to short-term, 'casual', 'occasional' employment),
(ii) a 'work biography' based upon life-long gainful employment (continuous work biographies versus 'puzzle' biographies),
(iii) age (the older the employee, the better he or she is protected),
(iv) in-plant employment with the legal status of an 'employee' (as opposed to freelance activity),
(v) amount of weekly working hours (full-time as opposed to part-time),
(vi) status within the plant hierarchy (skilled as opposed to unskilled labour),
(vii) size of the firm (the bigger the firm, the more likely threshold requirements for the application of laws are met).

The 'ideal-type' of employment extrapolated from these criteria (the SER upon which the social protection system is based) is, long-duration full-time skilled employment in a medium-sized or large firm.

Three aspects to do with skilled work may be noted in relation to present challenges. First, the German system is based to a large extent on skilled labour (20 per cent unskilled, 60 per cent skilled within a dual system, 20 per cent extraordinarily skilled (including academic freelance), compared to the United States with a 40:20:40 ratio (Kern 1996)). However, under conditions of decentralisation of production, tertiarisation of the economy, and fragmentation of the workforce, 'atypical employment' is gaining ground among the three groups of employees. The resulting segmentation within the system of social protection promotes social exclusion (the 'two thirds-society'). Secondly, the SER has a gender bias, as the biography associated with that of the crafts*man*. Women, oriented towards unpaid work and discontinuous work biographies often fail to meet the requirements for social protection. Thirdly, there is increasing awareness of the economic rationales for better protection of so-called atypical work.

The result of this second decentration trend—decentration of the economic enterprise—with respect to governance is twofold. The regulatory power of economic actors supported by the state is systematically weakened by the internationalisation of economic power. Self-regulating power, a fundamental prerequisite of the 'autonomy' of the social partners, has lost many of its 'centres', those centralised enterprises and enterprise-based union branches who are responsible bargaining agents vis-à-vis employers and employees. Bargaining is replaced by 'regime-shopping' by conglomerates or by individual agreements within the firm—both incompatible with traditional governance.

This reinforces the case for implementation of universal basic rights (Somavia 2001). The question is how to develop regulatory power on a transnational level, to produce transnational (ILO, WTO) and supranational (EU) standards. Also, how the self-regulating power of autonomous social partners can be re-established, in forms of cross-national representation of workers (European works councils or global works councils, as in the car industry); or collective bargaining structures covering global regions rather than national sectors, combined with new 'virtual' forms of communication and organisation (Somavia 2001).

As regards new forms of work, universal protection is needed which allows for change on the one hand, and security on the other. Concerning new forms of representation, a particular concern is how to integrate marginalised groups of workers, giving voice to service sector employees, women, young people, the highly skilled. Universal standards reduces the scope for regime competition between the different regions of the world and incentives for 'regime-shopping'.

De-centration of the family and the individual?

In the traditional system of governance in Europe, besides the actors and agencies dealing with the production of goods and services, there are actors or agencies dealing with the re-production of the human basis of the society. These too are addressed by governance, as subjects to regulation and as beneficiairies of autonomy.

Family structures form a net of solidarity and subsistence, a sort of 'fall-back' structure, beyond market constraints. The very existence and the shape of family support can diminish or increase the constraint to enter gainful employment. Family networks, apart from other societal provisions for the independence of the individual (infrastructure, neighbourhood, public assistance, basic income, etc), have a double function with respect to work and employment. They can provide the individual greater independence from subordinate employment, and they can thereby contribute to an improvement of working conditions, as individuals have the choice whether to enter into employment.

For example, particularly significant is the role of family structures in relation to child poverty (and child labour). Children are an increasing victim of poverty all over the world (*cf* Huston 1994 and the contributions in Huston 1991). Combating child poverty requires intimate knowledge of changes and developments in family structures.

Here again, traditional governance is losing ground. Traditional governance of socialisation and care was, very roughly speaking, based on gender contracts and generation contracts (*cf* the classical studies of Shorter 1975; Donzelot 1977). The gender contract consisted of a distribution between men and women of house/care and gainful work, and a corresponding income distribution and redistribution within the family. The generation contract consisted of a mutuality between care activities of parents with respect to their young children and those of the children vis-à-vis their aged parents. It is on the basis of these contracts that, within traditional governance, a system of self-regulation could work, with remarkable results as regards the functions of socialisation and care (*cf* Donzelot's expression 'la police des familles', 1977). They gave rise to a relatively high degree of autonomy and a relatively low degree of state regulation.

However, here too there are processes of erosion so that 'decentration' seems to be applicable. The multi-generation family may be regarded as a well-structured 'centre' with a relatively high internal problem-solving capacity. Decentration, again, operates in both directions. On the one hand, 'individualisation' has occurred with respect to modes of life, fertility, life styles and inter-generation contacts, leading to the erosion of the multi-generational family as a prototype of socialisation and care. On the other hand, the sphere of socialisation and care, in cash or in kind, has been increasingly taken over by the state or other public and/or intermediate institutions, and thereby have been centralised (education, health, welfare, old-age provision, etc).

The basic trends may be summarised in the literature (*cf* McColdrick/Carter 1982; Walsh 1982; Kaufmann 1990; Mitterauer/Ortmayr 1997; Fthenakis 1998; Backes 1999; Fthenakis 2000) as regards the European case:

—a decrease in the number of first marriages;
—an increase in age at first marriage;
—a changing attitude towards marriage, with an increasing number of non-married couples;
—an increasing number of formerly a-typical households; single households, lone-parent families, step-parent families and 'living-apart-together' households;
—a reduced fertility rate and increasing childlessness;
—an increase in the number of divorces;
—due to increasing life expectancy and individualisation, an growing vertical and diminishing horizontal complexity of families;
—closer relationships between children and their grand or great-grand parents, with a new intensive engagement of grandparents within family life.

Though these trends are extrapolated from Europe, they could have equivalents in other regions of the world (*cf* the classical studies of Gould 1963; Hajnal 1965, though convergence theories (Gould 1963) need to be revisited (Mitterauer/Ortmayr 2000)).

Behind both trends are processes which can be characterised as the erosion of the gender contract and the generation contract. The changing roles of women in society and in the labour market are the hallmarks.

What is clear, however, is that the equilibrium between regulation and autonomy implied in traditional governance is no longer intact. Within small, one- or two-generation families and single-parent families, the traditional methods of social control through which family regulation was enforced and implemented (Donzelot 1977) no longer exist or are ineffective. Similarly, the capacity for self-regulation, as a prerequisite of factual 'autonomy', is scarce due to the lack of resources as compared with those available under the shelter of a multi-generation family. The resulting erosion of traditional governance creates an increasing need for a broader 'societal', solidarity and points to the expiry of traditional governance and the need, and factual emergence, of new governance.

Individualisation

Two other trends besides decentration (economic-political), are individualisation (sociocultural) and dualisation (socio-economic). They can be dealt with more shortly because they are closely linked to decentration, so how they challenge traditional European governance is similar to a large extent.

'Individualisation' (Giddens 1984; Beck 1986) describes the outcome of the processes of decentration from the perspective of the individual person. The everyday-life of the individual, under traditional governance, was shaped and structured by the traditional 'centres' controlling the worlds of production and reproduction, mainly enterprise and family. From the perspective of the individual, these centres had a double role. They provided a social and societal framework, a social bond, protection, but also a social identity, self-esteem, 'sense'. They simultaneously 'governed' the individual, determining economic, social, gender and inter-generation roles and patterns of behaviour (eg the patriarchal implications of the traditional gender contract).

Given this ambiguity (autonomous identity, regulation) of the traditionally 'centred' mode of governance with respect to the members of society, 'individualisation' carries a corresponding ambiguity. Due to the processes of decentration, individuals, to a certain extent, lose both the protection and the constraints of traditional governance. They lose many elements of the social bond traditionally provided by 'centred' governance. But at the same time they gain a degree of autonomy and self-determination which they never had before.

Both trends are linked in a paradoxical manner. In order to survive as a member of society and be integrated into society, individuals under new governance are obliged to determine themselves, permanently, and so are forced towards autonomy. New governance implies the duty of every member of society to control his/her own biography, to autonomously take basic decisions concerning education and training, career, family, life-style, etc.

This implies enormous challenges for new governance. Individualised members of society are frequently 'overcharged' by the 'burden' of their new status of self-determination. They can only make practical use of their new autonomy when, and insofar as, society provides them with skills, new social linkages and networks. Linkages and networks are increasingly necessary to 'produce' the conditions of the new autonomy. Socialisation, education, gender-role, self-esteem, career, life-style can no longer be taken for granted, but rather have to be elaborated in a new mutual exchange between the self-determining individual and the societal framework providing conditions for practical self-determination.

This is the point made by the Nobel prize winner Amartya Sen in his category of 'capabilities' (Sen 1999: ch 1). Under conditions of individualisation, human beings have to develop 'themselves' in order to get access to freedom. Education, training and further training, increasingly in a virtualised IT manner (Somavia 2001), acquire great importance. 'Life-long learning' becomes imperative

(European Commission 2000) not only for professional reasons, but for the successful pursuit of the individual's life-course.

New governance, to a large extent, consists of building these linkages and networks. This is why 'civil society' plays such an outstanding role in new governance (*cf* Cohen/Arato 1992). Those linkages and networks exist, or have to be built up, in new forms of communication and co-operation, of neighbourhoods and communities, in new social and civil dialogues, relations of trust and confidence. They require, given the processes of decentration, a local and a global character. They have to replace, as much as possible, the bonds of traditional governance. This substitution is necessary not only in the fields of traditional 'centred' governance (state—economy—reproduction), but also in the new fields of 'de-centred' governance (supranational—regional—local), fields which are frequently decoupled from the legitimation centres of traditional governance.

Individualisation as an irreversible trend means there is no way of avoiding the challenges it puts on the agenda. The neo-liberal belief in a 'Robinson Crusoe' self-determination capacity of the individual without any societal frame and support has proved to be a great scientific as well as practical error (*cf* Mückenberger/Deakin 1989). In the words of Émile Durkheim, if society does not proceed from mechanical to organic solidarity, it will end up with a state of 'anomie'—a state of total individualisation without coherence, without interaction, without society itself.

Dualisation of society?

This is the link to the third trend, dualisation. Processes of individualisation are often accompanied by a divide between 'winners' and 'losers'. Winning and losing does not take place only on an individual level, but rather also on an agglomerate collective level. Here, ascriptive characteristics, 'stigmata', play a role rendering groups within a given society victims of segmentation, discrimination, exclusion or even oppression against 'minorities'.

Segmentation creates dichotomies. According to ascriptive characteristics members of society are divided into those who belong to the 'majority' and those who belong to a 'minority'. Gender, ethnicity and religion, skills and education, abilities and disabilities, age, poverty—all contribute to inequality, a structured inequality, a double form of 'structuring' society which can also be called 'governance'. First, there is discrimination against what is labeled 'minoritarian'. Being female, black, unskilled, disabled, old, poor implies being subject to further disadvantages. Secondly, advantages and disadvantages tend to cumulate. There is a mechanism of 'spill-over' and of downward and upward spirals, so that advantages and disadvantages occurring in one 'sphere' tend to be reinforced in other 'spheres'.[4] Some discriminations arise separately, others in a cumulative form. A

[4] The term 'sphere' refers to Michael Walzer's 'Spheres of Justice'—a concept the paradigm of which consists in prohibiting the spill-over as mentioned in the text.

black unskilled woman bears social disadvantages from which a white skilled man may profit.

The effect of this diversification of segmentation and discrimination is manifold. On the one hand, it hides the fact that there is domination in society, There is no longer a 'ruling' and an 'oppressed' class, there is just a great diversity of individuals with different signs and labels. On the other hand, a numerical minority will be able to dominate a numerical majority simply by cumulating positive characteristics.

The danger of anomie is less evident than in the context of individualisation, but it is clearly there. A divided society ('two-thirds-society', 'elbow society', etc) bears the risks of individual deviance as well as of collective conflict and upheaval. It threatens social integration, not only as a means of sociocultural inclusion, but also of economic prosperity and political wellbeing and cohesion.

The Result of the Crisis—New Governance, New Voice

A new uncertainty

The outcome of the erosion of the old system of governance and voice implies what Jürgen Habermas called 'new uncertainty' *('Neue Unübersichtlichkeit')*. The old centres of governance have not been clearly substituted by new ones. Both coexist. Besides the traditional, new arenas, actors, forms of voice and public attention and issues emerge (*cf* Standing 1999: pp 42 *ff*). The latter operate in a sort of 'no-man's-land'—according to self-set rules, co-operating with self-chosen actors, in coalitions and networks for self-established ends, set up, not through well-centred and hierarchically legitimised democratic procedures, but rather through a new type of governance, the autopoietical or procedural (Teubner 1989; Rogowski/Wilthagen 1994).

The question of legitimation re-emerges in a twofold manner. First, how the components of new governance legitimise their action in the no-man's-land ('simple legitimation'). Secondly, how the 'legitimation relationship' between different 'competency-competing' actors and agencies is organised, particularly between those who possess formal legitimation, but not enough influence to exert it, and those who exert influence without proper formal legitimacy ('reflexive legitimation').

The reason for this new uncertainty about legitimacy is clear. Old governance relied upon modes of interaction corresponding to the areas of state (hierarchy) and market (equality), namely regulatory act and contract. In contrast, new networks lack a proper, original and authentic mode of interaction. They make use of both of the traditional modes, but in an alienated, sometimes perverse way. The relationship between state and individuals/organisations becomes more controlled by contracts. Economic actors, rather than behaving as equals, exercise regulatory norm-setting power with respect to citizens/organisations.[5]

Civil Society

All these trends form a sort of essential background for the debate on 'civil society'. Civil society, in classical political theory, is the foundation which constitutes—via real or ficticious 'social contracts'—states, and from which the latter derive their *ratio essendi*, their legitimacy. When those constituted and legitimised 'centres' break up, or erode into a dispersed policentricity, thc question of legitimation arises on the agenda. The process called 'decentration' is reflected in two recent discourses on civil society.

At international level, civil society disputes the legitimacy of global actors—global economic players as well as politically hegemonic powers. New actors emerge from civil society, 'NGOs'. They proclaim new programs, eg 'agenda 21', fair trade clauses, social and ecological standards in transnational agreements and contracts etc Perhaps later they will be regarded as the fore-runners of a legitimised world-wide regime of 'eternal peace' (I Kant). But, for the moment, they operate in a no-man's-land with no proper rules and sanctions. Instead, they have recourse to opaque modes of 'voice', lobbying, and sanctions such as 'bans', 'blacking', moral condemnation, kamikaze-like strategies. These are new forms of voice, detached from the traditional levers of enforcement, and hence bound to enforcement through 'legitimacy' rather then 'legality'—what Hannah Arendt called 'communicative power'.

At subnational level, voluntary associations, 'citizens' initiatives, again 'NGOs', play an increasing role. They too, to a certain extent, substitute political influence for traditionally legitimised bodies. This is a sort of 'direct democracy', but without a formal mandate, without safeguards against partial and biased composition and lobbying. It may be argued that they are the fore-runners of a new system of voice—a new regional, and inter-regionally linked, network regime. But again, for the moment, they represent a somewhat amorphous—without rules—opposition of civil society emerging from the alienation suffered by the 'chain of legitimation' of existing political and economic actors and powers.

Civil society aims to re-constitute itself, society as well as states, in an international as well as a decentralised dimension. However, it is not as powerful as global political and economic actors are. It lacks the two basic media/resources on which the latter build, money and administrative power. But it possesses something they lack, and need, legitimacy, 'communicative power' (H Arendt) and 'influence' (T Parsons).

The new concept, as formulated by Cohen and Arato (1992) and Habermas (1994), tries to systematically explain civil society, with its discursively developed

[5] *Cf* trade-norms, standard contracts, but also the rule-setting competency of the EU social dialoge according to Articles 138–139 EC.

claims, so as to gain influence on the dominant economic and political subsystems and their media/resources of control, money and administrative power. The concept accepts both the relative autonomy of the subsystems, economy and state, as a result of societal differentiation, and the fact that their media/resources, money and power, have an important impact on decision-making in society. It aims, however, to enable civil society and its representatives to acquire countervailing power vis-à-vis economy and state, which:

—is anchored in the life-world of the citizenry,
—is competent in, and committed to, communicative rationality,
—bundles up, articulates, and makes public the communicatively founded life-world claims of civil society hitherto sacrificed to the dominant system and the media/resources of power and money,
—thereby provides public attention, 'communicative power' (H Arendt), legitimacy, 'influence' (T Parsons), an influence which does not articulate itself through power or money, but which nevertheless exerts an indirect impact on the decision-making of economic and political actors and agencies,
—which thereby does not only, defensively, protect the life-world against further 'colonisation' (J Habermas), by the system and the subsystems, but rather, proactively, undertakes steps forward to 'de-colonise' the life-world.

The basic questions remain, whether discursively built communicative power will really be able to enforce civil society's legitimate demands, or remain powerless; and what will be the future relationship between the informal way of influence and the formally legitimised bodies of political and economic power? Who are the new actors and agencies, beyond the state and the economy? Which media/resources can be used, if not money and power? Which societal framework of governance is capable of accommodating the coexistence of a variety of actors and agencies using diverse resources.

The New Concept of Civil Society

The revised concept of civil society, as proposed eg by Cohen/Arato or Habermas, differs from the traditional concept, say of John Locke or of A de Tocqueville, in one fundamental respect. The latter conceived of civil society within the dichotomy, 'civil society—state' (economic activity was just one field, not of the state, but rather of the activity of society). As against that, the former replaced the old dichotomy with a new triangle, 'state—economy—civil society'. Cohen and Arato thereby categorise state and economy under the heading of 'the system', civil society under the heading of 'life-world' (categories developed by Lockwood).

Within the old dichotomy, the economy was still an undistinguished ingredient of civil society. However, this is incompatible with the discourse-ethical claim to properly distinguish strategic/instrumental action from 'communicative action' (Habermas)—ie action which is guided by the media/resources power and money from that guided by discursive rationality. By introducing the triangle State—economy—civil society, it becomes theoretically possible to distinguish resources/media controlled sub-systems from civil society, the latter a communicatively controlled group of actors, with a proper/or more than one proper life-world based identities.

This is a necessary, if not sufficient prerequisite of the constitution of societal actors—and a new type of 'agora' and 'voice'. Paradigmatic for civil actors are 'voluntary associations' and 'public spaces'/'agoras'. This was the case already for de Tocqueville (1835–40), when describing the American democracy, and it is still more so in the new concepts of civil society. The assumption is that, in order to cope with all major or minor everyday-life problems, people have to associate with one another in a variety of associations and to mobilise, via voice, a variety of public spheres. Only in this way can they, under democratic circumstances, achieve the aims which, under pre-democratic conditions of inequality, single influential persons have been able to achieve.

Thus was de Tocqueville's reasoning, still on the basis of the dichotomy, state—society. It becomes more plausible with the new triangle, State—economy—civil society. Here the inegalitarian subsystem, economy, is dealt with as subsystem, whereas civil society remains a sphere which is controlled by discursive rationality and voice rather than by the media/resources of power and money. The problem with de Tocqueville's argument is that the human competence, and capacity, for building and participating in associations is, from both a quantitative and a qualitative point of view, limited. At the level of Europe, this may be to overestimate its capacity, and limit this approach.

Newly established actors—associations and public spheres—need influence enabling them to give voice to the communicatively-based life-world demands vis-à-vis the resources/media controlled subsystems. The legitimacy of civil society's claims and the mode of their public deliberation tend to reinforce one another.

System and life-world have to achieve a reflexive relationship (in Giddens' meaning) to one another—ie a relationship which excludes neither the relative autonomy of each nor the chance of mutual impact and 'learning'. In order to be capable of such reflexivity, both components require an overlapping societal constitutional framework which shapes the rules for their relationship. This framework will establish 'sensors', 'receptors' the objective of which is information, exchange, 'early-warning' and preventive co-ordination.

Within this constitutional framework, civil society's voice still has no direct sanctioning power. It remains restricted to argument and conviction. Nevertheless within a recognised system of sensors, receptors, and mechanisms of resonance, the refusal to communicate can be publicly identified, proved, and condemned.

These general observations apply also in the field, the territorial life-world, of workers' and citizens' demands, via voice, for equality and participation therein. The new democratic culture of communication, participation and co-operation replaces the former culture of distrust and competitiveness. It thus contributes to a proactively defined wellbeing of the citizens. It is a culture of voice, of actors (not of mere subjects or recipients), a culture of polis and agora and civil dialogue (not of an alienated bureaucratic and paternalist 'welfare state'). The culture of voice is a new relationship between civil society, on the one hand, and the administrative and economic power on the other. It does not deny the latter systems' relative autonomy, but it ties them, via a developed system of 'sensors', public discourses, and processes of moderation and mediation, to the common good within a given territory.

References

Backes, GM, (1999) *Individualisierung und Pluralisierung der Lebensverhältnisse: Familie und Alter im Kontext der Modernisierung, Zeitschrift für Familienforschung* 10, pp 5–29.

Beck, U (1986) *Risikogesellschaft* (Frankfurt, Suhrkamp).

Bercusson, B, Deakin, S, Koistinen, P, Kravaritou, Y, Mückenberger, U, Supiot, A and Veneziani, B, (1996) *A Manifesto for Social Europe* (Brussels, ETUI).

Bonfiglioli, S and Mareggi M (eds), (1997) *Il tempo e la città fra natura e storia* (Roma, Urbanistica Quaderni).

Boulin, J-Y and Mückenberger, U, (1999) *Times of the city and quality of life* (Dublin, BEST 1/1999).

Clegg, HA, (1979) *The Changing system of Industrial Relations in Great Britain* (Oxford, Basic Blackwell).

Cohen, JL and Arato, A, (1992) *Civil Society and Political Theory* (Cambridge, Mass, and London, England, The MIT Press), xxi and 771 pp.

CRPM, Conférence des Régions Périphériques Maritimes, (1998) (L'Europe polycentrique, Rennes, CRPM).

Donzelot, J, (1977) *La police des familles* (Paris, Les Éditions de Minuit).

Dorf, MC and Sabel, CF, A Constitution of Democratic Experimentalism, Columbia Law Review 98 (March 1998) p 2, pp 267–473.

European Commission, (2000) *Memorandum on Life-Long Learning,* (Brussels) 30. 10. 2000—SEC(2000) 1832.

European Court of Justice, (1995: 15.12.95); Case C-415/93, *Bosman.*

Fthenakis, Wassilios F, (1998) *Family transitions and quality in early childhood education,* Europena Early childhood Education Research Journal 6, pp 5–17.

—— (2000) *Kindergarten—eine Institution im Wandel,* Amt für Soziale Dienste Bremen (ed), *Kindergarten—eine Institution im Wandel* (Bremen, Temmen), pp 11–91.

Giddens, A, (1984) The Constitution of Society, Outline of the Theory of Structuration (Cambridge, Polity Press).

Gould, W, (1963) *World Revolution and Family Patterns* (New York, McMillan, Free Press).

Habermas, J, (1992) *Faktizität und Geltung. Beiträge zur Diskurstheorie des Rechts und des demokratischen Rechtsstaats* (Frankfurt, M Suhrkamp).

Hajnal, J, (1965) *European Marriage Pattern in Perspective,* Glass, DV/DE C Eversley (eds), Population and History (London, Arnold), pp 101–45.

Herdegen, M, (1999) Europarecht, 2. Ed (München, Beck).

Hirschman, AO, (1970) *Exit, Voice, and Loyalty. Responses to Decline in firms, Organizations, and States* (Cambridge, Mass, Harvard).

Homann, K and Suchanek, A, (2000) Ökonomik, Tübingen: Mohr Siebeck.

Huston, AC (ed), (1991) *Children in Poverty Child development and public policy* (New York, Cambridge University Press).

—— (1994) *Children in poverty: Designing research to affect policy*, Social Policy Report, Vol VIII, 2, pp 2–12.

Kern, Horst, (1996) *German Capitalism. How Competitive will it be in the Future?* Conference 'The Restructuring of the Economic and Political System in Japan and Europe: Past Legacy and Present Issues', Milano, May 15, 1996, mimeo.

Leibfried, S, Pierson, P, (1995) *European social policy. Between fragmentation and integration* (Washington, the Brookings Institution).

Littmann, P, Jansen, SA, (2000) Oszillodox. Virtualisierung—die permanente Neuerfindung der Organisation (Stuttgart, Klett-Cotta).

Marks, G,Scharpf, FW, Schmitter, PC and Streeck W (eds), (1996) *Governance in the European Union* (London, SAGE).

—— Nielsen, F, Ray, L, and Salk, J (1996) *Competencies, Cracks and Conflicts: Regional Mobilisation in the European Union*, Marks *et al* 1996, pp 40–63.

Marshall, TH, (1950) *Citizenship and Social Class* (Cambridge, Cambridge University Press).

McColdrick, M and Carter, EA (1982) *The family life cycle*, Walsh 1982, pp 167–95.

Mückenberger, U, (1985) *Die Krise des Normalarbeitsverhältnisses*, Zeitschrift für Sozialreform, pp 415 *ff*, 457 *ff*.

—— (1989) *Non-Standard Forms of Work and the Role of Changes in Labour and Social Security Regulation*, International Journal of the Sociology of Law, vol 17, pp 381–402.

—— (1992) *Non-Standard Forms of Employment in the Federal Republic of Germany: The Role and Effectiveness of the State*, Gerry und Janine Rodgers (Hg.), *Precarious Jobs in Labour Market Regulation*, Genf 1992: International Labour Organisation (ILO), pp 267–85.

—— (1994) *Social integration or anomy? The Welfare State challenged by individualism*, J Ferris and R Page (eds), *Social Policy in Transition. Anglo-German perspectives in the new European community*, (Avebury), pp 57–69.

—— (1995) *Aktuelle Herausforderungen an das Tarifwesen*, Kritische Justiz, vol 28, p 1, pp 26–44.

—— (1996) *Towards a new definition of the employment relationship*, International Labour Review, vol 135, no 6, pp 683–95.

—— (2000) Zeiten der Stadt, 2nd edn, (Bremen, Temmen).

—— Deakin, S, (1989) *From deregulation to a European floor of rights*, Zeitschrift für ausländisches und internationales Arbeits- und Sozialrecht, pp 153–204.

—— Offe, C, Ostner, I, *A Basic Income Guarateed by the State: A Need of the Moment in Social Policy*, Offe 1996, pp 201–21.

Naschold, F, Oppen, M, Wegener, A, (1997) *Innovative Kommunen. Internationale Trends und deutsche Erfahrungen* (Stuttgart, Kohlhammer).

OECD, (2000) *Facts about European NGOs Active in International Development. Development Centre Studies* Adèle Woods (Paris, OECD).

Offe, C, (1996) *Modernity and the State* (Cambridge, Polity Press).

Osborne, D and Gaebler, T, (1992) *Re-Inventing Government* (New York).

Parsons, Talcott, (1972) *Das System moderner Gesellschaften*, German translation of *The System of Modern Societies* (München, Juventa).

Polanyi, K, (1944/1995) *The Great Transformation*, German translation (Frankfurt, Suhrkamp 1995).

Rogowski, R and Wilthagen, T, (1994) *Reflexive Labour Law. Studies in Industrial Relations and Employment Regulation* (Kluwer).

Sainsaulieu, R (ed), (1992) *L'Entreprise—une affaire de société* (Paris, Presse de la Fondation Nationale des Sciences Politiques).

Scharpf, FW, (1996) *Negative and Positive Integration in the Political Economy of European Welfare States*, Marks *et al*, 1996, pp 15–39.

Sen, A, (1999) *Development as Freedom* (Oxford, Oxford University Press).

Shorter, E, (1975) *The Making of the Modern Family* (New York, Basic Books Inc).

Sieverts, T, (1997) *Zwischenstadt—zwischen Ort und Welt, Raum und Zeit, Stadt und Land*, (Braunschweig/Wiesbaden, Vieweg).

Somavia, J, (2001) *Die Zukunft der Arbeit. Sind wir für die Globalisierung gerüstet?* Frankfurter Allgemeine Zeitung, v. 4. 1. 2001.

Standing, G, (1999) *Global Labour Flexibility. Seeking Distributive Justice* (Macmillan, St Martin's Press, London/New York).

Supiot, A (ed), (1999) *Au-delà de l'emploi. Transformation du travail et devenir du droit du travail en Europe* Rapport pour la commission européenne (Paris, Flammarion).

Sydow, J and Wirth, C (eds), (1999) *Arbeits, Personal und Mitbestimmung in Unternehmensnetzwerken* (München und Mering, Rainer Hampp Verlag).

Teubner, G, (1989) *Recht als autopoietisches System* (Frankfurt, Suhrkamp).

Tocqueville, A de, (1997) *Über die Demokratie in Amerika* (1835/40), selected and edited by JP Mayer (Stuttgart, Reclam, 391 S).

Walsh, F (ed), (1982) *Normal Family Process* (New York, The Guilford Press).

Walzer, M, (1983) *Spheres of Justice. A Defense of Pluralism and Equality* (New York, Basic Books).

Weber, M, (1978) *Economy and Society* (Berkeley, University of California Press).

Williamson, OE, (1975) *Markets and hierarchies* (New York).

World Bank, (2000) *Entering the 21st Century. World Development Report 1999/2000* (Oxford, Oxford University Press).

12

The Originality of Transnational Social Norms as a Response to Globalisation

M-A MOREAU*

Economic globalisation leads to a search for new responses in terms of regulation: both the creation of new regulatory techniques and the identification of legal norms. Social regulation within the context of globalisation poses new challenges and raises a series of theoretical questions (Murray and Trudeau 2004). One of the main questions is how internationalisation of the new model of labour is to be regulated, on what basis and with what objectives (Hepple 2005).[1]

The argument of this paper is, first, that globalisation triggers off a search for new regulation that responds to the specificities of the dominant model of multinational corporations (hereinafter MNCs). Secondly, it is suggested that innovative European transnational social norms have a quality of originality which is consistent with the theoretical features of transnational social norms as a response to globalisation.[2]

One preliminary point should be emphasised: the distinction between globalisation and the internationalisation of commerce is relevant in the light of the evolution of legal norms. Some authors consider globalisation only as an extension of international trade over the preceding four centuries, the present stage being the 'third globalisation' (Cohen 2004). From a legal point of view, however, the most important thing is not that the current state of international trade is different, broader and institutionalised (by the WTO). Rather, that an interdependence of factors creates a new international division of labour, with a change of paradigm regarding the model of production (Murray, Belanger, Giles and Lapointe 2004).

More precisely, the new organisation of MNCs at the global level, the globalisation of financial markets and the new rules of the WTO are interdependent factors explaining the specificities of globalisation (Michalet 2000, 2002). It is this interdependence which explains the strategy deployed by global firms. This

* Professor at the Law Department, European University Institute, Florence. CRIMT is the Centre de recherches interuniversitaires sur la Mondialisation et le Travail, Montréal, Canada, www.crimt.org.

[1] Discussion of these questions is developed very broadly by B Hepple; also by the author in *Normes sociales, droit du travail et mondialisation* (Paris, Dalloz, 2006) 416. See also G Murray and G Trudeau, 2004.

[2] This paper draws on a set of other papers written between 2002 and 2005 and published in different journals in France and Canada. They present a more detailed analysis of each aspect examined here.

interdependence must, therefore, be taken into consideration when searching for new forms of regulation or new methods of governance (Report OIT 2004).

One response to the expansion of international trade consisted in the development of private international law rules (rules of conflicts of law) for the coordination of national laws. The latter, as laid down in the 1980 Rome Convention on the conflict of laws for international contracts, can be a useful solution to problems of international contracts of employment of those (generally white collar workers) working for MNCs, given the need for mobility in global firms (Hepple 2005, Robin Olivier 2005). But this does not suffice for the international business of MNCs. Instead, new norms called '*lex mercatoria*', independent of national legal orders, were created in response to the new conditions of MNCs' business evincing the need for transnational norms. In the same way, transnational norms could be useful for the new employment relationships created in global firms (Moreau 2005; Jacquet, Delbecque, Carneloup, 2007).

Changes brought about by globalisation have great consequences for labour relations. The most important changes are to be found on the employer's side.[3] Employers are no longer national companies, but international groups with strategies based on the international division of labour. These strategies include the possibilities of new global organisation offered by 'global networking', a choice of the location/relocation of economic activities by 'global switching', the concentration of specific functions (research and development, finances) and a choice of sites by 'global focusing'. The workforce may still be located on the national sites and establishments, but activities become mobile[4] (Mucchieli 1998) and decisions are taken not at national but at the global level. In this context, national labour laws and national systems of industrial relations are unable to respond to the challenges of the transnational economic relationships created by MNCs.

Accordingly, it is fundamental, first, to analyse the theoretical features of transnational norms which could be adapted to the specific labour relations created in MNCs, (I). This in order to propose, secondly, that European transnational social norms possess an interesting and original quality responding to the new paradigm created by globalisation in the field of legal norms (II).[5]

[3] Traditionally, the employer manages the corporate structure. There are exceptions where judicial definitions look to the community of workers on which the employer exercises authority. But in a complex organisation of companies, as with MNCs, it is very difficult to lift the corporate veils and identify one unique employer. There is an old and interesting French case law (1986) on this topic, but nowadays the corporate group is not in itself considered as the employer, though this could be very useful in international disputes.

[4] Economic activities are marked by the same degree of mobility. This is not so important where industries have important investments in activities with sunk costs, or for services which need proximity to customers. Generally, it is possible to say that there are varying degrees of mobility and, consequently, MNCs interest in relocating activities in order reduce costs. Moreau 2005b.

[5] This paper does not aim, however, to analyse in detail corporate social responsibility, nor the European social dialogue, nor the possibilities available through the Open Method of Coordination (see Moreau 2005c, 2006; Vigneau 2005)

Definition and Features of Transnational Social Norms

The definition of transnationality in the *Dictionnaire Capitant*[6] is as follows: 'transnational implies the crossing of a frontier and/or what is exercised beyond the border, independent of state action'.[7] A transnational approach implies that different countries are concerned, but outside the power of a state or of different states. The transnational approach goes beyond the hierarchy of norms in traditional legal analysis; it is neither national, looking to state action, nor international, looking to action by an international institution (as with the ILO or UN). In the field of the *lex mercatoria*, transnational norms are elaborated by private actors, as in international contracts including international arbitration clauses enforceable by way of international arbitration. Scholars such as Christian Joerges and Gunter Teubner emphasise the evolution from a national elaboration of norms to the elaboration of transnational norms, by the way of private actors able to develop norms in their own sphere of activity, due to the incapacity of states with respect to transnational regulation.

The transformation can be observed whereby norms elaborated by a central state are now created at the periphery by private actors within a constellation (Teubner, 1996, 2002). The rules governing this transformation from central to peripheral formulation of norms must be created. The question of the regulating authority remains crucial, as it is in the sphere of labour relations to be discussed in this paper.

As regards the regulation of labour relations, the central issues are not only the loss of power of national states in the context of globalisation, or the capacity of private actors to regulate. In labour law, a large part of the norms evolves from collective bargaining, based on the recognition of collective autonomy (Report Sciarra 2004). The situation differs from country to country, however, it is an important feature of that labour law that it results from the sharing of regulatory power between states and social partners.

The most important challenge posed by globalisation results from the fact that labour laws were constructed within territorial boundaries and with national norms because the main parties to the employment relationship—employer and worker—were located in a territorial/national sphere (Moreau 2003). The territoriality of labour law is due not only to state sovereignty, but also from the location of the labour force on the territory.

In the global context workers are employed in the national context, but the employer exercises his power at a global level. The employer has the capacity to locate/relocate economic activities, whether in a traditional organisational structure based on the labour force, or in a business organisational structure involving

[6] The French reference book for legal definitions.

[7] '*(. . .) est transnational ce qui suppose le franchissement d'une frontière ou/et s'exerce par-dessus d'une frontière indépendamment de l'action des Etats*'

an international supply chain based on commercial law. Labour relations involving a community of workers located in one country and an employer exercising power at national level is no longer relevant in the field of international business. The balance of power is altered in favour of the employer when the latter enjoys a transnational power, while both workers' rights and collective action remain at national level.

Consequently, in the context of these transformations, the new labour relations should expand workers' rights in the face of the MNCs' global power. This can be called 'the principle of concordance', one element in a theoretical perspective on the new regulatory instruments responding to globalisation.[8] The general idea is quite simple: if the employer's power is transnational, workers' rights should also be recognised at a transnational level. If labour relations operate in a transnational dimension, social norms must also be developed (not only at the national level but) at the transnational level. Some examples may illustrate the relevance of transnational social norms.

Examples illustrating the importance of transnational social norms

The case of the restructuring of global firms provides the strongest arguments for the transnationalisation of labour norms. When Levi-Strauss, General Motors or Alcatel announce mass dismissals in Europe, the decision is a private one by the central management in one country, but has consequences in different countries. Despite the multinational dimension of the employer, the public employment institutions of a country affected by the decision on dismissals has no direct influence on the central head office of the MNC. The state concerned has no direct power to modify the central management's global decision.[9] However, a group of states representing a relevant market share could have an influence. Thus, at the European level, the European Commission is likely to have some degree of influence if the MNC has strategic interests in the European market. The conclusion is that there is a need for a transnational institution able to act in the sphere of the transnational markets where global firms operate.[10]

In the face of a threat of relocation (for example, of Canadian firms to Mexico, or European firms to Poland, Latvia or Hungary), trade unions need first to evaluate the seriousness of the threat: is it real or virtual. The firm's financial accounts at the global level can reveal the ability of the employer to move the establishments. Consequently, if the trade unions' rights to information are limited to those in the national territory of the establishment—which is usually the case in national labour laws—there is no basis for effective action.

[8] This idea of concordance was first developed by MA Moreau and G Trudeau in 2000 and in Dalloz, 2006. The need for new responses to globalisation in terms of norms and governance is emphasised in the report on the Social Dimension of Globalisation published by the ILO in February 2004.

[9] Except in the USA.

[10] See the orientation of the European Commission in a Communication published in March 2005 on the possible action of the European Union on restructuring, Moreau 2005c.

In the *Michelin affair* of 1994 in France the French Supreme Court required the employer to produce the consolidated accounts of the group at global level ('*comptes consolidés*') in order to evaluate the economic situation of the firm and the need for dismissals. In this case, a balance between the global firm and the trade unions is re-established by the obligation to provide transnational information.

Yet, this possibility does not exist in many countries. For instance, in Canada/Quebec, it is not possible for trade unions to evaluate the seriousness of a relocation threat (Moreau and Trudeau, 2000). The lack of balance between the financial information available to the management side, and used at global level to organize the firm, and the limited national information given to trade unions on the firm's economic situation argues for the development of regulation on the provision of transnational information.

In the *Hoover affair* of 1993, the absence of transnational coordination between the French and Scottish trade unions enabled the employer to relocate the French plant to Scotland, having negotiated the reduction of labour costs in Scotland. No arguments opposing the move were raised by the trade unions concerned, reflecting their lack of transnational coordination. In the absence of any transnational countervailing power of action, or any transnational *corpus* of collective bargaining, MNCs have great power to organise global strategy so as to obtain the economic conditions most favourable to them in production for the European market.

However, in the *Renault affair* of 1997, great pressure was put on the company after the decision to close a plant in Vilvoorde (Belgium) due to litigation initiated by the European works council. A French judge issued an injunction against Renault in a judgment enforceable in Belgium. This transnational jurisdiction was exceptional and resulted from the judge's power in the specific area of the market concerned: Europe in this case. The decision, however, thus had consequences for the MNC at the global/European level. It was the rapidity of the judicial response that proved to be crucial in imposing a legal restraint on the MNC based on European law (Moreau 1997). In contrast, in the *Metaleurope affair*, a plant was closed because the Swiss management refused to comply with French environmental standards. Litigation procedures against the main company in Switzerland were so slow that the workers concerned were unable to achieve any solution.

In general, it appears that European and international procedures fail to address sudden and rapid closure decisions. Many other examples could be put forward to illustrate that national norms are usually ineffective in the fact of MNCs' transnational capacity to act.

The principle of concordance

The principle of concordance provides a basis for the development of transnational social norms in order to confront the challenge posed by the transnational organisation and actions of MNCs. The principle of concordance results from the need to adapt norms—and social regulations in general—to the scope of the power of MNCs.

The elaboration of transnational social norms in itself will not suffice to modify significantly social regulation at global level. However, social norms limited to territorial and national scope are not an alternative; such norms will not facilitate any change to or for the social actors.[11] However, the elaboration of transnational social norms may be expected to bring about a profound reformation of the power of social actors in terms of their actions and reactions to globalisation effects, such as relocation and restructuring (Moreau 2005).

Strategies of MNCs aim to achieve the highest rate of profitability, regardless of the means of obtaining it (CA Michalet, 2002). Their economic strategies are driven by financial profitability, not by employment considerations nor by the volume of their economic activities. This is one particular result of the globalisation, and is a mechanism created by and mainly of financial markets (CA Michalet 2002, Aglietta and Reberioux, 2004). MNCs frequently take decisions at the global level (for example, a collective redundancy) because of their expectation that the profit created by the decision, due to its impact on the financial markets, exceeds in itself any profit resulting from the labour cost savings due to elimination of the jobs.

This lack of connection between the decision (mass dismissals) and the expected result (increase in share value) should lead trade unions to adapt their collective action to the employer's fear of financial losses. As the exercise of management power at the global level changes relations at different levels, as the scope of decisions is no longer national but transnational, and as decisions are taken simultaneously across the globe, such exercise of management power presupposes a reactive capacity with the same dimensions and synchronicity. In other words, when management power is exercised at a global level, so that a single corporate decision can result in a multiplicity of territorial/national consequences, the situation calls for the development of a countervailing reactive power equivalent in its scope and nature.

Labour law aims at protection of the workforce and at reduction of inequalities. Nowadays, national labour laws are unable to cope with the new challenges posed by the global dimension of MNCs, and are unable to fulfil these primary objectives. It is argued, therefore, that social norms must be adapted to the new global organisation of MNCs in order to pursue the essential objectives of labour law; in particular, by the implementation of the '*principle of concordance*'.

The principle of concordance prescribes that social norms must match the power of MNC, in particular, at three different levels: (i) concordance of scope, (ii) concordance of time, (iii) concordance of action.

Concordance of scope

If the power of MNCs is exercised in different countries in accordance with a global strategy, applicable legal norms should have the same scope: on trans-

[11] See infra, 2-2, evaluation of European Works Councils.

national information, transnational representation of workers, transnational collective bargaining.

Concordance of time

The decisions of MNCs can be implemented with great speed; judicial or social responses must be available with similar swiftness. This requires that a court can adjudicate on a situation located in another country using procedures for timely and effective enforcement against the MNC (such as injunctions) (see Hepple 2005). It is necessary to match the speed of such procedures to the decision-making time frame of the MNC's activities (for example, the action '*en référé*' in the case of economic redundancies in France).[12]

Concordance of action

To coordinate the actions of the social actors in response to MNC power requires a number of capabilities: the capacity to exercise freedom of association in all the workplaces of the MNC; the capacity to bargain in the different establishments specifically on transnational subjects (which may include restructuring, training, health and safety, etc); and the capacity to organize collective action at the level of the MNC.

The principle of concordance provides a general framework for transnational social norms, though the question of their precise content remains open. Regulation cannot be through the unilateral action of the main transnational actor—the employer. In international commercial law, the '*lex mercatoria*' is determined by the actors, and respects the equality of the parties and their choice of arbitration as a form of 'private' international justice. In labour law, however, unilateral elaboration of transnational social norms, for example, by MNCs' codes of conduct, lack international legitimacy and their content does not even systematically meet the ILO's core labour standards.[13] This 'normative self-service', as Supiot calls it (Supiot, 2004), results from the absence of a transnational institution willing to regulate these transnational codes of conduct (neither the European Commission nor the ILO). By way of illustration, analysis of norms on corporate social responsibility (CSR) (Sobczak 2002, 2004, Moreau 2005a) highlights, first, the importance of transposing labour law guidelines to the level of transnational norms; and, secondly, for regulation, as matter of prime concern, to respect the

[12] In 1996, the French *Cour de Cassation* authorised the works council, in case of economic dismissals, to use an emergency procedure called '*réferé*'. This is available for use under restrictive conditions in a very short time (*référé d'heure à heure*: 'hour to hour'). The result was that workers' representatives can obtain a judgement in the time frame of the management's decision-making procedure; in other words, before the letters of dismissal, and this has a useful effect towards improvement of the social plan consequent on any dismissals.

[13] The ILO Declaration of 1998 specifies four core labour standards. However, in the majority of codes of conduct, generally there are provisions prohibiting child labour and forced labour, often discrimination, and but only sometime provisions on freedom of association and the right to bargain.

need for a specific balance as between employers and trade unions, in light of the unequal situation of the parties.

What is at issue is to identify representative transnational actors for transnational collective bargaining, or legitimate institutions able to draw up transnational social norms. One can infer from the principle of concordance that transnational norms, to adequately address the challenges of globalisation, should:

(i) result from a transnational elaboration, to reflect and integrate the transnational dimension of the different actors;
(ii) have a transnational content, so as to reflect the specificity of transnational labour relations;
(iii) be enforceable at transnational level through an effective (transnational) mode of control.

A wide range of new responses to globalisation demonstrates the willingness of social actors to introduce new methods of governance through new regulatory techniques.[14] Yet many of the latter fail to take account of the above-mentioned characteristics (Moreau 2005b). In my view, the most interesting responses come from the European Union. The transnational social norms mapped out at the European Union (EU) level in order to cope with the challenge of globalisation illustrate the originality of its approach based upon the transnationality of social norms.

The Originality of European Transnational Norms

The case of the European Union is instructive. MNCs have significant experience in the field of transnational collective labour relations as a result of the Single European Market's internationalisation of employment, but the latter's lacking any legal framework (Moreau 2005c). In particular, global firms, characterised by new complex organisations (Daugareilh 2000), faced new challenges regarding the creation of global synergies between their workforces. Progressively, transnational social issues have made their way from the first European agreement creating a European works council (Danone in 1986) to the European Work Council Directive in 1994.

In terms of evolution, two key points may be highlighted. Firstly, three particular European directives contributed to develop a European model of transnational social norms. Secondly, even if the new European social regulations suffer from limited implementation, they undoubtedly contribute to the evolution of trans-

[14] For example, collective agreements negotiated through the European social dialogue, including codes of conduct at European sectoral level; social clauses in international contracts; international collective agreements concluded by international trade union confederations and global firms; unilateral management standards of CSR; labels, certifications, and various types of soft law (Moreau 2005 a–b, 2006).

national bargaining. Both aspects provide interesting theoretical elements to the formulation of responses to the challenge of globalisation.

The European 'model' of transnational social norms

Three EU directives have been adopted in response to internationalisation of employment at European level (Blas-López 2005).

Council Directive 94/45/EC of 22 September 1994[15] concerns the establishment of a European Works Council or a procedure in Community-scale undertakings and Community-scale groups of undertakings for the purposes of informing and consulting employee (hereinafter, EWC Directive). This directive creates a transnational representation mechanism, based on the principle of the autonomy of the social actors representing workers and employers in the European Union, for the involvement of workers on decisions affecting transnational employment issues.

Council Directive 2001/86/EC of 8 October 2001[16] supplements the statute for a European Company (SE) with regard to the involvement of employees. This directive establishes a social model for the European Company based on the capacity of workers' representatives in the different countries involved in the European Company (SE) to establish an autonomous framework for the representation of workers in the new SE.

Council Directive 2003/72/ EC of 22 July 2003 supplements the Statute for a European Cooperative Society with regard to the involvement of employees. It is almost the same statute as for the SE, but for a European non-profit enterprise which will group together cooperatives established in different countries into one European Cooperative Society.

These three directives aim to provide a unified framework for the transnational representation of workers adapted to the global/European enterprise. They were forged with a view of a 'common model' and confirm that European labour laws are able to adapt the representation of workers to the conditions prevailing in MNCs (Rodière 2002, Hepple 2005, Blas-López 2005, Moreau 2005a).

This European model of representation of workers in a MNC established in at least two Member States rests on a common foundation.

Diversity and legitimacy

The guarantee of a transnational representation of workers reflecting their geographic and cultural diversity is to be achieved by the setting up of a representative, transnational negotiation body, the so-called Special Negotiation Body (hereinafter, SNB). The SNB, representative of the employees of the MNC's subsidiaries and/or establishments, will negotiate the transnational framework of involvement of the employees.

[15] OJ L 254/64. Council Directive 97/74/EC of 15 December 1997 extended the Directive to the United Kingdom; Directive 94/45/EC. OJ L 10/22.

[16] OJ L 294/22.

The composition of the SNB reflects the national representation of the workers communities and the proportion of workers within each country.[17] The SNB can thus be said to reflect two dimensions of representation: both nationality and the number of workers are taken into account. SNB members are chosen in accordance with the national legal criteria of each country involved in the process, thus respecting national social culture and the diversity of choices in Europe regarding the question of workers' representation.[18]

The formation of an SNB with national representatives (from trade unions, works councils, shop stewards/elected representatives, etc) provides a clear advantage: European social diversity is respected and stronger links are promoted between national representation structures and the European level. This is particularly important for a European works council that has to deal with national representatives in each country.

The SNB is characterised by proportional representation of the workers at Community level. A specific cultural orientation is given to the European-level transnational representation when a majority of workers are from one particular country. For instance, in the French enterprise ELF Aquitaine, more than half of the workers are French; in such a case, the EWC is influenced by French social culture. In the case of the European Company, the issue of cultural dominance proves to be even more crucial due to the choices in the involvement of employees in the company management (German social culture, Dutch social culture). Transnational representation arises from the accommodation of different national social identities. European legitimacy is built upon national legitimacies.

Collective autonomy

The role of the SNB is to negotiate a framework for transnational workers' representation. Provisions lay down that where the SNB decides not to open negotiations or to terminate negotiations already opened, the 'subsidiary requirements' in the Annex to the EWC Directive shall apply.[19] However, the directives greatly encourage the SNB to reach an agreement and provide a useful framework for negotiations. In this way, the collective autonomy of the social partners within European enterprises is at the heart of the elaboration of those transnational social norms (Vigneau, 2002).

[17] '(. . .) by allocating in respect of a Member State one seat per portion of employees employed in the Member State which equals 10% or a fraction thereof, of the number of employees employed by the participating companies and concerned subsidiaries or establishments in all the Member States taken together' (Art 3).

[18] It can be briefly recorded that the reason why it took approximately 30 years for the European Company Statute to be adopted stems from a conflict between the Member States over the mode of workers' representation (Davies, 2004, Vasquez 2003, Moreau 2001). German trade unions would not renounce their right to co-determination ('*co-gestion*') while Spanish employers refused to accept a co-determination system. This reveals how the European Union is characterised by sharply opposing trends.

[19] Similarly, no European company or European cooperative society can be registered if no agreement is reached.

The exercise of collective autonomy in the creation of the European works council, also incorporated into the two other directives, aims to preserve the former rights of the workers. Employers establishing European companies or European cooperatives cannot suppress or reduce the rights of the workers. Collective autonomy will operate with consideration of this principle (the so-called '*before and after*' principle)[20] whereby the rights of the transnational body of representation established prevents the SE being used as a way of undermining existing national provisions on board level participation (Davies 2003).

Information and consultation

The objective of these transnational structures of workers' representation is to reach an agreement, through social dialogue, on workers' information and consultation procedures within the European company, group of enterprises or cooperative. The agreement may include provisions concerning the involvement of workers at the management level.

The quality and relevance of the information provided to the representatives is a basic condition to ensure the efficacy of the social dialogue. Information must enable the representatives to express their views, in particular, regarding (i) the European/global economic situation of the employer, and (ii) transnational employment issues. The EWC Directive sets guidelines, but the social actors are free to give more prominence to workers' participation. The other directives are also oriented towards the possibility of concluding agreements to achieve the function of information and consultation in the European company (Vasquez, 2003, Laulom and Vigneau 2005).

To sum up, collective autonomy exercised through transnational bargaining can give rise to the creation of transnational social norms. There is not a unique model of transnational representation. The directives attest that social pluralism is recognised in the European Union and the European social partners co-define the precise content of the transnational representation provisions. However, the European framework does set some mandatory conditions. All employees of the enterprise must be represented, according to geographic and proportionately quantitative criteria, and the representation agreement must include, as a minimum, the functions of information and consultation.

Evaluation: the principle of concordance and European transnational norms

It is possible to obtain some first impressions from experience emerging from the operation of European works councils. The outcomes from the other two

[20] For a complete analysis of the directive on involvement of employees in a European Company, see F Vasquez. The provisions are quite complex because the constitution of the European company can have different features (by establishing a holding company, through a merger, etc).

directives are much more difficult to evaluate: the European company statute has been in effect for too short a time—and the absence of specific tax provisions makes it incomplete—while the third directive is not yet in force. Over the first eight-month period, only two companies have had recourse to negotiating an SE statute. A certain success was achieved in the case of Nordair. However, all social provisions were violated in the second case: no collective bargaining was undertaken, which led to a complaint from the trade unions.

Regarding the EWC Directive, however, there are been significant developments. No fewer than 750 European works councils have been created by agreement. The concrete operation of European works council differs substantially from one to another. Although the agreements setting out activities generally provide for transnational information once or twice a year, the scope of that information and the possibility for social dialogue/consultation presents considerable variation.

Nonetheless, the action of EWCs has produced strong and significant developments in some important enterprise such as Arcilor, Renault and EDF (Moreau 2003, 2005; Berthoux, 2006). These are visible in various actions throughout the European Union in the fields of health risks and safety, workforce adaptation within the group, discrimination, and working conditions aimed to prevent restructuring. Bargaining has produced codes of conduct on working conditions (eg safety) and fundamental social rights.

In 2005, an average of one agreement per week was reached on an EWC. This demonstrates the considerable demand for collective bargaining within MNCs established in Europe. As claimed by Antoine Lyon-Caen (Lyon-Caen, 1997) Directive 94/45 has created a model of transnational collective bargaining that is now used by global firms established in the European Union. To this may be added a new development: international collective bargaining between global firms and international federations of trade unions; about 49 agreements were concluded since 2000. In most cases, the EWC was shown to have acted as a 'facilitator' promoting the synergy between the employees of the global firm and the international trade unions (Daugareilh, 2005; Drouin, 2007).

As a result of this transnational social culture, European works councils provide a new function within the transnational social relations in the EU as a partner in social innovation with expertise in transnational social dialogue. Nevertheless, this movement is still in its early stages and remains limited to some firms (Daugareilh, 2005). The great majority of the European work councils play only an information role, which is minor if compared to the powers of the national employees' representatives.

The transnational social norms that have emerged from the EU framework may set the scene and open opportunities for synergies in European global firms (Bethoux, 2004). But European works council still have weak positions with respect to the transnational decision-making power of European global enterprises. The latter's actions still depend on the firm's shareholding structure and culture.

Nonetheless, EWCs act as unique structures of representation. They can be extremely useful in European firms when the employer wishes to embark upon a social dialogue or transnational megotiation. Most of the agreements concluded by the European works councils in 2004/2005 generated codes of conduct in the framework of corporate social responsibility. These codes of conduct were given greater legitimacy because they were not elaborated unilaterally. The EWCs are useful negotiation bodies because codes of conduct are also transnational regulatory techniques (Daugareilh, 2005).

Undoubtedly, European works councils have a limited field of action. They only apply to specified situations: European or global firms established in at least two EU Member States). They cannot act at a global scale, though some firms have made a breakthrough, extending the European works council to include countries outside the European Union, thus creating new global works councils. This evolution is still unclear, mainly because of the somehow 'gloomy' relations between the regional and international levels of the trade unions.

The intention of this paper was to demonstrate that three EU directives provide a legal framework in accordance with the principle of concordance on many points. Although the absence of provisions on the transnational enforcement of these norms is regrettable, it should not overlooked that the European Court of Justice has the possibility—as illustrated with the Renault case—to interpret and enforce the agreement concluded by the European works council. The *Bofrost case*[21] demonstrates that the Court can require a company, even if its corporate headquarters are established outside the EU, to provide the workers and their representatives with the necessary information about the composition and structure of a European group. The cases show that the Court is willing to ensure the directives are of useful effect to regulate questions of internationalisation of labour relations. The most important effect of European social norms in the context of globalisation may be that a European regional court—instead of a national judge from one of the Member States—may adopt an autonomous and teleological approach in favour of workers' social integration (Robin-Olivier 1999).

The Originality of Transnational Social Norms as a Response to Globalisation

Several conclusions may be drawn from this brief analysis of common elements of the European model of transnational regulation.

[21] *Betriebsrat der bofrost Josef H Boquoi Deutschland West GmbH & Co. KG, Straelen v bofrost Josef H Boquoi Deutschland West GmbH & Co. KG Straelen*, Case C-62/99, [2001] ECR I-2579. See also *Gesamtbetriebsrat der Kuhne & Nagel AG & Co KC v Kuhne & Nagel AG & Co KC*, Case C-440/00, ECJ, 13 January 2004; *Betriebsrat der Firma ADS Anker GmbH v ADS Anker GnbH*, Case C-349/01, ECJ, 15 July 2004.

Transnational regulation within a regional legal order

The theoretical debate mainly focused on the possible recognition of a global or transnational legal order generated by the social actors themselves (as in the *lex mercatoria*) parallel to the traditional legal order. The example of the EU demonstrates that transnational social norms can also emerge from a legal order and draw legitimacy from an institutional framework. This is not formation of 'global law without the state'; rather, it is transnational regulation within a regional legal order. From that perspective, the EU legal order has no equivalent in the world. It can contribute relevant solutions to the challenges of globalisation, all the more so given the EU plays a central role in global markets (Moreau and Trudeau 2000).

Legitimacy and unilateralism

It is essential that social actors acting at a transnational level enjoy normative legitimacy; that they do not unilaterally establish '*ex nihilo*' social norms or regulatory techniques, not even soft law. Unilateral regulation is unacceptable in the field of social regulation. The European Commission should, therefore, aim to regulate working conditions in the EU apart from codes of conducts, labels and forms of certification. However, the procedural regulations required for this have not been sufficiently developed.

Effective judicial procedures

The concordance of time and action between transnational norms and their enforcement is not adequately achieved. Judicial action is at the level of national procedures, with their natural limits. The speed with which complaints may succeed is conditioned by national judicial procedures, without consideration for global challenges.

Articulating the national and transnational

Social actors should seek to integrate the new actors of the globalisation/antiglobalisation debates into the legal framework in order to give transnational norms a coherent effect. In particular, this implies the articulation of national norms with transnational norms, especially as regards effective enforcement.[22]

Diverse forms of hard law and soft law regulatory instruments were created in the framework of the EU or NAFTA market integration treaties (Moreau 2005 b). From a close scrutiny, it is suggested that European social norms elaborated for workers' transnational representation provide the most interesting responses to globalisation, with respect to traditional labour law objectives and the structures of global corporate management.

[22] B Bercusson, 'Application du droit du travail: les interactions entre droits nationaux et communautaire', *Travail et Emploi*, 2004 (octobre), no 100; Ministère de l'emploi, du travail et de la cohesion sociale, France, pp 27–38 (also in English, pp 39–46).

References

Aglietta, M et Rebérioux, A, *Dérives du capitalisme financier* (Paris, Albin Michel, 2004) 391.

Andreff, W, *Les multinationales globales*, éd La Découverte (1995, Paris) 212.

Bercusson, B, 'Application du droit du travail: les interactions entre droits nationaux et communautaire', *Travail et Emploi*, 2004 (octobre), n° 100, 27–38 (also in English, 39–46).

Bethoux, E, 'Les comités d'entreprise en quête de légitimité', *Travail et Emploi*, 2004, n° 98, 21–35.

——, 'Entreprises multinationales et représentation des salariés en Europe : l'expérience des comités d'entreprise européens', *Thèse de l'Université Paris X Nanterre*, décembre 2006.

——, 'Entreprises multinationales et représentation des salariés en Europe : l'expérience des comités d'entreprise européens' *Thèse de l'Université Paris X Nanterre*, décembre 2006.

Bourque, R, 'Les accords-cadres internationaux et les fédérations syndicales internationales', Institut International d'études sociales, 2005, Genève, ILO, DP/161/2005.

Blas-López, ME, 'La mutation des partenaires sociaux en Europe en réponse à la globalisation de l'économie', *RSCAS, EUI Working Paper*, 2006, www.iue.it.

Cohen, D, *La mondialisation et ses ennemis* (Paris, Hachette littérature, 2004).

Daugareilh, I, 'La responsabilité sociale des entreprises transnationales et les droits fondamentaux de l'homme au travail : un contre-exemple des accords internationaux' in *Mondialisation, travail et droits fondamentaux* (Bruxelles-Paris, Bruylant-LGDJ, 2005) 349–84.

Davies, P, 'Workers on the Board of the European Company?' (2003) 32 *Industrial Law Journal* 75.

Drouin, R-C, 'Les accords cadre internationaux', *Les cahiers de droit*, 2007, vol 1, 135.

Hepple, B, *Labour Laws and Global Trade* (Oxford, Hart Publishing, 2005).

Daugareilh, I, 'Les sources juridiques des règles appliqués aux travailleurs des entreprises transnationales à structure complexe', *Syndicalisme et société*, 2000, vol 3, 83–109.

Jacquet , J-M, Delbecque, P, Corneloup, S, *Droit commercial international* (Paris, Dalloz, 2007) 844.

Laulom, S et Vigneau, C, 'Actualité du rapprochement des législations en matière de relations professionnelles', *Droit social* 2005, 526.

Lyon-Caen, A, 'La négociation collective dans ses dimensions internationales', *Droit social* 1997, 352.

Michalet, CA, *Qu'est ce que la mondialisation?*, éd La Découverte (Paris, 2003) 210.

——, 'Les métamorphoses de la mondialisation: une approche économique', dans dir E Loquin et C Kessedjian, *La mondialisation du droit* (Paris, Litec, 2000) 2–42.

Moreau, MA et Trudeau, G, 'Le droit du travail face à la mondialisation de l'économie', *Rel Indus* 1998, vol 53, n° 1, 55–87.

——, 'Globalization and Labour Law, World Congress of Industrial Relations, Tokyo, 2000', *Impact of Globalization on National and Regional System of Industrial Relations*, vol 2, 72–84.

——, 'A propos de "l'affaire Renault"', *Droit social* 1997, 493,

——, 'L'implication des travailleurs dans la société européenne', *Droit social*, 2001, 967.

——, 'Des rattachements territoriaux à la transnationalité des normes du travail', dans *Les lieux du droit du travail*, *La semaine sociale Lamy*, suppl.n° 1140, 20 octobre 2003, 82–8.

——, 2005b 'La recherche de nouvelles techniques de régulation sociale, quelles fonctions, quelles complémentarités', *IUE Working Paper P/*2005.

——, 2005c 'L'internationalisation de l'emploi et les délocalisations en Europe: perspectives juridiques in *Délocalisations, normes du travail et politiques de l'emploi, vers une modialisation plus juste?* , dir P Auer, G Besse, D Meda, éd La Découverte (Paris, 2005)177–206.

——, *Normes sociales , droit du travail et mondialisation*, (Paris, Dalloz, 2006) 416.

Mucchielli, J-L, *Multinationales et mondialisation*, (Paris, Points Seuil, 198) 375.

Murray, G et Trudeau, G, 'La régulation sociale de l'entreprise mondialisée? Introduction', *Relations Industrielles* 2004, vol 59-1, 3–26.

Murrray, G, Belanger, J, Giles, A, Lapointe P-A, *L'organisation de la production et du travail, vers un nouveau modèle?* (Canada, Presses de l'Université Laval, 2004) 261.

OIT, Rapport de la World Commission, *La dimension sociale de la mondialisation*, 168, www.ilo.org.

Robin-Olivier, S, La référence aux droits sociaux fondamentaux dans le Traité d'Amsterdam, *Droit social*, 1999, pp. 609–21.

——, 'La mobilité internationale du salarié', *Droit social* 2005, 495.

Rodière, P, *Droit social de l'Union européenne* 2ème éd (Paris, LGDJ, 2002).

Sciarra, S, 'L'évolution des droits du travail dans l'Union européenne, 1992-2003', Rapport de synthèse, 2004, www.europa/comm.empl, European publications, Brussels, vol1 and vol 2, 2005.

Sobczak, A, *Réseaux de sociétés et codes de conduite : un nouveau modèle de régulation des relations de travail des entreprises européennes* (Paris, LGDJ, 2002) 355.

——, 'La responsabilité sociale de l'entreprise : menace ou opportunité pour le droit du travail?', *Relations Industrielles*, 2004, vol 59-1, 26–51.

——, dir *La responsabilité globale*, suppl *La semaine sociale Lamy*, 18 octobre 2004, n° 1186, 11.

Supiot, A, *Du nouveau au self-service normatif. Etudes offertes à Jean Pelissier, Analyses juridiques et valeurs en droit social* (Paris, Dalloz, 2004) 541–58.

Teubner, G, *De la pyramide au réseau, Pour une théorie dialectique du droit*, PU saint Louis, Bruxelles, 2002.

——, (ed), *Global Law without a State*, (Aldershot, Dartmouth, 1997).

Vasquez, F, 'Commentaires sur la directive sur l'implication des travailleurs dans la Société européenne' , dans *La société européenne, Liaisons sociales Europe*, septembre 2003, 25–117.

Vigneau, C, ' Etude sur l'autonomie collective au niveau communautaire', *RTDE* 2002, 653.

INDEX

Please note that page references to footnotes will have the letter 'n' following the number